T0244256

"Digging All Night and Fighting All Day"

The Civil War Siege of

SPANISH FORT

and the Mobile Campaign, 1865

PAUL BRUESKE

SB

Savas Beatie
California

First edition, first printing

ISBN-13: 978-1-61121-710-0 (hardcover)
ISBN-13: 978-1-61121-711-7 (ebook)

Library of Congress Cataloging-in-Publication Data

Names: Brueske, Paul, author.
Title: "Digging All Night and Fighting All Day" : The Civil War Siege of
    Spanish Fort and the Mobile Campaign, 1865 / by Paul Brueske.
Other titles: Civil War siege of Spanish Fort and the Mobile Campaign, 1865
Description: El Dorado Hills, CA : Savas Beatie, [2024] | Includes
    bibliographical references and index. | Summary: "The bloody two-week
    siege of Spanish Fort, Alabama (March 26-April 8, 1865) was one of the
    final battles of the Civil War. The siege and battle that unfolded on
    the rough and uneven bluffs of Mobile Bay's eastern shore, fought mainly
    by veterans of the principal battles of the Western Theater, witnessed
    every offensive and defensive art known to war. It is an outstanding
    study of a little-known but astonishingly important event rife with acts
    of heroism that rivaled any battle of the war"-- Provided by publisher.
Identifiers: LCCN 2024026636 | ISBN 9781611217100 (hardcover) | ISBN
    9781611217117 (ebook)
Subjects: LCSH: Spanish Fort, Battle of, Spanish Fort, Ala., 1865. | Mobile
    Campaign, 1865. | Spanish Fort (Ala.)--History--19th century.
Classification: LCC E477.94 .B76 2024 | DDC 976.1/2106--dc23/eng/20240625
LC record available at https://lccn.loc.gov/2024026636

SB

Savas Beatie
989 Governor Drive, Suite 102
El Dorado Hills, CA 95762
916-941-6896 / sales@savasbeatie.com / www.savasbeatie.com

All of our titles are available at special discount rates for bulk purchases in the United States. Contact us for information.

For my dad, Ken Brueske, and my uncles Raymond and Franklin.
I wish you guys were all still here to read this book.

TABLE OF CONTENTS

TABLE OF CONTENTS

(continued)

LIST OF MAPS

by Hal Jespersen

Photos have been placed throughout the text for the convenience of the reader.

Preface

When historians discuss the Civil War in the winter and spring of 1865, they understandably tend to focus on the events transpiring between the principal armies in Virginia and the Carolinas. Comparatively speaking, few books have been written on the 1865 Mobile campaign, and a dedicated book has never told the story of the often-overlooked siege of Spanish Fort.

The History of the Campaign of Mobile; including the cooperative operations of Gen. Wilson's Cavalry in Alabama (1867) by U.S. Brig. Gen. C. C. Andrews, a participant in the campaign, is a valuable primary source overview. Andrews incorporated reports and accounts from the commanding officers from both sides of the conflict. Published in 1867, the events were fresh on the minds of the participants who contributed accounts to Andrews. This book persists as the foundation upon which historians have built and expanded.

A hundred and twenty-four years after Andrews's book was published, Arthur Bergeron produced *Confederate Mobile* (1991). Bergeron's well-researched book provides an overview of Mobile's Confederate-controlled era. He succeeds in illustrating Mobile's continual importance after the South's loss in the battle of Mobile Bay. However, in its 198 pages, Bergeron's book dedicates only one 19-page chapter to the Mobile campaign.

Two years later came Chester Hearn's *Mobile Bay and the Mobile Campaign* (1993). As the title implies, Hearn's book examines the 1864 battle of Mobile Bay and the 1865 Mobile campaign. However, Hearn focuses most of his attention on the battle of Mobile Bay. He does an excellent job of pointing out that the siege of Mobile came late in the war when the technological and tactical nature of the war had evolved. Hearn asserts that the campaign foreshadowed the future of warfare. He reveals how ironclads, submarines, torpedoes, land mines, hand grenades, advanced rifled artillery and repeating rifles, coordinated amphibious assaults, elaborate earthen fortifications, instantaneous electronic battlefield reports via telegraph, and skilled deployment of troops were utilized. Hearn's account however, provides only scant detail on Spanish Fort.

In *Mobile, 1865: Last Stand of the Confederacy* (2001), Sean Michael O'Brien chronicles the final Union efforts to capture Mobile. O'Brien concludes that this campaign was "completely unnecessary." He argues that Mobile's significance had already been "neutralized" with the Federal capture of the bay. O'Brien cites Grant's hindsight assessment that the campaign needlessly cost lives on both sides. While it is true that an earlier capture of the city might have altered the course of the war, O'Brien fails to recognize the city's continued significance after the battle of Mobile Bay. The city's logistical importance in 1865, however, made it an essential place for the Confederates to defend and the Federals to attack. *Mobile, 1865* provides a good overview of the Mobile campaign. However, those wanting more on tactics and the battles themselves will likely be frustrated by the lack of attention to detail.[1]

At only 89 pages, John C. Waugh's *Last Stand at Mobile* (2001) offers a brief overview of the battle of Mobile Bay and the 1865 Mobile campaign. This narrative is a concise account of the fighting around Mobile. It is not, however, an in-depth study. Only eight pages cover the events that unfolded at Spanish Fort.

Russell W. Blount's *Besieged, Mobile* (2015) provides an overview of the Mobile campaign. The book, however, is not an in-depth campaign study. Blount delivers a concise account but references only a small number of primary sources. Like O'Brien, Blount fails to acknowledge the logistical importance of Mobile late in the war when Union forces planned their expedition.

Christopher McIlwain's *Civil War Alabama* (2016) dedicates attention to the political history and understanding of the war's course and consequences in Alabama. McIlwain admittedly omits a detailed analysis of critical military components. He diminishes the siege to a lone sentence, "Canby was basically unmolested during his pounding, thirteen-day siege of Spanish Fort." This book, however, will show that the defense of Spanish Fort was more substantial than McIlwain suggests.[2]

John Sledge's *These Rugged Days: Alabama in the Civil War* (2017) provides a detailed study of the war in Alabama. Sledge's book is a must-read for anyone seeking an overview of Alabama's Civil War history. It is an excellent guide to the

---

1 Sean O'Brien, *Mobile, 1865: Last Stand of the Confederacy* (Santa Monica, 2001), 233–234.

2 Christopher L. McIlwain, *Civil War Alabama* (Tuscaloosa: The University of Alabama Press, 2016), 262.

military actions occurring within the state. Sledge admittedly writes for a general audience and does not bog down the casual reader with tedious details regarding troop dispositions. Despite lacking original maps, Sledge delivers a well-written narrative history of Alabama's Civil War events, including a 22-page chapter on the Mobile campaign.

My first writing venture, *The Last Siege: The Mobile Campaign, Alabama 1865* (2018), presented an overview of the 1865 campaign for Mobile. *The Last Siege* and the afore mentioned books covered Spanish Fort to varying degrees. *"Digging All Night and Fighting All Day,"* however, is the first dedicated, detailed, and objective study of the siege of Spanish Fort, the events leading up to it, and its aftermath, which led to the final Confederate surrender east of the Mississippi River.

This book also seeks to illuminate the leadership of Spanish Fort's commander, Randall Lee Gibson, the unlikely 33-year-old Southern general who, at the beginning of the war, had no military experience. Gibson, nevertheless, developed into a distinguished and battle-hardened leader. As Confederate Maj. Gen. Dabney H. Maury put it: "General Randall L. Gibson had been in action in the Western army. He it was who closed an honorable record by his masterly command of the defenses near Spanish Fort, on the eastern shore of Mobile Bay, in the last great battle of the war between the States." At Spanish Fort, he led a garrison that resisted a Federal force that outnumbered his own ten to one. Maury declared Gibson's nearly two-week defense of Spanish Fort "one of the most spirited defenses of the war."[3]

As the late historian Richard Sommers once jokingly pointed out, the defense of Spanish Fort and Fort Blakeley enabled Mobile to hold out even longer than Richmond, the Confederate capital. The siege of Spanish Fort, indeed, ended up being one of the last battles of the Civil War. It proved to be an intense, pitched battle between two armies vastly different in size. The struggle occurred on the rough and uneven bluffs of Mobile Bay's eastern shore, mainly by veterans of the principal battles of the Western theater. Maury noted that these men "brought to it the experience of four years of incessant conflict, and in the attack and defense of that place demonstrated every offensive and defensive art then known to war." It was an intense and bloody siege, rife with acts of heroism that rivaled any battle of the war.[4]

3 Dabney H. Maury, *Recollections of a Virginian in the Mexican, Indian, and Civil Wars* (New York, 1894), 149; Dabney H. Maury, "Defence of Mobile in 1865," *Southern Historical Society Papers*, vol. 3, no. 1 (Jan. 1877): 7.

4 Maury, "Defence of Spanish Fort," 130.

The battlefield now lies within a peaceful, suburban neighborhood known as Spanish Fort Estates. It is hard to imagine this suburban enclave being the former scene of such a desperate struggle. Sadly, much of the fort and earthworks have long since been destroyed, yet some traces remain discernible. Driving through Spanish Fort Estates, one can still see eroded breastworks in some yards. Over the years, property owners of the critical locations of the siege have allowed me to explore the same terrain and earthwork remnants where thousands of men fought and died nearly 160 years ago. There is no better way to experience faint, momentary glimpses of the past. Relic hunters, some of whom have scoured the battlefield for nearly 50 years, have shared valuable insight with me. Fort McDermott, the Confederate's most vital position, is maintained by the local Admiral Semmes Camp 11 of the Sons of Confederate Veterans and is open to the public. Also, the scene of the Federal assault is now a public green space complete with hiking trails. Old Spanish Fort, the Red Fort, and U.S. Battery #22 are on private property but remain in good condition.

Maury notes that the Spanish first built and occupied this earthen fort during the colonial period. Though it has long been held that the Spanish first erected the fort, no documentation of its construction during the 1780–1813 period has surfaced in Spanish archives. Whatever the exact origin of the name in the area's colonial days, the term Spanish Fort became etched in Civil War history due to what happened there in the spring of 1865. My intent in writing this book is to provide an impartial study that sheds further light on the struggle between the Union and Confederate armies during this understudied battle.[5]

Acknowledgments

Many people graciously assisted me while preparing this work. Kirk Barrett, Roger Hansen, and the late Mike Randall were indispensable during the research process. Kirk and Roger have studied the Mobile campaign for many years and were instrumental in constructing the casualty and prisoner lists and order of battles, and lending their expertise on the finer points of the siege. Mike had a great knack for finding obscure facts and images.

My deepest gratitude goes to Bill Rambo and Robert Bradley for taking the time to read and critique my manuscript for accuracy. They were tremendously helpful and readily shared their vast knowledge of Alabama's Civil War history.

Special thanks to Sheritta Bitikofer, Mike Bunn, Amy Delcambre, Dr. Stephen North, Tom Root, Wayne Sirmon, David Snyder, and Dr. Phillip Theodore for

5 See Appendix 12 for more information on the origins of Spanish Fort. Maury, "Defence of Spanish Fort," 133.

offering writing suggestions. Special thanks to Slade Watson for his prodding to write this book and his critical eye. Moreover, the following individuals assisted me with my research: Mike Bailey, Fort Morgan Historian (retired); Bill Barnhill, Spanish Fort, AL; Donnie Barrett, Director Fairhope Museum (retired), Fairhope, AL; Ken Barr, Alabama Department of Archives and History; Kirk Barrett, Point Clear, AL; Chris Becker, New Orleans, LA; Nick Beeson, History Museum of Mobile, Mobile, AL; Sheritta Bitikofer, Crestview, FL; Robert Bonner, New Orleans, LA; Tim Bode, Belleville, MI; the late David Brasell, Malbis, AL; Robert Bradley, Alabama Department of Archives and History (retired); Sharee Broussard, Mobile, AL; Mike Bunn, Director, Blakeley State Park; Miriam Cady, West Virginia and Regional History Center; Dr. Glen C. Cangelosi, MD, New Orleans, LA; Calvin Chapelle, Director, Confederate Memorial Park, Marbury, AL; Amelia H. Chase, Digital Assets Archivist, Alabama Department of Archives and History; Dr. Charles Collins, New Orleans, LA; Barry Cowan, LSU Archives and Special Collections; Brian DesRochers, Interpretative Ranger, Blakeley State Park; A. J. Dupree, Mobile, AL; Laura Eliason, Indiana State Library; Valerie Ellis, Mobile Local History Library, Mobile, AL; Ken Flies, St. Paul, MN; Pat Galle, Mobile, AL; Larry Garrett, Pensacola, FL; Kerry Gossett, Springville, AL; Aaron Haley, Alabama Department of Archives and History; Ben Hannan, Mobile, AL; Roger Hansen, Demps Mountain, GA; Dean Hargett, State Historical Society of Missouri; Richard Holloway, Senior Ranger, Fort Randolph and Buhlow; Dr. Robert Houston, University of South Alabama (retired); Russell Horton, Wisconsin Veterans Museum; the late Ronnie Hyer, Viti Levu, Fiji Islands; Garret B. Kremer-Wright, The State Historical Society of Missouri; Dr. Richard Marksbury, Spanish Fort, AL; Dr. Henry McKiven, University of South Alabama; Samantha McNeily, Auburn University-Montgomery; Hesper Montford, Mobile Local History Library; Clay Miller, Spanish Fort, AL; Tim Noakes, Special Collections, Stanford University, the late Norman Nicolson, Mobile, AL; Mike Nicholson, Charlotte, NC; Vanessa Nicholson, Marion Military Institute Archivist, Marion, AL; Steve North, Daphne, AL; Bob Peck, Minnie Mitchell, Mobile Historical Society, Mobile, AL; Dave Pederson, Nashville, TN; Becki Plunknett, Special Collections Archivist/Coordinator, State Historical Society of Iowa; Bill Rambo, Alabama Historical Commission (retired), Marbury, AL; Mike Randall, Hurley, MS; Rick Reeves, Tampa, FL; Timothy Rey, University of Alabama ROTC; Joe Ringhoffer, Mobile, AL; Tom Root, Mobile, AL; Ron Manzow, Plainview Minnesota Historical Center, Plainview, MN; Patricia Ricci, Confederate Memorial Hall Museum, New Orleans, LA; Lori Schexnayder, Tulane University Special Collections; Charles B. Schmitz, Picayune, MS; Dr. Ben Severance, Auburn University-Montgomery; Wayne Sirmon, University of Mobile; John Sledge, Architectural Historian for the

City of Mobile; the late Dr. Richard J. Sommers, Senior Historian of the U.S. Army Heritage and Education Center, PA; Fred Spaulding, Mobile, AL; Bryce Suderow, Washington, D.C.; Elizabeth Theris, Mobile Local History Library, Mobile, AL; Gordon Thrasher, Ozark, AL; Dr. Steven Trout, University of Alabama; Bud Urquhart, Mobile, AL; Don Urquhart, Mobile, AL; Tom Van Antwerp, Mobile, AL; John Weaver, West Lafayette, IN; Wes Wilson, DePauw University Archives.

A special thanks goes out to Theodore P. Savas and the editorial staff at Savas Beatie for accepting my work for publication and helping to preserve America's military history. I especially want to thank Veronica Kane, production supervisor, and editor David Snyder for their skillful assistance.

"The defense of Spanish Fort was the last death grapple of the veterans of the Confederate and Federal armies."

— Major General Dabney H. Maury,
Confederate Commander of the District of the Gulf[1]

1 Dabney H. Maury, "Defence of Spanish Fort—Some Comment by the Confederate Commander on Mr. P. D. Stephenson's Article," *Southern Historical Society Papers* 39, no. 1, (Apr. 1914): 130.

Key Commanders Referenced

Confederates

Lt. Gen. Richard S. Taylor, commander, Department of Alabama, Mississippi, and East Louisiana

Maj. Gen. Dabney H. Maury, commander, District of the Gulf

Commodore Ebenezer Farrand, commander of Mobile's naval squadron

Brig. Gen. John R. St. Liddell, commander, Eastern Division of the District of the Gulf, Commanding Officer of Fort Blakeley

Brig. Gen. Randall L. Gibson, commander of Spanish Fort

Brig. Gen. James T. Holtzclaw, commander, left wing of Spanish Fort (3/31–4/8/65)

Brig. Gen. Bryan M. Thomas, commander, left wing of Spanish Fort (3/26–3/31/65)

Col. Isaac W. Patton, Spanish Fort's Chief of Artillery

Lt. Col. Philip B. Spence, commander, 12th Regiment Mississippi Cavalry

Federals

Maj. Gen. Edward R. S. Canby, commander, Military Division of West Mississippi

Acting Rear Adm. Henry K. Thatcher, commander, Western Gulf Squadron

Maj. Gen. Gordon Granger, commander, XIII Army Corps

Maj. Gen. A. J. Smith, commander, XVI Army Corps

Brig. Gen. Eugene A. Carr, commander, Third Division, XVI Army Corps

Col. James L. Geddes, commander, Third Brigade, Third Division

Brig. Gen. Cyrus B. Comstock, Aide-de-Camp to General Canby

Brig. Gen. James C. Veatch, commander, First Division, XIII Army Corps

Prologue

Battle of Mobile Bay, August 1864

Admiral David Farragut, commander of the U.S. West Gulf Blockading Squadron, struggled during the first three years of the war to stop the Confederate blockade-running in and out of Mobile Bay. So, on August 5, 1864, he launched what became known as the battle of Mobile Bay. The Federals defeated and captured the Confederate flotilla along with Forts Morgan, Gaines, and Powell, thus sealing the mouth of Mobile Bay and ending the blockade running.[1]

The capture of the forts at the entrance of Mobile Bay effectively ended the running of the Confederate blockade. Despite the significant victory, the city of Mobile remained in Confederate hands. As one U.S. Army officer summed it up: "The two great guards to Mobile Bay had fallen, the gallant fleet rode safely in the harbor, but the city of Mobile and its splendid land defenses did not yield."[2]

At the time of the battle, the Confederates had depleted Mobile's garrison to reinforce their armies elsewhere. The city had strong lines of earthen fortifications, yet few soldiers were available to defend them. Had the Federals known how few men defended Mobile, they probably could have captured the city with minimal loss.[3]

---

1 Benjamin C. Truman, "The War in the Southwest," *New York Times*, Feb. 28, 1865, 1.

2 Truman, "The War in the Southwest."

3 Titus M. Coan to Hattie Coan, Jan. 14, 1865, Titus Munson Coan Papers, New York Historical Society, hereafter Letter, TNC to HC, Jan. 14, 1865; Arthur Bergeron, *Confederate Mobile* (Jackson, MS, 1991), 196; Christopher C. Andrews, *History of the Campaign of Mobile* (New York, 1867), 20.

Maury claimed that when the Federals commenced their attack upon the defenses of the lower bay in August of 1864, there were hardly any troops in Mobile's land defenses. "Even the artillery garrisons, consisting of the 1st Louisiana artillery and the 1st Mississippi light artillery, had been called away by General Stephen D. Lee to aid in repulsing the column which, under Maj. Gen. A. J. Smith had advanced from Memphis as far as Harrisburg," he remembered. Maury later speculated that with a demonstration by Farragut's fleet on the city artillery batteries, U.S. forces could have successfully landed near Dog River and then captured Mobile without severe loss.[4]

On August 15, 1864, Farragut performed a reconnaissance in the USS *Metacomet* within 3 ½ miles of Mobile. The strong defenses protecting the city, the main channel wholly obstructed, and a row of piles guarded by mighty forts deterred him. A naval attack alone could never take Mobile. Their drafts restricted Farragut's larger warships to the bar channel and the lower fleet anchorage, so they could not get within 20 miles of the barriers. The obstructions could not be removed under heavy fire from the Confederate batteries. Even the fleet's shallow draft ironclad river monitors could not reach the city of Mobile.[5]

With the surrender of Fort Morgan, Farragut felt he had accomplished enough for the time being. After all, he had sealed the bay to blockade running, his fleet enjoyed free movement throughout most of Mobile Bay, and he held the forts at the mouth of the bay. He determined that capturing the city itself was unnecessary and would prove difficult to hold with Granger's small land force. "If I did not think Mobile would be an elephant to hold," he stated, "I would send up the light-draft ironclads and try that city, but I fear we are not in a condition to hold it." Major General Edward Richard Sprigg Canby, commander of the U.S. Military Division of West Mississippi, concurred. He also felt it "unwise" to attack Mobile directly until he had a larger force. Farragut estimated that 20,000–30,000 men were needed to take the city. In fact, at that time, half that number might have been able to march up the bay's western shore and capture the city with little resistance.[6]

---

4 Dabney H. Maury, "Souvenirs of the War," *New Orleans Daily Crescent*, Mar. 19, 1866, 4.

5 United States War Department, *Official Records of the Union and Confederate Navies in the War of the Rebellion*, Series 1, vol. 21, pp. 529–530, 612, hereafter cited as *ORN*. All references are to Series 1 unless otherwise noted; Viktor Von Scheliha, *A Treatise on Coast-Defence: Based on the Experience Gained by Officers of the Corps of Engineers of the Army of the Confederate States* (London, 1868), 157. Monitors were ironclad warships with revolving turrets. They were designed for use in shallow harbors and rivers.

6 Loyall Farragut, *The Life of David Glasgow Farragut, First Admiral of the United States Navy, Embodying His Journal and Letters* (New York, 1879), 468–470; Andrews, *Campaign of Mobile*, 20; *ORN* 21, 523, 530, 612.

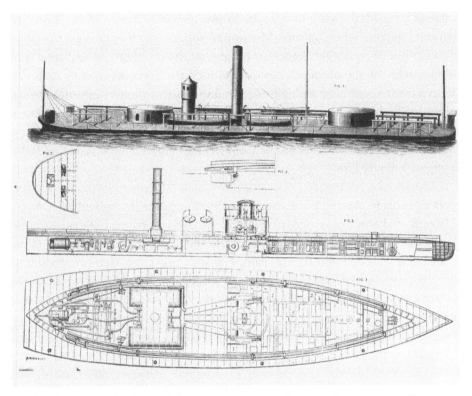

Thatcher's fleet utilized iron-clad river monitors to navigate the shallow waters of upper Mobile Bay. *Naval History and Heritage Command*

As more troops could not be spared, the U.S. naval fleet in Mobile Bay maintained a menacing presence in sight of the Confederates. Nearly eight months would pass before enough soldiers were available to launch the land campaign for Mobile. By that time, the Southerners could send in reinforcements to meet the threat from Canby's forces. Next to Richmond, Mobile endured as the second-largest city under Confederate control in 1865.[7]

Strategic Importance of Mobile

Why did General-in-Chief Ulysses S. Grant still deem the capture of Mobile important after the battle of Mobile Bay? The answer lies principally with the city's

---

7 Charles J. Allen, *"Some Account and Recollections of the Operations Against the City of Mobile and Its Defences, 1864 and 1865," Glimpses of the Nation's Struggle—A Series of Papers Read Before the Minnesota Commandery of the Military Order of the Loyal Legion of the United States* (St. Paul, MN, 1887), 68–69; Andrews, *Campaign of Mobile*, 20.

value as a logistical center, with access to two navigable rivers and two principal railroads linking the Alabama-Mississippi theater to the Georgia-Carolinas theater. Federal authorities wanted to occupy southern and central Alabama, with Montgomery as the ultimate objective point of the 1865 invasion of Alabama. With its year-round river and railroad communication into the heart of Alabama, capturing Mobile would greatly facilitate that objective. Mobile remained essential for the Confederates to defend and the Federals to attack. The loss of Mobile would not only further dampen the Confederacy's waning morale but also deal it a mighty military blow.

Indeed, the Mobile & Ohio and the Mobile & Great Northern Railroads were essential to moving Confederate forces and supplies throughout Mississippi, Alabama, and much of Georgia. The Mobile & Great Northern Railroad terminus was opposite Mobile on Mobile Bay's eastern shore. This rail line connected to the Alabama & Florida Railroad at Pollard, Alabama, providing Mobile rail access to Montgomery and beyond. The Mobile & Ohio Railroad (M&O) served as the primary supply line for Gen. John B. Hood's Tennessee campaign. The M&O remained crucial to the Confederate war effort throughout the conflict. Federal raiding parties damaged the M&O line during Maj. Gen William T. Sherman's Meridian campaign in early 1864, and again by Brig. Gen. Benjamin H. Grierson's U.S. Cavalry raid later in December of that year. However, the Confederates repaired it in time to send the Mobile garrison reinforcements and supplies. Mobile's railroad access still allowed the uninterrupted transportation of much-needed reinforcements and ordnance stores in early 1865.[8]

Mobile's location at the outlet of one of the most considerable river systems in the South made its possession important to both sides. The Mobile River, formed by the merger of the Alabama and Tombigbee, flows into the bay in front of the city. The Tombigbee and Alabama Rivers were essential to the Confederacy, especially as large steamers navigated them to Montgomery. The Federals still considered the capture of Mobile, with its year-round railroad and river access into the interior, one of the keys to subduing the state of Alabama and the Deep South. "In our possession, the entire territory of Middle and Northern Alabama and Middle and Northern Mississippi is at our mercy," the *New York Times* reported.[9]

---

8 Andrews, *Campaign of Mobile*, v, 9, 32; Lucius F. Hubbard, "Civil War Papers," 618, Library of Congress; Allen, "Operations Against the City of Mobile," 55; Andrews, *Campaign of Mobile*, 10; *ORN* 22, 41; "Grierson's Great Raid," *New Orleans Times Picayune*, Jan. 20, 1865, 1; United States War Department, *War of the Rebellion: Records of the Union and Confederate Armies*, Series 1, vol. 45, part 2, p. 753, hereafter cited as *ORA*. All references are to Series 1 unless otherwise noted.

9 Andrews, *Campaign of Mobile*, 9; Allen, *Operations against the City of Mobile*, 55; "The War in the Southwest," *New York Times*, Feb. 26, 1865.

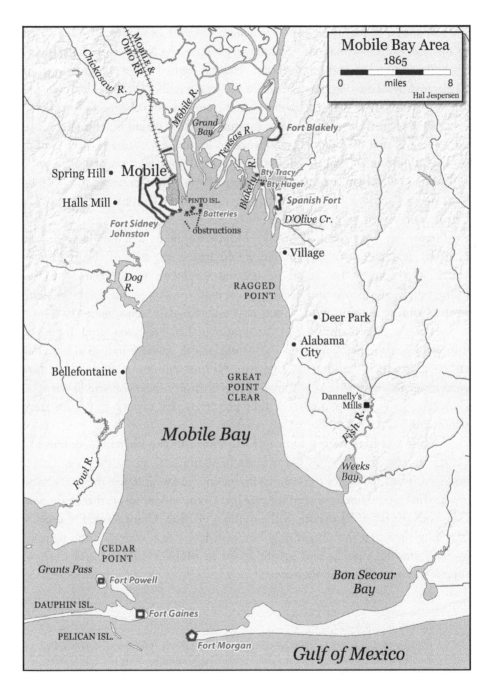

After the battle of Nashville on December 15–16, 1864, the Federals could finally spare enough troops and vessels to attack Mobile. Even though the Confederates could no longer use the city as a port, U.S. Maj. Gen. Henry Halleck still recognized its logistical value. He believed Mobile would make an ideal base to operate against Selma and Montgomery, where the Southerners had a large stockpile of supplies and ammunition. Halleck figured the war's end could be accelerated by destroying the railroads in the region and capturing Selma. He also knew an invasion of south Alabama "would prevent any of Hood's force from being sent against Sherman, and the capture of Selma would be as disastrous to the enemy as that of Atlanta." He advocated invading Alabama from the south because, as he put it: "Mobile was less swampy, and, moreover, the operating army could be supplied by steamers on the Alabama River." On December 30, 1864, he suggested to Grant to send elements of the Army of the Cumberland to the Gulf Coast to aid Canby in taking Mobile.[10]

Grant—who had wanted to take Mobile earlier in the war—agreed with Halleck's assessment. Taking Mobile would hasten the end of the war as he saw it. On January 18, 1865, he ordered Canby to move against Mobile, Montgomery, and Selma and destroy roads, machine shops, and anything useful to the Confederate war effort. Grant also ordered Maj. Gen. James H. Wilson to launch the largest cavalry raid the continent had ever seen from Tennessee into central Alabama. Capturing the Confederacy's military-industrial complex at Selma remained the ultimate objective. Wilson's raid and Canby's expedition were mutually supportive operations. Wilson's cavalry incursion would keep Lt. Gen. Nathan B. Forrest occupied, thus preventing his cavalry command from reinforcing Maury at Mobile.[11]

Mobile had long been a source of frustration to the Federals—Mobile and Galveston were the last Gulf Coast cities of significance to fly the Confederate flag—yet it became one of the last major cities of the South to feel the heavy hand of war. That would not have been the case had Grant had his way earlier in the war. Ever since the fall of Vicksburg in the summer of 1863, Grant wanted to capture Mobile to prevent it from benefiting the Confederacy as a blockade-running port; by the following year, he also sought access to Mobile's rail lines and rivers to supply Sherman's invasion of Georgia.[12]

---

10 *ORA* 45, pt. 2, 419–420.

11 George S. Waterman, "Afloat-Afield-Afloat," *Confederate Veteran* VII, (Nov. 1899): 490; Ulysses S. Grant, *The Personal Memoirs of U. S. Grant*, vol.2 (Mount MacGregor, New York, 1885), 583; James H. Wilson, *Under the Old Flag; Recollections of Military Operations in the War for the Union, the Spanish War, the Boxer Rebellion, Etc.*, vol. II (New York, 1912), 237–238. Wilson's book indicates Selma as the second largest military industrial base in the Confederacy next to the Tredegar Iron Works in Richmond, Virginia.

12 Phillip D. Stephenson, "Defence of Spanish Fort," *Southern Historical Society* 3, no. 1 (Jan. 1877): 123; Grant, *The Personal Memoirs of U. S. Grant*, 2:545–548, 584.

After capturing Vicksburg, Grant urged his superiors to allow him to do more before the Southerners could recover, and "while important points might be captured without bloodshed." Grant suggested a campaign against Mobile to then General-in-Chief Halleck, starting from Lake Pontchartrain. Halleck declined Grant's request, reasoning that the 'possession of the trans-Mississippi region was a more significant priority than moving against Mobile. Instead, Grant remained on the defensive as he had been a year before in Tennessee.[13]

Had Grant been allowed to attack Mobile earlier, some argue that the bloody battles around Chattanooga would never have occurred, nor would Sherman have had the arduous and costly task of fighting his way to Atlanta. "It would have been an easy thing to capture Mobile at the time I proposed to go there. Having that as a base of operations, troops could have been thrown into the interior to operate against General Bragg's army," Grant later lamented. The Confederate forces in the interior depended on supplies shipped in from the port of Mobile. Grant believed Bragg would have had to detach portions of his forces to meet this threat in his rear. If he had not done this, the Federal army from Mobile could have inflicted inestimable damage upon much of the region. Convinced capturing Mobile would hasten the end of the war, he continued to push the importance of capturing the city. Halleck, however, refused all his requests.[14]

Maury's recollections support Grant's notion that taking Mobile would have been easier earlier in the war. The city had been put in a state of defense from the onset of the war. Maury, however, remarked that in May of 1863, the defenses around Mobile were "not nearly completed." With the fall of Vicksburg, the anticipation of Grant's forces attacking Mobile aroused anxiety. Confederate authorities tried to provide enslaved laborers to complete and strengthen the defenses around the city. By the winter of 1863, the earthen fortifications were so strong that some officials estimated a garrison of 10,000 troops in them would compel the enemy to devote 40,000 troops and ninety days to capture the place. One Federal officer even declared the earthworks around Richmond "trifling compared with the fortification to protect Mobile."[15]

Though short-handed, the extra time allowed Maury to strengthen his defenses until the Federal advance in 1865. Mobile became the best-fortified city in the Confederacy next to Richmond. However, immediately after the battle of Nashville,

---

13 *Personal Memoirs of U. S. Grant*, 2:340–341.

14 Isaac H. Elliott, *History of the Thirty-Third Regiment Illinois Veteran Volunteer Infantry* (Gibson, IL, 1902), 48; *Personal Memoirs of U. S. Grant*, 2:340–341.

15 Clement A. Evans, *Confederate Military History: A Library of Confederate States History*, vol. VII (Atlanta, GA, 1899), 43; Maury, "Souvenirs of the War," 4.

Brigadier General Randall Lee Gibson, commander, Spanish Fort. *Library of Congress*

U.S. forces in the West finally turned their attention toward Mobile.[16]

After the devastating setback at Nashville, Confederate Lt. Gen. Richard S. Taylor, the commander of the Department of Alabama, Mississippi, and East Louisiana, realized the South had little hope of winning the war. Nevertheless, he remained resolute in trying to protract the struggle to secure the best terms possible at the negotiating table. "The duty of a soldier in the field is simple— to fight until stopped by the civil arm of his government, or his government has ceased to exist," Taylor asserted in his memoir. The men who fought at Spanish Fort demonstrated this commitment to duty. They were as stubborn and gallant as soldiers anywhere and performed their duty as if the war's outcome depended on them.[17]

Randall L. Gibson exemplified this fierce determination. In 1861, he was a young, highly educated, wealthy, well-connected Louisiana lawyer and a slave-owning planter. He lost his bid for a congressional seat in Louisiana's newly formed secessionist state government. The following month, he enlisted in the Louisiana state forces and soon became an officer in the 1st Louisiana Regular Artillery Regiment. In April, the Confederate Army fired on Fort Sumter, thus beginning the Civil War. Little did Gibson know the critical role he would play at Spanish Fort, one of the war's last battles.[18]

16 Maury, "Souvenirs of the War," 4; "The Attack on Mobile," *New York Times*, Apr. 7, 1865, 1.

17 Richard Taylor, *Destruction and Reconstruction: Personal Experiences of the Late War* (New York, 1879), 206, 218; Wilson, *Under the Old Flag*, 237–238; "In Mobile Bay," *Osage City* [KS] *Free Press*, Nov. 29, 1888, 2. Taylor was the son of former President Zachary Taylor.

18 Mary G. McBride, *Randall Lee Gibson of Louisiana: Confederate General and New South Reformer* (Baton Rouge, LA, 2007), 60, 66–68. McBride's biography is suggested for further reading. Before joining the Confederate Army, Gibson sold his 31 slaves, livestock, and cane crop to his father Tobias.

Chapter 1

"Time Is Everything to Us Now"

Confederates

On May 19, 1863, Maj. Gen. Dabney H. Maury took command of the District of the Gulf with headquarters at Mobile. The Confederate military leadership burdened the 43-year-old with the monumental task of leading the defense of the Mobile Bay area. He was, however, well qualified for the job. He was born into a prominent Fredericksburg, Virginia family. His uncle, Matthew Maury, the noted oceanographer and naval cartographer, raised him after his father died of yellow fever. A West Pointer, Maury graduated in 1846 with Civil War notables such as Confederate generals Thomas "Stonewall" Jackson, A. P. Hill, George Pickett, and future U.S. General George McClellan—a close friend. He served in the Mexican War and remained in the U.S. Army until the Civil War. Before he arrived in Mobile, the Virginian had commanded divisions in the Pea Ridge, Iuka, and Corinth battles. President Jefferson Davis wanted Maury at Mobile, presumably for his experience supervising heavy artillery against gunboats at Vicksburg.[1]

Soon after Maury assumed command at Mobile, Lt. Col. Arthur James Lyon Fremantle of the British Army visited the city on his tour of the Confederacy. While sightseeing the defenses of Mobile Bay, the ubiquitous Englishman overheard Maury remark: "Well, I never should have believed that I could have lived to see the day in

---

1 Bergeron, *Confederate Mobile*, 28–29; Ezra J. Warner, *Generals in Gray: Lives of the Confederate Commanders* (Baton Rouge, LA, 1959), 215–216; Taylor, *Destruction and Reconstruction*, 202.

Major General Dabney H. Maury, commander of the District of the Gulf.

Library of Congress

which I would detest that old [U.S.] flag." Fremantle described Maury as a "very gentlemanlike and intelligent but diminutive Virginian."[2]

Indeed, he was small—only about five feet three inches tall. Some of his men called him "puss in boots" because his large cavalry boots seemed to cover a good portion of his person. Despite his diminutive appearance, many regarded him as a gallant and efficient leader.[3]

On August 15, 1864, Lieutenant General Taylor took command of the Department of Alabama, Mississippi, and East Louisiana, and thus Maury's District of the Gulf. Taylor described Maury as "intelligent, upright, and devoted to duty." Taylor noted that he had gained the respect and confidence of the people of Mobile, enabling him to supplement his force with the local militia. He recalled: "It was a great comfort to find an able officer in this responsible position, who not only adopted my plans but improved and executed them."[4]

Lieutenant Colonel James M. Williams, 21st Alabama, did not share Taylor's sentiments. Williams had evacuated the dangerously exposed Fort Powell to save his garrison after Farragut's fleet entered the bay in August 1864. Disgusted with Williams's decision, Maury temporarily removed him from command. Disgruntled by what he perceived as unjust treatment, Williams harbored resentment toward his commander. In an October 1864 letter to his wife, he grumbled: "I am coming to

2 Sir A. Fremantle, *The Fremantle Diary: Being the Journal of Lieutenant Colonel James Arthur Lyon Fremantle, Coldstream Guards, on His Three Months in the Southern States* (London, 1956), 103–104; Sidney Adair Smith and C. Carter Smith, eds., *Mobile: 1861-1865* (Chicago, 1964), 19.

3 Philip Daingerfield Stephenson, *The Civil War Memoir of Philip Daingerfield Stephenson, D. D.: Private, Company K, 13th Arkansas Volunteer Infantry, and Loader, Piece No. 4, 5th Company, Washington Artillery, Army of Tennessee, CSA*, ed. Nathaniel C. Hughes (Conway, 1995), 358359.

4 Taylor, *Destruction and Reconstruction*, 202.

Lieutenant General Richard Taylor, commander of the Department of Alabama, Mississippi, and East Louisiana. *Library of Congress*

have a perfect contempt for the corrupt and imbecile administration of our military department here." In a letter written a few months later, Williams claimed that Maury had "been irreverently dubbed the Lord of Panic" by some for his belief that Mobile would be attacked at any moment.[5]

Fall 1864

Despite Williams's cynicism, intelligence reports made it clear to Maury that Mobile would be next in line for an attack. He knew that grand-scale preparations were being made to capture the city. After all, it was the only Gulf Coast city of magnitude remaining under Confederate control, east of the Mississippi River. Within sight of the Confederate camps, Federal gunboats anchored in Mobile Bay were constant reminders of the pending attack. Maury did all within his power to prepare for the Federals. "We could only bide the time when he was ready to move inland," remembered Brig. Gen. St. John R. Liddell, commander of the Eastern Division of the District of the Gulf. Meanwhile, the Graybacks kept throwing up defensive earthworks and preparing to give the U.S. Army a "warm reception."[6]

---

5 James M. Williams, *From That Terrible Field: Civil War Letters of James M. Williams, Twenty-first Alabama Infantry Volunteers*, ed. John Kent Folmar (Tuscaloosa, 1981), 147,157. Maury temporarily relieved Williams of command after the battle of Mobile Bay for evacuating Fort Powell. Maury felt Williams prematurely retreated, that he should have continued to fight his guns despite being greatly exposed to the Federal gunboats in his rear in Mobile Bay. The military court exonerated Williams, but he evidently resented Maury for the treatment he had received.

6 William R. Plum, LL. B., *The Military Telegraph During the Civil War in the United States: with an Exposition of Ancient and Modern Means of Communication, and of the Federal and Confederate Cipher System; also a Running Account of the War Between the States* (Chicago1882), 297; St. John R. Liddell, *Liddell's Record*, ed. Nathaniel C. Hughes (Baton Rouge, LA, 1985), 189.

Brigadier General St. John Richardson Liddell, commander of the Eastern Division of the Gulf District. *Confederate Memorial Hall*

Shortly after the battle of Mobile Bay, Maury assigned Liddell, 50 years old, the command of the Eastern Division in September of 1864 with headquarters at Blakeley. Liddell owned a plantation near Harrisonburg, Louisiana, before the war. He had briefly attended West Point before being removed in 1835 for poor academics and an alleged fight with two classmates. Although he lacked extensive military training, Liddell proved to be a capable and hard-nosed brigade and division commander at Chickamauga, Perryville, Murfreesboro, Missionary Ridge, and Red River. His biographer Nathaniel C. Hughes described him as "active and often violent, a doer, a fully engaged human being." Maury entrusted him with affairs on the eastern shore of Mobile Bay in preparation for Canby's expected expedition.[7]

After U.S. forces captured the lower defenses of Mobile Bay in August 1864, the Graybacks anticipated an attack on the city. In the months preceding the campaign for Mobile, Confederate authorities continued to fortify their defenses and send in reinforcements to the city. Though some considered Mobile's western shore defenses as strong as any place in the South, engineers recognized the vulnerability of the eastern shore. They determined strong land fortifications on the bluffs of the Blakeley River were needed to protect the two existing artillery batteries, Huger (pronounced *HU-gee*) and Tracey. The two batteries were located in the marsh at the Apalachee and Blakeley Rivers junction to prevent the U.S. fleet from gaining access to the rivers. The land fortifications would also be used to threaten Federal columns advancing from the east.

7 Warner, *Generals in Gray*, 187; Liddell & Hughes, *Liddell's Record*, 8; "U.S. Federal Census, 1860, Slave Schedules," FamilySearch, accessed February 7, 2023, https://www.familysearch.org/ark:/61903/3:1:33S7-9BSC-9CFW?i=10&cc=3161105&personaUrl=%2Fark%3A%2F61903%2F1%3A1%3AWK27-WW6Z. In 1860, Liddell enslaved 88 people in Catahoula Parish, Louisiana.

Recognizing the imminent threat facing Mobile, Taylor sent the highly regarded Col. Samuel Lockett, the chief engineer for the Department of Alabama, Mississippi, and East Louisiana, to oversee the construction of the defenses. An 1859 graduate of West Point, Lockett designed Vicksburg's defenses, where he surrendered with the garrison on July 4, 1863. The two principal earthen fortifications in Baldwin County—Spanish Fort and Fort Blakeley—were thus hurriedly thrown up under his supervision.[8]

Besides Fort Gaines and Fort Morgan, Mobile's fortifications were made of earth. With advancements in artillery, earthen fortifications offered better protection than masonry. In his book *Treatise on Coast Defense*, Mobile's chief engineer, Viktor Von Scheliha, argued: "Earth, especially Sand-works, properly constructed, is a better protection against Modern Artillery than permanent Fortifications built on the old plan." Scheliha noted that when the U.S. Navy continually bombarded the earthen Fort Powell from February 22–March 2, 1864, "not a single gun had been dismounted, not a single traverse had been seriously damaged, nor had the parapet and the bomb-proof lost any of their strength, all damage done by the exploding shells being at once repaired by throwing sand-bags in the opened craters."[9]

Batteries Huger and Tracey were the first fortifications built near the eastern shore long before Colonel Lockett arrived in Mobile. One artillerist posted at Huger stated: "It is not such a place as I would select for a summer residence, but then it will do under the circumstances." The Confederates had long recognized that Federal vessels might attempt to pass up the Blakeley River or the Apalachee River and then come around through the Tensaw, arriving in Mobile. The two marsh batteries were built on low ground near the river to close this route, with piles driven for a foundation. At the Blakeley and Apalachee Rivers junction point, Huger featured four bastions and was open at the north end. Battery Tracey, an enclosed fort on the west side of the Apalachee River, was about 1,060 yards north of Huger. Huger was just over 3,100 yards from Spanish Fort, Tracey about 4,190 yards. To further obstruct access, piles were driven across the Apalachee and Blakeley Rivers; many torpedoes were anchored in different parts of the bay.[10]

8 "The Attack on Mobile," *New York Times*, Apr. 7, 1865, 1; Allen, "Operations against the City," 59, 69; *ORA* 45, pt. 2, 779–780; accessed Sep. 2, 2017, http://battleofchampionhill.org/lockett1.htm.

9 Viktor Von Scheliha, *A Treatise on Coast-defence: Based on the Experience Gained by Officers of the Corps of Engineers of the Army of the Confederate States* (London, 1868), 29, 36.

10 Mark Lyons to Amelia Horsler, Mar. 30, 1865, War Letters of Mark Lyons, Alabama Department of Archives and History, hereafter ML to AH, Mar. 30, 1865; Waterman, "Afloat-Afield-Afloat," 22; *Liddell's Records*, 190; Maury, "Defence of Spanish Fort," 133; Andrews, "Campaign of Mobile," 70–71. Period estimates of the distance from Huger and Tracey to Spanish Fort varied between 1700–2500 yards. Modern maps reveal the distance between Huger and Spanish Fort to be about 3,075 yards. A fort (Tracey) is a closed structure, while a battery (Huger) is open-backed.

Colonel Samuel Lockett, Chief Engineer, Department of Alabama, Mississippi, and East Louisiana. *Alabama Department of Archives and History*

The two marsh batteries supported each other and commanded the Apalachee and Blakeley Rivers. They boasted powerful artillery pieces. Huger featured 11 guns, including two massive 10-inch columbiads mounted in the center on a 25-foot high bombproof; Tracey had five 7-inch rifled guns.[11]

The prevailing reason for the two batteries' location was their distance from the hills on the eastern shore. In a January 12, 1865, letter to Confederate headquarters at Richmond, Lockett opined that these works should have been located closer to Fort Blakeley. Still, there had already been too much time and labor expended to justify abandoning them. "I have scrupulously avoided making any material alterations in work at this point," he explained, "as this policy has already been pursued almost to a ruinous extent, resulting in a great increase of expense and retardation of operations that long since should have been completed."[12]

Maury feared the U.S. Army might occupy the site of the 18th-century Spanish Fort and silence Huger and Tracey. His engineers decided to build a fortification there to protect the two river batteries from bombardment from the eastern shore and to threaten Federal columns that might advance in that vicinity from Pensacola, Fort Morgan, or other points from the east. On August 11, 1864, while the Federals besieged Fort Morgan at the bay's mouth, plans to construct earthen fortifications were pushed forward around the old Spanish Fort. The

---

11 *ORA* 45, pt. 2, 779–780; Waterman, "Afloat-Afield-Afloat," 22; Gordon Thrasher, *Selma Brooke Guns of Mobile* (Ozark, AL, 2022), 4. The Selma Naval Gun Foundry and Ordnance Works logbook indicates they shipped a Brooke S-125, an 11-inch rifle for Battery Huger—the only one of its kind— to Mobile on March 17, 1865. It is not clear if the cannon made it to Huger.

12 *ORA* 45, pt. 2, 779–780.

Confederates built Fort Blakeley, about four miles upriver, to protect their line of communication with Spanish Fort and the two marsh batteries.[13]

On August 10, 1864, Col. John H. Gindrat proposed building the new and improved Spanish Fort around the remnants of the existing colonial fort; Scheliha wholeheartedly agreed. "A sufficient number of hands have arrived to justify us in making the most earnest endeavors at securing that important position permanently," Scheliha informed Gindrat the following day, "and, if time be allowed, there can be no doubt of our success." Gindrat supervised the construction of the fortifications under tremendous pressure. "Time is everything to us now, and we have to make the best use of the short respite the enemy seems willing to grant," Scheliha pointed out. "You know our wants as well as I do. Please push the work and call for any assistance you may require." Work began on Spanish Fort around August 19, 1864, about the same time Colonel Lockett arrived in Mobile.[14]

In early September, Gindrat assumed command of all engineering operations on the eastern shore, including Spanish Fort and Fort Blakeley, and the strengthening of the existing marsh batteries, Huger and Tracey. He worked tirelessly and with a sense of urgency. Within a month, his enslaved labor force had nearly built Redoubt 2 and commenced erecting Redoubt 3. They also cleared timber in front of and between these works to provide a clear field of fire. Gindrat reported that his laborers cut the timber for bombproofs and magazines.[15]

Maury and Lockett, however, determined no bombproofs should be constructed at the eastern shore forts in early October. Lockett reasoned the construction of bombproofs for the protection of the garrison to be "inexpedient" and would require more workforce than circumstances allowed. He believed the main attack on these works would be infantry and light artillery combined with a long-range bombardment from the gunboats in the bay, so bombproofs were not essential. Lockett reported to Richmond: "I have had no bombproofs for the garrison made, as I think experience in this district indicates very plainly that such temptations to the garrison to leave its post on the parapet are extremely dangerous, or, at least, of doubtful propriety."[16]

13 Maury, "Defence of Spanish Fort,"133; *ORA* 39, pt. 2, 772; Allen, "Operations against the City of Mobile," 72. A line of communication refers to the route that connects an operating military unit with its supply base. Supplies and reinforcements are transported along the line of communication.

14 *ORA* 39, pt. 2, 772; Janet Hewitt, ed., *Supplement to the Official Records of the Union and Confederate Armies*, Part I, vol. 7 (Wilmington, NC, 1994), 940.

15 *ORA* 39, pt. 2, 815, 819, 842. A redoubt is a small fort, an enclosed defensive work. Bombproofs are underground shelters for protection against artillery fire.

16 *ORA* 39, pt. 3, 792; *ORA* 45, pt. 2, 779–780.

The Confederates built a heavy battery at Redoubt 1, also known as the old Spanish Fort. Designed to prevent gunboats from ascending the river and removing torpedoes and obstructions, Redoubt 1's commanding position over the Blakeley River made it nearly impossible for the U.S. Navy to reduce Batteries Huger and Tracey, which Scheliha believed were their most important works.

Fort McDermott (Redoubt 2) undoubtedly occupied the strongest position of the Spanish Fort's defenses. The Confederates built McDermott 800 yards away from Redoubt 1 on a 145-foot hill. The fort overlooked Redoubt 1, with an elevation difference of 58 feet. Engineers determined that Fort McDermott had to be fortified to prevent the U.S. Army from mounting artillery there and subduing Old Spanish Fort. Scheliha believed this lunette-shaped work to be the key to the whole position and could not be made too strong.[17]

Due to a shortage of labor, materials, and tools, strengthening the fortifications around Mobile posed a challenge. Concerned about the slow progress of the works around the city, Taylor made the controversial decision to send a detachment of United States Colored Troops (USCT), captured by Forrest in Tennessee, to be employed as laborers at Mobile. These soldiers of color, some of whom were once reportedly enslaved in Mobile, were dressed in standard-issue blue U.S. uniforms. [18]

Federal authorities considered the formerly enslaved men to be soldiers and expected them to be treated as prisoners of war. Under a flag of truce, Granger sent a letter of protest to Maury over the use of captured Black soldiers to labor upon the fortifications of Mobile. Granger threatened that an equal number of prisoners in their hands would be similarly employed if Maury allowed the practice to continue. Maury's response confirmed that 200 USCT prisoners captured by Forrest were laboring upon the fortifications of Mobile, "just as other slaves are and have been almost since the commencement of the war employed by both the Governments of the United States and the Confederate States." He made the Confederacy's position clear: they were legal property and not considered prisoners of war at the date of their capture. He further defended this stance by pointing out that they operated by Confederate law and "the Constitution and laws of the United States." The Virginian dismissed Granger's threat: "The employment, then, of white men, prisoners of war, whose social and political character is that of freemen, is not justified by the circumstances, and is neither fair nor in accordance

---

17 Hewitt, *Supplement to the Official Records*, pt. 1, vol. 7, 956; *ORA* 39, pt. 3, 796; "General Orders 120," *Mobile Advertiser and Register*, Mar. 28, 1865. Maury ordered the redoubt to be named in honor of 2Lt. Edward J. McDermott who was killed on Lake Maurepas, Louisiana, while leading an attack during a special mission on March 13, 1865.

18 Taylor, *Destruction and Reconstruction*, 210; *ORA* 49, pt. 1, 957; "Mobile Items—A letter from Mobile," *Richmond Dispatch*, Oct. 18, 1864, 1.

with the established usages of warfare." Maury claimed that the prisoners themselves declared that they were taken away from their homes and their lawful owners in Confederate territory by invading parties of U.S. forces, placed in the army, or employed for other military purposes against their will. "These negroes are well fed and provided for and generally content in their present situation," Maury replied. "They express the utmost reluctance and indisposition to be returned to the dominion of the United States, and restored to involuntary service with their armies, and are earnest in their desire to return to their lawful owners, from whom they were unwillingly taken away." He added that he intended to restore them to their lawful owners, who would receive just compensation for the labor of these enslaved men.[19]

Winter 1864–65

In December, earth and sod were transported to Huger and Tracey to strengthen their magazines. Lack of powder and shipping of stores from Corinth delayed torpedo manufacture. Progress on the eastern shore fortifications had slowed considerably due to the lack of hands available.[20]

Maury received an ominous dispatch on Christmas day. From his Meridian headquarters, Taylor wired him of General Hood's "severe reverse" in Tennessee and conveyed his grim belief that Mobile would be seriously threatened as soon as Canby received reinforcements. He urged Maury to make "steady and energetic preparations" for the anticipated attack, instructing him to "push forward with all possible vigor, and, if necessary, you should employ your soldiers" to complete the works.[21]

The Confederate military leaders did not want to risk the capture of the Spanish Fort garrison. Unknown to most of the common soldiers, officers took measures to withdraw them if all hope for further defense was lost. Toward the end of December 1864, instructions were received to begin the construction of a narrow wooden treadway bridge from the rear of Spanish Fort across the marsh to communicate with Huger and Tracey. The plans called for small piles driven in the swamp by hand, with light cross pieces joining them together. Observers described the narrow bridge as 18 inches to four feet wide and three or four feet above the marsh. The Confederates did not complete the roughly mile-long treadway until

---

19 *ORA*, Series 2, vol. 8, pt. 1, 354–355.

20 *ORA* 45, pt. 2, 678, 735.

21 Ibid., 734.

March 30, after the siege began. Just before the investment of Spanish Fort, Maury sent 1Lt. John T. Elmore of his staff to Gibson to manage the completion.[22]

Colonel Isaac W. Patton, commander of the 22nd Consolidated Louisiana Regiment, commanded the small garrison at Spanish Fort during its construction in mid-August of 1864. Born in Fredericksburg, Virginia, on February 4, 1828, Patton came from a distinguished military family. Early colonist Hugh Mercer, his great-grandfather, later became a general in the Revolutionary War, losing his life at the battle of Princeton. Patton had five brothers who faithfully fought for the Confederacy. One of his brothers, Col. George S. Patton, commanded the 22nd Virginia Infantry Regiment of the Army of Northern Virginia and is the grandfather of the famous World War II general.[23]

Educated at the Fairfax Institute near Alexandria, Patton first gained military experience as a second lieutenant in the 10th United States Infantry under Gen. Zachary Taylor during the Mexican War. After his stint in the U.S. Army, he moved to Louisiana in 1855 to become a cotton planter. In early 1862, the Virginian joined the Confederate Army and participated in the organization of the 22nd Louisiana. When the Federal fleet opened its attack below New Orleans in April 1862, Patton's command manned the artillery at Chalmette. They fired the first shots and fought until they exhausted their ammunition. Forced to fall back to New Orleans, Patton's command then dispersed and headed to Vicksburg, where they manned heavy artillery. He commanded the largest and most important fort on the Confederate line at Vicksburg. During the siege, he suffered a severe wound to the hip and became a prisoner of war.

In early 1864, after the fall of Vicksburg, Gen. Leonidas Polk created the 22nd Louisiana Consolidated Regiment by merging several Louisiana units—the remnants of the 3rd, 17th, 21st, 22nd, 27th, 29th, and 31st Louisiana regiments. They received the designation 22nd Louisiana because most of the men came from that regiment. Patton's command rarely numbered more than 250 men. After Vicksburg, he went to Mobile to serve as Maury's artillery commander, staying the remainder of the war.[24]

---

22 *ORA* 45, pt. 2, 746; *ORA* 49, pt. 1, 317; Maury, "Defence of Spanish Fort," 131; *ORA* 49, pt. 2, 1129; John T. Elmore, Compiled Service Records, RG 109, NARA; Hewitt, *Supplement to the Official Records*, pt. 1, vol. 7, 942.

23 Andrews, *History of the Campaign of Mobile*, 70; "Col Isaac W. Patton (CSA), Mayor of New Orleans," Geni_family_tree, last modified June 29, 2019, https://www.geni.com/people/Col-Isaac-W-Patton-CSA-Mayor-of-New-Orleans/6000000004088656026.

24 Andrews, *History of the Campaign of Mobile*, 70; "Col Isaac W. Patton"; Arthur W. Bergeron, Jr., "They Bore Themselves with Distinguished Gallantry: The Twenty-Second Louisiana Infantry," *The Journal of the Louisiana Historical Association* 13, no. 3 (Summer 1972): 264–282.

Colonel Isaac W. Patton, 22nd Consolidated Louisiana, commander of Spanish Fort's Artillery. *Admiral Semmes Sons of Confederate Veterans Camp 11*

Patton's lieutenants attempted to reinforce Fort Gaines during the battle of Mobile Bay. The machinery on their steamboat transport did not work properly and was delayed. They arrived at the lower bay in time to witness the naval engagement but had to make a hasty retreat back to Mobile. Had they come an hour earlier, they would have been doomed to capture with the rest of the garrison of Fort Gaines.[25]

On January 21, 1865, Lockett notified Patton that all hands constructing fortifications at Spanish Fort were to be transferred to Mobile to put up new works there. Lockett wrote, "I hope your lines are now secure, or, at least, in such condition that the troops can finish the necessary work." However, storms during the middle of January interfered with having the earthworks sodded. Much work was still needed to prepare the fort to repel a U.S. Army attack. Lockett arranged tools for Patton's small garrison to continue with the work required to strengthen Spanish Fort. He directed Patton to have his men plant sub-terra shells in front of Redoubt 2, place head-logs on infantry parapets and make fascines to replace sandbags, and then use the sandbags to make loopholes out of which the infantry could shoot.[26]

Spanish Fort occupied the high ground with an estimated length of about two miles. Its southern flank rested on the Blakeley River; it's left on Minette Bay. The

---

25 W. H. Tunnard, *A Southern Record. The History of the Third Regiment Louisiana Infantry* (Baton Rouge, LA, 1866), 304–305.

26 *ORA* 45, pt. 2, 803. Fascines are a bundle sticks, bound together used for strengthening the sides of embankments, ditches, or trenches.

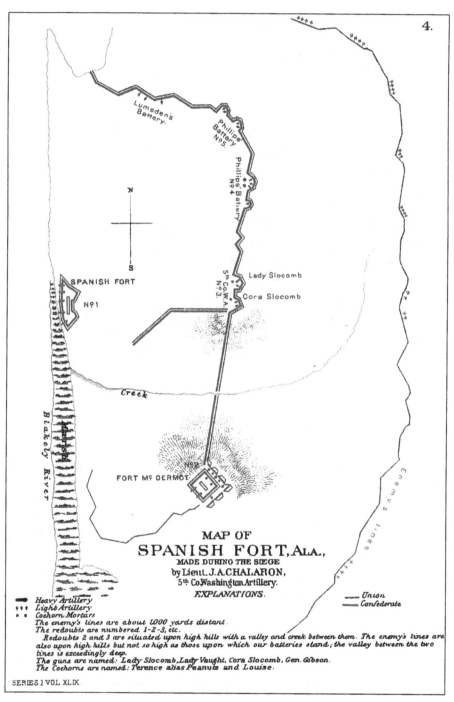

1Lt. Joseph A. Chalaron, 5th Company, Washington Artillery, drew this map during the siege. *History Museum of Mobile*

breastworks ran in a semi-circle around the inside rim of the highland. The fort looked a lot like "a horseshoe pressed open."[27]

Officers on both sides considered Spanish Fort the key to Mobile. The importance the Confederates placed upon its position in the city's defenses was evident by the superior engineering skill displayed in its construction and the numerous heavy artillery pieces it brandished.[28]

Although the earthworks were indeed substantial in many places, they were not complete when the siege began. Maury later admitted that the ground was difficult to defend. "The works were badly placed," Maury observed, "they were light and incomplete." On the extreme left, for example, a section of the fort remained sparsely protected by works, owing to the marshy character of the ground. Some of the Confederates recognized it as their weak point. However, in a sense, it was also a strong point. The Confederate engineers felt the dense swamp would be sufficient to deter an attack. Only a picket line would be placed there.[29]

The breastworks were made of logs piled three to four feet high. The Confederates dug dirt from the 5-foot-deep trench before the logs and packed it down on top of them. Breastworks had to be packed down. Otherwise, hit by an artillery shell, the falling or splintering logs might cause more damage than the projectile. Head-logs were placed along the top of the works to protect the men's heads "from the missiles of the Yankee pickets." Head-logs were placed a few inches off the top of the breastworks by smaller limbs so that the defenders could aim and shoot at the enemy while minimizing their exposure. A formidable ditch in front of the breastworks added to the strength of the place. It was five feet deep and eight feet wide, but the ditch in front of Fort McDermott was even deeper and broader.[30]

Large trees in front of the fort were cut down for a few hundred yards, providing a clear field of fire. "Every ravine had borne a heavy growth of hardwood, which having been slashed made, with the underbrush and vines, an almost impassable obstruction," noted one U.S. soldier. In front of the main works were numerous advanced rifle pits for skirmishers. Along the entire front existed an elaborate

27 *ORA* 49, pt. 1, 314–315; Allen, "Operations against the City of Mobile," 72.

28 Sanford Huff, M.D., *The Annals of Iowa* (Iowa City, 1866), 948.

29 Stephenson, "Defence of Spanish Fort," *Southern Historical Society* 3, no. 1 (Jan 1877): 123; Richard L. Howard, *History of the 124th Regiment Illinois Infantry Volunteers: Otherwise Known as the "Hundred and Two Dozen," from August, 1862, to August, 1865* (Springfield, IL, 1880), 295; Hewitt, *Supplement to the Official Records*, pt. 1, vol. 7, 964.

30 J. S. E. Robinson, "Reminiscence of the War between the States," Auburn University Montgomery Library, Archives and Special Collections; A. A. Stuart, *Iowa Colonels and Regiments: Being a History of Iowa Regiments in the War of the Rebellion* (Des Moines, IA: Mills & Company, 1865), 191; Howard, *124th Regiment*, 295.

Fort McDermott from the Union XIII Corps' position. *Alabama Department of Archives and History*

line of abatis fifteen feet wide. The tops of the fallen trees were pointed outward, trimmed, and sharpened, forming a continuous brush fence. A line of *cheval de frise*, medium-sized logs wired together at the ends with sharpened stakes passed through them, intervened between the ditch and the abatis.[31]

Despite Lockett's earlier directive, Patton set his men to work making bombproofs and ammunition magazines behind their breastworks. Some of these bombproofs were as large as 16x20 feet and 10–12 feet deep. The artillerists encamped at Spanish Fort cut down large trees and rolled the trunks over the hole. They put a layer of brush and dirt, then another layer of heavy logs crosswise, and then a layer of scrub and soil until the roof was as high as eight feet. Bombproofs proved indispensable to the garrison.[32]

Artillery of all kinds and calibers bristled along the walls. All the batteries were on a high and commanding ground. The real strength of the Spanish Fort consisted of two firmly enclosed and bastioned forts, the Old Spanish Fort (Redoubt 1) and the most vital position, Fort McDermott (Redoubt 2). This fort was heavily armed, including columbiads and Brooke rifled guns.[33]

---

31 Howard, *124th Regiment*, 295–296; Elliott, *Thirty-Third Regiment*, 228. Abatis is a defensive obstacle formed by felled trees with sharpened branches facing the enemy.

32 Stephenson, "Defence of Spanish Fort," 121–123; Waterman, "Afloat-Afield-Afloat," Vol. VIII, Jan. 1900, 24.

33 Howard, *124th Regiment*, 296; "Later From Spanish Fort," *The Times Picayune*, Apr. 5, 1865, 4.

The total number of guns inside the Spanish Fort amounted to 46 pieces. Moreover, Huger had 11 guns, while Tracey had five seven-inch rifled guns.[34]

Several of the guns were received during the siege. "Hence we had more to contend against," recalled one soldier of Carr's Division of the XVI Corps, "providing the earthworks were equally strong and well manned than at Vicksburg, where the enemy had but little artillery which he could make effective against us."[35]

The Brooke guns were made in the Confederate Naval Ordnance Works at Selma. The iron came from Bibb and Shelby Counties, Alabama. General Maury declared that Brierfield, Alabama, produced "the best iron for making cannon in the world." The Selma Brookes were rifles (11-inch, 7-inch, and 6.4-inch calibers) and smoothbores (11-inch, 10-inch, and 8-inch calibers). Four twenty-four-pounder bronze howitzers at Spanish Fort were captured from a Federal gunboat on the Yazoo River.[36]

Coehorn mortars were freely used at Spanish Fort. Maury had the mortars cast at the Skates & Company Foundry in Mobile. He also had wooden mortars made of gum tree stumps, hollowed out to eight and ten-inch calibers. They were hooped with iron and lined with sheet iron. These wooden mortars could only be used at short range and with minimal charges.[37]

The Confederates incorporated numerous innovations to defend the city against the imminent Federal attack. In case their cannons were silenced, they placed sub-terra shells, also known as torpedoes, in front of the breastworks of Spanish Fort to prevent an assault. In the weeks preceding Canby's arrival, the

34 *ORA* 49, pt. 1, 150–151; Waterman, "Afloat-Afield-Afloat," Vol. VIII, Feb. 1900, 55.

35 Howard, *124th Regiment*, 296; *ORA* 49, pt. 1, 314.

36 Maury, "Spanish Fort," 133; Maury, "Defense of Mobile," 4; Thrasher, *Selma Brooke Guns of Mobile*, 3–5; *ORN* 21, 881–882; Maury recalled about a year before the siege of Spanish Fort, six 24-pounder bronze howitzers were captured from a Federal gunboat on the Yazoo River. Ross's Brigade of Texas Cavalry along with Owens' Arkansas Light Battery operating in Mississippi along the Yazoo River opened on the gunboat, causing her to surrender. Having no boat available to receive the surrender of the ship, several Confederates stripped down nude and swam out to receive the crew's formal surrender. Six twenty-four pounder bronze howitzers were removed from the vessel and sent to Mobile, where their carriages were changed to suit land defense. Four of them were mounted in the works of Spanish Fort. There was an 11-inch Brooke rifle sent to Mobile, the only one of its kind. Maury erroneously claimed not one of the Selma Brooke guns "was ever bursted or even strained" during the defense of Mobile. However, Lt. Col. James M. Williams, 21st Alabama, reported that a defect in a 7-inch Selma Brooke gun at Fort Powell caused it to burst on February 29, 1864.

37 Maury, "Souvenirs of the War," 4; Confederate Papers Relating to Citizens or Business Firms, complied 1874–1899, documenting the period 1861–1865," NARA-Confederate Citizens File. [Online version, www.fold3.com/image/52052683, Dec. 31, 2020.] The only extant invoice for them is one from Skates & Company Foundry, for ten 24 pounder mortars, dated Nov. 1863. The wooden coehorn mortar had simple design: a tube, often copper or bronze alloy, bolted to a wooden bed set to a 45-degree angle. Straps on each side enabled the weapon to be picked up by 2–4 men to be moved around the lines.

small garrison at Spanish Fort planted torpedoes along the ground in the woody marsh in their front and on the roads approaching the fort. "We planted our front pretty thoroughly with mines, consisting of large shells buried with caps that would explode at the touch of a foot on a trigger," recalled one soldier of Lumsden's Battery. The torpedoes in front of the fort were marked by little stakes and pieces of white cloth to alert their comrades.[38]

The subterranean shells were typically 7-inch, 8-inch, and 11-inch explosive shells with percussion fuses fixed on top. They were placed lightly under the soil so the slightest pressure would trigger an explosion.[39]

"The torpedoes were the most striking and effective of the new contrivances for defense which were used during these operations," Maury later touted. Submarine torpedoes (submerged mines) littered the water approaches to Mobile. The Confederates innovatively built their best torpedoes from beer casks charged with gunpowder. An iron chain linked to a mushroom-shaped concrete block anchored and concealed the deadly mines about two feet below the water's surface. These torpedoes prevented vessels drawing three feet of water from getting within cannon range of the city's defenses.[40]

In addition to powerful artillery and torpedoes, several other military innovations were incorporated into the defense of Spanish Fort. Screens, "made by plates of steel"—or "mantlets," as the soldiers called them—shielded their cannon embrasures. Made of "wrought iron," these plates were about two feet by three feet square and half an inch thick; these "mantlets" protected cannoneers against enemy sharpshooters. They were secured to the inner faces of the embrasures and were quickly lowered and raised as the gun ran into the battery or recoiled from the embrasure upon firing.[41]

Sandbag embrasures protected the sharpshooters in the rifle pits. Before the siege began, General P. G. T. Beauregard gave Maury the model of a wooden

38 Howard, *124th Regiment*, 296; Elliott, *Thirty-Third Regiment*, 228; Stuart, Iowa Colonels, 191; George Little and James Maxwell, "A History of Lumsden's Battery, C. S. A," Gutenberg, accessed July 2, 2020, https://www.gutenberg.org/files/26455/26455-h/26455-h.htm; John N. Chamberlin, *Captaining the Corps d'Afrique: The Civil War Diaries and Letters of John Newton Chamberlin* (Jefferson, NC, 2016), 110.

39 "Mobile," *New York Herald*, Apr. 9, 1865, 1. Land mines were referred to as sub-terra shells or torpedoes. There are numerous accounts of sub-terra shells at Spanish Fort. One long time relic hunter that has metal-detected Spanish Fort for decades, however, told the author that he doubts these reports. He noted that neither he, nor anyone he knows, has ever found any physical evidence of sub-terra shells at Spanish Fort.

40 Maury, "Spanish Fort," 133.

41 Dabney H. Maury, "Defence of Mobile in 1865," *Southern Historical Society Papers* 3, no. 1 (Jan. 1877): 11–12; Waterman, "Afloat-Afield-Afloat," 53; Hewitt, *Supplement to the Official Records*, 942.

embrasure to be used by sharpshooters. Sandbags in the rifle pits covered these embrasures. The old veterans of the Army of Tennessee found them far superior to the head-logs, but demand for them exceeded Maury's ability to provide them.[42]

An invention of Maury's chief of artillery, Col. William E. Burnet, greatly facilitated the maneuvering of siege guns. His innovation dispensed with eccentrics entirely, thus allowing the heaviest cannon to be moved into a battery with one hand.[43]

Although the Federals commonly believed they would not meet much resistance, the Confederates had no intention of giving up Mobile without a fight. Despite limited manpower and time, the capable Confederate engineers: Lockett, Gindrat, Scheliha, and the men under their direction worked tirelessly to construct the best defensive system possible.

---

42 Maury, "Spanish Fort," 135; Maury, "Defence of Mobile in 1865," 11–12; *ORA* 49, pt. 2, 1179.

43 Maury, "Souvenirs of the War," 4; Maury, "Defence of Mobile in 1865," 12.

Chapter 2

"The Longer Mobile Can Be Held the Better"

Confederates

General P. G. T. Beauregard, commander of the Department of the West, knew the Confederacy no longer had the strength to fight pitched battles and execute costly frontal assaults. On November 17, 1864, the Louisianan counseled Taylor to adopt a Fabian defensive system, avoiding senseless assaults in favor of wearing down the enemy through skirmishing and indirection.[1]

"Don't run the risk of losing your force and guns to hold any one place or position, but harass the enemy at all points. Hannibal held the heart of Italy for sixteen years and then was defeated. Be cool and confident, and all will yet be right," advised Beauregard. General Hood's Army of Tennessee was on its ill-fated expedition into Tennessee when Beauregard sent the telegram. Hood had rejected the Fabian system of fighting employed by his predecessor, Gen. Joseph Johnston. His aggressive approach would have devastating consequences during the battles of Franklin and Nashville. Hood's failures undoubtedly convinced Taylor about the soundness of Beauregard's directive.[2]

Indeed, Taylor shared Beauregard's sage advice with Maury. Before the siege at Spanish Fort began, Maury asked him whether he should fight to the last man to

---

1 William R. Plum, LL.B., *The Military Telegraph During the Civil War in the United States* (Chicago, 1882), 248.

2 Plum, *The Military Telegraph*, 248.

save Mobile. "The answer must be, save the troops and abandon the City," Taylor replied in a confidential letter from his Meridian headquarters on February 16, 1865, "but the practical question before us is, will the consequence of the loss of Mobile be such as to justify us in risking the loss of the garrison by attempting to hold the city? This has been affirmatively decided." Taylor's instructions did not mean Maury should give up the city without a fight. On the contrary, he wanted him to hold his position as long as he could but without risking the capture of his garrison. "No troops would have been withdrawn from the Army of Tennessee to reinforce your garrison had it been contemplated to abandon Mobile," he emphasized. Taylor made it clear that an attempt to defend the city had to be made. "The longer Mobile can be held, the better for the cause, as other operations of the enemy will be delayed, and time afforded us to march an army to its relief."[3]

Privately, Beauregard endorsed a Fabian strategy to Taylor. Publicly, however, he tried to instill confidence in the garrison's ability to hold the city. On January 20, 1865, the esteemed Louisianan visited Mobile, and in a speech, he assured the citizens that the city should be held at all hazards—it would not be given up without a fight.[4]

Without the assistance of Forrest's cavalry, though, the Graybacks could not hope to prevent Mobile's ultimate capture. Nevertheless, they understood it would require a much larger army to take the city than to defend it. Confederate authorities thus deemed it good tactics to hold the large force under Canby and Thatcher in the vicinity with their comparatively smaller force. By defending Mobile, they hoped to tie them down and prevent them from reinforcing their armies in the east.[5]

The Army of Tennessee had to confront Sherman's forces in North Carolina. There was no way they could return to help lift the siege of Mobile. Forrest offered the only hope of outside help. Taylor believed he would defeat Wilson's cavalry raid from the north. Forrest could come to his aid if Maury could hold out a week.[6]

Maury hurried the preparations for the anticipated invasion. In the days leading up to the expected attack, Mobile newspapers were filled with military orders. The Virginian issued numerous orders, including the prohibition of all

---

3 Richard Taylor to Dabney H. Maury, Feb. 16, 1865, Richard Taylor Manuscript Collection, Louisiana Research Collection at Tulane University, hereafter Richard Taylor to Dabney Maury, Feb. 16, 1865.

4 *ORA* 48, pt. 1, 681.

5 Hubbard, "Civil War Papers," LC.

6 Maury, "The Defense of Mobile in 1865," 6; Taylor, *Destruction and Reconstruction*, 218–219; *ORA* 49, pt. 2, 1160–1161, 1167.

liquor sales, calling in all artillerists from throughout his district to report at once, and sending away an excess number of enslaved persons due to lack of provisions. After a reasonable time, all enslaved men between 18 and 45 years of age would be enrolled and put in the army.[7]

Confederate Navy

On August 8, 1864, following the capture of Admiral Franklin Buchanan at the battle of Mobile Bay, the 58-year-old Commodore Ebenezer Farrand assumed command of Mobile's small flotilla. He had commanded the naval station at Selma before arriving at the blockaded port city.[8]

With 42 years of experience, Farrand—a New York native—had risen to the rank of commander in the U.S. Navy. He was stationed at the Pensacola Navy Yard during the early stages of the secession crisis. On January 12, 1861, Confederate militia arrived at the gates of the Pensacola Navy Yard and demanded its surrender. Farrand cooperated conspicuously during the surrender of the naval station to the Confederates. Observers witnessed him shaking hands with them, seemingly unsurprised at their arrival. Rumors spread that Farrand strongly influenced the aging commanding officer of the Navy Yard, Commodore James Armstrong, to surrender. Once the Secessionists occupied the Pensacola naval base, he resigned on January 30, 1861, and promptly joined the Confederate Navy.[9]

The highlight of Farrand's Confederate service occurred in May 1862. As commander of the Confederate naval defenses at Drewry's Bluff in northeastern Virginia, his shore batteries turned back the invasion of five Federal gunboats from the James River. This victory prompted the Confederate Congress to pass a resolution expressing thanks to the New Yorker "for the great and signal success achieved over the naval forces of the United States in the engagement."[10]

7 "Canby," *Philadelphia Inquirer*, Apr. 3, 1865, 3; *Mobile Advertiser and Register*, Apr. 1, 1865, "From Mobile, Augusta, Etc.," *New Orleans Times-Democrat*, Apr. 12, 1865, 1.

8 "Summary of News," *New Orleans Times-Democrat*, Aug. 14, 1864, 4. On Aug. 9, 1864, the *Mobile Tribune* and later, on Aug. 14, 1864, the *New Orleans Times-Democrat* reported "Farrand succeeds Buchanan."

9 Edward S. Cooper, *Traitors: The Secession Period, November 1860–July 1861* (Madison, NJ, 2008), 70–72; George F. Pearce, *Pensacola During the Civil War: A Thorn in the Side of the Confederacy* (Gainesville, 2000), 21–23; Scharf, *History of the Confederate States Navy*, 601; "Ebenezer Farrand," CSN Foundation, 290, accessed Sep. 21, 2016 https://sites.google.com/site/290foundation/290-standing-orders/ebenezer-farrand-csn.

10 "Civil War Reference Web Page," accessed July 12, 2015, http://www.civilwarreference.com/people/index.php?peopleID=719.

Commodore Ebenezer Farrand, commander of the Confederate Naval Squadron, Mobile Bay. *Alabama Department of Archives and History*

Before the land campaign against Mobile, the army and navy did not work well together. Maury complained to Taylor about Farrand's lack of cooperation.[11]

In a February 4th letter to President Davis, Taylor expressed his dissatisfaction with Mobile's navy squadron, calling it "a farce." He grumbled that the navy's "vessels are continually tied up at the wharf, never in cooperation with the army. The payment of its expenses is a waste of money."[12]

In fairness to Farrand, he did not have much to work with after the battle of Mobile Bay. One observer described his sailors as "soldiers of fortune," mainly Scots, Irish, English, Italian, and German. He inherited a small fleet, including the ironclads *Tuscaloosa, Huntsville, Nashville*, and the gunboats *Morgan* and *Baltic*. An officer of Smith's XVI Corps noted: "The Rebs have two ironclads here equal to the celebrated *Tennessee* captured by Farragut at the fall of the forts Morgan, Gaines & Powell at the mouth of the Bay." Newspaper reports, moreover, indicated that the *Nashville* seemed "as strong as the *Tennessee* at all points at which she will be exposed in a fight." Though the Southern ironclad vessels may have appeared as formidable as the *Tennessee* to the besiegers, the *Tuscaloosa* and *Huntsville* were never fully completed. The *Nashville's* armament included three 7-inch Brooke rifles and a 24-pounder howitzer. Despite an intimidating appearance, the side-wheel steamer was only partially armored. The *Morgan* escaped capture at the battle of Mobile Bay in 1864. A deserter reported that the *Morgan* had two 6-inch rifled guns and

11 *ORA* 49, pt. 1, 934–935, 951.

12 *ORA* 49, pt. 1, 955.

two 6 and 7-inch rifled Brooke guns. Once an ironclad, the converted riverboat *Baltic* had its armor removed and transferred to the *Nashville*.[13]

Although smaller, the *Tuscaloosa* and *Huntsville* were intended to be similar to the *Tennessee*. They were only partially armored, however, and their engines were defective. Neither had a full complement of guns, although they were reportedly identically armed with a 7-inch Brooke rifle, a 7-inch Blakely rifle, and four 32-pounders. The obstacles that impeded the Confederates during the construction of the two vessels, lack of resources and men, grew daily in magnitude. The ironclads were never fully completed.[14]

Despite his low opinion of Mobile's small flotilla, the lack of cooperation between Farrand and Maury concerned Taylor. On February 22, he offered Maury wise counsel: "A divided command has, with few exceptions, always been a source of weakness, of discord, and not infrequently of irredeemable disaster."[15]

Federals

Meanwhile, Canby began his deliberate preparations for the overland campaign to capture Mobile. It would be the 48-year-old's first substantial expedition under his command.

A Kentucky-born West Pointer, class of 1839, Canby had served in the Seminole and Mexican Wars. Early in the Civil War, while commanding the Department of New Mexico, the Confederates defeated his forces at the battle of Valverde. Five weeks later, other troops in his department not under his immediate command beat the Graybacks at Glorieta Pass. This victory prevented the Confederacy's westward expansion into the New Mexico Territory.[16]

13 William L. Cameron, "The Battles Opposite Mobile," *Confederate Veteran* 23 (1915): 306; James F. Drish to wife, Mar. 3, 1865, Illinois State Historical Society, hereafter JFD to wife, Mar. 3, 1865; "From the South" *Detroit* (MI) *Free Press*, 4; *ORN* 22, 59–60, 225–226; George S. Waterman, "Afloat-Afield-Afloat. Notable Events of the Civil War," *Confederate Veteran* 12 (1899): 490; John T. Scharf, *History of the Confederate States Navy from Its Organization to the Surrender of Its Last Vessel: Its Stupendous Struggle with the Great Navy of the United States; the Engagements Fought in the Rivers and Harbors of the South, and Upon the High Seas; Blockade-running, First Use of Iron-clads and Torpedoes, and Privateer History* (New York, 1887), 592. Reports of the guns of the *Huntsville*, *Tuscaloosa*, and *Morgan* varied and came from deserters.

14 Waterman, "Afloat-Afield-Afloat," 490; William N. Still, Jr., *Iron Afloat The Story of the Confederate Armorclads* (Nashville, 1975), 223; *ORN* 21, 35; Franklin Buchanan Letterbook, Sep. 12 1862–Nov. 20 1863, Southern Historical Collection, University of North Carolina, Chapel Hill, NC.

15 Richard Taylor to Dabney Maury, Feb. 16, 1865.

16 "Edward R. S. Canby," National Park Service, accessed Mar. 10, 2016, http://www.nps.gov/resources/person.htm?id=57.

Confederate Ironclad *Nashville* aided the besieged Spanish Fort garrison during the siege.
Naval History and Heritage Command

Canby had a "by the book" reputation. He was highly regarded for his administrative skills and prudent judgment and served as a staff officer in Washington, D.C., for much of the war. In July 1863, Secretary of War Edwin M. Stanton sent Canby to New York City to restore order after the draft riots. Upon arriving at the city, *New York Tribune* editor Horace Greeley described Canby: "He is a man full of fire and energy, and evidently will not be trifled with, with impunity." On May 11, 1864, Canby replaced Nathaniel P. Banks as commander of the Military Division of West Mississippi after the disastrous Red River Campaign. The New Orleans *Times-Picayune* reported that Canby "joins a high sense of professional and patriotic duty with a rigorous regard for individual rights."[17]

In his memoirs, Grant remembered:

General Canby was an officer of great merit. He was naturally studious and inclined to the law. There have been in the army but very few, if any, officers who took as much interest in reading and digesting every act of Congress and every regulation for the government of the army as he. His knowledge gained in this way made him a most valuable staff officer, a capacity in which almost all his army services were rendered up to the time of his being

17 Max L. Heyman, *Prudent Soldier: A Biography of Major General E.R.S. Canby, 1817-1873: His Military Service in the Indian Campaigns, in the Mexican War, in California, New Mexico, Utah, and Oregon; in the Civil War in the Trans-Mississippi West, and As Military Governor in the Post-War South* (Glendale, California, 1959), 195, 201–202; Robert Conner, *General Gordon Granger: The Savior of Chickamauga and the Man Behind "Juneteenth"* (Havertown, 2013), 151–152; "Edward R. S. Canby," National Park Service; "All Hail Mobile!," *The Times Picayune*, Apr. 12, 1865, 4.

Major General Edward R. S. Canby, commander of the Army of West Mississippi. *Library of Congress*

assigned to the Military Division of the Gulf. He was an exceedingly modest officer, though of great talent and learning.[18]

Gordon Granger and A. J. Smith—both experienced and proven generals—served as Canby's corps commanders for the Mobile Campaign.

As the commander of the Military Division of West Mississippi's reorganized XIII Corps, Major General Granger would play a prominent role in the spring 1865 expedition. A veteran of the Mexican War, he fought at Wilson's Creek, New Madrid, Corinth, Chickamauga, Missionary Ridge, and the battle of Mobile Bay. The 44-year-old New York-born West Pointer displayed reckless courage, ambition, and a quick wit. He relished the pleasures and honors of a soldier's life.[19]

Journalist William Shanks, a contemporary of Granger, portrayed him as "a man equally courageous morally as physically, and pursued an object, or criticized a subject or person without the slightest regard to others' opinions. He never shirked a responsibility—in fact, would rather act without authority than not, as giving zest to the undertaking. A gruff man, not only in his criticisms but in his language, Granger never disliked a man without showing it."[20]

The *Boston Daily Advertiser* reported, "Troops who will not follow where he leads will follow never" and printed this glowing description of him:

18 Grant, *Personal Memoirs*, 650.

19 "More Seven Thirties," *Richmond* (IN) *Weekly Palladium*, 3; Johnson, "In Camp and Field," 7; John C. Palfrey, "The Capture of Mobile, 1865," in *The Mississippi Valley, Tennessee, Georgia, Alabama, 1861–1864* (Boston, 1910), 539.

20 Conner, *General Gordon Granger*, 2.

For the gallant General is the gentleman in his parlor, a man in all circumstances, a brave soldier in the field, an experienced and able officer and leader. He is all life, all energy, all activity; nothing escapes his observation, and he disposes of his army as easily as a merchant of his ledgers. The General is an old pioneer and backwoodsman, although only forty years of age, is a great hunter and splendid shot, and can follow the trail with 'Kit Carson.' It is for these reasons that he is particularly fitted for the command he holds, and for these reasons that I do not know, among the many major-generals of our service, one who could fill the place of General Granger.[21]

Granger possessed a commanding stature; he was easy and natural in manner and agreeable in conversation. Known for being a strict disciplinarian—yet far from tyrannical—Granger enforced obedience. His command loved and respected him. At the battle of Chickamauga, seeing Gen. George H. Thomas in danger of being routed, Granger disobeyed orders and led his men into action in time to prevent catastrophe. For his actions that day, the New Yorker became known as the "Savior of Chickamauga."[22]

News reports and the men who served under him widely recognized Granger as an admirable commanding officer, yet Grant disliked him. "General Granger had got down to New Orleans, in some way or other, and I wrote Canby that he must not put him in command of troops," Grant recalled in his memoirs.[23]

Halleck expressed his high opinion of Granger in a private letter written to Canby on February 28, 1865. Still, he informed Canby that Grant "found much fault with the latter in the West and does not deem him competent for a large command." Halleck did not know the reasons for Grant's low opinion of Granger but shared his emphatic message to Canby "not to give Granger any large command, for if he does, he is certain to fail."[24]

Grant's aversion to Granger probably originated in 1863 when he (Granger) served under him in east Tennessee. Despite Granger's record of heroic exploits, his occasional abrasive personality and unprofessional behavior rubbed both Grant and Sherman the wrong way. Consequently, Sherman removed him from command of the IV Corps before the Atlanta campaign.[25]

Grant continued to try to derail Granger's career. In February 1865, he informed Halleck: "I think orders should go to General Canby to put Maj. Gen.

21 "The Advance on Mobile," *Boston Daily Advertiser*, Apr. 13, 1865, 2.

22 "General Gordon Granger," *Hillsboro* (OH) *Highland Weekly News*, Feb. 10, 1876, 3.

23 Grant, *Personal Memoirs*, 584.

24 *ORA* 48, pt. 1, 1001–1002.

25 Conner, *General Gordon Granger*, 134–148.

Major General Gordon Granger, commander of the XIII Army Corps, Army of West Mississippi. *Library of Congress*

F. Steele in command of the new corps formed." Fortunately for Granger, Canby disregarded what he interpreted as Grant's suggestion and gave him command of the XIII Army Corps. Granger's new command had plenty of experience, having fought at Vicksburg and the Red River Campaign.[26]

President Abraham Lincoln called Granger's cooperative effort with Farragut against the Mobile Bay forts a "brilliant success." His land operations performance against Fort Gaines and Fort Morgan undoubtedly gave Canby complete confidence in his leadership ability.[27]

Major General Andrew Jackson Smith, a 50-year-old Pennsylvanian and Mexican War veteran, led the XVI Corps. Appointed to West Point in 1834 by Andrew Jackson, for whom he was named, he graduated 36th in the class of 1838. Smith came down to Mobile after the Battle of Nashville.[28]

Smith enjoyed a stellar record, having repeatedly distinguished himself. His command built a strong reputation at Corinth, the battles of the campaign for Vicksburg, and Tupelo. Credited with saving Nathaniel Banks's ill-fated Red River expedition during their retreat, many regarded Smith as the "main agent of destruction of Hood's army at Nashville." Halleck touted Smith's ability in a letter to Canby, declaring, "You will find him all you can desire in the field."[29]

His men affectionately nicknamed him "Whiskey" and "Old Dad" and thought Smith invincible as a corps commander. "Such a thing as defeat with him in command never for one moment entered our heads, no matter what the odds

---

26 *ORA* 49, pt. 1, 864, 907; Conner, *General Gordon Granger*, 164.

27 *ORN* 21, 543; Conner, *General Gordon Granger*, 160.

28 "Was A Veteran of Two Wars," *St. Louis-Dispatch*, Jan. 31, 1897, 5; Allen, "Operations against the City of Mobile," 70–71. Andrew Jackson Smith was more commonly known as A. J. Smith.

29 "A Veteran Dead," *Logansport* (IN) *Reporter*, Feb. 1, 1897, 1; James K. Newton & Stephen E. Ambrose, "The Siege of Mobile," *The Alabama Historical Quarterly* 20 (Winter 1958): 598; *ORA* 48, pt. 1, 1001–1002.

against us," remembered one soldier from Ohio who served under him. As one newspaper put it, Smith "has a place in history as a commander who was never defeated when in charge of a battle or campaign."[30]

A letter written by a soldier of the 14th Indiana Artillery to his brother provides further insight on Smith:

> Old Smith, our general, is one of the boys or men, whatever you may call him. I will tell you something about him. When we were at Duck Creek, there were three armies to cross the creek on one bridge, it would take them at least two weeks to cross if we would have waited on one bridge, but Old Smith thought we were not crossing fast enough and so he had another bridge built. When he got it built, Gen. Wood wanted to cross on it, but Smith couldn't see it all. Smith told Wood that he was a better man than he was, and he had a better army than he had, and if he didn't believe it, he could try it, but Wood couldn't see to try it.[31]

Sherman greatly valued Smith's services. "I have two officers at Memphis that will fight all the time—A. J. Smith and Mower," proclaimed Sherman. He repeatedly tried, without success, to bring Smith back to his command during the summer of 1864. General Nathaniel Banks would not spare Smith. "Indeed, it appears that Smith's force is the real substance of his army," Sherman observed. Later, he appealed directly to Smith: "Your command belongs to me and is only loaned to help our neighbors, but I fear they make you do the lion's share. However, do as General Halleck orders, and as soon as possible, come to me."[32]

U.S. Navy

Acting Rear Admiral Henry K. Thatcher commanded the naval squadron in Mobile Bay. A 42-year veteran, Thatcher had served most of the war with the North Atlantic Blockading Squadron and had participated in the two battles for North Carolina's Fort Fisher.[33]

On January 24, 1865, the 59-year-old Thatcher took the helm of the West Gulf Blockading Squadron after the successful capture of Fort Fisher. On February 19, 1865, he arrived at Mobile Bay and replaced Commodore James S. Palmer,

---

30 "Gen. A. J. Smith," *The National Tribune*, Sep. 20, 1906, 3; Newton & Ambrose, "The Siege of Mobile," 598; "Was A Veteran of Two Wars," *St. Louis-Dispatch*, Jan. 31, 1897, 5; "A Veteran Dead," 1.

31 Rolland J. Gladieux, *The 14th Indiana Light Artillery* (Kenmore, New York, 1978), 25.

32 *Miscellaneous Document of the House of Representatives for the First Session of the Fifty-Second Congress, 1891–1892* (Washington D.C., 189), 121; *ORA* 32, pt. 3, 479; *ORA* 39, pt. 2, 370.

33 David D. Porter, *The Naval History of the Civil War* (New York, 1886), 780.

Major General A. J. Smith, commander of the XVI Army Corps, Army of West Mississippi. *Library of Congress*

who had temporarily assumed command when Admiral Farragut went home on leave due to health issues. Palmer felt it "unfortunate" to be superseded just before the invasion. Nonetheless, he vowed to stay on and assist Thatcher with "cheerfulness and zeal."[34]

Upon assuming command at Mobile Bay, Thatcher inherited an imposing fleet of over 30 vessels, including six ironclads, all for operations against Mobile. Soon after his arrival, he quickly opened communication with Canby and offered full cooperation toward their shared objective of capturing Mobile.[35]

Federal Strategy

Canby had hoped that Mobile would fall under its own weight. He thought that the Confederates would decide that the force required for its occupation and defense could be used more advantageously elsewhere than in trying to defend a blockaded seaport. However, spy intelligence, naval reconnaissance, and even newspaper reports eventually made it clear that the city would not be abandoned without a fight.[36]

Mobile's strong defenses and unique geographical features limited Canby's possible avenues of attack. He had personal knowledge of the western approaches to the city from his service in the area as a brigade adjutant while stationed at

34 Loyall Farragut, *The Life of David Glasgow Farragut: First Admiral of the United States Navy, Embodying His Journal and Letters* (New York, 1879), 472–474; *ORN* 22 (Jan. 24), 32, 47.

35 *ORN* 22, 56-57; Porter, *Naval History*, 780–781.

36 Hubbard, "Civil War Papers," LC; "Department of the Gulf," *New York Times*, Mar. 20, 1865, 8.

Acting Rear Admiral Henry Knox Thatcher, commander of the West Blockading Squadron, U.S. Navy. *Naval History and Heritage Command*

Pascagoula, Mississippi, in 1848, after returning from the Mexican War.[37]

The city's natural defenses influenced Canby's decision. A vast marsh to the north of the city extending to Three-Mile Creek made it nearly impossible for the Federals to attack from that direction. The bay also posed challenges to an invading fleet. The peculiar indentations of the upper bay made it difficult for large warships to get within several miles of the city. At the time, the Dog River Bar reached across a large portion of the bay from the mouth of that river. The shallowness of this sandbar prevented Thatcher's fleet from approaching near enough to the western shore to assist in reducing the numerous shore batteries. Moreover, the Dog River meanders through the low, marshy ground close to the rear of the outside line. This natural barrier would have made it difficult for troops to attack under fire.[38]

Besides Mobile's natural defensive advantages, Canby understood its well-deserved reputation as one of the best-fortified places in the Confederacy. The city's strong western shore fortifications also influenced his grand invasion tactics. Confederate engineers prepared the city's defensive fortifications for nearly four years. They built three strong lines of earthworks west of the town, its chief defense.[39]

37 "Camp Jefferson Davis 1848 Rosters," RG 94 Cartographic and Architectural Archives, NARA.

38 "Mobile," *Philadelphia Inquirer*, Feb. 14, 1865, 2; Truman, "The Siege of Mobile," *New York Times*, Apr. 21, 1865, 8; "Department of the Gulf," *New York Times*, Mar. 20, 1865, 8.

39 James L. Nichols, "Confederate Engineers and the Defense of Mobile," *Alabama Review*, July 12, 1959, 191.

Through intelligence reports from deserters, Canby knew that the city's western land approach defenses featured three strong lines of earthworks with massive ditches eight-foot-wide and five-foot-deep in front of them. The water approaches were crammed with every kind of obstruction that human ingenuity could invent: shore batteries, underwater channel obstructions, and gunboats. In addition, deadly submerged torpedoes littered the water approaches to the city and thus kept the U.S. fleet a safe distance away. Some reports suggested it would require at least 40,000 soldiers and 90 days to capture the city.[40]

The tremendous obstacles and defenses on the western shore proved a potent deterrent. Mobile's western fortifications were so strong that Canby decided not to move directly against the city. He believed it a sound policy to avoid attacking the Confederates where they expected. Instead, he chose to flank them. He determined the longest way around would be the quickest way to reach his objective. As the Graybacks suspected, he planned to march up the eastern shore with naval support on his left in Mobile Bay. He would move first against the two Baldwin County forts, Spanish Fort and Blakeley, to access the Tensaw and Alabama Rivers and thus flank Mobile.[41]

His plan called for the navy to engage Spanish Fort's water battery while his land forces attacked the fort from the east. After capturing the fort, its guns would turn on Batteries Tracey and Huger, compelling their evacuation. Thatcher's gunboats would then pass up the Blakeley and Apalachee Rivers and down the Tensaw River directly in front of Mobile. By flanking the city's defensive works this way, the Confederates would be forced to surrender or evacuate the city. To keep Maury guessing, he would also incorporate two feint movements. One would consist of a brigade on the west side of Mobile Bay. The other would be Major General Fred Steele's column from Pensacola; they would feint north to Pollard, Alabama, before making a sharp turn to the west to attack Fort Blakeley. If he found reducing the eastern shore forts would take too long, he would bypass them and move directly on Montgomery. Canby and his army, however, would soon learn the Confederates had plans of their own, utterly devoid of Southern hospitality. Taking Mobile would be no small task.[42]

---

40 "The Defenses of Mobile," *Cincinnati Enquirer*, May 20, 1865, 1; Nichols, "Confederate Engineers and the Defense of Mobile," 191; "Our New Orleans Correspondence," *New York Times*, Mar. 20, 1865, 8; "From Mobile," *Detroit Free Press*, Feb. 14, 1865, 4; Maury, "Souvenirs of the War," 4.

41 Andrews, *History of the Campaign of Mobile*, 31; Truman, "The Siege of Mobile," *New York Times*, Apr. 21, 1865, 8; Samuel H. Byers, *Iowa in War Times* (Des Moines, 1888), 402–403.

42 *ORA* 49, pt. 1, 92-93; Byers, Iowa, 402–403.

Chapter 3

"Take Mobile and Hold It"

Confederates, Winter 1864 & Spring 1865

After the disastrous Nashville battle, the Confederacy's foremost concern became the safety of Gen. Robert E. Lee's army at Petersburg. Richard Taylor, therefore, sent most of the Army of Tennessee to North Carolina to interpose between Sherman and Lee's rear. He also knew Canby would attack Mobile in the spring. Taylor wanted to hold the city with a small but sufficient force to compel a large army to reduce it. He sent French's Division, Gibson's and Holtzclaw's Brigades, and most of the artillery of the Army of Tennessee to south Alabama.[1]

Although the Confederacy had suffered a series of demoralizing setbacks, many citizens of Mobile determined to continue the war with all of their available resources. On February 18 and 19, 1865, a "large and enthusiastic meeting" occurred at a Mobile theater. To promote the cause for southern independence, a series of resolutions were adopted at this meeting. These resolutions declared an unalterable purpose to sustain the civil and military authorities in their efforts to achieve independence; that "victory or death" should be the battle cry moving forward, that the government should immediately place one hundred thousand black men in the army; that reconstruction was no longer an open question; and that an order reinstating Gen. Joseph E. Johnston to the command of the Army of

---

1 Clement A. Evans, *Confederate Military History: A Library of Confederate States History*, Vol. X (Atlanta, 1899), 157–158; Taylor, *Destruction and Reconstruction*, 201–202, 217–218.

Tennessee would restore confidence, increase the army, and secure the successful defense of Alabama, more than any other order that could be issued from the war department.[2]

On February 3, 1865, the Hampton Roads Peace Conference occurred between Confederate representatives and President Lincoln and Secretary of State William Seward. The meeting happened on Hampton Roads, off Fort Monroe, aboard the U.S. steamer River Queen. During the conference, President Lincoln maintained an inflexible position. He insisted on restoring the Federal government's authority in all states and refused to back down on the issue of emancipation. Surrender was the only way to end the war. With no authority to accept Lincoln's rigid terms, the dejected Southern commissioners returned to Richmond. The negotiations lasted just four hours. Jefferson Davis dispatched Vice-President Alexander Stephens, Virginia Senator Robert M. T. Hunter, and Assistant Secretary of War John A. Campbell of Mobile, to meet with Lincoln and Seward. The failed meeting, however, led to a renewed commitment to the war effort. President Jefferson Davis—hoping to discredit the peace movement—denounced Lincoln's surrender demand as a "degrading submission." He defiantly declared that the South must fight on and never submit to the "disgrace of surrender."[3]

Mobile's garrison, well-informed by newspaper reports on Hampton Roads, discussed the prospects of peace. Some men favored the acceptance of the terms offered by Lincoln, while others were opposed to it. One Alabamian of Holtzclaw's Brigade expressed his resolve to continue the struggle: "If we quit now, there will be a party who will always say we could have whipped them if we had kept on, and that element would foment trouble in the future. So, let's fight it out. We will be the gainers by it, for if we get whipped, it will settle the question for all time to come." A soldier of Cockrell's Division shared a contrasting viewpoint: "Disguise the fact as we may, the real sentiment of this brigade and this division is for peace on almost any terms."[4]

Despite the significant disparity in numbers and resources, many defenders appeared eager for the coming fight. "Mobile is a very strong place, and the enemy seems inclined to try it soon. I am in hopes that we will be able to thwart him in

2 Anonymous, *The American Annual Cyclopedia and Register of Important Events of the Year 1865*, Vol. 5 (New York, 1870), 9–10.

3 James M. McPherson, *Battle Cry of Freedom: The Civil War Era* (New York, 1988), 822–825; Bruce Levine, *The Fall of the House of Dixie: The Civil War and the Social Revolution That Transformed the South* (New York, 2013), 248–250. At the meeting, Lincoln remained willing to discuss the possibility of the federal government providing compensated emancipation to slave owners.

4 Edgar W. Jones and C. David A. Pulcrano, *Eighteenth Alabama Infantry Regiment* (Birmingham, 1994), 62–63; Chambers, *Blood & Sacrifice*, 202–203.

all his plans," touted Capt. Clement S. Watson, Gibson's Louisiana Brigade, in a letter to his wife. "I would like to see them make an assault upon some of our positions. I think we could teach him a lesson that would be of long service." After enduring nearly four years of unimaginable hardship, toil, and horror, Watson still believed the South could prevail if everyone would perform their "duty like a man and patriot should."[5]

While the Confederate troops prepared to receive the attack on Mobile, the Confederate Congress debated the enrollment of enslaved men into the army. Opinions on the subject differed among the soldiers at Mobile. "We know but little of the policy of such an act but look upon it with dread as to the consequences but willingness if it is for the public good," noted one Alabamian of Holtzclaw's Brigade. "However, politics is not my forte, so I will leave such things to wiser heads." A Texan of Ector's Brigade summed up the debate in a letter to his father on February 22: "The Negro question is up pretty high. Some of the soldiers are in favor of it, and some are opposed to it. I am in favor of anything before subjugation."[6]

Some soldiers believed enslaved men would make valuable additions to the army. "Let their sable faces be seen in every military and civil department where they can be employed with advantage," argued a 19-year-old 16th Confederate Cavalry trooper. He declared in a February 10th letter to the *Mobile Evening News* and the *Mobile Register and Advertiser* that "our negroes will fight better than those of the enemy." He urged the Confederate Congress to act immediately.[7]

Conversely, a Mississippian of Cockrell's Division recorded in his journal that he believed the measure was "not right." Cockrell's Division, nonetheless, passed a resolution on February 18th affirming "that the best interests of the country demanded that the negroes" be enlisted in the service.[8]

Gibson issued a public appeal on March 16, 1865, to drum up deserters to defend Mobile. "Some men, belonging to the regiments of this brigade, remain

5 "Spanish Fort Fight Near Mobile Bay," *The Times Picayune*, Sep. 24, 1899, 24; Clement S. Watson to his Wife, Mar. 5, 1865, Clement Stanford Watson Papers, Louisiana Research Collection, Tulane University, hereafter CSW to Wife, Mar. 5, 1865.

6 James M. McPherson, *For Cause and Comrades: Why Men Fought in the Civil War* (Oxford, 1997), 109–114; James A. Durrett and Henry Durrett, The Letters of James A. Durrett, accessed July 20, 2019, https://durrettblog.wordpress.com/Carlock and Owens; *History of the Tenth Texas*, 226–227.

7 R. C. Beckett, "A Sketch of the Career of Company B, Armistead's Cavalry Regiment," in *Publications of the Mississippi Historical Society*, Vol. 8, ed. Franklin Lafayette Riley (Oxford, MS, 1905), 42–43.

8 Chambers, *Blood & Sacrifice*, 202–203. "First Missouri Brigade," *Mobile Advertiser and Register*, Mar. 4, 1865. Cockrell's Division had previously been known as French's Division.

away from their colors, having in the first instance overstayed their furloughs, while others have attached themselves to commands nearer their own homes," Gibson wrote. "Both classes of absent soldiers are guilty of desertion—a military crime fatal to the cause of their country, whose laws punish it with death." Gibson's last appeal to the men from his Louisiana Brigade called for them "to rejoin their commands, whose heroic deeds and disciplined valor have covered their old banners with the luster of enduring fame." He asserted that the brigade would "soon be stronger than it has ever been" with many men already coming in. Gibson declared: "Your old battle flag still flaunts defiance to the foe; your old comrades still stand shoulder to shoulder, with ever-increasing confidence in themselves and the cause."[9]

As they awaited the arrival of Canby's forces, the Confederates encamped around the city. Besides discussing the prospects for peace and arming Black soldiers, they spent their time fishing, going to Mobile on passes, and attending religious services. "We had preaching in our regiment today for the first time in many months," Private Durrett informed his sister. "I heard a very good sermon. I wish I could hear as good as one every Sunday."[10]

Federals, Winter 1864 & Spring 1865

Meanwhile, the Federals arrived at their staging camps about 30 miles south of Mobile, on Dauphin Island, and Mobile Point near Fort Morgan. They traveled aboard transports from New Orleans. Granger's XIII Army Corps, except one division, camped at Mobile Point, while Smith's XVI Corps and a division of the XIII Corps bivouacked on Dauphin Island near Fort Gaines.[11]

Many of the soldiers were Midwestern farm boys and had never seen the beaches of the Gulf Coast. The sugary white sand reminded them of snow. "All along the Gulf Shore, the sand is piled up in banks as white as snow," observed one soldier from Illinois.[12]

---

9 Randall L. Gibson, "Drumming Up the Rebel Deserters to Defend Mobile," *New York Daily Herald*, Apr. 9, 1865, 8.

10 Jones and Pulcrano, *Eighteenth Alabama*, 62–63; Durrett, The Letters of James A. Durrett.

11 JFD to wife, Mar. 3, 1865. Canby's troops traveled on transports from New Orleans, often under adverse weather conditions. They were well equipped and armed with 1863 and 1864 Springfield rifled muskets. Two brigades from Gen. C. C. Andrews's Division of the XII Corps were detailed to General Fred Steele's column, encamped at Fort Barrancas near Pensacola, Florida. Bivouac means temporary encampment under little shelter.

12 Moses A. Cleveland, *The Civil War Diary of Moses A. Cleveland: 7th Battery Mass. Light Artillery; the Red River Campaign and the Campaign Against Port Of Mobile, Alabama, 1864-1865*, ed. Olga

"The Island, low and wet, is mostly a white sand, which is blown up into ridges and hills, on the gulf side, which protects the camps from the prevailing winds," noted a New Yorker of James Veatch's Division, XIII Corps, in a letter to his sister. "The roar of the gulf shore is a pleasing contrast to the comparative quiet of the bay."[13]

The coastal camps provided a notable change of rations for the Bluecoats. Oyster beds were abundant in the shallow waters near the U.S. Army camps. "Oysters are plentiful and of fine quality," exclaimed a member of the 7th Massachusetts Light Artillery, XIII Corps. "Can buy plenty of oysters (large ones) for 12 cents a dozen. I never saw finer ones than are obtained here." Oysters were so plentiful that six mule teams were driven upon the beds during low tide, and wagons were loaded with them. They were shoveled out in piles in camp, and everyone was allowed to help themselves. The men ate them raw, roasted, stewed, baked, or fried.[14]

The blue-clad veterans often played baseball. Organized regimental teams played each other. "We played ball with the 47th Indiana today," a private of the 29th Wisconsin wrote in his diary while at Dauphin Island. "Beat them." The day before, his regiment lost to the 11th Wisconsin.[15]

Besides gathering and dining on oysters and playing baseball, the soldiers "played cards, marbles, pull sticks, run and jump, or stand and jump, wrestled, boxed, or played shake hands." The recruits drilled while on the island, but there was not enough room for company or regiment drills. The men did have time to keep their skills sharp through target practice. "Standing gun drill in the forenoon a bore to those who have been through the manual of the piece so many times," noted one Federal. They also performed fatigue duties, such as working on the pier and unloading artillery pieces from incoming vessels.[16]

Strange occurrences occasionally broke the monotony of camp life. One day, lightning killed an Illinois soldier, while others near him were stunned by the shock. A Massachusettsan recorded a morbid discovery in his diary: "I saw

Fairfax (Nacogdoches, TX, 2011), 66; Robert Ridge, Diary, Mar. 16, 1865, Abraham Lincoln Presidential Library, Springfield, IL, hereafter Ridge Diary, Mar. 16, 1865.

13 John F. Francis to his sister, Feb. 18, 1865, Edmund Family Collection, New York Historical Society, NY.

14 David W. Reed, *Campaigns and Battles of the Twelfth Regiment Iowa Veteran Volunteer Infantry* (n.d), 226; Cleveland, *Diary of Moses A. Cleveland*, 66–67.

15 Henry P. Whipple, *Diary of a Private Soldier* (Waterloo, WI, 1906), 64–66.

16 E. Stockwell, *Private Elisha Stockwell, Jr., sees the Civil War*, ed. B. R. Abernathy (Norman, OK, 1958), 160; John Thomas, Diary, Mar. 8, 1865, Dolph Briscoe Center Archives, University of Texas, Austin, TX, hereafter Thomas Diary, Mar. 8, 1865; Cleveland, *Diary of Moses A. Cleveland*, 68; Whipple, *Diary of a Private Soldier*, 64–66; Ridge Diary, Mar. 17, 1865.

bleached human bones—perhaps what is left of some hero who went down with the Tecumseh sunk at the taking of the Forts. His bones the playthings of the waves—the moaning of the solemn pines his requiem."[17]

After their triumphs at Atlanta, Franklin, and Nashville, many of the Bluecoats believed that the Rebels would not put up much resistance defending Mobile. "Papers say the South have robbed the cradle and the grave to recruit her armies," one Bluecoat jotted down in his diary. "The north will never have to resort to such an extremity, and her other resources are equal to her men." There were even rumors that Mobile had been evacuated. "I don't think we will have much fighting to do to capture Mobile," predicted an officer of the 122nd Illinois.[18]

The Federals were indeed confident in their ability to capture Mobile. "Away up the bay, hid among her strongholds, and protected by fortifications, forts, and torpedoes, which guarded all avenues of approach, lay the defiant rebel city, which thus far in the war, had eluded the visitation and grasp of the Union armies," recalled a soldier of the 95th Illinois after the war. "Silently, she awaited the bursting of the storm gathering at her doors, and in the stupendous preparations culminating around her, was conscious of a fate similar to that which had befallen her rebellious sister cities, one by one, all along the Atlantic coast."[19]

Canby's men were left in the dark regarding his plans. They assumed they would attack Mobile but could only speculate on the details. "I don't know anything about our plan in regard to the attack, but if we lay siege to the city, we can starve them out without much loss of life," an Illinoisan officer informed his wife. "There is a very large fleet here to cooperate with the army in the reduction of the city." A captain of 28th Wisconsin did not believe the war would end soon: "I hope it may, but hardly think it will. Be that as it may, much is being done towards ending the war, and it does seem that the rebels must soon be overcome—conquered. When that is done, the war is ended—and not till then."[20]

Before the start of the campaign, Chaplain Elijah E. Edwards, 7th Minnesota, Marshall's Brigade, suffered from an affliction and had to be hospitalized for some time. Edwards could have requested a discharge due to the seriousness of the illness, but he could not resist the strong allure of the coming battle. As he put it:

---

17 Cleveland, *Diary of Moses A. Cleveland*, 67, 70.

18 Ibid., 68–69; JFD to wife, Mar. 3, 1865.

19 Wales W. Wood, *A History of the Ninety-Fifth Regiment* (Chicago, 1865), 163.

20 Thomas N. Stevens and George M. Blackburn, *"Dear Carrie...": The Civil War Letters of Thomas N. Stevens* (Mount Pleasant, MI, 1984), 302.

"There is something dreadful and yet fascinating about a great battle, and I for one cannot keep away."[21]

The ever-cautious Canby moved deliberately in his preparations for the coming expedition. Grant, however, knew the potential threat posed by the Rebels arming black men if Canby did not set out soon. On February 27, he impatiently ordered Canby to "get all the negro men we can before the enemy puts them in their ranks." Fortunately for the Union army, the Confederacy's general order authorizing the enrollment of black soldiers did not occur until March 23, just a few days before the siege of Spanish Fort began, too little and far too late to make an impact for the South. On the same day, Grant dispatched his trusted aide, Brevet Brig. Gen. Cyrus B. Comstock, to report to Canby for special duty, with a letter urging Canby to get moving.[22]

In a private letter dated February 28, 1865, Halleck cautioned Canby, "General Grant is very impatient at delays and too ponderous preparations." Canby's deliberateness, indeed, annoyed Grant. However, circumstances beyond Canby's control hindered him. Incessant storms for three weeks delayed the movement of troops and supplies. Lack of transportation also held up the campaign for Mobile. Despite sending to Mobile Bay all the Mississippi steamers that could make the voyage, Canby still lacked enough vessels to transport his men to the staging camps at Dauphin Island, Mobile Point, and northwest Florida's Fort Barrancas. He complained that the delay could have been avoided had the light draft, sea-going steamers he requested three months earlier had been furnished. Canby wanted his expedition to set out on March 5, but the unusual amount of rainfall and lack of transportation made that date uncertain. He informed Halleck of all these issues. It is unknown if Halleck forwarded these explanations to Grant. Grant felt left in the dark and was anxious to see everything pushed forward.[23]

March 1865

On March 7, Canby wired Halleck: "For the last forty days, we have had but seven days of favorable weather. During all the rest of this time, heavy easterly and southeasterly gales and dense fogs have prevailed, rendering the transportation of troops and supplies both tedious and dangerous." He explained that although

---

21 Elijah E. Edwards, Journal, Mar. 25, 1865, *Minnesota Historical Society* (MNHS), St. Paul, MN, 237, hereafter Edwards Journal, Mar. 25, 1865.

22 *ORA* 49, pt. 1, 781; "Confederate Law Authorizing the Enlistment of Black Soldiers, Mar. 13, 1865, As Promulgated in a Military Order," Freedmen and Southern Society Project, accessed June 14, 2020, https://www.freedmen.umd.edu/csenlist.htm; *ORA* 49, pt. 1, 780–781.

23 *ORA* 48, pt. 1, 1001–1002; 789; 907.

Brigadier General Cyrus B. Comstock, Aide-de-Camp, General Canby's Staff. *Library of Congress*

they had 12 steamers that could carry 10,000 men, a sandbar obstructed a Mississippi River pass out of New Orleans and delayed their arrival to Mobile Bay. Canby also pointed out that the Navy would not be ready for several days.[24]

Back at Nashville, Gen. George H. Thomas wired Grant on March 9 that he received a communication from Canby at the beginning of the month. Thomas told him that incessant rains in February had delayed Canby. Despite Thomas's insight, Grant remained irritated. Three months earlier, Grant showed the same impatience toward Thomas when he did not immediately attack Hood's Army of Tennessee due to freezing weather conditions.[25]

A requisition for railroad construction material from Canby prompted Grant to send a scathing letter. Almost in despair for the campaign against Mobile, Grant fumed:

> I wrote to you long ago urging you to push forward promptly and to live upon the country and destroy railroads, machine shops, etc., not to build them. Take Mobile and hold it, and push your forces to the interior to Montgomery and Selma. Destroy railroads, rolling-stock, and everything useful for carrying on the war, and when you have done this, take such positions as can be supplied by water.

Colonel Lucius F. Hubbard, 5th Minnesota, later reflected on Grant's terse dispatch: "There was no mistaking the purport of these instructions, and their tone fairly implied that if Canby did not proceed along the line indicated more promptly, somebody else might be designated to 'take Mobile.'"[26]

---

24 *ORA* 49, pt. 1, 856–857.

25 *ORA* 49, pt. 1, 869; "Battle of Nashville: Enemies Front and Rear," American Battlefield Trust, last modified Dec. 20, 2019, https://www.battlefields.org/learn/articles/battle-nashville-enemies-front-and-rear.

26 Grant, *Personal Memoirs*, 584–585; *ORA* 49, pt. 1, 875; Hubbard, "Civil War Papers," 620, LC.

Upon his arrival on March 12 at Dauphin Island, Colonel Comstock handed Canby a two-week-old letter from Grant. "I am extremely anxious to hear of your forces getting to the interior of Alabama," urged Grant. In the letter, he warned Canby of Forrest's probable presence near Jackson, Mississippi. Grant made it clear that he wanted to see the Confederates broken up in the west before they had time to collect their deserters and reorganize themselves.

Grant probably sent Comstock to keep an eye on Canby and apply pressure to expedite the campaign's progress. Before he arrived at Mobile Bay, Comstock had a similar assignment with Gen. Godfrey Weitzel during the attack on Fort Fisher. Canby assigned Comstock to special duty as aide-de-camp on his staff at Dauphin Island, collecting intelligence on roads and defenses.[27]

On March 16, Granger canceled the evening drill for the XIII corps. Instead of drilling, they finally received orders to march at daybreak with three days' rations in their haversacks. The long-awaited campaign for Mobile would begin the next morning.[28]

27 Cyrus B. Comstock, *The Diary of Cyrus B. Comstock*, ed. Marlin E. Sumner (Dayton, OH, 1987), 311–312; *ORA* 49, pt. 1, 780–782 *ORA* 49, pt. 2, 294, 311; Comstock, *Cyrus B. Comstock*, 297–303, 314–315.

28 William H. H. Fisher, Diary, Mar. 16, 1865, Special Collections, Pennsylvania State University, PA, hereafter Fisher Diary, Mar. 16, 1865; Stevens and Blackburn, *"Dear Carrie,"* 303.

Chapter 4

"The Bottomless Pit of Alabama"

Federals

Friday, March 17, 1865: Before dawn on St. Patrick's Day, Granger's XIII Corps cooked coffee and took down their tents. After about six weeks of waiting, they finally set out from their camps near Mobile Point to a predetermined rendezvous point by the Fish River.[1]

One Bluecoat camped near Canby's staff tents and heard some fine singing from them as they prepared for the march. "I catch the words 'Go where glory waits for us' yes indeed, but I should prefer the glory of being mustered out," he jotted down in his diary.[2]

The men carried a heavy load of clothing, ammunition, and rations; all told, nearly 30 pounds of gear. This consisted of a rifle-musket, bayonet, 45 rounds of ammunition, three days' rations of bread, meat, and sugar, a knapsack with blankets, and a piece of shelter tent. In addition to this, each company added three axes and three shovels to the load. Soon after starting, the soldiers began unloading the surplus clothing by throwing away everything unnecessary.[3]

---

1 Fisher Diary, Mar. 17, 1865.

2 Cleveland, *Diary of Moses A. Cleveland*, 70.

3 Elliott, *Thirty-Third Regiment*, 228; Willis V. Tichenor, "Reminiscences of the capture of Mobile," Twenty-Eight Wisconsin Volunteer Infantry, accessed Apr. 11, 2020, http://www.28thwisconsin.com/letters/tichenor_1893.html.

As the general movement began, Canby's plan began to be understood by his officers. "I am much pleased with the arrangement as it shows a disposition to concentrate our forces instead of scattering them, which has often resulted in disaster," Gen. James Slack, XIII Corps, informed his wife. "The column which moves from Pensacola and our column will be within easy supporting distance of each other."[4]

With over 13,000 troops under Granger, each regiment would systematically join the march, necessarily leaving at different times. Some regiments departing later in the morning organized baseball games as they waited their turn to join the march.[5]

Major Charles J. Allen of the Corps of Engineers and the 4th Wisconsin Cavalry (Knowles's Scouts) went out before the XIII Corps to scout the roads toward Fish River. Upon their return, they met Granger riding at the head of his staff. Allen informed him of the nature of the roads ahead—good when dry, nearly impassable after heavy rain.[6]

Federal Army's Feint to Fowl River

Saturday, March 18, 1865: On "a fine, warm day," a feint movement on the western shore of Mobile Bay set out to draw attention away from his main body's activity on the eastern shore. For the mission, Canby sent Col. Jonathan B. Moore's First Brigade of the Third Division, XVI Corps, to draw the Rebel's attention while the main body landed on the other side of the bay. Canby ordered Moore to display his force to give the impression they were the advance of a more substantial force.[7]

Moore's Brigade proceeded on its diversionary movement to the southwestern shore of Mobile Bay. At noon, the navy ferried approximately 2,000 men from the 95th and 72nd Illinois, 44th Missouri, and 33rd Wisconsin on the vessels *Swain*, *Groesbeck*, and *Mustang* on a short trip to Cedar Point, located in plain sight of Dauphin Island. The tinclads number 44 and 47 shelled the woods before the troops disembarked, driving off a small force of about 20 gray-coated scouts.

4 James R. Slack to Wife, Mar. 17, 1865, James R. Slack Papers, Indiana State Library.

5 Alexander Millard, Diary, Mar. 17, 1865, Auburn University Libraries, Auburn, AL, hereafter Millard Diary, Mar. 17, 1865; Thomas Diary, Mar. 17, 1865.

6 Allen, "Operations against the City," 72.

7 "Civil War Diary of Henry M. Dryer," GenWeb of Monroe County, NY, accessed Sep. 27, 2021, https://mcnygenealogy.com/book/diary.htm; Ridge Diary, Mar. 18, 1865.

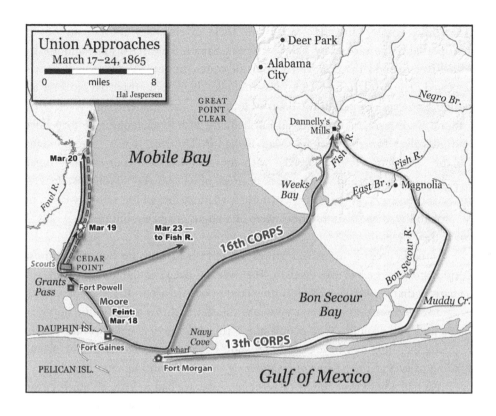

The cavalry scouts were lurking in this vicinity, watching the movements of the Federal army.[8]

They landed on a long, narrow pier near the remnants of Fort Powell, which the Confederates had evacuated during the August 1864 battle. On reaching the end of the dock, the Unionists discovered that the planking had been torn up for a few yards, compelling the men to jump a foot or two on the sand below. Anticipating an invasion at this location, the defenders had prepared a deadly surprise for their unwelcome guests. "We found a lot of torpedoes in the sand just as we stepped off the pier that the rebs fixed to blow some of us up with," an Illinois soldier recorded in his journal. One of the men discovered a partially buried torpedo where the planking had been torn up. The Bluecoats soon found five torpedoes in the vicinity before a tragedy occurred. Once safely upon the shore, the men noticed the unusual appearance of the two forts and breastworks, which were made entirely of oyster shells and reported to be a half-mile in length.[9]

8 Ridge Diary, Mar. 18, 1865; Wood, *A History of the Ninety-Fifth Regiment*, 164.

9 Wood, *Ninety-Fifth*, 164–166; Ridge Diary, Mar. 18, 1865.

While Moore's Brigade set out on their diversionary movement, Smith transported his command by water to Week's Bay on the eastern shore and up the Fish River to hold the designated point of concentration. About twenty vessels departed Dauphin Island at 9 a.m. It would take them about three days to ferry all of Smith's Corps. Several of the boats were stuck in the mud entering Weeks Bay. Around 11:30 a.m., they moved cautiously up the Fish River, looking for torpedoes and guerrillas. On the contrary, Maj. Benjamin Truman—a war correspondent for the *New York Times* embedded with the XVI Corps—reported that "eager multitudes of blacks and whites, of both sexes, of all ages and conditions, flocked to the shores, and rent the very air with their vociferations of joy. In many cases, in all probability, these manifestations were of a bogus character, but on the whole, I think they were sincere."[10]

Truman noted the unusual features of the Fish River to be "one of the most curious streams" he had ever been on. The river was deep enough for large boats yet so narrow that vessels over 280 feet long could not turn around. The crooked river caused some vessels to run their bow into the shore, throw a line to the opposite bank, and pull around. "The people along the shore was actually wonderstruck, and why shouldn't they have been to see some of the most gorgeous and luxurious floating palaces of the Mississippi wandering such a stream," he reported.[11]

"We had a hard time the first day we got here; we had to leave all our baggage on the Island, and we had nothing but a little dog tent that we could not set up straight in. We got into camp at night; it was raining hard," an officer from Illinois wrote his wife. "We pitched our tent and laid down; in the morning, we found ourselves floating. The tent was on the low ground & leaked; besides, the water had run under us." While Smith's Corps ferried its way through Week's Bay and up the Fish River to their camp by Dannelly's Mill, Thatcher's fleet extended naval demonstrations further up the bay toward Spanish Fort.[12]

Meanwhile, the XIII Corps continued its arduous march to the predetermined rendezvous point at Dannelly's Mill. In the weeks preceding the movement, however, the never-ending rains left much of the roads nearly impassable. "On the second day, we arrived at the bottomless pit of Alabama," groaned an officer of the 28th Wisconsin. The swampy nature of the south Baldwin County roads slowed Granger's march to a snail's pace. Artillery pieces and wagons sank to their axles. "I have been running through sand, mud, & water all day," complained one

10 Benjamin Truman, "The Attack on Mobile," *New York Times*, Apr. 7, 1865, 1.

11 Comstock, *Diary of Cyrus B. Comstock*, 312; "The Attack on Mobile."

12 JFD to wife, Mar. 24, 1865; *ORA* 49, pt. 1, 93. Contemporary sources spelled Dannelly's Mill in a variety of ways.

Vermonter of Benton's Division, XIII Corps. Granger's troops were forced to cut trees to make corduroy roads.[13]

*   *   *

Sunday, March 19, 1865: On this hot and muggy day, Moore's Brigade proceeded on its feint movement on the west side of the bay. Although they avoided sub-terra shells upon disembarking, they could not escape the constant and unbearable assault of mosquitoes. "I never saw anything like it. They sting like bees. Shoe leather does not impede them from boring your toes," grumbled one Bluecoat. The mosquitoes were relentless and "seem bound to have their fill of Yankee blood, which luxury they have not been able to procure until lately."[14]

That afternoon, Moore's troops broke camp and marched north 9 miles in a battle line, making as much noise as they could. Additionally, they were supported by shelling from the gunboats as they skirmished with the Confederates in their front. On the march, the Yankees found a Southern trooper and his horse lying near each other, "both dead, killed by one of the shells." Moore marched several miles north before stopping at dusk, where his four regiments camped in line of battle in the thick pine woods.[15]

Moore used his regimental bands to further the ruse. He ordered them to beat three tattoos in the morning and evening, varying the tunes each time to try and convince the Confederates that they were a large force of twelve regiments.[16] The band of the 44th Missouri, however, had only recently been formed with unskilled musicians. Their noticeably poor playing ability may have unwittingly revealed Moore's subterfuge. The 44th band's musical demonstrations were so pitiful that the men could not restrain themselves and burst into irrepressible laughter, making the woods ring for a long distance around.[17]

Across the bay, the XIII Corps awakened early, broke camp, and prepared for another day's march. Some regiments set out soon after sunrise, while others had to wait until the roads were corduroyed. They trekked over higher ground, and

13 Willis V. Tichenor, "Reminiscences of the capture of Mobile," Twenty-Eight Wisconsin Volunteer Infantry, accessed Apr. 11, 2020, http://www.28thwisconsin.com/letters/tichenor_1893.html; Fisher Diary, Mar. 18, 1865; Allen, "Operations against the City," 74. Corduroy roads were used to improve road conditions. Corduroying roads involved placing logs perpendicular to the direction of the road over a low or swampy area.

14 Edward O. Nye, Diary, Mar. 19, 1865, Charles H. Hooper Collection, John Pelham Historical Association, Hampton, VA, hereafter Nye Diary, Mar. 19, 1865.

15 Nye Diary, Mar 19, 1865.

16 A tattoo is a musical performance or display of armed forces.

17 Wood, *Ninety-Fifth*, 167–169.

the roads were better than the previous day. Very few houses and no people were seen. "At one time, we came in sight of the Bay," recalled one Vermonter, "then quite a distance through dense woods silent and gloomy." Although the roads were improved, they still experienced difficulty during the day's march. Cactus grew in profusion, penetrating and tearing at clothes and shoes. Along the way, they had to wade across a stream waist-deep. Moreover, warm and muggy conditions caused the men to cast off their excess clothing, overcoats, and blankets. Tired and hot, the men were relieved when they finally stopped for a couple of hours for dinner. After the dinner break, they continued the march for several miles. The long day concluded when they arrived at a deserted Confederate camp at about dusk. They remained there until the morning, all the while rumors continued to circulate that Mobile had already been captured.[18]

While the XIII Corps endured a hard march, vessels transported Smith's XVI Corps piecemeal across Mobile Bay from Dauphin Island to Dannelly's Mill. The 12th Iowa did not get onboard their gunboat transport until dark. After passing through Week's Bay, they entered the Fish River, described as "a very small crooked stream." They traveled slowly for several miles on the river before they disembarked at Dannelly's Mill and went into camp in the pine forest bordering the west side of the river. A soldier of the 12th Iowa described the location: "The entire country has a swampy, alligator appearance. There are no cultivated fields but several turpentine ranches, they too are deserted."[19]

Confederates

Back at Fort Blakeley, scouts brought Liddell intelligence of Canby's movements in the southern part of Baldwin County. That evening, he forwarded to Maury information that the Federal army was encamped at Dannelly's Mill, although he remained uncertain where they were headed. The small garrisons at Spanish Fort and Blakeley were urged to push forward their work without delay, ready to give the Bluecoats "a warm reception at any moment." Liddell ordered Lt. Col. Philip Brent Spence, 12th Mississippi Cavalry Regiment, to set out and discover the Federal's intentions.

Spence—a Princeton-educated 29-year-old from Davidson County, Tennessee—had crossed the state line into Alabama to join the Confederate army before his home state seceded. He had previously served on the staff of Gen. Leonidas

18 Fisher Diary, Mar. 19, 1865; Whipple, *Diary of a Private Soldier*, 66.

19 Whipple, *Diary of a Private Soldier*, 64–66; William L. Henderson, Diary, Oct. 3, 1861–Mar 20, 1865, The University of Iowa Libraries, Iowa City, IA., hereafter Henderson Diary, Mar. 19, 1865.

Polk until after the battle of Chickamauga before joining the 12th Mississippi. He fought in numerous engagements, including the defense of Atlanta.[20]

The Tennessean commanded about 500 troopers, detached from Col. Charles G. Armistead's Cavalry Brigade. Previously known as the 16th Confederate Cavalry, special orders were issued on March 24 that constituted ten companies under Armistead as the 12th Mississippi Cavalry, separating Lewis's Alabama Battalion. About 20 troopers—locally raised 15th Confederate Cavalry members—were detailed as guides and scouts because of their firsthand knowledge of the area. Although vastly outnumbered, his horsemen actively scouted and harassed the advancing blue columns.[21]

The Federal columns presented many challenges to Spence's small cavalry regiment. Before they advanced, Spence's men enjoyed abundant rations of freshly caught seafood from the bay. "During our short service on the bay, after leaving Gen. Sherman's front in Georgia, we had commenced thinking that to be a Confederate soldier with oysters and fish for rations was not a hard life after all, and we greatly enjoyed the change from the scanty supply we received while in front of Gen. Sherman in North Alabama and Georgia," remembered Spence.[22]

Unfortunately for Spence's mounted troopers, U.S. Navy gunners ended their seafood feasts. Acting Rear Admiral Thatcher's gunboats shelled the woods from Point Clear to Blakeley Bar to clear them out. Although the gunboats did not cause much damage, they prevented the horsemen from catching fresh seafood. "We were not long permitted to enjoy a luxurious living, as the United States Navy shelled my commissary squads whenever they appeared upon the shore," recalled Spence. He added: "An old soldier would take hazardous chances to get something good to eat, and fishing was first class, but the heavy guns of the United States Navy were more than we could stand, so we had to go back to cornbread and sorghum."[23]

---

20 *ORA* 49, pt. 2, 1128–1129; Philip B. Spence, "The Last Fight," *Louisville* [KY] *Courier-Journal*, Mar. 31, 1892, 7; "Colonel Philip B. Spence," *Confederate Veterans Magazine* 23 (1915): 181.

21 Maury, "Defence of Mobile in 1865," 2–3; *ORA* 49, pt. 2, 1148; R. C. Beckett, "A Sketch of the Career of Company B, Armistead's Cavalry Regiment," *Publications, The Mississippi Historical Society* 8 (Feb 1905): 32–50 9; *Dispatch Book, Eastern Division, District of the Gulf, Mar.–Apr. 1865, Vol. 100, Chapter II* (War Department Collection of Confederate Records, 1865), 49, 75; Andrews, *Campaign of Mobile*, 44. Troopers detached were from prominent Baldwin County families such as Sibley, Stapleton, Greenwood, D'Olive, and Durant. These surnames are still common in Baldwin Country.

22 Spence, "The Last Fight."

23 *ORN* 22, 66; Spence, "The Last Fight." Due to shortages caused by the naval blockade, Confederates often used sorghum—a grain used for sweetening—in place of cane sugar.

Federals

Monday, March 20, 1865: The morning began foggy, yet warm and pleasant. Scouting reports of Moore's movement from Cedar Point reached authorities in Mobile. That afternoon, Maury sent down Gibson's Louisiana Brigade, who were encamped south of the city.[24]

Moore's Brigade skirmished hard nearly all day as the Confederates slowly fell back. A lieutenant colonel in the 72nd Illinois recorded in his diary: "We gave them every chance for a fight but think they had not force enough." Moore's regiments reached Fowl River and halted. That evening, they returned to the edge of the timber and camped for the night. Around dark, a rain deluge occurred. "One of the heaviest rainstorms I ever experienced came up. All got soaking wet." complained one Illinoisan.[25]

Moore's feint occupied Gibson's Brigade long enough to provide a distraction from the primary movements on the eastern shore. While they skirmished in Mobile County, the remainder of Smith's 16,000 troops continued to be ferried from Dauphin Island to Fish River unmolested. Here, the Confederates possibly missed an opportunity to strike a blow while Smith disembarked and established his camp. Maury, however, had not received sufficient intelligence to understand Smith's vulnerability. He could have sent over reinforcements if he had figured out Canby's movements earlier. Liddell then might have been able to concentrate his forces to attack before Granger and Smith united.

Near Dannelly's Mill, Smith's Corps camped upon a high ridge under the pine trees. Canby issued orders that every position must "at once be fortified." Accordingly, the men threw up strong breastworks around their camp, but no significant Confederate force in their vicinity yet opposed them. They had sufficient time to cut large pine trees and pile them up about five feet with dirt thrown against the outside.[26]

Granger's XIII Corps broke camp at sunrise. His men appeared in good spirits after a night's rest, but their mood would change during the day. The roads were in poor condition, primarily dry sand. One Massachusettsan jotted down in his diary: "The topsoil is quicksand and mighty quick too. Let a loaded wagon standstill an hour, and it will settle into the ground halfway to the axle or more." To the dismay

---

24 "Civil War Diary of Henry M. Dryer"; Joseph Stockton, *War Diary of Brevet Brigadier General Joseph Stockton* (Chicago, 1910), 29; William P. Chambers, *Blood & Sacrifice: The Civil War Journal of a Confederate Soldier* (Huntington, WV, 1994), 208.

25 Stockton, *General Joseph Stockton*, 29; Nye Diary, Mar. 20, 1865.

26 Reed, *Twelfth Regiment Iowa*, 227.

of the men, they were led in the wrong direction for several miles. The subsequent backtracking prompted significant profanity.[27]

The men were ordered to carry their knapsacks—something they had never done before—but the roads were terrible and growing worse, so the horses' welfare took priority. To lessen the burden, some men again tossed their extras with regret. "Goodbye blanket and retain overcoat and rubber blanket to shield and spread on the ground," noted a blue artillerist, "fortunate for us that the weather will grow warmer."[28]

That evening, it rained, yet Granger's men remained undaunted. They pitched their tents in a grove, made coffee, and ate a meal and hard bread for dinner. Some soldiers were detailed to cut trees and build corduroy roads for the artillery to get along. Others built breastworks around their camp to protect against a Confederate attack.[29]

Further north up the bay, Thatcher's gunboats shelled the eastern shore—from an area called Rock Creek to the Village (modern-day city of Daphne)—from 2:00 p.m. to dark. Houses were damaged, and a shot passed through the telegraph office, but no lives were lost. One Mobile newspaper reported: "The innocent women and children, of course, got out of the way and saved themselves from being killed by representatives of 'the best government the world ever saw.'" At about dusk, the gunboats withdrew, some back to the fleet, others down the bay.[30]

Confederates

Liddell gathered as much information as he could from his cavalry scouts. He received reports that Federal gunboats were shelling the shore around Point Clear. Spence's horsemen had moved toward Dannelly's Mill but had not reported back. They could not yet determine conclusively where Canby planned his main attack. Liddell, however, correctly surmised that the hard rain would delay Canby's movements, allowing him time to prepare for their attack. He did all he could to put his small force in a state of readiness. He knew Spanish Fort needed more

---

27 Cleveland, *Diary of Moses A. Cleveland*, 71; Whipple, *Diary of a Private Soldier*, 66–67.

28 Cleveland, *Diary of Moses A. Cleveland*, 71.

29 Fisher Diary, Mar. 20, 1865.

30 *ORA* 49, pt. 2, 1129–1130; "From Below," *The Morning Herald*, Mar. 24, 1865; Henry C. Fike, Diary, Mar. 24, 1865, State History Society of Missouri, Columbia, MO, hereafter Fike Diary, Mar. 24, 1865.

preparation than Blakeley, so he requested reinforcements from Mobile to occupy and hasten the completion of the works there.[31]

Federals

Tuesday, March 21, 1865: Considerable wind, heavy thunder, and rainstorms made transportation by land and water difficult and tedious for the Federals.[32]

Canby and Comstock arrived at Dannelly's Mill after staying all night on a steamer at the mouth of Fish River. After disembarking, they went up to Smith's headquarters. Canby, Smith, Brig. Gen. John McArthur, and Brig. Gen. Kenner Garrard rode past the 12th Iowa's camp, "seemingly looking over the ground with a view to fortifying or establishing a base until a better one can be had." One Iowan described Canby as "rather a plain looking man, not very dignified, or even remarkably intellectual looking." In addition to fortifying their positions, the XVI Corps assembled a pontoon bridge for the XIII Corps to cross the Fish River.[33]

Moore's Brigade remained in camp all day on the western shore due to the hard rain. Confederate scout reports revealed the advancing Bluecoats that landed at Cedar Point to be a small force and probably just a feint. Recognizing that the Federal advance to Fowl River was just a ploy, the Louisianans returned to camp in the afternoon.[34]

Granger's Corps struck tents and moved out at sunrise. After marching a short distance in the hard rain, the men found the roads impassable for their heavily loaded wagons. Wagon teams trying alternate paths were soon mired. In all directions, wagons were sunk down to their axles. The animals nearly buried themselves in their struggles to haul the wagons. Arms were stacked, and fatigue parties went to work corduroying the road for two miles. Soldiers lifted wagons out of the deep sand and pushed them forward. Logs used for corduroying were typically carried by two men and laid lengthwise across the road in the mud and water. The men performed well despite the taxing work. "Carrying green pine logs is not easy work, but we hope to strike firmer land as we advance," wrote a soldier of the XIII Corps.[35]

31 *ORA* 49, pt. 2, 1129–1132.

32 *ORA* 49, pt. 1, 93.

33 Comstock, *Diary of Cyrus B. Comstock*, 312; Henderson Diary, Mar. 21, 1865.

34 Nye Diary, Mar. 21, 1865; Chambers, *Blood & Sacrifice*, 208.

35 William B. Kinsey, Journal, Mar. 21, 1865, New York State Military Museum, Saratoga Springs, NY, hereafter Kinsey Journal, Mar. 21, 1865; Holbrook, *7th Regiment of Vermont*, 162; Robert H. Crist to Peter M. Crist, Spared & Shared 10, last modified July 28, 2015, https://sparedshared10.

Mule hooves sometimes got stuck between the corduroy logs, causing their legs to break. The men would pull the injured mule off the road a few yards, shoot it, and then "leave it to stink." Dead mules were frequently left by the road, sometimes three or four per mile . Burying or burning them took too much time.

The thunderstorms left the men "wringing wet" as they slowly proceeded through the sparsely populated region. Few houses or cultivated fields were seen. Moreover, the condition of the roads caused their supply trains to fall behind. "Alligator steak became common and shoe-soup was spoken of before we reached Fish River," recalled one soldier of the 94th Illinois. The rain finally stopped at about 3 p.m. They went into camp around 8 p.m. after a demanding day building miles of log roads.[36]

That evening, the vanguard of the XIII Corps—Col. Henry Bertram's Brigade—arrived at Fish River, opposite Dannelly's Mill. Having constructed a pontoon bridge, Canby directed Bertram to move to the north side of Fish River the following morning.[37]

Confederates

Spence and his scouts hovered near Montrose while they gathered intelligence for Liddell. He reported advancing infantry—a reference to Granger's movement—and seven gunboats, a transport lying off Point Clear, and the U.S. Army camp near Dannelly's Mill.[38]

Liddell sent multiple dispatches to Spence that evening. "Keep on until you meet the enemy and skirmish with him," the Louisianan ordered, adding to use his discretion but to skirmish with the Federals with all or part of his horse soldiers. He urged the Tennessean to capture some pickets and gather intelligence from them on Canby's force.[39]

wordpress.com/2015/07/27/1865-robert-h-christ-to-father/, hereafter RHC to PMC; Cleveland, *Diary of Moses A. Cleveland*, 71.

36 RHC to PMC; Cleveland, *Diary of Moses A. Cleveland*, 72; Kinsey Journal, Mar. 21, 1865; Whipple, *Diary of a Private Soldier*, 67; J. C. W. Bailey, ed., *A Gazetteer of McLean County* [...] (Chicago, IL, 1866), 49.

37 *ORA* 49, pt. 1, 141; *ORA* 49, pt. 2, 59.

38 *ORA* 49, pt. 2, 1136–1137.

39 Ibid., 1137–1138.

Chapter 5

"Devastating Columns of Yankees"

Federals

Wednesday, March 22, 1865: The morning started a bit cold, but the weather became pleasant as the day progressed. On the western shore near Cedar Point, Southern scouts fired upon one of Moore's pickets and retreated. That afternoon, the Bluecoats headed back to the landing. Confederate horsemen followed them down to within a few miles of Cedar Point but were driven off by a few cannon shots from Moore's forces. They had to wait at the landing until the tide rose that evening before they could board transports to rejoin their corps on Fish River. In the evening, they anchored near the mouth of Fish River and enjoyed a sumptuous oyster feast.[1]

Meanwhile, at Dannelly's Mill, Canby shared the privations of his men. He and his entire staff stayed in shelter tents. Comstock described their temporary headquarters as "not very luxurious."[2]

Smith's men were tough, mainly composed of Midwestern farm boys. When Gen. Nathaniel P. Banks first saw the rough-looking troops during the Red River Campaign, he disparagingly said: "Those are ragged guerillas. If a general can't dress his troops better than that, he should disband them." Banks changed his opinion when they saved his forces from obliteration during their retreat. "This

---

1 John Nelson, Journal, Mar. 22, 1865, MNHS, St. Paul, MN, hereafter, Nelson Journal, Mar. 22, 1865; Ridge Diary, Mar. 22, 1865.

2 Comstock, *Diary of Cyrus B. Comstock*, 312.

corps was made up entirely of Western men and was typical of the "free and easy" discipline which pervaded many of the organizations hailing from that section of the country," recalled Col. William C. Holbrook, 7th Vermont. "No deference was paid to rank, and it was often impossible to distinguish an officer from a private."[3]

Spence's cavalry attacked U.S. Army sentries near the Federal encampment. The shooting prompted the din of drums and bugles calling the men to arms and excited apprehensions of an impending battle. Smith's men hurried to the front but found the Graybacks had already fallen back. Anticipating future attacks, men were soon put to work preparing entrenchments. They made earthworks by cutting down pine trees, piling them up, and throwing dirt on the outside. The practice of throwing up entrenchments continued around every future encampment, further slowing Canby's forces' movement.[4]

Before he arrived at Mobile Bay, Smith wired Washington seeking an official designation for his command. "I am now without a heading or identity for my command. Unless I receive a number or a name for my command, I must style myself the Wandering Tribe of Israel," wrote Smith. Halleck responded: "Continue on in your exodus as the Wandering Tribe of Israel. On reaching the land of Canby, you will have a number and a name." Later that month, the "Guerillas" became officially known as the XVI Army Corps.[5]

Smith's Guerillas had a reputation for plundering. "All alike believed in the inalienable right to forage as much as they pleased," observed Colonel Holbrook, "and it was a common saying that after the Sixteenth Corps had been ten minutes in camp, no chicken was ever heard to crow within a circuit of five miles."[6]

One evening, some turkeys belonging to Canby were stolen. The commanding general suspected the "Guerrillas" might be responsible for the theft, so he asked Smith about it.

"General, I understand your men sometimes take things that do not belong to them," Canby asked.

"Yes, by G-D-, we will take Mobile," replied Smith, "and it don't belong to my men."

"No, no, not that," Canby said.

---

3 "A. J. Smith's Guerillas," *The National Tribune*, 4; Holbrook, 7th *Regiment of Vermont*, 164; David D. Porter, *Incidents and Anecdotes of the Civil War* (New York, 1886), 219; Shelby Foote, *The Civil War: A Narrative, Volume 3: Red River to Appomattox* (New York, 1974), 31. Novelist Shelby Foote referred to Smith's men as "Gorilla-Guerrillas" in Volume 3 of his Civil War narrative.

4 Aurelius T. Bartlett, "Reminiscences of Aurelius T. Bartlett," in Bartlett Family Papers, Missouri Historical Society Archives, 57; Henderson Diary, Mar. 22, 1865.

5 *ORA* 49, pt. 1, 132, 669.

6 Holbrook, *7th Regiment of Vermont*, 164

"Well, then, what is it?" Smith asked.

"Why, my cook procured a half dozen turkeys last night," Canby replied, "and put them in a coop beside my tent, and this morning, I find four of them have been taken."

"Couldn't have been my men, not my men," the Pennsylvanian exclaimed, "they would have taken them all, taken them all!"[7]

Chaplain Edwards, 7th Minnesota, observed in his journal: "Smith's Corps has behaved on the whole very well as there is nothing to plunder." Despite their notorious reputation, they were widely regarded as an outstanding fighting force.[8]

Per Canby's orders, Bertram's Brigade of the XIII Corps crossed the pontoon bridge that morning and moved into a battle line with the XVI Corps, expecting an attack. Low on rations, Smith shared a small amount with Bertram until his supply train came up.[9]

The remainder of the XIII Corps endured hardship and toil— corduroying the swampy roads—as they slowly trekked to Dannelly's Mill. "My clothes are getting stiff with the gum and turpentine which oozes from the green logs, but it cannot be prevented as we cut and carry them by hand," complained a soldier from Massachusetts.[10]

The supply trains lagged behind the column. Granger, however, remained undaunted and pushed his men forward, much to their irritation. "Boys are swearing mad because they are obliged to work hungry," noted a soldier of the 7th Vermont. The supply train eventually came up later that evening so the men could eat.[11]

Meanwhile, the natural defenses were evident to the U.S. Navy in Mobile Bay. The shallow waters made it difficult for Thatcher's gunboats to approach closer than three miles off Spanish Fort.[12]

7 Mildred Throne, "Nashville and Mobile," The Palimpsest 50 / University of Iowa Research, 127–134, last modified 1969, https://ir.uiowa.edu/palimpsest/vol50/iss2/10.

8 Edwards Journal, Apr. 17, 1865, 262.

9 ORA 49, pt. 2, 59.

10 Cleveland, Diary of Moses A. Cleveland, 72.

11 Fisher Diary, Mar. 22, 1865; Cleveland, Diary of Moses A. Cleveland, 72.

12 George W. Perrigo, Diary, Mar. 18, 1865, West Virginia and Regional History Center, Morgantown, WV.

Confederates

At 8:00 a.m., Spence reported to Liddell that he failed to capture any Federals pickets as they were too close to the main force. Scouts did, however, provide numerous reports that confirmed suspicions that Canby aimed to capture Spanish Fort to gain access to the Alabama River for subsequent operations against Selma. "I now think there can be no longer any doubt upon the subject," lamented Liddell in a telegram to Col. George G. Garner, Maury's chief-of-staff. "It is sad to think of the desolation that will follow the traces of these devastating columns of Yankees." Certain of an imminent attack, he concluded: "I don't think we will be permitted to remain in quiet long." He requested reinforcements be sent at once to make every defensive preparation possible in time to receive Canby's attack.[13]

Some conflicting reports perplexed Maury. He wanted a full explanation of why Spence could not ascertain the accurate location of Canby's main force. The lack of credible and discernible scouting reports prevented him from sizing up the situation sooner. The miscommunication may have occurred because some scouts did not belong to Spence's regiment and were scattered at various points in Baldwin County. Maury thus directed him to report "nothing but what you know to be facts concerning the force and movements of the enemy." He angrily ordered Spence to arrest laggards, who were incautious against surprise and failed to gather accurate information, and always to keep his pickets and scouts' insight of the Federals.[14]

Liddell also ordered Spence to Fish River to gather intelligence on the type and number of vessels there, adding: "I will have to rely upon your energy and enterprise alone." But that was easier said than done. The nature of the terrain limited the Tennessean's ability to observe Canby's force safely; the Federals quickly spotted his troopers on the level ground.[15]

Federals

Thursday, March 23, 1865: Moore's Brigade raised anchor in Weeks Bay and started up the Fish River on a warm, clear day. They took most of the morning to rejoin their corps at Dannelly's Mill. Upon landing, they threw up a line of earthworks around their camp, half a mile from the river.[16]

---

13 *ORA*. 49, pt. 2, 1141–1142.

14 Ibid., 1143.

15 *ORA* 49, pt. 2, 1143; Spence to Captain Lewis, *Dispatch Book*, 42.

16 Ridge Diary, Mar. 23, 1865.

The Union camp near Dannelly's Mill lay within a beautiful pine forest, the trees nearly 150 feet high. Sparse underbrush and trees far enough apart allowed mule teams to drive between them. Locals raised a few vegetables and sweet potatoes in some places, but for the most part, nothing grew in the sandy soil except the pine trees. "The soil was literally good for nothing, but the lumber and resin business had been, and still might be an institution," observed Chaplain Richard L. Howard of the 124th Illinois. Most of the pine trees had been boxed for turpentine near Fish River and in many other portions of the country, which the soldiers in blue passed. The soldiers often remarked in their journals about the sparsely populated county. "There were but few houses, and they were inhabited by a people as forsaken as the land where they dwelt," recalled Howard.[17]

While encamped on Fish River, the men continued to fortify quite heavily to protect themselves from a surprise attack. They piled up logs and tossed dirt on them; the light soil made shoveling easier. The necessity for the work, however, seemed superfluous to the average soldier. "Our force appeared strong enough to whip anything that could be brought against us here, without any protection," Howard recalled.[18]

Besides fortifying their position, Smith's men occupied their time with activities such as brigade drills and writing to friends and family. "We rather enjoyed our marching under the grateful shade of these trees, especially as the fallen leaves made it soft for our feet," noted Chaplain Howard. "But had we been mules, we should not have liked the sand, and more particularly in some treacherous places where the thin wet crust easily gave way and revealed the quicksands below."[19]

As the troops were about to have an inspection in the morning, lively musketry firing occurred on the right side of their defensive lines. Confederate cavalry drove in the pickets and tried to stop fatigue parties from working on the entrenchments. Soldiers were quickly summoned to fall into a battle line behind the fortifications, ready to fend off any attack, but the Graybacks did not push their assault.[20]

During the day, Canby drafted a reply to Grant's letter of March 9: "You cannot regret more than I do the delays that have attended this movement. We have been embarrassed and delayed by rain and wind storms that have not been paralleled in the last forty years." He explained the difficulties caused by

17 John Scott, *Story of the Thirty Second Iowa Infantry Volunteers* (Nevada, IA, 1896), 331–332; Howard, *124th Regiment*, 286.

18 Howard, *124th Regiment*, 287

19 Ibid., 286.

20 Charles Henry Snedeker, et al., *The Civil War Diary of Charles Henry Snedeker*, 23 Mar. 1865 Auburn University Archives, 1966; Nelson Journal, Mar. 23, 1865.

the inclement weather to his transportation but assured Grant they were moving forward with the operation. "We have had now two consecutive bright days, the only two in a month, and a footing upon the fairground," he noted, adding that if the XIII Corps arrived that day, he would move out in the morning for Blakeley and endeavor to open the Alabama River for Thatcher's gunboats.[21]

The XIII Corps struck tents early in the morning and had their coffee, then set out with half-day rations in their haversacks, all that remained from their last ration distribution. During the day, Col. William P. Benton's Division crossed the pontoon bridge over Fish River and went into camp in a pleasant grove. "This point is called Danly's Mills," observed an officer of the 28th Wisconsin. "I don't see the Mill."[22]

Confederates

Liddell ordered Col. Bush Jones of Holtzclaw's Alabama Brigade to send down 20 picked men to Spence. They were to aid him in discovering Canby's objectives, infantry, and artillery strength. He also forwarded him a supply of ammunition. Spence intended to move out upon their arrival but reported at 4:50 p.m. that the soldiers Jones sent refused to advance upon Canby's forces.[23]

Liddell demanded Jones to send better men and sent a telegram to Maury requesting the 15th Confederate Cavalry—a reliable locally raised regiment—be sent over. He pointed out that the Federals were so heavily bogged down in places that the 15th Cavalry's familiarity with the region would enable them to interfere with Canby's communications. Maury sent Brig. Gen. Randall L. Gibson from Mobile to reinforce Liddell at Blakeley. That evening, Liddell notified Spence: "Quite an infantry force will be sent to your support tomorrow." Liddell ordered Gibson's Brigade to join Spence at 8:00 a.m. with two regiments of Holtzclaw's Brigade under Colonel Jones, including Lt. Col. James M. Williams of the 21st Alabama. Gibson's infantry moved out with Spence toward Fish River to observe Canby's movements.[24]

21 *ORA* 49, pt. 2, 66; Grant and Canby knew each for many years. In July 1848, Canby and Grant were stationed at Pascagoula, Mississippi's Camp Jefferson Davis together after the Mexican war.

22 Fisher Diary, Mar. 23, 1865; *ORA* 49, pt. 1, 141; Stevens and Blackburn, *"Dear Carrie,"* 302.

23 Andrews, *History of the Campaign of Mobile*, 45–46; *Dispatch Book*, 46, 49

24 Andrews, *History of the Campaign of Mobile*, 44–45; *Dispatch Book*, 49; *ORA* 49, pt. 1, 313; *ORA* 49, pt. 2, 1146; *Dispatch Book*, 51.

As Canby's forces marched up the eastern shore, Maury published orders in the local newspapers instructing all Creoles and free persons of color to report to his headquarters to participate in the defense of Mobile.[25]

Randall Lee Gibson

Gibson, the son of a wealthy Louisiana slave-holding sugar planter, was born on September 10, 1832. In 1849, he enrolled at Yale University, where he excelled, graduating with the class of 1853. One classmate recalled Gibson's impressive presence when he stood and delivered the class oration at graduation: "In his presence and appearance were united that which was comely and fascinating in the beauty of youth and scholarly in speech and that which was commanding in intellect, above all the impressiveness and dignity of an earnest purpose to do well his part."

He returned to Louisiana from Yale, where he studied law in New Orleans at the University of Louisiana. In 1855, he received a law degree. Following his law studies, he went to Europe for three years of study and travel. There, he worked for six months as an attaché at the U.S. embassy in Madrid, Spain. After traveling around Europe, he returned to Louisiana in 1857 to pursue both a law career and planting. Gibson bought a sugar cane plantation in 1858 while he practiced law in nearby Thibodaux.[26]

An ardent secessionist, Gibson set aside his comfortable lifestyle and enlisted in the Confederate army after Louisiana seceded. Soon after enrolling, he received a promotion to captain of an artillery company. The 13th Louisiana—a regiment comprised mostly of men from New Orleans—quickly elected him their colonel. Gibson, who had no training in military affairs, soon realized a weakness of the Southern army. As he put it: "I should judge this army needed West Pointers."[27]

Seven years after the war, Gibson recalled:

25 "Depredations of the Enemy at Fish River," *Mobile* [AL] *Evening Telegraph*, Mar. 23, 1865.

26 United States Congress, *Memorial Addresses on the Life and Character of Randall Lee Gibson, (a Senator from Louisiana): Delivered in the Senate and House of Representatives, Mar 1, 1893, and April 21, 1894* (Washington D.C., 1894), 45, 70. McBride, *Randall Lee Gibson of Louisiana*, 56–58, 60. In 1860, Tobias Gibson's, Randall's father, holdings included 204 enslaved people and 6,000 acres of land. Gibson sold his 700-acre plantation on Bayou Lafourche in 1860. He moved back to his father's property in Terrebonne Parish and ran one of his plantations while searching for land of his own. The University of Louisiana was incorporated into Tulane University in 1884.

27 Randall L. Gibson to Tobias Gibson, Dec. 2, 1861, The Gilderman Institute of American History, New York, NY, hereafter RLG to TG, Dec. 2, 1861; Donald E. Dixon, "Randall Lee Gibson," Master's thesis, Louisiana State University, 1971, 30.

Brigadier General Randall Lee Gibson.
Tulane University Archives

You know, at that time, I was ignorant of the military art as it was possible for a young civilian-bred man to be. I had never seen one man shoot at another. I had never heard a lecture or read a line on the subject. We were all tyros— all the rawest and greenest recruits— Generals, Colonels, Captains, soldiers. I recollect one thing, and that was the majestic presence, the magnificent appearance of General Johnston—he looked like a hero of the antique type, and his very appearance on the field was a tower of more than kingly strength.[28]

Gibson committed himself to learning military tactics and the art of war. He intently studied Maj. Gen. William J. Hardee's *Rifle, and Light Infantry Tactics*. "Colonel Gibson, an exceedingly bright man, soon mastered tactics and was never after at a loss in handling regiment or brigade," remembered Capt. John McGrath, 13th Louisiana. After a competitive drill competition at Tullahoma in 1863, General Hardee addressed Gibson's command: "You are one of the best-drilled regiments I ever saw." This is a high compliment from the author of the acclaimed 1855 textbook on tactics.[29]

Gibson maintained strict discipline and insisted on exacting officers. In a letter sent to his father in late 1861, he emphasized that "unless troops be drilled & disciplined, they can't be relied on." Gibson drilled his soldiers hard, enforced discipline, and soon won their respect. General Joseph Wheeler recalled: "I knew him in the camp, earnest and devoted in administering to the wants of his men and

28 McBride, *Randall Lee Gibson of Louisiana*, 65. McBride's book *Randall Lee Gibson of Louisiana: Confederate General and New South Reformer* is recommended for further reading on Gibson.

29 John McGrath, "In a Louisiana Regiment," *New Orleans Picayune*, Sep. 6, 1903; Dixon, "Randall Lee Gibson," 30; *Life and Character of Randall Lee Gibson*, 95.

performing a tedious routine of duty. I knew him on the march, always sharing with his devoted soldiers' labor, fatigue, suffering, and privation."[30]

Early in the war, Gibson met Ulysses Grant, with whom he would later have friendly post-war relations. General Leonidas Polk chose him to accompany Gen. Frank Cheatham for a prisoner exchange meeting after the battle of Belmont. Under a flag of truce, they met with the Federals at a location between Columbus, Kentucky, and Cairo, Illinois. In a December 9, 1861, letter to his father, Tobias, Gibson described his remarkable meeting with the future President:

> General Grant has somewhat the appearance of a gentleman, but the rest seemed to me impudent upstarts. Some among them made known their confidence in their 'on to New Orleans' intention, and all of them declared they were fighting for us—that they came to save, not destroy. Genl Grant even saying he would resign his commission if war should be made against slavery—but it was evident from the whole tenor of their remarks that their purpose individually was subjugation & confiscation. I was thoroughly disgusted with the whole party.[31]

George Norton of the 13th Louisiana Regiment accompanied Gibson to that meeting. Grant immediately recognized Norton, observing they were relatives and that he had spent many happy days in the Norton home in New Orleans during the Mexican War. Norton carried a letter from his father in the hope of just such a lucky meeting with the Federal general, and he handed Grant his father's greetings, which concluded: "I have instructed George, when you are captured, to bring you directly to my house, No 12. Dauphine, where you will find a room prepared for you, a plate at the table, and as cordial a welcome as in the days of yore." Later, during the 1876 presidential election, Gibson and Grant established a friendly rapport and shared a good laugh recalling their earlier chance meeting. Norton would continue serving as Gibson's acting assistant adjutant-general until the war ended.[32]

Gibson overcame the vindictiveness of the irascible Gen. Braxton Bragg, a pre-war acquaintance and a neighbor in Terrebonne, Louisiana. Although they were never close before the war, the relationship soured beyond repair before the battle of Shiloh. Gibson became frustrated when Bragg failed to communicate orders adequately to him. He mentioned the issue to him in the presence of Gen.

---

30 *Life and Character of Randall Lee Gibson*, 93–94; RLG to TG, Dec. 2, 1861; Dixon, "Randall Lee Gibson," 30.

31 RLG to TG, Dec. 9, 1861.

32 McBride, *Randall Lee Gibson of Louisiana*, 73; *New Orleans Daily Picayune*, Oct. 31, 1878.

Sidney Johnston—who turned to Bragg and asked how the mistake was made. Gibson had inadvertently committed a breach of military etiquette with Bragg in front of Johnston. Disgruntled, Bragg would not forget the supposed slight.[33]

At Shiloh's "Hornets' Nest," Bragg made a grave error when he ordered Gibson's Louisianans to assault a firmly entrenched Federal position. Gibson later described it as a march "through an open field under heavy fire and halfway up an elevation covered with an almost impenetrable thicket." His command bravely attacked the position, but the Federals repulsed them four times. "Colonel Gibson's horse was shot under him and fell within five feet of me. This, of course, created great confusion, and we were ordered to fall back and reform, which we did," remembered a soldier of the 4th Louisiana. While valiantly carrying out Bragg's impossible order, Gibson lost almost a quarter of his brigade. Unwilling to accept the failure himself, Bragg unfairly reported that Gibson's Brigade had been driven back "due to want of proper handling."[34]

Military historians have widely dismissed Bragg's harsh remarks as unjustified. Despite Bragg's censure, Gibson's men retained confidence in his leadership. One soldier even noted that he had done "all that any brigade commander could do." Numerous accounts contradict Bragg's unfounded criticism of Gibson. General Wheeler stated that his Louisianans "gained immortal renown for courage and heroism from the time it first met the shock of battle on the field of Shiloh." Bragg's report greatly embittered Gibson, who later described Bragg as an "imbecile, coward, tyrant."

Official reports frequently cited Gibson for conspicuous bravery in the many battles in which he afterward engaged. His brigade led a tremendous assault at the battle of Stones River, driving back the Federal line with heavy causalities. "It could not be that the column which advanced with such thorough desperation and such impetuous force upon our lines that day could have had a calm and deliberate leader," recalled Capt. Charles F. Manderson, 19th Ohio. At Jonesboro, he heroically seized the colors of one of his regiments and led a charge to the Federal works, generating enthusiasm throughout his command. After the crushing repulse at Nashville, Gibson's Brigade served as "a rearguard of the rear guard" to check the pursuing Federals. General Hood praised his conduct: "General Gibson, who

---

33 McBride, *Randall Lee Gibson of Louisiana*, 75, 77–78; Thomas C. Robertson, Company C "Delta Rifles," 4th Louisiana Infantry wrote about this experience at the battle of Shiloh (Apr. 6–7, 1862). His letter appeared in the *Woman's Enterprise* on Apr. 7, 1922. Thomas C. Robertson, "4th Louisiana at Shiloh Part 1," Civil War Louisiana, last modified Apr. 6, 1862, https://www.civilwarlouisiana. com/.

34 Robertson, "4th Louisiana at Shiloh Part 1," Civil War Louisiana, last modified Apr. 6, 1862, https://www.civilwarlouisiana.com/; McBride, *Randall Lee Gibson of Louisiana*, 77–78.

evinced conspicuous gallantry and ability in the handling of his troops, succeeded, in concert with [Henry D.] Clayton, in checking and staying first and most dangerous shock, which always follows immediately after a rout." While retreating from Nashville, he crossed the Tennessee River in open boats in the presence of the enemy, near Florence, Alabama. His corps commander, Stephen D. Lee, reported, "a more gallant crossing of any river was not made during the war."[35]

Gibson was an intelligent and conscientious man but also a tenacious fighter. He favored an aggressive, offensive strategy and heartily endorsed General Hood. Despite the widespread condemnation of Hood's disastrous campaign in Tennessee, Gibson defended Hood's assertion that the assaults he ordered were necessary to reinvigorate an army demoralized by constant retreats. Gibson's propensity for aggressiveness would be evident during the long siege of Spanish Fort.[36]

"After traveling from one end to the other of the Confederacy," Gibson told his father, "I must tell you it is no small Country—It is much larger than many a proud Empire in the old world. I shall deem myself fortunate in sacrificing my life to assist in the achievement of its Independence." Gibson would risk his life in many battles through his final fight as the commander of Spanish Fort.[37]

35 McBride, *Randall Lee Gibson of Louisiana*, 80–82; *Life and Character of Randall Lee Gibson*, 95, 57–58, 98.

36 McBride, *Randall Lee Gibson of Louisiana*, 110–111.

37 RLG to TG, Dec. 2, 1 861.

Chapter 6

"They Are Unlike Northern Woods"

Federals

Friday, March 24, 1865: Canby's force camped on the north bank of the Fish River near Dannelly's Mill. They waited at the rendezvous point for the last of Granger's Corps to arrive on this fine, warm day.

Smith's XVI Corps had finished building breastworks around their camp. "Our camp is high & dry, water good, plenty of wood to cook rations & that is all we need for here," observed Cpl. William B. Chilvers, Company B, 95th Illinois.[1]

An officer of the 122nd Illinois, whose regiment had camped at Dannelly's Mill for five days, did not share Chilvers's enthusiasm. "This is the poorest country I ever saw they can't raise anything except sweet potatoes, and we haven't been able to find any of them," he complained in a letter to his wife, adding: "I am hopes we will find a better country as we go out into the interior." The mill owner, Dannelly, reportedly owned thousands of acres of pineland. He ran a lucrative turpentine pitch rosin and pine lumber business, worked by countless hands before the war. He noted that the Confederates conscripted Dannelly and took him to Mobile a few days earlier, leaving his wife and family. They had nothing to eat as the Federals took all their food the first day they arrived.[2]

---

1 William B. Chilvers to aunt, Mar. 24, 1865, William Burnham Chilvers, 1835–1914, Nebraska State Historical Society; "Civil War Diary of Henry M. Dryer."

2 JFD to wife, Mar. 24, 1865.

Despite the persistent rumors in camp about the evacuation of Mobile, the men prepared for the coming attack. The men drew four days' rations and received orders to march at daylight the following morning. Presumably sent by Grant to push Canby forward, General Comstock grew impatient and anxious. "Quite warm in shelter tent—where I write. It is hot," complained Comstock in his diary. "Hope we may start in the morning—I would have done it this morning or perhaps yesterday."[3]

Most of Granger's XIII Corps arrived at Dannelly's Mill during the previous two days. As they waited for the rest of the corps to appear, they camped on a high dry ridge, relaxing and bathing in the Fish River. During the morning, portions of Veatch's Division were still marching along the Fish River. Around noon, they began crossing the pontoon bridge.[4]

Confederates

Spence's cavalry scouts continued to try to ascertain the size and movements of the Union column. They also sought to harass the Bluecoats when possible.

At 2:00 p.m., Spence's scouts attacked the advance wagons of the supply train of Veatch's Division as they approached Dannelly's Mill. "A party of guerrillas made a dash on our wagon train, which was stuck in the mud below Fish River," the Federal-controlled newspaper *New Orleans Times* reported three days after the engagement, "and captured ten mules and eight drivers, and one straggler. Two mules were killed. All the wagons and stores were brought in." The "guerrillas" in the *Times* report were a small but determined contingent of gray-coated horsemen. The rear guard of the brigade was painstakingly trying to get the main body of the train over a lousy piece of road at the time. Granger reported eight teamsters and 14 animals were captured while no wagons or stores were destroyed.[5]

Confederate 2Lt. Artemus O. Sibley—a 36-year-old Baldwin County native and prominent local mill-owning family member—led the attack on Veatch's Division supply train. He belonged to Capt. Thomas C. Barlow's Company C of the 15th Confederate Cavalry. Due to Sibley's extensive knowledge of Baldwin County, Liddell ordered him to assist the 12th Mississippi. Sibley sent a dispatch

---

3 ORA 49, pt. 2, 77; Ridge Diary, Mar. 24, 1865; Nelson Journal, Mar. 24, 1865; Comstock, *Diary of Cyrus B. Comstock*, 312.

4 Kinsey Journal, Mar. 24, 1865; Fisher Diary, Mar. 24, 1865.

5 "Yankee Accounts from Mobile," *Mobile Advertiser and Register*, Apr. 8, 1865, 1; Originally printed in the *New Orleans Times* on Mar. 27, 1865; ORA 49, pt. 1, 141; "The Expedition to Mobile," *The Times-Democrat*, Apr. 1, 1865, 1; Federal accounts varied from seven to eight teamsters/drivers and one straggler captured, 10 to 14 mules captured or killed. The straggler appears to have been Allen Rutherford, a drummer boy of the 47th Indiana. He rode in one of the wagons due to overly sore feet.

from a plantation called Greenwood to Liddell about his successful attack. His message differed from the *Times* and Granger's report. He informed Liddell that they killed eight mules to take away their means of transportation and captured 21 prisoners. "I learn from prisoners General A. J. Smith has a command somewhere on the western shore, intending to operate with this against Mobile," reported Sibley. He also suggested to Liddell that further cavalry attacks would be effective on the rear of the Federal column.[6]

News of Sibley's action delighted Liddell. Later that night, he proudly forwarded Sibley's dispatch to Maury, adding: "Lieutenant Sibley has been behaving handsomely." In the same message, Liddell informed Maury of vessels near the mouth of the Fish River. He correctly surmised these vessels had offloaded Smith's command at Dannelly's Mill and that Canby had not yet advanced.[7]

Meanwhile, Gibson halted his command near the Village (present-day Daphne), eight miles south of Spanish Fort, not getting as far as Liddell had intended.[8]

Federals

Saturday, March 25, 1865: The XVI and XIII Corps, over 32,000 men, prepared to march to Spanish Fort on this pleasant and cool day. Both corps, led by Canby in person, began the grand movement at daylight. "Off at last," noted Comstock before joining General Smith at the head of the column.[9]

Before the march of the XVI Corps began, a soldier of the 108th Illinois was found dead by the side of a log. "But it was so sad to think of a brave soldier's coming so far from home and loved ones, to die alone by the side of a log in the darkness of the night," lamented Chaplain Howard. The cause of death remained unknown, but Howard suspected a congestive chill.[10]

Smith's Corps set out before Granger's did. The "Guerillas" moved out in a column up the Blakeley Road—Brig. Gen. John McArthur's First Division

---

6 David Williamson, *The 47th Indiana Volunteer Infantry: A Civil War History* (Jefferson, NC), 268, 407. *ORA* 49, pt. 2, 1148–1149; *Dispatch Book*, 75. Williamson's book indicates that three Sibleys served in the 15th Confederate Cavalry: brothers Artemus and Walter, and Origen Jr., all members of the prominent Baldwin County family. Artemus and Walter were the sons of 76-year-old mill owner Cyrus Sibley. Artemus worked as an overseer before the war and lived next door to his father. First Lieutenant Origen Sibley Jr., 25 years old, was the son of 66-year-old Origen Sibley. Cyrus and Origen were brothers and their mills were 4 miles apart. Liddell sent Sibley 20 hand-picked troopers from Baldwin County who were well acquainted with the country to help him scout.

7 *ORA* 49, pt. 2, 1149.

8 *ORA* 49, pt. 2, 1149; Andrews, *History of the Campaign of Mobile*, 45.

9 Wood, *A History of the Ninety-Fifth Regiment*, 169; Comstock, *Diary of Cyrus B. Comstock*, 312.

10 Howard, *124th Regiment*, 287.

in advance—without throwing out skirmishers. Truman, the *New York Times* correspondent, noted that this was the first time they had not thrown out skirmishers since Perryville. Under Brig. Gen. Kenner Garrard, the Second Division closely followed McArthur, while Carr's Third Division remained in the rear to guard the wagon train.[11]

Canby's two corps marched in a northwest direction. A correspondent described the low ground during the first few miles from Fish River as "level as a ballroom." There were no signs of cultivation, only a vast pine forest for miles in all directions, with an occasional group of water beeches "shading the never-failing springs with which the country abounds." Nearly all the large trees were tapped for resin and turpentine.[12]

The area seemed devoid of human inhabitants. "I did not see a house all day," noted one Illinoisan. As they progressed, the land became hilly, with deep ravines and gullies, and covered with a young growth of pines, alternately thickly wooded and open in some places. "They are unlike northern woods—all pine trees are alike—no lodges or streams to guide, no moss, no farms, or fences," an officer of the 1st Indiana Heavy Artillery observed in a letter to his father.[13]

The march soon became enlivened by skirmishing in their front. The First Division had not proceeded far when shots from Spence's horseman began whizzing through the air, General McArthur narrowly escaping injury. Future Minnesota governor Lucius Hubbard, commanding the First Brigade, had a ball graze his clothes.[14]

Another future Minnesota governor, Gen. William R. Marshall, commanding the Third Brigade, did not have the same luck. While he sat on his horse at the head of his brigade, Confederates fired a volley from the brush on his left flank. Suddenly, Marshall fell to the ground, shot through the left side of the back of his neck. His brigade surgeon soon arrived at his side. The musket ball narrowly missed his jugular vein, but the injury was slight. After the surgeon dressed his wound, Marshall remounted his horse and continued to command his brigade,

11 Truman, "Near Spanish Fort, Opposite Mobile," *New York Times*, Apr. 17, 1865, 2; *ORA* 49, pt. 2, 78. At Perryville in 1862, Rebels made a dashing assault on the U.S. Army column.

12 Truman, "Near Spanish Fort, Opposite Mobile"; Snedeker, *The Civil War Diary of Charles Henry Snedeker*, Mar. 25, 1865.

13 "The Siege of Mobile," *New York Times*, Apr. 17, 1865, 2; Ridge Diary, Mar. 24, 1865; RHC to PMC.

14 Reed, *Twelfth Regiment Iowa*, 227; Truman, "The Siege of Mobile," *New York Times*, Apr. 17, 1865, 2.

much to the great satisfaction of his men. One Iowan noted in his diary: "He is a very fine man, a real gentleman, and as brave a soldier as ever rode a horse."[15]

Spence's small force, primarily the 12th Mississippi Cavalry, constantly disputed the Federal advance. Knowing the land, his horsemen skillfully avoided close-quarter combat while taking every advantageous position to pour fire on the blue-coated soldiers.[16]

Canby, cautious to a fault, insisted his men entrench every time they came to a halt. Some of his officers saw this as a needless precaution, recognizing only a small scouting party opposed them. "A line of battle was formed at the crack of every gun in the distance," recalled Col. Isaac Elliot of the 33rd Illinois.[17]

Some of Granger's regiments got off as early as 8:00 a.m., while others did not fall into line until the afternoon. They cooked, washed clothes, and packed up as they waited their turn to join the column. Except for Bertram's Brigade, they followed Smith's Corps directly from Dannelly's Mill to Deer Park. Meanwhile, Bertram moved by Montrose Road. The roads were better than the quagmire they endured before arriving at Dannelly's Mill. Yet their march continued to progress slowly. High banks made it difficult to cross the trains over a couple of streams. They were further delayed while the pioneers built a bridge over one stream.[18]

Bertram's Brigade passed through Alabama City (present-day Fairhope) on the bay. Speculators had bought up the land a few years before the war and divided it into lots. However, the would-be city failed to develop. The *New York Times* reported "that four horses, a few negroes, and many dogs, perpetuate its name."[19]

Canby's men went into camp between 5:00 p.m. and sunset, tired after marching eight or nine miles. They camped in line of battle, throwing up works along their line. "Many of our pioneer men were in the siege of Vicksburg and knew the 'tug of war' by experience," noted a private of the 7th Massachusetts Artillery. "One says 'Plenty of hellfire' and brimstone before we get into Mobile.

---

15 Ebenezer B. Mattocks, Diary, Mar. 25,1865, MNHS, St. Paul, MN, hereafter Mattocks Diary, Mar. 25, 1865; Scott, *Thirty Second Iowa Infantry*, 333–334; Bartlett, "Reminiscences," 57; Minnesota Board of Commissioners on Publication of History of *Minnesota in Civil and Indian Wars, Minnesota in the Civil and Indian Wars, 1861–1865*, Vol. 2 (St. Paul, 1890), 624.

16 Allen, "Operations against the City," 74.

17 Elliott, *Thirty-Third Regiment*, 57.

18 Fisher Diary, Mar. 25, 1865; William E. Davis, Diary, Mar. 25, 1865, Tom Perry Special Collections, Brigham Young University, Provo, UT, hereafter Davis Diary; *ORA* 49, pt. 1, 93; Kinsey Journal, Mar. 26, 1865; Thomas Diary, Mar. 25, 1865.

19 Truman, "Near Spanish Fort, Opposite Mobile." Alabama City is today known as Fairhope, a picturesque community on Mobile Bay.

Our labors here will not be equal to Vicksburg, but I feel pretty sure that Mobile will be taken by the forces that have started to do it."[20]

Bertram's Brigade halted further west at an area called Rock Creek. Meanwhile, the remainder of the two corps went into camp at Deer Park, on a grassy knoll with a stream of water nearby. A northern journalist on the scene described it as "one of the most beautiful and picturesque sections of country in the South." Truman, the *New York Times* correspondent, reported: "Deer Park is no park at all, as I could see. Phillip, the negro guide, who tells 'we'uns' where to go, says Deer Park existed only in the imagination. A few years ago, he says, a gentleman from Mobile bought up the land and staked it off, but the deer never put in an appearance, and the park was never made." Yet the remnants of the enclosure for the deer, a half-buried palisade, remained.[21]

Canby issued orders prohibiting foraging. His men, however, sometimes disregarded this order. Captain John A. Williams, the officer of the day for the 3rd Brigade of Benton's Division, came upon one of the 7th Vermont boys, who carried a fat goose triumphantly. Williams promptly confiscated the goose from the man, but his ethics did not stop him from wishing to have a dainty morsel for his supper, so he turned it over to his servant to cook and invited Capt. Thomas N. Stevens of the 28th Wisconsin to have dinner with him. Now, it so happened that Cpl. Henry R. Carlin, Company C, 28th Wisconsin, found out about the goose and how it came into Capt. Williams's possession. He secretly watched the cook and the camp kettle, believing it unfair and wishing to play a prank on him and have a feast. The cook entered the tent at dusk to prepare for the officer's dinner. At that exact moment, Carlin stepped out of the bushes, grabbed the well-cooked goose from the fire, and disappeared with it. The cook returned in a few moments and found, to his dismay, that the goose was missing, and no trace of it could be found. Carlin and his squad had a fine feast that night, and the exasperation of the captain can well be imagined. A few days afterward, Carlin asked Captain Stevens how he enjoyed his goose supper with Captain Williams the other night. Stevens laughed and replied: "Corporal, I guess you know what became of that goose."[22]

20 Henderson Diary, Mar. 25, 1865; Cleveland, *Diary of Moses A. Cleveland*, 72; Comstock, *Diary of Cyrus B. Comstock*, 312; *ORA* 49, pt. 1, 93.

21 *ORA* 49, pt. 1, 93; "Operations In Front of Mobile," *New York Herald*, Apr. 9, 1865, 1; Truman, "Near Spanish Fort, Opposite Mobile"; Howard, *124th Regiment*, 287–288; Comstock, *Diary of Cyrus B. Comstock*, 312.

22 Lauren S. Barker, "28th Wisconsin Regiment: The Captain's Goose and What Became of It," Twenty-Eighth Wisconsin Volunteer Infantry, last modified 1888, https://www.28thwisconsin.com/campfire/goose.html.

Canby ordered the advance division to throw up breastworks when they halted each night. "We had before been made to realize that we were now under the direction of a somewhat cautious commander," remembered Colonel Hubbard. "At every bivouac on our advance, we had been required to entrench our front, a new experience for the Sixteenth Corps, and we had otherwise been impressed with the fact that conservative influences were in control of the army."[23]

Confederates

After the war, Maury recalled the conservative nightly fortification efforts were "especially absurd to us, who knew that there was no force in Canby's front except about five hundred cavalry under Colonel Spence." Maury also acknowledged Spence and his efforts against the numerically superior Federal force:

> It is true, Spence handled his men with excellent skill and courage, and no doubt had even praying in a quiet way every night; for he made 40,000 Federals move very circumspectly every day and entrench themselves every night against him, and here I will say Colonel Spence was one of the most efficient and comfortable out-post commanders I ever had to deal with. He always took what was given to him and made the most of it. He was devoted, active, brave, and modest and did his whole duty to the very last day of our existence as an army.[24]

That morning, Liddell remained at Spanish Fort. He mistakenly believed that only the XIII Corps approached and judged from the bad roads that the divisions would be separated. Liddell and his subordinate generals planned to offer battle the following day on the north bank of D'Olive Creek, about two miles south of Spanish Fort. Gibson placed two brigades in a line of battle on the north hill of D'Olive Creek. Their plan called for Gen. Francis Cockrell's three brigades to be positioned on Gibson's left, with Holtzclaw in the rear, ready to move around and strike the Federals on their right flank. The force would be roughly 4,500 men, Gibson having already positioned three thousand in a line of battle that afternoon. Meanwhile, Liddell continued to actively elicit intelligence from his scouts. One of Gibson's scouts captured a Federal prisoner with a map of the eastern shore. The map illustrated Canby's plan to reduce the two Baldwin County forts, Blakeley and Spanish Fort. Spence stayed in front of Bertram's Brigade, which he mistakenly

---

23 Reed, *Twelfth Regiment Iowa*, 227; Hubbard, "Civil War Papers," 625–626, LC.

24 Maury, "Defence of Mobile in 1865," 2–3.

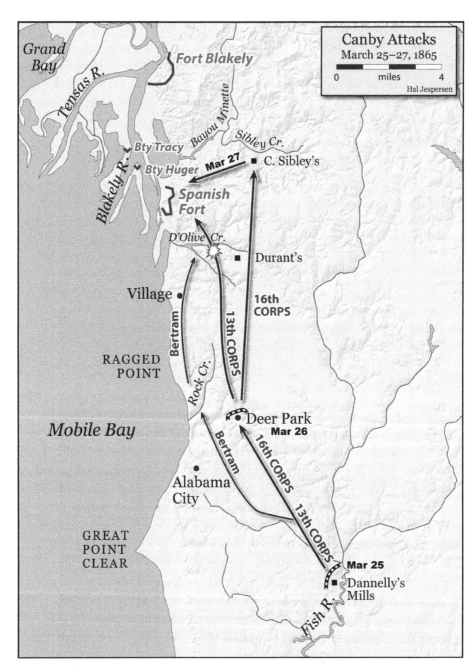

believed to be a division. He followed closely his orders to skirmish with them and keep Liddell updated.[25]

25 *ORA* 49, pt. 1, 313; *ORA* 49, pt. 2, 1152–1153; Andrews, *History of the Campaign of Mobile*, 45–46.

Chapter 7

"War Should Be Waged by Demons and Savages"

Federals

Sunday, March 26, 1865: Canby's army remained full of confidence; they figured that Spanish Fort's garrison would give them some trouble but believed Granger's men could handle them while Smith's troops continued further north to Blakeley.

The Federals set out on two separate roads. At daybreak, Granger's command was ready to move out. The order to march, however, was rescinded for some of the regiments, who had to stand around with their knapsacks for over two hours. They eventually got off and proceeded in a northerly direction. "Road good; houses frequent—deserted," noted a Wisconsinite from Bertram's Brigade. The XIII Corps traveled on the left, nearer the bay, heading directly for Spanish Fort. Meanwhile, Smith's XVI Corps on the right headed for the south branch of Bayou Minette.[1]

Before leaving Deer Park, Brig. Gen. Kenner Garrard's Division, XVI Corps, took the lead, with the 10th Kansas thrown out as skirmishers. Some soldiers called on divine intervention. "May God Help Us," Pvt. Frank Wittenberger, Company C, 14th Wisconsin, recorded in his diary before the march. "Very soon Gen. Canby and Gen. Osterhaus came riding by, it being the first time we had

1 "Civil War Diary of Henry M. Dryer"; *ORA* 49, pt. 1, 93; Comstock, *Diary of Cyrus B. Comstock*, 312; Edward G. Miller, *Captain Edward Gee Miller of 20th Wisconsin: His War 1862–1865*, ed. W. J. Lemke (Fayetteville, AK, 1865), 30; William M. Macy, "Civil War Diary of William M. Macy," *Indiana Magazine of History* 30, no. 2 (June 1934): 193.

seen our commander, and directly after we saw a house—the first since leaving Fish River," observed Chaplain Howard.[2]

The Federals found the weather pleasant and the ground higher and dryer than the previous day. Large pine trees covered the land, but the soil remained marshy in places. The area was rural; they marched by only three or four houses. "We passed a place called Durants about 10 a.m. Here, the country commences to roll a little and continues until the ridges pass into hills, and the great pines become monsters in their stateliness," Truman reported.[3]

From 9:00 a.m. to 1:00 p.m., heavy skirmishing occurred all along the line. The 10th Kansas had their hands full from the instant they engaged the Graybacks. Spence's omnipresent 12th Mississippi Cavalry, aided by the small detachment of the 15th Confederate Cavalry, kept up a barrage and made occasional stands on favorable ground. The Federal skirmishers advanced gradually, loading their guns at one tree before running to the next to fire.[4]

By 8:30 a.m., the blue-coated skirmishers from Kansas had exhausted their ammunition and had to be reinforced by the 6th Minnesota. The Graybacks resisted the advance as much as they could, but Canby's overwhelming numbers gradually forced them back.[5]

The firmer soil made the march considerably easier since leaving Fish River. However, the fierce resistance of Spence's horse soldiers negated some of the benefits of good roads. His troopers burned several rosin and turpentine barrels, causing enormous flames to impede the progress of the Federals. The fires were described as "hotter and larger" than the ones set by Sherman on his march through Georgia yet brought no distress to local inhabitants since there were few residents between Fish River and Spanish Fort. The gathering darkness around the fires also concealed the gray-coated soldiers from view. From their hidden position, they fired a single volley at the lead elements of the advancing corps before falling back.

---

2 Truman, "Near Spanish Fort, Opposite Mobile"; Frank Wittenberger, "Frank Wittenberger Civil War Diary," Richfield Historical Society, Richfield, WI, accessed Apr. 8, 2020, https://richfieldhistoricalsociety.org/story_frank_wittenberger.html; Howard, *124th Regiment*, 288. Major General Peter J. Osterhaus served as Canby's chief of staff.

3 Snedeker, *The Civil War Diary of Charles Henry Snedeker*; Truman, "Near Spanish Fort, Opposite Mobile."

4 Truman, "Near Spanish Fort, Opposite Mobile"; Snedeker, *The Civil War Diary of Charles Henry Snedeker*; Nelson Journal, Mar. 26, 1865; Charles S. Hill, *War Papers and Personal Reminiscences: 1861–1865. Read Before the Commandery of the State of Missouri, Military Order of the Loyal Legion of the United States* (St. Louis, 1892), 179.

5 Nelson Journal, Mar. 26, 1865; "Operations In Front of Mobile," *New York Herald*, Apr. 9, 1865, 1.

To some misunderstanding, several Union soldiers in the line immediately opened fire, putting their advanced skirmishers in grave danger.[6]

As the defiant Southerners resisted their advance, the U.S. soldiers soon discovered another deadly threat: sub-terra shells, also known as torpedoes. "The roadsides were filled with torpedoes, buried in the ground so that if man, horse or wagon should step on or pass over one so as to strike the plug, it would explode and scatter the missiles of death in every direction," recalled one Iowan.[7]

As they neared the fort, they regularly heard the noise of heavy detonations of the sub-terra shells, or "devil's paving stones," as the Federals called them. The Confederates buried the shells on the anticipated approach of the Federals. "A negro woman, who informed our men of the whereabouts of some of these torpedoes, said that just over the hill, the rebels had 'buried some cannons,'" reported a *New York Herald* correspondent. The *Herald* reported that so many sub-terra shells were planted that the Federals called it the "Yankee shell road." They proceeded with caution, scrutinizing the road as they went along.[8]

Several horses were killed during the day, and one man was seriously wounded. While inspecting the Confederate position in the afternoon, Granger and his staff rode along the turnpike leading towards the bay. He crossed a bridge, on either side of which, it afterward appeared, several sub-terra shells were buried in the sand where a soldier or wagon would likely travel. Not more than twenty minutes after Granger had crossed, a single horseman attempted to cross—almost in their very footsteps—and exploded one of these sub-terra shells.[9]

Confederates

The Confederates posted a force about two miles south of Spanish Fort to resist Canby's advance on the north hill of D'Olive Creek in the morning. They believed that the column from Fish River had about twelve thousand men and expected they would march by the river road with their left covered by the fleet. In round numbers, the Confederates had about 4,500 infantry and ten guns, including most

6 Hill, "The Last Battle of the War," 179; Crooke, *Twenty-first Regiment of Iowa Volunteer Infantry*, 146–147; Spence, "Last Fight," 7.

7 Scott, *Thirty Second Iowa Infantry*, 334.

8 William George Crooke, *The Twenty-first Regiment of Iowa Volunteer Infantry: A Narrative of Its Experience in Active Service, Including a Military Record of Each Officer, Non-commissioned Officer, and Private Soldier of the Organization* (Milwaukee, WI, 1891), 146–147; "Mobile," *New York Herald*, Apr. 9, 1865, 1; Truman, "Near Spanish Fort, Opposite Mobile."

9 "The Advance on Mobile," *Boston Daily Advertiser*, Apr. 13, 1865, 2; Truman, "Near Spanish Fort, Opposite Mobile."

of French's Division under Cockrell, Gibson's Louisiana Brigade, Thomas's Brigade of "Alabama boy-reserves"—as Maury described them—the 3rd Missouri battery, and Culpeper's battery.[10]

But they soon recognized how badly outnumbered they were and the threat to their left flank by the rapid movement of Smith's Corps. Liddell thus deemed it unwise for his main infantry to risk engaging the numerically superior Federals at D'Olive Creek. After consulting with Maury, they decided to fall back into their works. "I felt confident then, and the light of experience justifies the confidence, that had Canby marched upon us with only twelve thousand troops, we should have beaten him in the field," Maury later reflected, "but he moved by a road which turned our position far to the left, and his force was near forty thousand men. I, therefore, moved the troops into Spanish Fort and Blakely and awaited his attack in them."[11]

Liddell returned to his headquarters at Fort Blakeley while General Gibson assumed the immediate command of Spanish Fort. Liddell permitted Gibson to communicate directly with Maury, who retired to his headquarters at Mobile. Maury had confidence in the two officers he charged with defending the eastern shore. As he put it: "They were both gentlemen of birth and breeding, soldiers of good education and experience, and entirely devoted to their duty."[12]

Gibson's men resisted the attacking army as they slowly fell back into Spanish Fort. "We fought them until they forced us back into the ditches of the fort," recalled one Confederate. During the first week of the siege, Gibson's troops mainly came from Louisiana, Arkansas, Georgia, Tennessee, Alabama, and Virginia (Patton). Many of these men were battle-hardened veterans of numerous historical campaigns.[13]

Gibson's Louisiana Brigade occupied the right wing of Spanish Fort. Colonel Francis Lee Campbell, 13th Louisiana Regiment, assumed brigade command during the siege. A 28-year-old with blue eyes and light hair and a distant cousin of Robert E. Lee, Campbell originally hailed from Lowndes County, Alabama.

---

10 *ORA* 49, pt. 1, 93; Maury, "Defence of Mobile in 1865," 6; Compiled Service Records, RG 109, NARA. Culpeper's battery fell back with Liddell to Blakeley. With the exception of one detachment with a 20lber Parrott transferred to Spanish Fort, most of the 3rd Missouri Battery transferred back to the western defenses across the bay.

11 Andrews, *History of the Campaign of Mobile*, 46; Maury, "Defence of Mobile in 1865," 6; *ORA* 49, pt. 1, 314. Maury noted that Cockrell's Missourians and Ector's Brigade were there. It is believed that most of French's Division were there, not just his brigade. Casualty reports indicate that at least some of Sears's Brigade were present.

12 Maury, "Defence of Mobile in 1865," 6–7.

13 Andrews, *History of the Campaign of Mobile*, 47, 165; Eli Davis, "That Hard Siege of Spanish Fort," *Confederate Veteran* 12 (1904): 591; Evans, *Confederate Military History*, 45.

Colonel Francis Lee Campbell, commander, Gibson's Brigade, Spanish Fort. *Library of Congress*

He attended West Point but failed to graduate due to his poor performance in math. He was wounded in the shoulder at Shiloh and proved a capable officer. Campbell and his fellow officers were characterized as "wealthy, refined, gentlemanly fellows." The officers were indeed highly educated, wealthy, and well-traveled. As one officer put it, they were: "Gay, bright, dashing young soldiers, ready at all times to dance or to fight. French Creoles, with a few exceptions, scions of families who had furnished soldiers to every war in which Louisiana ever engaged, and to whom honor was dearer than life." In contrast, the men of the brigade were more diverse. For example, a report described the 13th Louisiana Regiment as "cosmopolitan [a] body of soldiers as there existed upon the face of God's earth." Many men were from New Orleans and had worked in various trades. They were mechanics, screwmen, longshoremen, sailors, barbers, and cooks. One officer who transferred to the regiment recalled his first encounter with them in camp:

> There were Frenchmen, Spaniards, Mexicans, Dagoes, Germans, Chinese, Irishmen, and, in fact, persons of every clime known to geographers or travelers of that day. Nor was that all, as it seemed to me that every soldier on the grounds, in addition to his jaunty zouave uniform, wore a black eye, a broken nose, or a bandaged head, having just been recruited, and only getting over the usual enlistment spree. In my gold-trimmed, close-fitting full-dress uniform, my young heartbeat with pride and ambition as I neared my destination, but I must confess a glance at the motley crowd of soldiers caused a sigh of regret that I had left my old company, even to assume higher rank.[14]

14 *ORA* 49, pt. 1, 318; Bruce S. Allardice, *Confederate Colonels: A Biographical Register* (Columbia, 2008), 88; McGrath, "In a Louisiana Regiment." Screwmen compressed and loaded pales of cotton

About three months earlier, Gibson's Brigade belonged to Lt. Gen. Stephen D. Lee's Corps at their previous fight at Nashville. With the rest of Maj. Gen. Henry D. Clayton's Division, Gibson's command repulsed two formidable assaults before it was compelled to retire due to two corps threatening to the rear. Lee recalled riding up to a brigade near a battery and trying to seize a stand of colors to lead the brigade against the Federals. The color-bearer from the 13th Regiment of Gibson's Brigade refused to relinquish his flag, and his regiment sustained him. Gibson had just appeared by Lee's side. He admiringly exclaimed: "Gibson, these are the best men I ever saw. You take them and check the enemy." He led them and checked the Federals. As Lee said, they were "as gallant as any in the service."[15]

Gibson's Louisianans suffered high casualties during many battles and were compelled to consolidate most of their regiments. The battered command reorganized accordingly: The 1st, 16th, and 20th Regiments; the 4th Battalion with the 25th Regiment; the 4th, 13th, and 30th Regiments and the 14th Battalion sharpshooters. The 19th Regiment remained the only unit unchanged. Early reports expressed confidence in Gibson's veterans at Spanish Fort. "All the old Louisiana troops that left New Orleans at its capture are there. Great confidence is felt, and food supplies are claimed to be abundant and sufficient for a long siege," one newspaper reported.[16]

While Gibson's troops held the right, Brig. Gen. Bryan M. Thomas—a 29-year-old West Pointer—commanded the 21st, 62nd, and 63rd Alabama Regiments on the left. Thomas previously served on the staff of Maj. Gen. Jones M. Withers and survived the battle of Shiloh. A West Pointer, class of 1858, the Georgian served in the U.S. Army.[17]

The veterans considered General Thomas's inexperienced brigade to be the weak link of the garrison. The 62nd and 63rd Alabama soldiers were mainly boys between 17 and 19 and some older men between 45–52. One Federal soldier later recalled that "both the cradle and the grave had been robbed" to furnish soldiers for the brigade. Some members of Thomas's Brigade gained combat experience at the battle of Chehaw Station on July 18, 1864. They defended the central rail link between Montgomery and Atlanta against U.S. Maj. Gen. Lovell H. Rousseau's raid. Despite their inexperience, they conducted themselves like veterans and

---

onto Mississippi River steamboats. Earlier service proved the Zouave uniforms lacked durability; they were probably not worn at Spanish Fort.

15 Stephen D. Lee, "Battle of Jonesboro," *Southern Historical Society Papers* 5 (Winter 1878): 131.

16 Clement A. Evans, *Confederate Military History: A Library of Confederate States History*, vol. X (Atlanta, 1899); "Defence of Mobile," *The Times Picayune*, Mar. 26, 1865, 3.

17 *ORA* 49, pt. 1, 318; "The War Is At Our Doors," *South Western Baptist* 16, no. 8 (July 1864): np.

Brigadier General Bryan M. Thomas, commander, Thomas's Brigade. *Alabama Department of Archives and History*

behaved "most gallantly." Afterward, Thomas's command came to Mobile, where they remained in the city's defenses. They stayed there until ordered to Spanish Fort, three days before the Federals arrived.[18]

After Nashville, Taylor sent most of the Army of Tennessee artillery—21 batteries—to help defend south Alabama. Five batteries went to Demopolis, while the rest went on to Mobile. Most of the artillery units had lost their guns during the fighting in Tennessee. During the defense of Atlanta, these batteries also lost and wore out their guns and material. Several companies had served from the start of the war and left dead comrades on more than a dozen great battlefields. At Spanish Fort, they would fight against men they had confronted at places like Shiloh.[19]

Colonel Patton, 22nd Louisiana, commanded Spanish Fort's artillery. Patton sub-divided his command. He managed all heavy artillery on the post, including the Batteries Huger and Tracey from his headquarters at Redoubt 1, while Capt. Cuthbert H. Slocomb of the Washington Artillery's 5th Company commanded all the field artillery batteries as a battalion within the works.[20]

18 63rd Alabama Infantry Regiment," Alabama Department of Archives and History, accessed Apr. 29, 2020, https://archives.alabama.gov; "62nd Alabama Infantry Regiment," Alabama Department of Archives and History, accessed Apr. 29, 2020, https://archives.alabama.gov; Howard, *124th Illinois Regiment*, 310. One member of Thomas's Brigade, Orderly Sergeant Thomas Seay, went on to become Governor of Alabama; "Rousseau's Raid," Encyclopedia of Alabama, accessed Apr. 29, 2020, https://www.encyclopediaofalabama.org/article/h-3596; "Our Forces in the Fight at Beasley's Farm," Selma [AL] *Morning Reporter*, July 27, 1864.

19 Larry J. Daniel, *Cannoneers in Gray: The Field Artillery of the Army of Tennessee* (Tuscaloosa, 2005), 182–183; Andrews, History of the Campaign of Mobile, 70.

20 Andrews, *History of the Campaign of Mobile*, 70; George S. Waterman, "Afloat-Afield-Afloat," *Confederate Veteran*, Vol. VIII, 23; Morning Report, Randall L. Gibson Papers, Louisiana and Lower Mississippi Valley Collections, Louisiana State University Libraries, Baton Rouge, LA, hereafter Morning Report, RLG.

At the start of the investment, Gibson's garrison only had about 2,100 men. This included Thomas's Brigade (about 950 men), Gibson's Brigade (about 500 men), and Patton's artillery (360 men). More than 300 artillerists were under Major Washington Marks, 22nd Louisiana, at Batteries Huger and Tracey. Except for Thomas's command, the men were mainly veterans from Hood's army.

To create an exaggerated impression of his numbers and to conceal his exact positions, Gibson detailed special parties to lay off a long line of battle as far in advance of the position as they could go and to make campfires along its whole length. His ruse worked. Federals variously reported the garrison's strength to be from three to ten thousand men. "The garrison consists of about 6,000 rebels," declared one soldier from Minnesota. "The position is very strong."[21]

To Gibson's dismay, he found the works at Spanish Fort incomplete. "It was apparent that an immense work with the spade, pick, and ax was before us and that some decisive measure must be adopted to prevent the large army already upon our front from coming upon us vigorously or by an onset," he later reported. A deficiency of tools exacerbated the problem. Undaunted, Gibson immediately set his men to work on the rifle pits, and they were kept busy around the clock with the available spades and axes.[22]

Maury—desperate for more soldiers—issued special orders that authorized and directed 27-year-old Capt. William F. Cleveland, Independent Scouts, to organize volunteers of Creoles and free persons of color into companies to report for duty. The special orders appeared in the *Mobile & Advertiser*. "It is hoped a cheerful response will be made to this order, as it requires duty of each man to defend his own home," Captain Cleveland stated in the notice.[23]

Federals

Granger's XIII Corps advanced slowly as they skirmished most of the day, though some regiments saw little to no fighting in the rear. After marching about eight miles, they crossed a shallow stream, formed a battle line, and began the investment by throwing up breastworks within a couple of miles on the southeast front of Spanish Fort. "The Rebs lay within speaking distance of our lines," observed one blue-coated soldier at the front on picket duty.[24]

21 Andrews, *History of the Campaign of Mobile*, 44; *ORA* 49, pt. 1, 314; "The Mobile Expedition," *New Orleans Times-Democrat*, Apr. 8, 1865, 2; Mattocks Diary, Mar. 26, 1865.

22 *ORA* 49, pt. 1, 314–315.

23 "Special Orders No. 85," *The Mobile Advertiser & Register*, Mar. 28, 1865.

24 Davis Diary, Mar. 26, 1865; James R. Slack, Diary, Mar. 26, 1865, Indiana State Library, Indianapolis, IN, hereafter Slack Diary, Mar. 26, 1865; Macy, "Civil War Diary of William M. Macy,"

Around 6:00 p.m., Brigadier General Veatch ordered 200 men of the Third Brigade, XIII Corps, to the left of the skirmish line of the First Brigade to connect with Colonel Bertram's line. Six companies of the 23rd Wisconsin set out accordingly.[25]

As the XIII Corps established its position, details helped set up field hospitals in their rear. One soldier noted in his diary that some men created hospital operating tables with arms and ammunition boxes.[26]

Confederate skirmishers hovered before the XVI Corps advance and kept up a continual barrage. By noon, they reached Cyrus Sibley's house and mill, located just off the Minette Creek. Here, they came upon a party of cavalry attempting to burn the bridge across Bayou Minette. General Garrard threw out the 178th New York regiment to reinforce the 10th Kansas. As Truman put it, the Graybacks became "quite doughty," and they fired a volley from the other side of the bridge but were driven off.[27]

Rifle pits were thrown up at the Sibley residence. The family had abandoned their home that morning, leaving many valuables behind, including "[a] rich library, furniture, piano, pictures, etc., and several Negroes who gave us all the information we wanted," noted an officer of the 177th Illinois. Cyrus Sibley owned the house and the mill near it. His brother Origen also owned a mill a few miles north. Both men had sons in the 15th Confederate Cavalry, attached as scouts to Spence's command. The commander of the 117th Illinois, Col. Risdon M. Moore, commandeered the house for his headquarters. Garrard's Division remained around Sibley's Mill to watch the Confederate movements on the Blakeley Road, protect the rear, and guard the wagon train of the XVI Corps. Canby ordered Smith to move back against the right of Spanish Fort at daylight with McArthur's and Carr's Divisions.[28]

Portions of the column crossed the creek a little before 1:30 p.m. The 124th Illinois formed a battle line and faced up the road when General Smith rode up and asked: "What regiment is this that is so _____ smart?" Colonel Howe saluted and responded: "The Hundred and two dozen Illinois." Though the men supposed

193; Thomas Diary, Mar. 26, 1865; *ORA* 49, pt. 1, 93.

25 *ORA* 49, pt. 1, 184–185, 187.

26 Cleveland, *Diary of Moses A. Cleveland*, 73; Hewitt, *Supplement to the Official Records*, 938.

27 "The Expedition to Mobile," *The Times-Democrat*, Apr. 1, 1865, 1; "Operations In Front of Mobile," *New York Herald*, Apr. 9, 1865, 1.

28 Edwin G. Gerling, *The One Hundred Seventeenth Illinois Infantry Volunteers: 1862–1865* (Highland, IL, 1992), 101; *ORA* 49, pt.2, 1157–1158; Truman, "The Siege of Mobile," *New York Times*, Apr. 17, 1865, 2; Wood, *A History of the Ninety-Fifth Regiment*, 170.

they were moving on Blakeley, Smith proceeded no further and, at 2:00 p.m., went into camp. Here, his men had a good wash in the creek and soon rested. Pickets were deployed within sight of the Confederates, and many shots were exchanged.[29]

Though the Confederates made no demonstrations from the fort that evening, the Federals expected a fight in the morning. "A Christian sabbath and Christians preparing to shoot each other to death," a U.S. soldier remarked in his journal. "War should be waged by demons and savages."[30]

29 "Spanish Fort and Fort Blakely Again," *The National Tribune*, Aug. 2, 1888, 3; Truman, "Near Spanish Fort, Opposite Mobile"; Alfred J. Hill, *History of Company E, of the Sixth Minnesota regiment of volunteer infantry* (St. Paul, MN, 1899), 28–29; Howard, *124th Regiment*, 288; "Operations In Front of Mobile," *New York Herald*, Apr. 9, 1865, 1.

30 Whipple, *Diary of a Private Soldier*, 67; Cleveland, *Diary of Moses A. Cleveland*, 72; Truman, "Near Spanish Fort, Opposite Mobile," *New York Times*, Apr. 17, 1865, 2.

Chapter 8

"Take the Bull by the Horns"

Confederates

Monday, March 27, 1865: The day turned out to be miserable, cold with strong southeast winds and constant rain. To make matters worse for the Union forces, they soon discovered—to their anguish—that the Graybacks had not left Spanish Fort as some supposed they might. "The fall of the city is conceded by the rebels themselves, and this work will delay us but a short time," the *New York Times* erroneously reported. On the contrary, they would soon learn they were in for a long, hard fight.[1]

In Meridian, Taylor wired General Lee at Richmond: "Enemy has thrown his large force to the eastern side of Mobile Bay, leaving nothing on the west side. I am ready to receive any attack he may make at Mobile." Taylor also informed Lee of his expectation that Forrest could whip James Wilson's cavalry raid and then help raise the siege of Mobile. He added: "I hope to protect our main interests here and personal communications."[2]

Gibson demonstrated his propensity for aggressive tactics at the onset of the investment. He ordered an attack before daylight to deter the Federals from

---

1 Andrews, *History of the Campaign of Mobile*, 50; Fisher Diary, Mar. 27, 1865; Snedeker, *Diary of Charles Henry Snedeker;* "The Attack on Mobile," *New York Times*, Apr. 9, 1865, 8; Comstock, *Diary of Cyrus B. Comstock*, 313.

2 *ORA* 49, pt. 2, 1160–1161.

assaulting and inspire the young troops of Thomas's Brigade. Lieutenant Colonel Robert H. Lindsay, 19th Louisiana, led the bold 550-man attack.[3]

Lindsey gallantly set out in a "very heavy skirmish line" toward a break in the Federal line, thus flanking the 47th Indiana's left. The sudden attack surprised Granger's blue-coated soldiers, allowing the Rebs to inflict a "severe blow." They poured a deadly volley down on the Federals. The "pretty brisk" firing drove back the Bluecoats, with a few wounded and one killed. The Federals soon returned in a heavy line of battle to repulse Lindsey and retake the ground lost. Before recalling his men, Lindsay managed to capture a few prisoners, many arms, and accouterments. "Our object seemed to be accomplished, for it was not until late in the evening that he advanced, feeling his way cautiously, and making no assault, invested our defenses," Gibson afterward reported.[4]

Mainly composed of artisans, the 21st Alabama was formed at Mobile in October 1861. The regiment had taken part in the battle of Shiloh, where it suffered heavy losses. In January 1864, two companies under the command of Iowa-born Lt. Col. James M. Williams were stationed at Fort Powell. About a month later, they withstood a bombardment from five gunboats and six mortar-boats from Farragut's fleet, which attempted to force an entrance through Grant's Pass.[5]

In early August 1864—during the battle of Mobile Bay—Williams found himself in an unwinnable situation. Fort Powell's defenses were oriented to receive attacks on its western front. However, once the Federal fleet ran past the guns of Fort Morgan and defeated Admiral Buchanan's small Confederate fleet, it left Williams's small garrison in a precarious position. The fleet inside Mobile Bay dangerously exposed his rear. Soon, a U.S. ironclad monitor came to within 700 yards of the rear of the work, seriously threatening to explode his magazine. Williams believed remaining in the fort was unjustifiable. He telegraphed Col. Charles D. Anderson at Fort Gaines that he would be compelled to surrender within forty-eight hours. Anderson replied: "Save your garrison when your fort is no longer tenable." Accordingly, Williams determined to evacuate his men and destroy Fort Powell rather than allow both to be captured. At 10:30 p.m. on August 7, 1864, Williams and his two companies marched out to Cedar Point and blew up the fort. The evacuation of Fort Powell infuriated Maury. "Colonel Williams should have

---

3 Andrews, *History of the Campaign of Mobile*, vii; *ORA.*49, pt. 1, 315.

4 Whipple, *Diary of a Private Soldier*, 67; "Mobile," *New York Herald*, Apr. 9, 1865, 1; Crooke, *The Twenty-first Regiment of Iowa*, 147; Slack Diary, Mar. 27, 1865; *ORA* 49, pt. 1, 315.

5 "21st Alabama Infantry Regiment," Alabama Department of Archives and History, accessed Apr. 28, 2020, https://archives.alabama.gov/referenc/alamilor/21stinf.html; Clement A. Evans, *Confederate Military History: A Library of Confederate States History*, vol. VII (Atlanta, 1899), 123.

Lieutenant Colonel James M. Williams, 21st Alabama, Thomas's Brigade.
Confederate Memorial Park / Anne B. Hearin

fought his guns," he angrily noted on Williams's report. "Fort Powell should not have been surrendered." Maury promptly removed Williams from command pending an investigation.[6]

The investigation took a couple of weeks while the anguished Williams awaited vindication. He desperately pushed to have his case resolved, but seemingly to no avail. When his case finally proceeded, the Confederate authorities contended Fort Powell could have held out a month. Williams pointed out in a letter to his wife that Fort Morgan resisted the Federal bombardment for eighteen days. The suggestion that his small fort could have held out longer than the vastly stronger masonry fort infuriated him. In another letter to his wife, he vented his frustrations, writing, "the proposition is ridiculous and eventually brings into disgrace those who have endeavored to ruin me."[7]

Although the military court acquitted Williams of all blame, Maury remained unsatisfied. At Maury's request, Taylor suspended Williams from command until the War Department reached a decision. Williams appealed the decision directly to the secretary of war, James A. Seddon, "in the name of Justice, and as a soldier of the Confederacy, whose honor is dear to him, and who has no other resort" for vindication. Seddon, however, declined to interfere. Williams—refusing to resign—begrudgingly waited for his reinstatement.[8]

In early December, Maury finally reinstated Williams to his regiment and assigned him command of Batteries Huger and Tracey. "I feel at home again now that I find myself behind the ramparts of a fort bristling with Brooke guns and Columbiads," he told his wife. "I take so much delight in my duties as a soldier

6 James M. Williams, *From That Terrible Field: Civil War Letters of James M. Williams, 21st Alabama Infantry Volunteers* (Tuscaloosa, 1981), 127–128, 137–147.

7 Williams, *From That Terrible Field*, 127–128, 137–147.

8 Ibid., 136, 140–150.

that I am wonderfully consoled whenever I look out on the works around me and the brave comrades who wait for the approach of the Yanks to perform their grand Southern symphony on the big guns."⁹

In early 1865, the 21st Alabama was assigned to Brig. Gen. Bryan M. Thomas's Brigade during the opening days of the fight before Spanish Fort. On the morning of March 27th, Williams's long-awaited opportunity came to redeem himself.¹⁰

Federals

Canby decided to surround Spanish Fort before giving any attention to Fort Blakeley. Smith ordered two divisions of his XVI Corps, the 1st (McArthur) and 3rd Divisions (Carr), to retrograde a few miles and take up a position in front of Spanish Fort on the right. His "Guerillas" were aroused early and by 6:00 a.m., were set in motion. His two divisions turned back in a southwest direction toward Spanish Fort. Garrard's Division remained entrenched near Sibley's house to guard against an attack from the Confederates at Blakeley and protect the supply trains. They busied themselves throwing up breastworks and an artillery battery.¹¹

With the 81st Illinois of Geddes's Brigade in advance, the column proceeded cautiously, wary of the dreaded sub-terra shells. They found three on the road in damaged condition, and one contained 60 lbs. of powder. The Federal soldiers passed the brow of the hill overlooking Minette Bayou when suddenly they were ambushed. A Confederate regiment fired a volley from their concealed position in the bushes on the farther side of the bayou, about four hundred yards distant. It was Williams who commanded this small regiment of about 225 men of the 21st Alabama. Smith, riding near the head of the advance, narrowly escaped while many shots took effect on the 81st Illinois Regiment. Leaving a regiment at this point to engage Williams's Alabamians, the remainder of Smith's command marched on, with the pioneers removing trees that had been felled across the roads to delay their advance.¹²

9 Ibid., 150–151.

10 Williams, *From That Terrible Field*, 150, 158; *ORA* 49, pt. 1, 1046. At Spanish Fort, the remaining companies of the 21st Alabama, except companies C and D, who remained at Fort Blakeley as Provost Guards for Liddell, under Williams, were placed in Bryan M. Thomas's Brigade, but later detailed to Holtzclaw's Brigade.

11 Hill, *History of Company E*, 29; Howard, *124th Regiment*, 290; Wood, *A History of the Ninety-Fifth Regiment*, 170; Ridge Diary, Mar. 27, 1865.

12 "Spanish Fort, Opposite Mobile," The *New York Times*, Apr. 17, 1865, 2; Andrews, *History of the Campaign of Mobile*, 51; Allen, "Operations against the City," 75; Howard, *124 Regiment*, 290.

"A countryman had been pressed into service as a guide; mounted on the sorriest of horses, he presented a most forlorn and, at the same time, laughable spectacle, surrounded by the staffs and orderlies of Smith and Carr," recalled on U.S. officer. Within about a mile of Spanish Fort, Smith ordered both his divisions to deploy in line of battle, McArthur on the left and Carr on the right. Smith rode with a stern countenance; he wanted his movements concealed from the Graybacks. At the sight of their "chief," the men of the 49th Missouri gave a cheer, which the Confederates heard distinctly. Thus foiled in his efforts to conceal the position, Smith rebuked his men in a few hasty words. In half a minute, a shell from Spanish Fort came screeching through the trees and dropped close to the 49th Missouri. It did not burst as it fell, and the men gave back a little. Seeing this, Smith yelled at them: "Stand up to it! You had no business cheering."[13]

By 9:00 a.m., Smith's advance arrived within range of the enemy's batteries. They proceeded in a southwest direction a short distance when they came upon rebel pickets. "Then it was a foot race to see who would get to Spanish Fort first. When the last rebel went over the works, our skirmish line was not over 100 yards behind them, and then, great guns! Didn't they open fire upon us! In a second, every man was out of sight or behind a stump or log," recalled a soldier of Carr's Division. Thomas's Brigade sustained heavy casualties while resisting Smith's advance outside the works on the Confederate left of the line. Company A of the 62nd Alabama, for example, lost 16 killed or wounded during the day.[14]

Brigadier General Eugene A. Carr recalled: "Old A. J. was very anxious 'till we got fairly settled to the siege." His two divisions managed to move into position under heavy fire. "We were greeted with quite a lively fusillade of shells and musket balls," an officer of McArthur's Division remembered, "and it seemed much like our advance on Vicksburg." By 10:00 a.m., the Federals had Spanish Fort completely hemmed in on the land side. Carr established his command on the right, his right flank resting by Minette Bay. "From the high grounds in our front, and from the right of the Bay, Mobile, the bone of contention and object of our present sanguinary strife, is plainly visible," reported one newspaper correspondent embedded with XVI Corps. McArthur was next to the left, connecting with Benton's Division of the XIII Corps.[15]

13 Allen, "Operations against the City," 75; Andrews, *History of the Campaign of Mobile*, 51–52.

14 "Spanish Fort and Fort Blakely Again," *The National Tribune*, Aug. 2, 1888; Reed, *Twelfth Regiment Iowa*, 227; Roger Hansen, "Confederate Wounded, 1865 Mobile Campaign" (unpublished manuscript, 2020).

15 Eugene A. Carr, *First Reunion of the Survivors of the Army of Tennessee, And Its Four Corps* (Logansport, IN, 1892), 26; Reed, *Twelfth Regiment Iowa*, 227; Elliott, *Thirty-Third Regiment*,

Early in the day, Union soldiers marched a young soldier to the rear. The boy, probably of Thomas's Brigade, had been captured on the skirmish line. Though he showed no signs of pain or emotion, an examination found a mini-ball had passed directly through his chest. This incident occurred before any provision had been made for receiving or caring for the wounded. A doctor directed the guard to assist the captive in getting into the ambulance, and as he lay down, a quantity of blood that had collected gushed from his chest wound in a large stream. "The quiet, brave little fellow remained with us and fared the same as our own wounded, and when at last he was sent to the general hospital, with them, he was doing well and probably recovered," recalled the doctor who first treated him.[16]

Around 10:00 a.m., the Federal artillery opened on Spanish Fort, and the Confederates returned the compliment. The artillery and musketry fire was continual, with no decrease to either. One 1st Indiana Heavy Artillery officer exclaimed: "I have never heard brush rattle so in my life, nor I never wanted to leave a place so much."[17]

After a few hours of observing the battle, Truman concluded the fortifications comprising Spanish Fort "were hard nuts to crack." In the constant cold rain, the besiegers had to lie down on their stomachs while shells flew around them. Some men were able to protect themselves by rolling behind logs and stumps. "We are on a side hill in plain sight of the Rebs & we got orders to lay down. It is raining shot & shell are coming fast," observed one Vermonter.[18]

The Federals made repeated attacks that morning in strong lines of skirmishers but were repulsed, with heavy losses around the whole lines and only a slight loss to the Confederates.[19]

One soldier of Benton's Division criticized what he perceived as carelessness on the part of the generals of the XIII Corps: "In the first day of the siege, there was much reckless and unpardonable risking of life. Some regiments, for no possible reason but the drunken bravado of general officers, were for hours held in the most exposed positions, in close formation, without shelter of any kind."[20]

57; *ORA* 49, pt. 1, 267; "From Mobile Bay. Operations before Spanish Fort," *New Orleans Times-Democrat*, Apr. 6, 1865, 2.

16 Bartlett, "Reminiscences," 57.

17 Fisher Diary, Mar. 27, 1865; RHC to PMC; Stevens and Blackburn, *"Dear Carrie,"* 302.

18 Truman, "Near Spanish Fort, Opposite Mobile," *New York Times*, Apr. 17, 1865, 2; Fisher Diary, Mar. 27, 1865; Miller, *Captain Edward Gee Miller*, 30; Sidney E. Weston, "Dear Parent," Vermont Civil War, Lest We Forget, accessed Apr. 4, 2020, https://vermontcivilwar.org/get.php?input=32074.

19 *ORA* 49, pt. 2, 1161–1162.

20 Sperry, *History of the 33d Iowa Infantry Volunteer Regiment*, 134–135.

Men on both sides believed that Canby would immediately follow up with an assault. All preparations for storming the fort were made, including stripping all superfluous weight off the men. They expected orders to storm the frowning works belching furious fire at them.[21]

Union batteries shelled the fort for nearly an hour without receiving a response. The Federals erroneously perceived this as a weakness. The Confederates, however, anticipated an assault and held back their fire. They had their big guns "double shotted with grape and canister all the time" in readiness for an expected attack, which many Bluecoats would not have survived. Battery F, First Missouri Artillery, posted on the extreme left of the line, less than 800 yards from the fort, fired a volley from six guns and burst six shells over the works. Cheers went around the entire Federal line . . . all too much for the Rebels to take in silence. "Quick as a flash, the masks of twelve embrasures were torn away, a dozen murderous muzzles were thrust out, and the awful thunder of twelve heavy guns was joined by the almost simultaneous squealing, hissing, cracking, crashing, and bursting of as many ponderous missiles of destruction," reported the *New York Times* correspondent. "The quiet which followed was ludicrous. Not a National soldier opened his mouth or stirred a limb. No Sabbath school was ever more quiet."[22]

Soon after arriving in front of the fort and after the works had been reconnoitered, Smith sent a staff officer to Canby's headquarters and requested an immediate assault by the XVI Corps upon the rebel works. Canby doubted Smith's ability to carry the works and asked General McArthur's opinion. After careful inspection of the fort, McArthur flatly replied: "My division will go there if ordered, but if the rebels stay by their guns, it will cost the lives of half of my men." Canby responded: "It won't pay." His inclinations toward engineering work were so strong that he opted for a siege. During the night, breastworks were built, and siege operations commenced in regular order.[23]

"Though surprised, we were by no means disappointed when it was ordered that the troops should establish a line of investment," remembered Colonel Hubbard. Earlier in the war, it would probably have been considered good military tactics to have made a direct assault, particularly against a fort seemingly in an incomplete and somewhat disorganized state. Though Hubbard believed an assault would probably have succeeded, he recognized heavy casualties might largely be

---

21 Truman, "Near Spanish Fort, Opposite Mobile," *New York Times*, Apr. 17, 1865, 2; Hubbard, "Civil War Papers," 626, LC.

22 Truman, "Near Spanish Fort, Opposite Mobile."

23 Reed, *Twelfth Regiment Iowa*, 228; Hill, *War Papers*, 180; Holbrook, *7th Regiment of Vermont*, 168; Allen, "Operations against the City," 76.

avoided through siege operations, and "consideration of humanity at that period of the war—evidently so near to its close—was no doubt a powerful factor in General Canby's policy."[24]

Though some officers preferred a direct assault, most considered pressing a siege would hurt the Confederates more, with less loss of life on their part. "These works are surrounded by ditches and sharp stakes in the ground. And, besides all this, they have a row of torpedoes surrounding their works, which explode when stepped upon. A charge would be very dangerous," a U.S. surgeon pointed out in a letter to his brother. Truman twice rode across the entire front of Spanish Fort during the day and concluded that had they assaulted immediately, they would "have sustained a repulse." Colonel Holbrook, 7th Vermont, echoed Truman's assessment, writing that "an attempt to storm these formidable defenses at that time would have been attended with very great slaughter." Another officer observed that the fort "is exceedingly strong work. Cannot be assaulted successfully & we don't propose to attempt it." Considering the fort's exposure to the Confederate ironclads on the Blakeley River and Batteries Huger and Tracey, Canby would have suffered further casualties trying to hold it.[25]

The Federals suffered substantial casualties the first day before earthworks and pits could be thrown up for the defense of the artillery and riflemen. "The enemy's fire was so heavy during the day that we were not able to do anything towards entrenching ourselves, and until dark, we lay on the ground exposed to a continuous fire," Colonel Holbrook recalled. "The colors of the respective regiments were planted in the ground and served as targets for the rebel artillerists."[26]

Granger boldly rode along the lines in front of the skirmishers during the day with Captain Cobb, his chief commissary, and an orderly carrying the corps flag. This daring act called the attention of the Confederate sharpshooters—armed with Whitworth and Kerr .45 caliber long-range sniper rifles—who showered them with bullets, shooting Granger's orderly in the face. His horse also received a wound in the foot, and his dog, which accompanied him, received a slight wound in the leg. Granger and Cobb managed to escape injury. "The enemy had an exceedingly efficient corps of sharpshooters," recalled an officer of the XIII Corps, "and any conspicuous exposure of the person was a hazardous operation." One bullet struck

24 Hubbard, "Civil War Papers," 626, LC.

25 Ebenezer B. Mattocks to sister, Apr. 7, 1865, "The Civil War Letters of E. Brewer Mattocks," MNHS, hereafter EBM to sister, Apr. 7, 1865; Truman, "Near Spanish Fort, Opposite Mobile"; Holbrook, *7th Regiment of Vermont*, 168; JFD to wife, Apr. 1, 1865.

26 "Later From Spanish Fort," *The Times Picayune*, Apr. 5, 1865, 4; Holbrook, *7th Regiment of Vermont*, 168–169.

Pvt. Charles H. Fadden, I Company, 7th Minnesota, in the back while he was lying face down and nearly passed through his entire body.[27]

Around dusk, Pvt. George C. Black, Company K, 124th Illinois, suffered a gunshot through the bowels and soon died. "There was something peculiarly sad about the death of poor Black," grieved Chaplain Richard Howell. He described Black as a good, faithful man and soldier and well-liked. A few months before, he had lost his voice and did not speak for a long time, save in a whisper. His comrades urged him to ask for a discharge. He insisted that he could continue to do his duty. Detailed as a cook due to his inability to speak, he served in that capacity for some time. Before the siege, he rejoined his infantry company, claiming he could do better service.[28]

The Federals also sustained some self-inflicted casualities. A piece of a shell fired from his rear hit 1Lt. Henry F. Folsom, C Company, 7th Minnesota, in his thigh. "Dan Smith and Cute Wilson were both wounded. It was through carelessness that they got hurt," remarked a soldier of Lowell's Artillery Brigade of the XVI Corps. "Dan was acting No. 1, and Cute was No. 3. Dan didn't pay enough attention to sponging the gun being hot, and consequently, the gun went off and blowed three of his fingers off and wounded Cute pretty bad."[29]

As soon as it became dark and their positions were concealed, fatigue parties threw up entrenchments to protect their positions. "We threw up opposing works and pressed our advance with vigor, the sandy soil allowing much more rapid excavation than at Vicksburg," noted an officer of the XVI Corps. "The enemy also were more active and waspish than at Vicksburg, keeping up a brisk fire of both artillery and musketry." The blue-coated soldiers had little time for rest as they toiled in the rain. One officer of the XIII Corps recounted in his diary: "We had a long wet, cold night." They diligently handled their picks and spades so that by the morning, they had constructed a good line of earthworks and rifle pits to cover the front. As one Alabamian later recalled: "If you want to see a soldier work, put him at work that is to protect him from the enemy's bullets. He will do his best work."[30]

27 *Dispatch Book*, 68; "The Expedition to Mobile," *The Times-Democrat*, Apr. 1, 1865, 1; Holbrook, *7th Regiment of Vermont*, 169; "Mobile," *New York Herald*, Apr. 9, 1865, 1; N. Buck to C. C. Andrews, June 4, 1866, C. C. Andrews Papers, MNHS, hereafter Buck to Andrews, June 4, 1866. The Confederate Dispatch Book notes that Liddell ordered some Whitworth riflemen from Blakeley to Spanish Fort on March 28. Over the years, relic hunters have discovered Whitworth and .45 caliber bullets at Spanish Fort according to Roger Hansen.

28 Howard, *124 Regiment*, 297.

29 N. Buck to C. C. Andrews, June 4, 1866; Rolland J. Gladieux, *The 14th Indiana Light Artillery* (Kenmore, New York, 1978), 27.

30 Elliott, *Thirty-Third Regiment*, 57; Holbrook, *7th Regiment of Vermont*, 170; Miller, *Captain Edward Gee Miller*, 30; Jones and Pulcrano, *Eighteenth Alabama Infantry*, 64.

The previous summer, Truman endured three weeks in front of Atlanta in a camp bombarded by shells night and day. "But there was more terror in three shells on the night of the 27th inst. then there was in three weeks of shelling last summer," he reported. It rained hard at the close of the day. General McArthur knew Truman's quarters were far away and invited him to stay at his headquarters. Exhausted, Truman went to sleep early; then, an awful shell explosion aroused everyone nearby. "What was that?" "Where did that come from?" No one knew. They believed that the rebel gunboats had opened upon them. Truman and his comrades went back to bed. An hour later, another monster launched and burst in the same place—in front of General McArthur's tent—"scattering enough iron to start a small foundry." A third came crashing through the camp and buried itself three feet in the earth, producing an earthquake-like sensation. The men subsequently dug out the giant shell. These extraordinary missiles were scattered throughout the camp that night. The next day, they learned that the shots came from either Battery Huger or Tracey or the gunboats in the river.[31]

The Union Navy was not in a position to drive off the Southern gunboats or silence the marsh batteries. Thatcher's ironclad river monitors struggled northward—to get close enough to support Canby—but had not yet crossed the Blakeley River sand bar. They were, therefore, not able to cause any damage to the fort.[32]

Carr's Division occupied the northern flank. Carr, a 35-year-old New York-born West Pointer, distinguished himself at Wilson's Creek, Pea Ridge, the Vicksburg campaign, and the Camden expedition. At Pea Ridge on March 7, 1862, he earned the Medal of Honor for gallant service. There, despite being wounded three times, he and his command held their ground for seven hours under heavy fire. The *New York Times* reported Carr was "[f]avorably known as a gallant soldier and an accomplished gentleman."[33]

In February of 1865, an uncharacteristic incident occurred involving Carr. He had been placed in charge of a specialized corps called the "detached brigade," supposed to be bound for New Orleans. Before he left, Carr attended a party onboard a river steamer at Devall's Bluff and reportedly returned to Little Rock drunk. Major General Joseph J. Reynolds, Carr's immediate supervisor, reported:

31 Truman, "Near Spanish Fort, Opposite Mobile." The author interviewed one relic hunter who reportedly found fragments of 7-inch Brooke shells in this area.

32 *ORA* 49, pt. 2, 1163; *ORN* 22, 67.

33 Carr, *First Reunion of the Survivors of the Army of Tennessee*, 26; "General Eugene A. Carr Dead," *The Allentown Leader*, Dec. 3, 1910, 5; "Death of General Carr," *Army and Navy Journal*, Dec. 10, 1910, 407; "Promotion of Brig. Gen E. A. Carr to a Brevet Major-General," *New York Times*, May 8, 1865, 2.

Brigadier General Eugene A. Carr, commander, Third Division, XVI Army Corps. *Library of Congress*

"He was under orders at the time, and it was generally known that he was under orders for important service." Reynolds immediately relieved Carr of command. "General Carr is now unassigned. He has been a long time in this department," he informed Canby. Then he added: "His habits, in my opinion, are bad and his influence detrimental to the best interests of the service. I respectfully request that the major-general commanding the military division will assign him to duty out of this department [of Arkansas]." Despite Reynolds's unfavorable report, Canby recognized Carr's ability and appointed him to command the 3rd Division of the XVI Corps.[34]

Carr's Division suffered heavily during the first few days of the siege. His men were positioned on the end of the Federal line, nearest Minette Bay and the Blakeley River. This left his right flank exposed to deadly fire from the Southern gunboats on the river. Canby could not do much about the Confederate vessels during the initial stages of the investment; obstructions and torpedoes blocked Thatcher's fleet from entering the river to drive them off. Consequently, they inflicted severe punishment on Carr's command. "The Rebel gunboats in the bay enfiladed our lines, and I saw a man cut in two by a piece of a big shell," remembered Carr.[35]

The heavy U.S. Army movement north from Dannelly's Mill, however, left the road destroyed, jeopardizing their line of communication. With rations nearly depleted, Canby turned to 39-year-old Brig. Gen. Joseph Bailey to oversee the construction of a wharf approximately five miles south of Spanish Fort. Bailey had experience supervising military engineering projects under pressure. In 1864, he received the thanks of Congress for overseeing the rapid construction of a remarkable dam on the Red River at Alexandria, Louisiana, rescuing Adm. David Porter's Mississippi River Squadron. At Mobile Bay, he had many of the same men

---

34 James T. King, *War Eagle A Life of General Eugene A. Carr* (Lincoln, NE, 1963), 70–71.

35 Carr, *First Reunion of the Survivors of the Army of Tennessee*, 26.

who built the dam at Red River, including the 96th and 97th (USCT) Regiments and the 1st Company of Pontoniers. Bailey pushed them hard, and they quickly made two pontoon landings from the shore, estimated to run 75–100 yards into the bay. "If the latter kept a diary," reported Truman, "a glance at its pages will show that during one week's time, he had four fights, a hundred wrangles, slapped the faces of three steamboat Captains, and nearly killed (with hard work) some three hundred members of the Ninety-seventh Colored." Bailey's autocratic leadership style produced results. The next day, his men completed Starke's Landing. The logistical efficiency of Canby's cooperation with Thatcher's fleet is noteworthy. The wharf significantly expedited the navy's ability to transport rations, reinforcements, artillery, and other much-needed supplies from Fort Gaines and Fort Morgan. Starke's Landing also allowed the Federals to transport their severe casualties by water quickly for medical attention.[36]

Confederates

On the Blakeley River, four Confederate gunboats supported their besieged fort. Gibson wired Liddell: "Why don't the gunboats open on the enemy's right? It could do great good. All going well. Huger's fire helps us."[37]

Taylor had called Farrand's small naval squadron a "farce" before the siege. Despite Taylor's aspersion, the squadron provided valuable support early in the defense of Spanish Fort. They tormented Carr's Division and fired over the fort into the Yankee camps. Farrand, moreover, ensured that his vessels brought supplies to the fort and exchanged fresh men for wounded and worn-out ones despite his limited resources. These movements occurred at night so that the Federals could not observe them.[38]

As the Federals attempted to advance their position, Gibson realized he had an immense amount of digging to do. His force stayed busy strengthening the defenses, but the lack of entrenching tools concerned him. Where shovels were available, the Confederate skirmishers held their ground and slowed the advance of the Bluecoats. They were, however, compelled to retire behind their main lines in places where they had none. During the day, Gibson blamed a lack of entrenching tools for the loss of five men killed and 44 wounded.[39]

---

36 Allen, "Operations against the City," 76; Benjamin C. Truman, "The Campaign in Alabama," *New York Times*, Apr. 24, 1865, 1; "Mobile," *New York Herald*, Apr. 9, 1865, 1.

37 *ORA* 49, pt. 2, 1161.

38 Cameron, "The Battles Opposite Mobile," *Confederate Veteran* 23 (1915): 305.

39 Ibid., 1162.

Gibson maintained constant telegraph communication with Liddell at Blakeley. He reported heavy Union skirmish lines advancing and stressed the need for more spades and axes. "Our casualties are fewer today than yesterday, but my men, of course, being up night and day and constantly engaged, are jaded. . . . The enemy is in very heavy force, presses me at all points, but I take the bull by the horns," he declared. Despite his optimistic facade, Gibson knew the vulnerability of the incomplete works on his left. Water covered the ground there, and bringing in more dirt was out of the question. He also did not have enough men to adequately man the works and strengthen his left with additional batteries.[40]

Yet his men bravely manned their positions and sincerely tried to "take the bull by the horns." Iron screens shielded the artillerists, helping them wreak havoc on the besiegers. "Slocomb knocked one of the enemy's batteries all to pieces," boasted Gibson that afternoon, adding: "We are all in good spirits and confident."[41]

The Federals, however, attacked the left and center and drove the skirmishers of Thomas's Brigade into the fort. "The Reserves not very steady," Gibson remarked in one dispatch. He pleaded with Liddell that his force should not be reduced but only replaced by experienced troops. "I would suggest that you send another brigade with tools to assist in completing the works so that everything may be ready in case of an assault. The boys are worn down already," he observed. He also urged Battery Huger and the gunboat on Blakeley River to open the besiegers' right.[42]

That evening, Confederate surgeons transferred over 100 dead and wounded soldiers to transport ships, where they were taken to cemeteries and hospitals in Mobile. Surgeons in Thomas' Brigade moved an additional 50–60 soldiers to the hospitals for various disabilities and fatigue associated with extreme hardships and the shock of close combat. Records indicate the surgeons were overly generous in assessing the boy soldiers on the night of March 27. On no other day would so many be allowed to leave the firing lines.[43]

The citizens of Mobile supported Gibson's efforts. One local newspaper reported that some people had volunteered to go over and assist with administering to the wants of the wounded. The paper encouraged residents to freely send over refreshments, such as coffee, bread, and butter, to comfort the men at Spanish

---

40 *ORA* 49, pt. 2, 1162–1164; Handwritten report, RLG, Apr. 16, 1865.

41 *ORA* 49, pt. 2, 1161.

42 *ORA* 49, pt. 2, 1162–1164.

43 Compiled Service Records, RG 94, NARA.

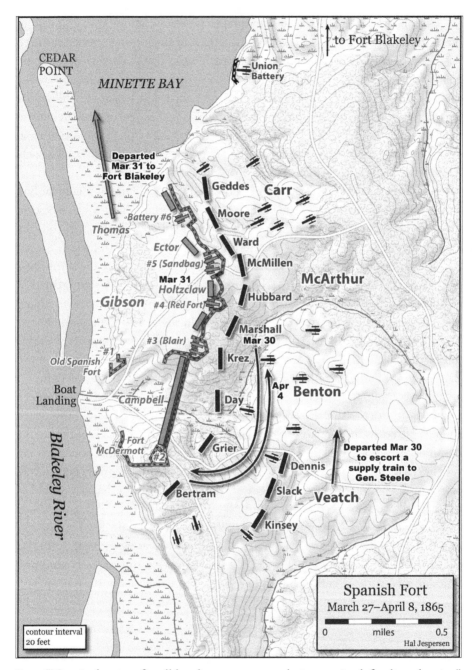

CEDAR POINT

MINETTE BAY

to Fort Blakeley

Union Battery

Departed Mar 31 to Fort Blakeley

Battery #6

Thomas

Geddes   Carr

Moore

Ector

#5 (Sandbag)

Ward

McMillen

McArthur

Mar 31 Holtzclaw

#4 (Red Fort)

Hubbard

Gibson

Marshall Mar 30

#3 (Blair)

Krez

#1

Old Spanish Fort

Boat Landing   *Campbell*

Apr 4   Benton

Day

Blakeley River

Fort McDermott

#2

Grier

Departed Mar 30 to escort a supply train to Gen. Steele

Dennis

Slack   Veatch

Bertram

Kinsey

Spanish Fort
March 27–April 8, 1865

0   miles   0.5

Hal Jespersen

contour interval 20 feet

Fort. "Now is the time for all loyal persons to act their parts in defending the city," urged the newspaper editor.[44]

44 "From the Confederacy," *The Times Picayune*, Apr. 14, 1965, 2.

Chapter 9

"A Perfect Roar"

Confederates

Tuesday, March 28, 1865: The weather improved from the previous rainy day. The fighting turned out to be lively, with heavy cannonading and continual siege operations.[1]

The Graybacks wasted no time in greeting the besiegers with shells and bullets. "This morning, the ball opened," noted one Bluecoat. The firing from the rifle pits created "a perfect roar." Near batteries Huger and Tracey, on the Blakeley River, two ironclads described as "formidable-looking monsters" and the wooden gunboat CSS *Morgan* patrolled. Maury and Liddell advised the Southern gunboats where to direct their fire; dispatches were sent by telegraph, in person, and by signals. These gunboats got the range of the Federal lines, allowing them to punish them severely.[2]

Early in the morning, the Confederates fired 7-inch conical shells near Smith's headquarters, all of which failed to explode. One landed within thirty-five feet of Smith's tent, burying itself in the earth and throwing dirt all over his encampment. A shell splinter instantly killed Sgt. John McGuire, Company C, 40th Missouri, while he sat in his tent. The uncomfortable proximity of the incessant cannonading

---

1 Howard, *124th Regiment*, 299.

2 Thomas Diary, Mar. 28, 1865; "From Mobile Bay. Operations before Spanish Fort," *New Orleans Times-Democrat*, Apr. 6, 1865, 2; *ORA* 49, pt. 1, 319–320; "The Expedition to Mobile," *New Orleans Times-Democrat*, Apr. 4, 1865, 1; Truman, "Near Spanish Fort, Opposite Mobile," *New York Times*, Apr. 17, 1865, 2; Slack Diary, Mar. 28, 1865.

compelled the XVI Corps to move their camps further to the rear. Colonel Patton had overall command of the 300 men garrisoned at batteries Huger and Tracey. He maintained telegraphic communication with Maj. Washington Marks, in personal command at Huger. About two hundred men from the 22nd Louisiana and Company C, 1st Mississippi Light Artillery under Capt. Lauderdale A. Collier manned Huger. Captain Ambrose Plattsmier, Company I, 22nd Louisiana, commanded Tracey, with Companies G, H, and I, of the 22nd Louisiana, a force of one hundred and twenty men.[3]

The combined shelling from the gunboats, marsh batteries, and the redoubts of Spanish Fort exacted a heavy toll on Carr's Division, which occupied the most exposed position of the Federal line. Part of Lowell's Artillery Brigade had advanced within 600 yards of the fort and commenced a fierce fire for a short time. The Southern gunboats soon silenced them and inflicted several casualties on the men building breastworks. "And the casualties, I regret to say, among our brave boys are not few, being nearly if not double that, of any other Division in the army," reported one newspaper.[4]

Federals

To counter the devastating enfilading fire from the gunboats and the marsh batteries, the Federals worked on establishing a battery of Parrott and Whitworth cannons on the bluff of Minette Bay. With his battery, Capt. W. H. Blankenship of the 1st Indiana Heavy Artillery had arrived from Fort Morgan and disembarked at Starke's wharf that evening. Blankenship and his men worked all night in the heavy rain to transport the battery to the top of the hill, in the rear of Smith's Corps.[5]

Garrard's Division remained entrenched around the Sibley house near Bayou Minette. They had little to do or see but time enough to listen to the almost continuous cannonading at Spanish Fort, which, however, soon ceased to be an object of remark except when, occasionally, the rush of the enormous shells from the Southern gunboats drew everyone's attention.[6]

Fort McDermott on the Confederate right of Spanish Fort boasted a heavy 6.4 Brooke rifle affectionately called the "Dog Towser" (big dog). It caused extreme annoyance to the XIII Corps. A detachment from Benton's Division went to the

---

3 Waterman, *Confederate Veteran Magazine*, VIII (Jan. 1900): 22; Maury, "Defence of Mobile in 1865," 9–10.

4 Gladieux, *14th Indiana*, 27; "From Mobile Bay," *New Orleans Times-Democrat*, Apr. 6, 1865, 2; *ORA* 49, pt. 1, 94.

5 *ORA* 49, pt. 1, 94; Andrews, *History of the Campaign of Mobile*, 81–82.

6 Hill, *History of Company E, of the Sixth*, 29.

front to relieve some skirmishers in the advance rifle pits at daylight. On their way, they passed through a ravine full of felled timber and commanded by the cannon of Fort McDermott. The rebel sharpshooters also had full range on this dangerous ravine. Despite the dangers, the men pushed on and drove some Graybacks from their advanced rifle pits. Several men were seriously wounded—one of them mortally. "It was a wonder all were not killed," remarked one Federal soldier.[7]

As a company of the 7th Vermont came off the skirmish line in the morning, the Rebels fired their cannons but did not hit any of them. One soldier, considered "the worst coward of the lot, cried & cursed to the rear." Skirmishers preferred to endure long shifts in the rifle pits during the day rather than risk exposure to the Confederate sharpshooters. After several men were wounded that morning, the futility of relieving skirmish lines during the daylight became evident. The men in the rifle pits were relieved at night to reduce casualties. As one Federal soldier recalled, "We had to go out and come in in the dark, for they picked us off so." Another Federal soldier described going out to the advance rifle pits at night: "It was almost pitch dark so that we could hardly see 10 feet ahead of us. We had to crawl through ravines and rifle pits and through abatis to our posts."[8]

An incident occurred that involved two enslaved men who had left the fort during the night and attempted to come into the Federal lines. A picket of the 40th Missouri ordered them to halt. One of them became frightened and tried to run before a Union soldier shot him down. "The poor fellows were too ignorant to exhibit any manifestations of friendship, whereupon one was shot dead and another mortally wounded," noted Chaplain Howard. The one who survived could not provide much useful intelligence. They did learn that a brigade of French's Division had reinforced the Southerners.[9]

Confederate artillery fire silenced the 2nd Iowa Battery and 3rd Indiana Battery. The blue-coated soldiers pushed forward their siege operations despite the heavy fire under which they came. Every available man worked, digging the approaches closer to the fort. They utilized local natural resources to strengthen their earthworks further. Each company detailed one man to go into the woods,

7 Samuel H. Byers, *Iowa in War Times* (Des Moines, 1888), 405; Allen, "Operations against the City," 78.

8 Fisher Diary, Mar. 28, 1865; *ORA* 49, Pt, 1, 154; Charles O. Musser, *Soldier Boy: The Civil War Letters of Charles O. Musser, 29th Iowa* (Iowa City, 1995), 198–199; Weston, "Dear Parent"; Snedeker, *Civil War Diary of Charles Henry Snedeker*, Mar. 28, 1865.

9 Richard L. Howard, *History of the 124th Regiment Illinois Infantry Volunteers: Otherwise Known as the "Hundred and Two Dozen," from August, 1862, to August, 1865* (Springfield, IL, 1880), 299; Snedeker, *Civil War Diary of Charles Henry Snedeker*, Mar. 28, 1865; Andrews, *History of the Campaign of Mobile*, 63.

Federal soldiers making Gabions and fascines. *Florida Center for Instructional Technology, College of Education, University of South Florida*

collect wild vines, and bring them in to make gabions. "It looked rather funny to see several hundred men scattered through the woods making baskets while a war is being fought," noted Cpl. Adolphus P. Wolf, Company F, 117th Illinois. The process involved five sticks, about three-and-a-half feet long with one end sharpened, driven in the ground a little way. Then, the men weaved vine to make a basket without a bottom and pulled it from the ground. Once filled with dirt, gabions provided substantial support to the earthworks. Corporal Wolf added: "You would hardly be surprised if I tell you that many an odd-shaped thing was brought into camp to pass for a basket."[10]

To make matters worse for the men, about 3:00 p.m., a light rain commenced, "and the day drizzled away in a most shabby manner." Nevertheless, heavy details of U.S. soldiers continued to dig day and night. A soldier of the 14th Wisconsin recalled: "Everyone wanted to shovel all the time, for the one resting would get cold and want to warm up." The sandy soil made shoveling less taxing. The

10 Henderson Diary, Mar. 28, 1865; Cleveland, *Civil War Diary of Moses A. Cleveland,* 73; Gerling, *The One Hundred Seventeenth Illinois Infantry Volunteers,* 101.

Gabions heightened by sandbags. *Library of Congress*

Graybacks, however, could see the bright shovels glisten in the moonlight and took potshots at them.[11]

The artillery fire grew heavier with time. However, the Federals got so close at some points that the Confederates could not depress their cannon low enough to injure them. The close proximity allowed one Bluecoat from Carr's Division to make an unusual observation. "Some of the boys in front of one of the portholes completely silenced the Gun it contained: nearly half of the cannoniers were negroes & I'm afraid some of them got hurt that day," observed a private of the 14th Wisconsin, Ward's Brigade. It is difficult to confirm the validity of the Wisconsinite's observation. Lumsden's Battery probably manned the redoubt he referenced. One veteran of Lumsden's Battery, however, recalled about a dozen

11 Howard, *124th Regiment*, 299; Stockwell, *Private Elisha Stockwell*, 163, 164.

enslaved persons attached to their battery, "some belonging to commissioned officers, others to privates, all subject to their master's orders, but of course subject to control by the officers of the company also." There is no known record of these enslaved men serving in official military roles.[12]

The nearness of the opposing forces created a deadly environment for both sides. They were so close that they dared not show their heads over the works lest a bullet strike them. Private James Williams, 40th Missouri, who accidentally raised his head over the breastworks, had it instantly blown off.[13]

Musketry and artillery fire continued unabated during the day. One soldier jotted down: "Shells are flying in every direction." The skirmishers in the advance lines kept low to avoid getting hit. Despite the caution, several men were killed during the day. "A sad casualty occurred today while we were eating dinner in the ravine a shell came into the headquarters of the 29th Illinois Infantry and bursting killed four and wounded eight," noted one private. He added that two of the killed were "torn to pieces—a terrible result of a stray shot."[14]

Both sides maintained continual telegraph communication throughout the siege. Canby ordered a telegraph line fifteen miles in length built around the forts on the eastern shore. They used this wire night and day, connecting his headquarters with all parts of the besieging line, including Stark's Wharf.[15]

U.S. Navy

The Federals completely invested the fort by land. The Confederates, however, still maintained control of the river system in their rear and full telegraph communication with Mobile. Canby hoped that Thatcher's fleet could gain access to the river and thus cut them off. However, the navy struggled to get closer because of the shallow waters and a far more dangerous obstacle that would soon reveal itself.[16]

---

12 Charles S. Hill, *War Papers and Personal Reminiscences: 1861–1865. Read Before the Commandery of the State of Missouri, Military Order of the Loyal Legion of the United States* (St. Louis, 1892),180; Newton & Ambrose, "The Siege of Mobile," *The Alabama Historical Quarterly* 20 (Winter 1958): 596–597; Little and Maxwell, "A History of Lumsden's Battery."

13 Ridge Diary, Mar. 28, 1865; "Rebellion in the Gulf States Dead," *Chicago Tribune*, Apr. 18, 1865, 3.

14 John M. Williams, *The "Eagle Regiment,": 8th Wis. Inf'ty. Vols. A Sketch of Its Marches, Battles and Campaigns. From 1861 to 1865. With a Complete Regimental and Company Roster, and a Few Portraits and Sketches of Its Officers and Commanders* (Belleville, WI, 1890), 96; Cleveland, *Civil War Diary of Moses A. Cleveland*, 73.

15 "From Near Spanish Fort," *New Orleans Times-Democrat*, Apr. 11, 1865, 8.

16 Slack to wife, Mar. 28, 1865.

Comstock went down to the Village to see the pier being built by Bailey. He then went to see Thatcher to get help driving off the troublesome gunboats *Nashville* and *Morgan* that were punishing the XVI Corps. The fleet worked tirelessly to get through the obstructions and shallow waters. They also removed several submerged torpedoes from their path.

Around noon, Thatcher sent five gunboats up the Blakeley River at Comstock's request, including the *Octorara* and the river ironclad monitors *Milwaukee*, *Kickapoo*, *Winnebago*, and *Chickasaw*. The ironclads successfully crossed over the bar. But the *Octorara* ran aground on the ridge of the bar in eight feet of water, experienced mechanical malfunctions, and could go no further that day. The *Winnebago* and *Milwaukee* continued to advance. The *Winnebago* fired a trial projectile when she first came to rest, demonstrating Spanish Fort was still too far for her guns. About sunset, both ironclads continued up the Blakeley River to within about a mile and a half of Fort McDermott, taking a position roughly off the left flank of the XIII Corps. They fired some shells at *St. Nicholas* while the garrison offloaded supplies at the landing below the fort. This compelled *St. Nicholas* to move up the river. Patton's artillery at Old Spanish Fort opened on the two monitors, and they exchanged a few shots. When the first shot came screeching up the bay at the fort, immense cheering occurred all along the Federal line. The *Milwaukee*, dropping with the current, her bow headed upstream, had got within two hundred yards of the *Kickapoo*, then at anchor, where boats had previously swept for torpedoes. Everything seemed to be progressing well, then a sudden shock and a terrific splash of water. Moments later, the stern of the monitor sunk. The ironclad had struck a torpedo on her port side about forty feet from the stern and went down in about ten feet of water. The distance from the fort made it difficult for Gibson to be sure that the *Milwaukee* had sunk.[17]

Lieutenant Commander James H. Gillis restored order and rapidly evacuated his entire crew to the *Kickapoo*. Every sailor made it to the deck alive despite the initial confusion. The stern sank in about three minutes, but the forward compartments did not fill for nearly an hour, giving the crew ample time to save most of their effects. Gillis then reported to the flagship *Stockdale* and obtained permission to proceed to Pensacola to get divers and a steam pump to aid in unloading the guns from his sunken vessel. Despite the sinking of the powerful double-turreted monitor, the U.S.-favoring *New Orleans Times-Democrat* newspaper erroneously

---

17 Comstock, *Diary of Cyrus B. Comstock*, 313; Andrews, *History of the Campaign of Mobile*, 67–68; TNC to HC, Mar 31, 1865; *ORA* 49, pt. 2, 1168.

The USS *Milwaukee* became the first victim of the Confederate torpedoes during the 1865 Mobile Campaign. *Naval History and Heritage Command*

---

predicted that the navy would sustain no further torpedo damage since most monitors were equipped with torpedo rakes.[18]

Confederates

In the Yankee camps, a rumor circulated that General Forrest was lurking with a strong cavalry force in the vicinity. Though the rumor proved false, Taylor still planned to send Forrest to Mobile. In a dispatch from Meridian, he reiterated to Maury his hopes that Forrest could whip Wilson's cavalry raids moving from North Alabama in a few days and would then be able to assist him with "all the force of the department."[19]

Gibson needed reinforcements. He did not have enough men to resist a general assault. His men were spread thin on considerable portions of the line. Liddell sent a boat to Spanish Fort to transfer Thomas's two reserve regiments to Blakeley. Gibson wired Liddell: "There are strong indications that the enemy will assault my lines in the morning. Allow me to keep the Reserve regiment until tomorrow night." Liddell permitted him to keep them. Thomas's Brigade, sometimes called the "boy militia," was composed primarily of teenage Alabamians. The Confederate conscription law of February 17, 1864, lowered the mandatory service age to 17 and raised the maximum service age to 50, with those aged 17–18 and 46–50 to serve only in their respective states as reserves. Several 16-year-olds joined with

18 Andrews, *History of the Campaign of Mobile*, 67–68; "From Another Correspondent," *New Orleans Times-Democrat*, Apr. 4, 1865, 1. Federal monitors were ironclad vessels with a rotating gun turret.

19 Davis Diary, Apr. 4, 1865; *ORA* 49, pt. 2, 1167, 1171.

their parent's permission. Thomas's Brigade included two Alabama regiments, the 62nd and 63rd, with many under 18, though officered by older veterans. The young Alabamians "excited the mingled grief and admiration" of Gibson's seasoned veterans. "In vain did we tell them when going to the skirmish line to shelter themselves as much as possible," one veteran remembered. "They thought it was 'not soldierly,' and they stood up and were shot down like sheep."[20]

Thomas and his officers were known to be competent leaders and led the young men of their regiment by example. "It is needless to say, Col. [Daniel E.] Huger is not in a bomb-proof," one soldier of the 62nd Alabama pointed out. "He can be seen at any time walking up and down the line encouraging the men, regardless of ball or shell. Major [Brunaugh F.] Yniestra, always at his post, never tires or fears in the discharge of his duty." The inspiring example of their officers boosted the morale of the young men of Thomas's Brigade despite the sizable besieging force in their front. The following excerpt written by a soldier of the 62nd Alabama to the editor of a local newspaper during the siege provides insight into their outlook:

Will it be encouraging to the citizens of Mobile to know that we are fully and firmly resolved to hold this fort—the gateway to the State of Alabama—to the last extremity? Our troops are in the highest spirits, confident of success, and only ask for food and powder. Without these necessary stimulants (and one is the twin sister of the other), man must be humiliated, but give us an ample supply of each, and we will immortalize every inch of dirt around Spanish Fort.

We care not for the force the enemy may bring against us. We are cognizant of but one thing: we are fighting for ourselves and not for a despotic power or tyrannical chieftain. So, rest assured, Spanish Fort is ours—will be ours as long as the flames of Liberty burn in the breasts of Southern patriots and Southern Generals.[21]

Federals

Under cover of darkness, Capt. James L. Noble, with 100 men of Company H, 21st Iowa, Slack's Brigade, went to the front on the extreme left. He also commanded 300 unarmed men from other regiments to build earthworks for a battery. While they labored on the earthworks, some stuck their bayonets and muskets in the ground. The Confederates heard the noise of the tools and sent

20 Maury, "Souvenirs of the War," 4; *ORA* 49, pt. 2, 1168, 1173; "Conscription," Essential Civil War Curriculum, accessed July 1, 2020, https://www.essentialcivilwarcurriculum.com/conscription.html; Stephenson, "Defence of Spanish Fort," 122.

21 "Letter from Spanish Fort—Casualties in the Sixty Second Regiment," *New Orleans Times-Democrat*, Apr. 12, 1865, 1. Most of Yniestra's records indicate his rank as Lieutenant Colonel.

out an attack party to drive off or capture the Yankees. About midnight, Noble's advance pickets were attacked amid a dark rainstorm. The Graybacks surprised him, but Noble rallied his men, and hand-to-hand combat ensued in the darkness. Some unarmed men ran back to camp and gave the alarm while Noble and the others struggled to keep the Confederates out of the earthwork. Help soon arrived, and the Graycoats were driven off, both sides having sustained casualties. The attack provoked heavy firing all along the skirmish line of the army.[22]

Wednesday, March 29, 1865: The morning opened with clouds and light rain. "The cannonading & sharp shooting came bright & early this morning & was kept up all day pretty steady," one soldier jotted down in his journal. The firing on both sides increased in severity. After three days of hard fighting, the Federal soldiers realized they were wrong in assuming the Confederates had no fight left in them. One officer of the XVI Corps summed it up: "The taking of Mobile is said to be a rather serious undertaking and will require more time than at first supposed and will require much more time."[23]

Once the soldiers adapted to the constant noise of battle, siege operations became somewhat monotonous. In the Federal camps, some men passed the time by cooking, playing cards, or writing letters home while others watched the artillery shells being fired. To protect themselves from the big shells they dubbed "camp kettles" that were fired at them from the Southern gunboats, they slept in bombproofs—when they did sleep. Around 10:30 a.m., men in the advanced lines "getting tired of doing nothing, gave a yell, as if about to charge, which proved a successful ruse, for immediately the rebel heads made their appearances above the works to look for the last time."[24]

That morning, as the men of Company C, 12th Iowa, retired back to camp from the engagement, they cut down a large tree to prevent Rebel shells from splintering it and injuring them. But, in falling, the tree smashed three tents, including their two headquarters' tents. No one was hurt, but the tents, medicine box, bass drum, and flagpole were damaged.[25]

Comstock went to the front lines in the morning and carefully examined the Confederate fortifications, which he concluded were "of about same strength as that of Vicksburg with a little more relief & a little better abatis." He took Maj. Gen. Peter J. Osterhaus, Canby's German-born chief-of-staff, to the part of the

---

22 Byers, *Iowa*, 405–406; *ORA* 49, pt. 1, 167.

23 Ridge Diary, Mar. 29, 1865; JFD to wife, Mar. 29, 1865.

24 Truman, "From Near Spanish Fort," *New Orleans Times-Democrat*, Apr. 11, 1865, 8; Fisher Diary, Mar. 29, 1865; Hill, War Papers, 182; "From Mobile," *Chicago Tribune*, Apr. 10, 1865, 1.

25 Henderson Diary, Mar. 28, 1865.

Major General Peter J. Osterhaus, Chief-of-Staff, Army of West Mississippi. *Library of Congress*

line he thought could be assaulted—the Confederate left flank. Osterhaus agreed with him.[26]

U.S. Navy

The *Mobile Advertiser & Register* pointed out the city's natural and man-made defenses: "We have advantages in this contest rarely, if ever before, accorded to the Confederate side—The Yankee navy is powerless to help in the attack. Shoal water and 'Rebel' guns keep them out of the fight, and there they lay in sight, but miles away to help in the infernal undertaking against the peace and rights and happiness of this community."[27]

Indeed, Thatcher's fleet struggled to get her gunboats into position to contribute to the fort's bombardment. "Thus far, the Navy has not assisted the Army much, but they are getting in position today to help us some," expressed one officer. At 2:00 p.m., the ironclad *Osage*, under Lt. Cmdr. William M. Gamble, lay at anchor inside the sandbar in company with four other vessels. A strong breeze blew eastward, and the *Winnebago* had dragged close alongside. To avoid a collision, the *Osage* weighed anchor and moved off to a safe distance on her starboard bow. Her commander stopped the vessel in two fathoms of water, and hands ordered ready to let go of the anchor. A torpedo exploded under the bow almost immediately, and the ship sank rapidly. The crew quickly searched below for the dead and wounded. Five sailors were killed and twelve wounded. The vessel submerged, with only her turret, smokestack, and the U.S. flag at its masthead visible. "At this rate, the whole ironclad fleet will be consumed within a week," lamented Dr. Titus Coan of the USS *Sebago*.[28]

---

26 Comstock, *Diary of Cyrus B. Comstock*, 313.

27 "The War at Home," *Mobile Advertiser & Register*, Apr. 7, 1865.

28 JFD to wife, Mar. 29, 1865; Andrews, *History of the Campaign of Mobile*, 70; TNC to HC, Mar. 31, 1865.

The USS *Osage* became the second victim of the Confederate torpedoes during the 1865 Mobile Campaign. *Naval History and Heritage Command*

The vicinity where she struck the torpedo had been thoroughly dragged with nets; the torpedo which struck her had likely drifted downstream. According to one naval officer, the Confederates would "place them in the water with a drag attached, which would allow them to drift down with the current just below the surface. The water being muddy prevented them from being seen." The navy was supposed to equip its vessels with "torpedo fenders" to safeguard against sea mines. This apparatus consisted of a thick rope stretched between two spars attached to the front of the boat. They were designed to detonate mines before they could strike the vessels. Admiral Thatcher failed to ensure that the *Osage* and *Milwaukee* had torpedo fenders. The *New York Times* correspondent criticized Thatcher's failure to take necessary precautions, pointing out that the two ironclads "were exploded on successive days, whence it appears that the warning of the first was not sufficient."[29]

The fleet cleared the channel of torpedoes as far as Starke's landing, the location of Canby's supply station, and some of the lighter draft gunboats had come up within shelling distance of Spanish Fort. Still, the shallow water, torpedoes, and

---

29 "In Mobile Bay," The National Tribune, Oct. 13, 1887, 3; Andrews, *History of the Campaign of Mobile*, 70; "The Attack of Mobile," 8; TNC to HC, Mar. 31, 1865.

rows of piles near Huger made it impossible for them to pass the fort and isolate it from Mobile and Blakeley as they had planned. One officer of Garrard's Division concluded: "This was an investment that did not invest."[30]

Torpedoes took a toll on the fleet. "They have a great many planted around the fort on land as well as in the bay quite a number have exploded killing or wounding a good many," recorded one soldier. Admiral Thatcher himself narrowly escaped the explosion of one torpedo. Seated on the deck of his flagship, he supervised as two sailors examined a torpedo they had "scooped up" from the bay. The crew believed the explosive mine had been emptied of its powder. But when the men unscrewed the percussion nipples, the torpedo exploded, wounding them both. Thatcher, seated only a few yards away, barely escaped injury.[31]

"Our torpedoes were very rude," recalled Maury. "Some were demijohns charged with gunpowder. The best were beer kegs loaded with gunpowder and exploded by sensitive primers. These were anchored in every channel open to an enemy." A vessel passing over them triggered an explosion that would blow a hole through the bottom and sink her.[32]

Bertram's Brigade had advanced farther than the division on the right, leaving his right flank exposed. At seven in the evening, seven companies of the 29th Illinois (3rd Brigade, Veatch's Division) went out to the front to open a line of works connecting with Bertram's right. While digging, sometime after 10:00 p.m., a force of Louisianans sallied out from the fort. Gibson's veterans boldly charged up almost to the main Union lines and "made a furious assault." Confusion reigned in camp for a few minutes, but the affair did not last long. The Graycoats captured several men before being repulsed.[33]

Before the break of dawn, another mishap happened in Benton's Division. During the evening, Capt. Lewis K. Myers, 29th Iowa, worked as brigade officer of the day and was charged with advancing rifle pits within 100 yards of the Rebel works. Under cover of darkness, Myers and four companies of men worked

30 Hill, *War Papers*, 182.

31 Perry, *Infernal Machines*, 186.

32 Dabney H. Maury, "How the Confederacy Changed Naval Warfare," *Southern Historical Papers* 22 (1894): 78; "In Mobile Bay," *The National Tribune*, Oct. 13, 1887, 3; Walter G. Smith, *Life and Letters of Thomas Kilby Smith, Brevet Major-General, United States Volunteers, 1820–1887* (New York, 1898), 383.

33 Sperry, *History of the 33d Iowa Infantry*, 141; Holbrook, *7th Regiment of Vermont*, 173; Andrews, *History of the Campaign of Mobile*, 72–73. A sally is a sudden attack from a defensive fortification. Federal accounts list the number of men captured varied between 100–200 men. Accounts on the exact time of this sortie vary from 10:00 p.m.–midnight.

Wreck of the "Osage" and "Milwaukee," from Harper's Weekly. *History Museum of Mobile*

diligently digging rifle pits to within 50 yards of the Confederate advance rifle pits. Gibson's Louisianans fired on Myers's work detail continually during the night.

A group of soldiers brought out a supply of ammunition for a company running low in the rifle pits. Myers quietly led these men in a single file line behind him to the detached rifle pits of that company. He inadvertently took the wrong path in the dark and ended up walking straight into the Confederate lines.

As Myers approached, he stated: "Boys, I am coming back again." A voice answered, "Come on." A few steps more brought him face to face with a Rebel officer, with a sword at his side, and at his left a few men with arms at a ready. Myers and his men realized the predicament they had gotten themselves in. The rebel officer looked him close in the face and asked: "Do you know where you are—do you belong to us?"

"Of course, we belong to you, ain't you Confederate soldiers?" replied Myers. He continued trying to bluff the Confederates until one Graycoat shouted, "Hold on, these are not our men!" The Federals quickly fired their guns as both sides retreated.

Myers suffered a gunshot wound in the right hip and fell to the ground. As the Southern sentinel who shot him turned to run, Myers managed to squeeze off two rounds from his revolver. "He fell within a few steps of me and lay quiet," Myers remembered. From their breastworks about fifty yards distant, the Confederates poured a heavy fire into the brush. "I could see day breaking fast and knew they

THE SIEGE OF MOBILE—WRECK OF THE "OSAGE" AND THE MONITOR "MILWAUKEE."

DESTRUCTION OF THE TIN-CLAD No. 48, April 1, 1865.

MUSHROOM ANCHOR TORPEDOES.

LANDING OF THE NATIONAL FORCES AT THE MOUTH OF FISH RIVER, BELOW MOBILE, March 23d, 24th, and 28th, 1865.

Mushroom anchor torpedoes crippled the Federal Fleet from *Harper's Weekly*. *History Museum of Mobile*

could soon see me," Myers recalled. "So, I began to crawl off. Could not stand on my wounded leg. Soon came to one of my boys, who had been with me and was lost in the brush." They managed to escape back into their lines.[34]

Confederates

A shell from Battery Huger went a little too far to the right the previous day, killing some men of the Spanish Fort garrison. Undaunted, Liddell urged its continued use. "I think the improper direction of the gun yesterday ought not to prevent us from using it today," Liddell wired to Maury's headquarters. "Solid shot or percussion-shell can be used effectively and will demoralize the enemy."[35]

At Battery Blair, Edward S. McIlhenny, 5th Company, Washington Artillery, lost his life during an artillery duel. One soldier of the 5th Company recalled: "I got a glimpse of his face as he fell, a face of agony. Alas, no time for thought, sorrow, or sympathy. Time only to move his body out of the way so that the gun could be worked. He was a quiet boy of 19 or 20 and a general favorite. He was sincerely mourned."[36]

34 Byers, *Iowa*, 406; Andrews, *History of the Campaign of Mobile*, 73–77; "Mobile," *New York Herald*, Apr. 9, 1865, 1.

35 "By Telegraph," *New Orleans Times-Democrat*, Apr. 11, 1865, 6; *ORA* 49, pt. 2, 1173.

36 Stephenson & Hughes, *Civil War Memoir of Philip Daingerfield Stephenson*, 363.

Chapter 10

"A Hard Nut to Crack"

Confederates

Thursday, March 30, 1865: Gibson's command showed no signs of giving up on this clear and pleasant day. One newspaper reported: "Spanish Fort, which we were to take so easily while on our way to Blakely, has proved a hard nut to crack, and our little job has settled into a siege." Even though Gibson fought from a defensive position, he continued to employ aggressive tactics.[1]

Spanish Fort's artillerists shelled the besiegers severely, causing quite a spectacle of extraordinary occurrences. One shell fell into the midst of about a dozen soldiers gathered around a fire preparing coffee for breakfast. When it impacted the ground, the earth trembled so that half the party was thrown down, and it knocked over the coffee pot and passed on without injuring a single man. Four mules were instantly killed by a shell passing through the bodies of three of them, and then it exploded, killing the fourth. Another shell, in its flight, cut down five pine trees. One correspondent, who had witnessed many prior battles, exclaimed: "In all my army experience, I have never seen such ponderous shot and shell thrown from the enemy's works."[2]

---

1 "From Near Spanish Fort," *New Orleans Times-Democrat,* Apr. 11, 1865, 8; Davis Diary, Mar. 30, 1865.

2 "Mobile," *New York Herald,* Apr. 9, 1865, 1; Whipple, *The Diary of a Private Soldier,* 68; Truman, "Siege of Mobile."

The artillerists at Huger remained optimistic as they fired away at the Federals. "Whilst I write, we are shelling the Yankees—the report is with good effect," noted a soldier of the 22nd Consolidated Louisiana from his post at Huger. "Skirmishing still continues at the (Spanish) Fort. I believe we are going to whip them." To boost morale at Huger, two bottles of whiskey were offered as a prize to the cannoneers who made the best shot.[3]

Federals

The blue-coated soldiers in the advance rifle-pits had more to worry about than just the Confederate shells and sharpshooters. "We were directly between the rebel fort and one of our own batteries," recorded a soldier of Benton's Division, "which opened during the day so that our own shots passed directly over our heads. One struck very near us and bounded over toward the enemy. Another exploded close to our ditch. By this, we began to fear our friends."[4]

The Federals improved their ditches by digging them deeper and throwing dirt over the front. As they worked, sharpshooters countered the Southern cannons. "The sharpshooters kept strong shooting all day to protect us," observed a soldier of Lyman Ward's Brigade. They closely watched the fort's embrasures for any sign of movement. "At one embrasure, they ran out a huge, grim monster of a siege gun, but we kept up such a peppering that they were glad to withdraw it without firing," recalled another veteran.[5]

Heavy shelling and long periods of fatigue or picket duty exhausted the men. They would go on duty before daylight and remain 24 hours. A soldier of the 33rd Iowa noted: "In the afternoon, I became so fatigued that I went to sleep, with shells bursting all around me, and the Minnie balls whizzing above. I never before imagined that one could sleep in such circumstances."[6]

The uneven topography around Spanish Fort complicated their work and made it more dangerous. Approaching the fort they often had to expose themselves to cross ravines with steep banks. Colonel Hubbard recalled: "Many a soldier practically dug his own grave while engaged in this work, as a shell would explode in his vicinity or the keen eye of a sharpshooter would detect an exposure perhaps impossible to prevent."[7]

---

3 ML to AH, Mar. 30, 1865.

4 Sperry, *History of the 33d Iowa Infantry*, 137.

5 Wittenberger, "Frank Wittenberger Civil War Diary," 137.

6 Ridge Diary, Mar. 30, 1865; Sperry, *History of the 33d Iowa Infantry*, 138.

7 Hubbard, "Civil War Papers," 627, LC.

The Bluecoats were worn out after a long day of duty under constant fire. Once relieved, they returned to the rear of their camps to draw rations and wash up. "We are out of range of the Rebel guns, and I am glad for we need rest for we are all tired out," expressed one exhausted Federal.[8]

Despite the dog-tired state of the troops, a journalist on the scene for the Union-friendly *New Orleans Times-Democrat* portrayed a positive image for the readers back home: "The condition of the army is splendid. Every man, enlisted man, and officer is in his place, and too much praise cannot be awarded to them. At the present writing, our advance lines are within thirty yards of Spanish Fort, behind strong breastworks, dealing death to every rebel who has the temerity to elevate his cranium."[9]

Around noon, the 1st Division (Veatch) of the XIII Corps received orders to escort a supply train to Major General Steele's column as it approached Fort Blakeley, four miles north. Later, at 6:00 p.m., Colonel Marshall's 3rd Brigade of the XVI Corps moved out of its place and temporarily transferred to the center of the XIII Corps line, where it took the place of Veatch's Division by 7:00 p.m. That evening, Veatch and his division moved two miles to the rear and camped for the night.[10]

Federal vessels brought much-needed supplies to Starke's Wharf. Sub-terra shells, however, disrupted the supply chain despite four being dug out of the road the day before. The *New York Times* reported that some of the first wagons that went over the road "were blown to splinters on Thursday by these treacherous machines." In one instance, a horse was "blown to atoms by a torpedo, and its rider fell into the hole uninjured."[11]

On the extreme U.S. right flank, the Confederates continued their bombardment of the XVI Corps. "They are shelling us very bad today," pointed out a soldier of Carr's Division to his aunt. "They have got splendid forts full of good guns & three very large water batteries with 3 or four heavy ironclad gunboats. The gunboats are doing us more damage than anything else. They have a clean sweep of our lines at easy range & our boats cannot get at them."[12]

Soldiers could see the shells coming but could not tell where they would hit. "It always looked like it coming right where you were, so those that were down at

8 Miller, *Captain Edward Gee Miller*, 30; Fisher Diary, Mar. 30, 1865.

9 "The Expedition to Mobile," *New Orleans Times-Democrat*, Apr. 4, 1865, 1

10 Reed, *Twelfth Regiment Iowa*, 229, 231; *ORA* 49, pt. 1, 95; Slack Diary, Mar. 30, 1865.

11 Truman, "Near Spanish Fort, Opposite Mobile."

12 Chilvers to aunt, Mar. 30, 1865.

the foot of the hill ran uphill, and those up the hill ran down," recalled one soldier of Ward's Brigade. "Everyone moved, and all were excited until it had hit when we would quiet down until the next one was on the way."[13]

Guns off to the right severely enfiladed Moore's Brigade. The 33rd Wisconsin suffered the most in Moore's front. The camp occupied by Carr's Division officers were at dinner in a valley in the rear, seated upon logs and camp chairs under the pines. As they discussed the progress of the siege over coffee, they heard a rushing sound from the missile approaching from the right and hustling and shrieking through the air, apparently not more than ten feet above their heads. "It seemed savagely to tear the air to pieces and to leave it empty," observed Chaplain Howard.

The startled officers instinctively turned their heads the way it went as the coffee cups dropped from their hands and, at the next instant, heard it strike amid the 33rd Wisconsin with a heavy thud as though a barrel of sand had been driven into the earth. "Another instant and there was a terrific explosion, followed by the ascent of logs, sticks, tents, dirt, guns, clothing, and we thought arms and legs, into the air," noted Howard. "Our heart fainted at the sight; it was horrid." They quickly started for the spot where they found several men struck and mutilated, and the scene beggared description. "There they lay groaning, poor fellows, with their legs broken and torn so that their feet only held by pieces of skin, some both feet, some a foot, and a hand, while the hole in the earth torn out by the shell was larger than a hogshead, and the debris lay scattered all around. The men were off duty, having been in the rifle pits all night, and it looked so hard to be slaughtered that way in their tents." A Brooke rifled gun on a rebel gunboat had fired the hundred-pounder shell.[14]

Two more shells soon came in. One exploded in the air, just over the left of the 8th Iowa. Two pieces of it, one of which was a ragged brass flange, came tearing down, killing two men. John Hervett, known as "Lager John" for his expressed fondness for the German national beverage, suffered a mortal wound. Howard recalled: "He clapped his hands to the place, calling out, 'My God, boys, I'm shot,' and fell dead." They had just been ordered on duty and were putting on their accouterments when they were killed. The casualties were indeed horrific; a Black cook named Henry of the 33rd Wisconsin had both his legs shot off during the bombardment. By this time, Carr's men had become terrified. "All our skill seemed to be set aside and rendered useless by this distant and yet deadly foe," noted Howard. "None of our works were able to resist such a monster shell. Our rifles

13 E. Stockwell, *Private Elisha Stockwell*, 161–162.

14 Andrews, *History of the Campaign of Mobile*, 90; Ridge Diary, Mar. 30, 1865; Howard, *124th Regiment*, 299–301.

were as jackstraws and our caves as films of gauze against such a weapon, at such a range. . . . But the rebels did not know what they were doing; only one more shell was fired, which did no damage."[15]

Despite the heavy artillery onslaught, Smith's "Guerillas" held their ground. All that afternoon and into early night, they spent strengthening the works and building bombproofs on their right. "We worked with a will," recollected Howard, "with the ghastly scenes of the day before our eyes." One Minnesotan recounted a less serious casualty: "Lieutenant Folrum, my messmate, was wounded in the seat of his trousers but repaired the breach by getting another pair and is earnest to his country and men. If a man is seriously wounded, he has sympathy enough. If ludicrously wounded as Folrum, he becomes a butt of good-natured jest."[16]

Confederates

Maury, accompanied by his staff officers, visited Spanish Fort. After examining the lines, he decided to relieve Thomas's Brigade with Holtzclaw's Alabama Brigade veterans from Fort Blakeley. That evening, Liddell sent two regiments of Cockrell's Division to relieve Holtzclaw at Blakeley. The latter called in his pickets and, about midnight, marched his brigade to the Blakeley landing, where it embarked on the steamers *Mary* and *Red Gauntlet* for Spanish Fort.[17]

Maury's order to remove Thomas's men vexed Gibson. He tried to get the order rescinded: "General Liddell and I both think that no men should be taken away for a few days. This is a school of instruction for the Reserves; they are daily improving as soldiers and are well pleased. The enemy presses at all points, especially my left flank. I have a great deal of work to do there upon the main line, and I must re-establish my skirmish line. For these reasons, I hope you will let matters remain as they are." The Virginian, however, had his mind made up and denied Gibson's request to keep Thomas's Brigade. Later that evening, Gibson wired Liddell: "The Reserves are now leaving."

Undaunted, the resilient Louisianan maintained a cheerful demeanor. Gibson encouraged his officers to visit the line and give the men "cheerful words" to encourage them. "Morale is our main bulwark in this position." During the day, he issued circulars to instruct and inspire his men:

15 Howard, *124th Regiment*, 301–302; Chandler A. Chapman, ed., *Roster of Wisconsin Volunteers, War of the Rebellion, 1861–1865*, vol. II (Madison, WI, 1886), 514; Howard, *124th Regiment*, 302. It is unclear if the fatal shots came from a gunboat or Battery Huger. Carr's men believed the shots came from the gunboat near the fort.

16 Howard, *124th Regiment*, 302; Edwards Journal, Mar. 30, 1865, 247.

17 Andrews, *History of the Campaign of Mobile*, 80.

I. The brigadier-general commanding desires to express to the troops the admiration of their valor and endurance and his entire confidence in their ability to defend this position.

II. Thousands of anxious hearts turn toward you.

III. Let every officer and man resolve to do his whole duty, to stand firm at his post, and to make the enemy pay dearly in blood for every inch he may advance, and by the blessing of Heaven we shall continue those successes which so far with scarcely any loss crowned your efforts.[18]

In another circular, he instructed his officers to keep picked men watching the Federal movements at all times. "Never permit him to gain a foot of ground without fighting for it and to hold any point from which, by a bold strike, you can dislodge him," he exhorted. He demanded continued work on the works to make them strong enough to resist heavy artillery fire. Gibson— anticipating an assault at any time—instructed his officers to be prepared by keeping a small force ready for any emergency "so that in the blink of an eye, it can be thrown into action." During a heavy shelling, he instructed the men to protect themselves carefully and, the moment it ceases, to be prepared for an assault.

He emphasized the need for vigilance against an assault, especially every morning before dawn, noon, and evening before dark. To further deter an assault, Gibson ordered his men to light more campfires at night to present an exaggerated impression of their numbers and the strength of the works. He also forbade communication with the Federals under any circumstance. With the ammunition supply running low, Gibson cautioned his officers to economize what was left. "It is not the frequency but the deliberate precision of the fire that produces results," he instructed. He ordered no firing from the mainline outside of the batteries unless in the case of an assault.

To counter the Federal sharpshooters, Gibson ordered his officers to place five sharpshooters to support each artillery piece. They were instructed to conceal themselves carefully, use the wooden screens, and be active whenever the batteries on either side began firing.[19]

Back at Fort Blakeley, Liddell faced a new threat: Maj. Gen. Fred Steele's column. Steele's force of over 13,000 men had marched out of Fort Barrancas near Pensacola, Florida. He had feinted toward Montgomery before sharply turning west at Pollard, Alabama. Steele approached Fort Blakeley from the vicinity of Stockton to the north. Liddell urgently telegraphed headquarters at Mobile for

18 *ORA* 49, pt. 2, 1176–1177.

19 Handwritten orders, RLG, Mar. 31, 1865.

2Lt. Artemus O. Sibley and his 15th Confederate Cavalry scouts. "One hundred cavalry are hovering around us, trying to join the enemy's force here, and it is important that they should be intercepted."[20]

Acting Master's Mate George S. Waterman of the Confederate Navy penned a series of articles for *Confederate Veteran* magazine after the war detailing his experiences at the battle of Mobile Bay and the 1865 Mobile campaign. He had many friends from his hometown, New Orleans, fighting at Spanish Fort. As a visiting officer, he could visit the fort to see and help his old schoolmates, many of whom served with the Washington Artillery's 5th Company. Before his journey to Baldwin County began, he received a sobering reminder of his old comrades' dire situation. While waiting for his transport on the wharf at Mobile, he observed a coffin brought ashore. "We raised hats in respect to the dead soldier but did not know the remains of Edward S. McIlhenny, a schoolmate, rested therein," recalled Waterman. "He was a member of the Washington Artillery and met a soldier's death on the line of duty." One artillerist of the Washington Artillery recalled McIlhenny as "a quiet boy, of 19 or 20 and a general favorite. He was sincerely mourned."[21]

Confederates

Friday, March 31, 1865: Early in the morning, a spectacle occurred with the arrival of over 1,500 soldiers from Fort Blakeley. Steamers transported General James T. Holzclaw's Brigade (931 men) and Ector's Brigade (575 men) under Col. Julius A. Andrews from the Blakeley Wharf south on the Blakeley River to Spanish Fort. They were sent to relieve Thomas's Alabama Reserves, who were transferred up to Blakeley. The exchange increased Gibson's strength by about 100 muskets. Under the cover of darkness, the blockade runners *Mary, Magnolia,* and *Red Gauntlet* were busy all night transporting the veterans of the Army of Tennessee. Upon debarking, Holtzclaw assumed command of the left-wing of the fort.[22]

Lack of transportation and fuel delayed the transfer of men. Mindful of the looming threat of Steele's column, Liddell anxiously pushed to complete the transfer. He telegraphed Gibson the evening before, notifying him that the *Mary*

20 *ORA* 49, pt. 2, 1176.

21 George S. Waterman, "Afloat-Afield-Afloat," *Confederate Veteran* VIII (Jan. 1900): 21; Stephenson & Hughes, *Civil War Memoir of Philip Daingerfield Stephenson*, 363. McIlhenny was killed on March 29th.

22 Morning report, RLG; *ORA* 49, Pt. 1, 315; *ORA* 49, Pt. 2, 1179, 1180, 1186; Waterman, "Afloat-Afield-Afloat," *Confederate Veteran* VIII (Feb. 1900): 53; Andrews, *History of the Campaign of Mobile*, 90.

and *Red Gauntlet* were headed his way. "Have the Reserves ready to place on them and also the wounded and useless persons, let there be no delay," He ordered. Gibson's reply confirmed their arrival: "It was already daylight when Holtzclaw's Brigade arrived, and I could not detain the boat and pull out the other Reserve regiment. I will send it up by the very first boat tonight."[23]

Later, Liddell also wired Maury: "All of Holtzclaw's Brigade has gone & but one Regiment of Reserves has reached here, no other boats reported for this service & the transfer is not completed in consequence. Unless the boats are required to remain here & supplied with wood from a tender, it will be impossible to effect a rapid transfer of troops when desired. Boats here are compelled to go back to Mobile for wood & time & labor, thereby lost, & when wanted, cannot be had. I beg your attention, especially on this matter, to prevent future disaster."[24]

Brigadier General James T. Holtzclaw was born in McDonough, Henry County, Georgia, on December 17, 1833. His family moved to Chambers County, Alabama, early in his childhood. Educated at the Presbyterian high school, he received an appointment to the U.S. Military Academy in 1853. He declined the appointment, however, on account of the death of an older brother. In 1854, he went to Montgomery and began studying law in the office of Elmore & Yancey. He earned admittance to the bar the following year. Although he never ran for office, Holtzclaw was one of the most influential men of his day in Alabama politics.[25]

Holtzclaw actively participated in military operations at the onset of the secession crisis. He first answered the call to arms in early 1861 as a lieutenant with the Montgomery True Blues. Before Alabama even officially seceded, Alabama Governor Andrew Moore ordered the 2nd Volunteer Regiment of Alabama, including the True Blues, to northwest Florida to seize the United States forts at Pensacola at the request of the governor of Florida. On January 12, 1861, he greeted Commodore Ebenezer Farrand with his militia to capture the Pensacola Navy Yard and Fort Barrancas. At Fort Barrancas, Holtzclaw's men un-spiked and

23 *Dispatch Book*, 77; *ORA* 49, pt. 2, 1180.

24 *Dispatch Book*, 77.

25 Clement A. Evans, *Confederate Military History: A Library of Confederate States History*, vol. VII (Atlanta, 1899), 417–418; *Confederate Regimental History Files*, SG024903, Alabama Department of Archives and History, Montgomery, AL; Benjamin C. Holtzclaw, *The Genealogy of the Holtzclaw Family, 1540–1935* (Richmond, 1936), 43; "U.S. Federal Census, 1860, Slave Schedules," FamilySearch, accessed Feb. 3, 2023, https://www.familysearch.org/ark:/61903/3:1:33S7-9YB6-9PHV?i=197&cc=3161105. In 1860, Holtzclaw owned 18 enslaved persons.

remounted the cannons, aiming them at Federally occupied Fort Pickens across Pensacola Bay on Santa Rosa Island.[26]

At Fort Barrancas, the True Blues reputedly fired the first shot of the war, even before Fort Sumter, albeit inadvertently. They were in charge of the sunset and sunrise signal cannon. One night, someone loaded the gun with a shot. At sunrise the following day, soldiers unwittingly fired the shot over the Federal garrison at Fort Pickens. In March of 1861, Holtzclaw's regiment was relieved and ordered back to Alabama. In April, all Alabama troops, including Holtzclaw's True Blues, were mustered out of the Alabama State Service and reorganized into the Confederate States Army.[27]

In August 1861, President Davis appointed Holtzclaw major of the 18th Alabama. At Shiloh in 1862, he suffered a gunshot wound through the right lung while standing by the colors of his regiment. The wound was considered mortal, but within 90 days, he rejoined his regiment. Holtzclaw's men helped capture the 8th Iowa at Shiloh, which they now faced again at Spanish Fort.[28]

At Chickamauga, while commanding his regiment, he was thrown from his horse and badly injured. He remained upon the field, his regiment suffering severe losses. In command of Henry D. Clayton's Brigade in the Chattanooga campaign, he took a gallant part at Lookout Mountain and Missionary Ridge.[29]

Holtzclaw's Alabamians opposed Sherman's forces in Georgia and actively participated in the fighting from Rocky Face Ridge to Atlanta. Upon the promotion of Clayton on July 8th, 1864, Holtzclaw became a brigadier general. He commanded the brigade during Hood's flank movement in North Georgia and the following Tennessee campaign. His brigade reached the position before Nashville first, which the army occupied the next day. On December 16th, he held a line directly across Franklin Pike and maintained his position against repeated Federal assaults.[30]

At Franklin, Gibson sacrificed a portion of Holtzclaw's Brigade to cover the retreat of his brigade across the Harpeth River. During the fighting, Holtzclaw followed orders to send a detachment of his brigade to fill a gap in the lines. In the

26 Evans, *Confederate Military History*, 417–418; "Gen. James T. Holtzclaw, Montgomery," *New Orleans Times-Democrat*, July 19, 1893, 1.

27 John H. Napier, III, "Martial Montgomery: Ante Bellum Military Activity," *Alabama Historical Quarterly* (Fall 1967): 127–129.

28 Evans, *Confederate Military History*, 418; Byers, *Iowa*, 406.

29 Evans, *Confederate Military History*, 418; *Confederate Regimental History Files*, SG024903, Montgomery, Alabama Department of Archives and History.

30 Evans, *Confederate Military History*, 418; *ORA* 45, pt. 1, 705–706.

chaos of battle, he lost communication with this detachment, which, unbeknownst to him, came into a position taken by Gibson, who was exhausted after running around the enemy's cavalry. Holtzclaw reported: "Without notice to myself or authority from the major-general, Brig. Gen. Gibson ordered this detachment of about seventy-five men to remain and cover the battery. Then, withdrawing with the battery, he withdrew his brigade while my small detachment, in obedience to his orders, held the position and covered the retreat of himself and the section. As a matter of course, they were overwhelmed by the enemy's cavalry, 2,000 or 3,000 of whom had surrounded them, three officers and five men only escaping." Although the tenor and tone of his after-action report seemed to indicate his vexation with Gibson, there is no further evidence of tension between the two generals.

In his official report on Nashville, Holtzclaw concluded: "I will say nothing of the hardships and exposures borne by my command; they but bore their part of the general burden; yet that part they bore with cheerfulness and spirit, and repulsed the enemy, with loss, whenever they encountered him on the soil of Tennessee. My officers and men conducted themselves to my entire satisfaction throughout all the fights and marches."[31]

One corporal of the 18th Alabama remembered Holtzclaw:

> [He] was in the prime of life and, in personal appearance, was handsome and commanding. In voice, I never heard his superior. Everyone seemed to love to hear Holtzclaw give a command. His voice was clear and ringing. In appearance, he represented an ideal military man. He received what nearly proved to be a mortal wound at Shiloh. His bearing on that occasion up to the time of being wounded was most gallant indeed.[32]

Another veteran recalled the arrival of Holtzclaw's Brigade. He described them as "pale but intrepid, sad but unsubdued, even though they must have known the end was not far off. We proudly welcomed these men, still dauntless and loyal through four years of almost constant fighting."[33]

While Holtzclaw oversaw the fort's left wing, Alabama native Col. Bush Jones, the 29-year-old commander of the 32nd and 58th Alabama Regiment, assumed command of Holtzclaw's Brigade. A resident of Perry County, he practiced law in Uniontown before the war. Described as young and handsome, Jones enlisted in January 1861 and fought at Manassas as a private in the 4th Alabama. He then went to Corinth, where he became a colonel of the 58th Alabama Regiment.

31 *ORA* 45, pt. 1, 706–707.

32 Jones and Pulcrano, *Eighteenth Alabama Infantry Regiment*, 14.

33 George S. Waterman, "Afloat-Afield-Afloat," *Confederate Veteran* VIII (Feb. 1900b): 53.

Brigadier General James T. Holtzclaw, commander of the left wing of Spanish Fort, March 31–April 8, 1865. *Alabama Department of Archives and History*

He led the 58th at Chickamauga, where his regiment lost 63% of its number. After sustaining heavy casualties there, the two regiments were consolidated under him. He had temporarily assumed brigade command during Holtzclaw's absence at the battle of Jonesboro. There, he rode along the line on his horse, talking as coolly and calmly as if no battle was going on. A witness described a perfect hail of bullets around him, but he was not struck. Nothing shielded him from the enemy, yet he showed no sign of fear.[34]

Though the official records failed to mention when Ector's Brigade arrived at Spanish Fort, it is presumed they came with Holtzclaw. Gibson made it clear in his after-action report that 27-year-old Col. Julius A. Andrews commanded those troops. Wounded at Chickamauga and near Nashville, Andrews led that brigade's 32nd Texas Dismounted Cavalry regiment at Farmington, Murfreesboro, Jackson, and the Atlanta campaign.[35]

Ector's Brigade experienced several changes in command during the previous year. Andrews emerged as the brigade leader after Gen. Matthew D. Ector suffered a severe wound during the defense of Atlanta. After sustaining heavy casualties at

34 Waterman, "Afloat-Afield-Afloat," 1900b, 24; *ORA* 49, pt. 1, 318; Willis Brewer, *Alabama, Her History, Resources, War Record, and Public Men: From 1540 to 1872* (Montgomery, AL, 1872), 496–497; Thomas M. Owen, *History of Alabama and Dictionary of Alabama Biography* (Chicago, 1921), 925; "Alabama County Marriages, 1809-1950," FamilySearch, accessed Feb. 3, 2023, https://www.familysearch.org/ark:/61903/3:1:939V-ZQSL-1P?i=58&cc=1743384&personaUrl=%2Fark%3A%2F61903%2F1%3A1%3AVRJ5-CGY; Jones and Pulcrano, *Eighteenth Alabama Infantry Regiment*, 25. His correct name was Bush, not Bushrod Jones. General Joseph Wheeler erroneously called him Bushrod in his book. The error perpetuated in subsequent narratives. Jones married Caroline C. Evans, the sister of Mobile's famous author, Augusta Jane Evans in 1863.

35 *ORA* 49, pt. 1, 318; "Andrews, Julius A," Texas State Historical Association, accessed Jan. 8, 2018, https://tshaonline.org/handbook/online/articles/fan61; "Ector's Brigade," Texas State Historical Association, accessed May 1, 2020, https://tshaonline.org/handbook/online/articles/qke01.

Allatoona, the brigade joined Hood's expedition into Tennessee, but too late to fight at Franklin. Andrews received his second wound during the pursuit of the Federals to Nashville. Colonel David Coleman, 39th North Carolina, therefore, assumed command at Nashville. In early 1865, Andrews had recovered enough to rejoin his brigade for the defense of Mobile.[36]

Andrews earned the respect of his fellow regimental commanders. On November 5, 1864, they all signed a petition requesting him to be commissioned a brigadier general. In a letter of recommendation for this promotion, his division commander, Brig. Gen. Francis Cockrell described the Texan as "a thorough tactician, [and] possessor of the qualities which enable a commander to govern men and is a most efficient and gallant officer."[37]

It is unclear what, if any, role Colonel Coleman played during the siege. His name appears in the official records before and immediately after the siege, but he is not mentioned at Spanish Fort.[38]

The men of Ector's Brigade, like the Holtzclaw and Gibson commands, were battle-hardened veterans of the Army of Tennessee. Composed of two regiments of North Carolinians and four regiments of Texans, they were recognized for gallantry in many of the principal battles of the West. They were hotly engaged at such significant battles as Murfreesboro and Chickamauga. In defense of Atlanta, Resaca, Altoona, New Hope Church, Peach Tree Creek, and other actions, they were under fire virtually every day and sustained heavy losses. During Hood's expedition into Tennessee, Lt. Gen. A. P. Stewart described them as a "firm and reliable body of men."[39]

36 "Andrews, Julius A"; "Ector's Brigade"; "Ector, Mathew Duncan," Texas State Historical Association, accessed May 1, 2020, https://tshaonline.org/handbook/online/articles/fec02; *ORA* 49, pt. 1, 318, 1046; *ORA* 49, pt. 2, 1225, 1245.

37 "Andrews, Julius A"; "Ector's Brigade."

38 *ORA* 49, pt. 1, 318, 1046 *ORA* 49, pt. 2, 1225, 1245; Waterman, "Afloat-Afield-Afloat,"1900c, 24. On Mar 10, the official records list Coleman as commanding Ector's Brigade. Gibson and others, however, reported Col. Julius A. Andrews commanded the brigade during the siege of Spanish Fort. It is unclear what role Coleman played during the siege of Spanish Fort, if any. His name is not found in the official records correspondence nor in Gibson's after-action report. Colonel Andrews is last mentioned in the official records on Apr 11, commanding an infantry force in charge of the trains during the evacuation. After the evacuation of Mobile, Coleman resumed command of French's Division on Apr 16 at Meridian, Mississippi. Andrews surrendered on May 9, 1865 in Meridian, while Coleman surrendered in June 1865 at Shreveport.

39 A. C. Avery, *Five Points in the Record of North Carolina in the Great War of 1861-5* (Goldsboro, N.C.: Nash Brothers, 1904), 56; "Ector's Brigade," Texas State Historical Association, accessed May 1, 2020, https://tshaonline.org/handbook/online/articles/qke01; Walter Clark, *Histories of the Several Regiments and Battalions from North Carolina, in the Great War 1861-'65, VOL. II* (Goldsboro, NC: Nash Brothers), 711, 720-721.

Colonel Julius A. Andrews, commander, Ector's Brigade, Spanish Fort. *Southern Methodist University*

Upon debarking, Holtzclaw assumed command of the left wing of the fort. His brigade occupied the works from the left of Battery Blair (Redoubt 3), opposite McArthur's Division. They were positioned from right to left as follows: the 21st Alabama (detached from Thomas's Brigade) and the 18th Alabama between Redoubts 3 (Blair) and 4; next, the 32-58th Consolidated and 36th Regiment extending to the sandbag battery (Redoubt 5); Ector's Brigade occupied the works between Redoubts 5 and 6, opposite Carr's Division.

The exact regimental positions of Ector's Brigade are unknown. Reportedly, the two North Carolina regiments were on the right and the four Texas Regiments on their left, holding the extreme Confederate left flank. The besiegers took note of the entrance of the two Confederate brigades. "The Rebs have been reinforced & have been to work mounting big guns," observed a soldier of the 7th Vermont.[40]

---

40 John Lozedon, "Flag of Ninth Texas Infantry," *Confederate Veteran* XVII (1909): 455; Waterman, "Afloat-Afield-Afloat," 24; Andrews, *Campaign of Mobile*, 89; *ORA* 49, pt. 1, 96, 134, 275; Kirk Barrett, "Confederate Soldiers Captured at Spanish Fort and Imprisoned at Ship Island" (unpublished manuscript, 2018); Fisher Diary, Mar. 31, 1865. Andrews's wrote that the two North Carolina regiments were on Ector's right and the four Texas regiments occupied the left. They held the extreme left flank of the Confederate line, but the exact positions of the brigade's regiments are questionable. One account stated that the 32nd Texas and 29th North Carolina were posted on the extreme Confederate left flank. U.S. Army after-action reports indicate about 200 Confederates were captured during the immediate assault on the evening of Apr 8. Barrett's Ship Island prisoner rolls list 31 men from the 32nd Texas regiment, and 82 soldiers from the 29th North Carolina and 75 prisoners of war from the 39th North Carolina. Only five men were captured from the 9th Texas, five men from the 10th Texas, and 13 men from the 14th Texas. This seems to suggest the possibility that the 32nd Texas, 29th North Carolina troops and not all four Texas regiments occupied the Confederate left flank. Moreover, Lozedon's article shows a photograph of the 9th Texas Regiment flag taken before the turn of the 20th century with a handwritten caption: "Battle Flag of 9th Texas Regiment, Confederate Army. This regiment supported Alabama State Artillery Company A (Garrity's Battery) at Spanish Fort, Alabama." This would place the 9th Texas on the right of Ector's Brigade adjacent to Redoubt 5.

Federals

Before the Federals arrived at the Spanish Fort, they had heard that only older men and boys defended Mobile. They realized they were mistaken. In a letter home, a soldier of the 94th Illinois remarked that he had "never seen as many good fighting men in the south as that we are contending against."[41]

Shelling grew more intense on this windy and warm day. The Bluecoats endured strong cannon and continual musket fire on the skirmish line. "For 12 hours, we were under the severest artillery fire I have ever seen," one Iowan recorded in his diary. The Confederates constantly shelled their rifle pits with mortars, siege guns, and guns of various calibers. Dirt frequently splattered them from the exploding shells.[42]

Despite the unexpected ferocity of resistance the Federals faced, they managed to erect additional artillery positions and gradually dug their way closer to the works of Spanish Fort. To counter the mounting casualties caused by the Confederate gunboats and the marsh batteries, the XVI Corps command erected battery #22 on Minette Bay's southeast bank or bluff. The 1st Indiana Heavy Artillery initially handled eight 30-pounder Parrotts and two Whitworth guns at the battery.[43]

The Federals intended to keep the batteries concealed behind the small trees growing at the bluff's edge until all the guns were in position and then open a crushing fire. The Confederates on the river observed the partially revealed battery during the night. As soon as the mist cleared and permitted a full view of the Indiana battery, Lt. John W. Bennett, the captain of the ironclad CSS *Nashville*, immediately communicated with Maj. Washington Marks at Huger and prepared to shell them. However, at 8:00 a.m., the Indiana artillerists opened up with their 30-pounder Parrots. The U.S. Army's artillery anticipated Bennett by about fifteen minutes. They unleashed a rapid and accurate fire upon his ironclad, in the midst of which he had to weigh the *Nashville*'s anchor. By the time Bennett raised anchor, the Indiana battery had the *Nashville* ranged exactly.[44]

The *Nashville* moved up a short distance and returned fire from her stern guns. The vessel's guns suffered from limited elevation, however, and could not reach

---

41 William R. Iseminger, *From McLean to Mobile: A History of the 94th Illinois Infantry Regiment Volunteers, 1862–1865* (2022), 223–224.

42 Henderson Diary, Mar. 31, 1865.

43 Fike Diary, Mar. 31, 1865; William M. Macy, "Civil War Diary of William M. Macy," *Indiana Magazine of History* 30, no. 2 (June 1934): 193; Wittenberger, "Frank Wittenberger Civil War Diary"; *ORA* 49, pt. 1, 138–139; Allen, "Operations against the City," 78.

44 Allen, "Operations against the City," 78; Waterman, "Afloat-Afield-Afloat,", 22; *ORA* 49, pt. 1, 320.

The author at the Indiana Battery with Minette Bay in the background. *Pam Swan*

the Indianans on the high bluff. Struck eight times, the *Nashville* moved north of Tracey, out of range. Her relatively light armor could not continue to withstand the repeated shots. With a leaking boiler and no further hope of harming the Indiana battery, the *Nashville* sought shelter and repair in Mobile.[45]

The Indiana battery targeted the former blockade runner, *Heroine*, during her stay at the fort. Another vessel, the *Dorrance*, brought five wounded men of Gibson's Brigade back to Mobile. One of the wounded, Captain Henry James of the 19th Louisiana, died during the voyage.[46]

The Minette Bay battery also bombarded Huger and Tracey. The Federals supposed their bombardment had silenced Huger and Tracey since, as Canby put it, they "gave us no further serious annoyance." To make matters worse for the Graybacks, artillery reinforcements from Dauphin Island arrived at Starke's Wharf. Mack's 18th New York Independent Battery—known as the Black Horse Battery—disembarked from the vessel *White Cloud # 2* and went into camp.[47]

45 *ORA* 49, pt. 1, 320; Waterman 1900c, "Afloat-Afield-Afloat,", 22.

46 "From the Confederacy," *The Times Picayune*, Apr. 14, 1965, 2.

47 *ORA* 49, pt.1, 94; Snedeker, *The Civil War Diary of Charles Henry Snedeker*, "Civil War Diary of Henry M. Dryer."

The Confederates used the blockade runner *Heroine* on the Blakeley River during the siege of Spanish Fort to transfer men and supplies. *Naval History and Heritage Command*

Confederates

The Southern defenders were running dangerously low on ammunition. At the two marsh batteries, Patton's artillerists were ordered not to reply to the Federal battery. Maury noted that there were less than 200 rounds left for the Brooke guns and maybe a little over 200 remaining for the ten-inch cannons. "There was no more to be had in the Confederacy," he recalled. The batteries preserved the ammunition to use against any attempt Thatcher's fleet might make to force a passage of the river. Therefore, the garrisons of Huger and Tracey covered their guns with merlons and sheltered themselves in bombproofs and any other way they could. The two marsh batteries silently received fire for ten days without replying.[48]

Although the new Federal battery drove off the *Nashville*, Huger and Tracey only sustained minor damage. "One of the environs of Huger's dining room was a pertinacious Indiana battery of Federal Parrott guns, 'which faced our way too much,' for between the mouthfuls of relished viands there soared away from the Bay Minette," recalled George Waterman. He had stopped off at Huger on his way from Mobile to Spanish Fort. "One of these Parrotts caged by Indianans was known to us by word of mouth, and its ears must have burned as we talked about

---

48 Maury, "Defence of Mobile in 1865," 9–10; Maury, "Souvenirs of the War," 4. Merlons are solid upright sections of a battlement.

it; for while we were still commenting, it let out a squawk and threw its projectile at a post nearby us, grazed the head of the sentry at the magazine, and cleared the quarters." One soldier of the 22nd Consolidated Louisiana tried to comfort his girlfriend in a letter he sent from Huger: "Do not be uneasy as they have only small guns planted. They have thrown several hundred shell and shot at us, and yet nobody hurt."[49]

About 70 men of the 5th Company of Washington Artillery from New Orleans manned Redoubt 3 near the center of Spanish Fort's defenses. The Confederates named the battery in honor of their company's late Lt. Thomas M. Blair, killed September 19, 1863, at Glass Mills, during the first day of fighting at Chickamauga.[50]

Captain Cuthbert H. Slocomb, 5th Company, Washington Artillery, commanded all the field artillery at Spanish Fort. Before the war, Slocomb ran a hardware business in New Orleans. By 1861, he was a prominent citizen of the city and owned a significant amount of real estate property. The war, however, prompted him to join the Washington Artillery on May 26, 1861. He became the first lieutenant of the 2nd Company, serving as the assistant quartermaster. Slocomb saw action at the battle of Bull Run but resigned on November 7, 1861, to become the first lieutenant of the newly formed 5th Company on March 6, 1862. Wounded in April 1862 at Shiloh, Slocomb received a promotion to captain and the company's command after the resignation of Captain Hodgson on June 13, 1862. He was again wounded at Jonesboro before returning to duty in December 1864.[51]

From Shiloh to Nashville, the 5th Company, like most veterans at Spanish Fort, had seen much hard fighting in the western theater and suffered heavy losses. After the battle of Farmington, they had been with Gibson's Brigade (previously

49 Waterman 1900c, "Afloat-Afield-Afloat," 22; Robert Tarleton and William Still, "The Civil War Letters of Robert Tarleton," *Alabama Historical Quarterly* 32, no. 1 (Spring 1970): 79; ML to AH, Apr. 1, 1865.

50 Morning report, RLG, Apr. 1, 1865; "Thomas McMillian Blair," Find A Grave, accessed May 12, 2020, https://www.findagrave.com/memorial/40613117/thomas-mcmillian-blair. Morning reports in Gibson's Papers indicated the number of men Slocomb's Battery reported present varied between 68–72 men during the final week of the siege.

51 Charles E. Slocum, *History of the Slocums, Slocumbs and Slocombs of America: Genealogical and Biographical, Embracing Twelve Generations of the First-named Family from A.D. 1637 to 1908, with Their Marriages and Descendants in the Female Lines as Far as Ascertained* (Defiance, OH, 1908), 508–509, https://archive.org/details/historyofslocums00sloc/page/n7/mode/2up?q=Cuthbert; William M. Owen, *In Camp and Battle with the Washington Artillery of New Orleans: A Narrative of Events During the Late Civil War from Bull Run to Appomattox and Spanish Fort* (Boston, 1885), 273–274; "Captain Cuthbert Harrison Slocomb," Find A Grave - Millions of Cemetery Records, accessed Nov. 27, 2021, https://www.findagrave.com/memorial/6884675/cuthbert-harrison-slocomb.

known as Adams Brigade). In late November 1863, they lost six guns at Missionary Ridge. During the previous year, they were in the siege of Atlanta for 34 days and nights and had their guns knocked to pieces several times. During the war, 143 of the battery's horses were killed in action.[52]

The 5th Company served as light artillerists throughout the war. At Spanish Fort, however, the nature of the defense required them to be reassigned to heavy artillery, an assignment they did not relish. The 5th Company and the other artillerists were furnished with rifles to further compensate for the lack of infantrymen. The men adapted quickly and mastered their new roles with a firm commitment. One artillerist of Lumsden's Battery noted, "Our shoulders got sore with the continued kick of the firing."[53]

Only two of the field artillery companies were relieved by fresh batteries from Mobile during the siege. After about a week, Maury went to see Capt. Slocomb and told him that other companies not yet engaged were ready to take the 5th Company's place. Slocomb replied: "Appreciating, General, your consideration for my men, I desire to submit the question to them." He soon returned to Maury and stated: "General, the company, grateful for your kind intention, desire to hold this position to the end. We respectfully decline to be relieved." Slocomb's second in command, 1Lt. Joseph A. Chalaron, who commanded the 5th Company at Battery Blair, recalled that the men wanted "the honor of fighting out to the end, and so it did."[54]

Federal soldiers continued to dig a parallel in front of the main works of Spanish Fort. Hand-picked sharpshooters, the best shots from their respective brigades, covered their advanced positions. They severely annoyed the Confederate artillerists for the remainder of the siege, sometimes even forcing them to abandon their cannons and fill the embrasures with earth.[55]

At Battery Blair, the Washington Artillery's 5th Company operated its heavy guns under deadly fire. Wooden embrasures and iron screens were essential to the company's safety. When the cannons were ready to run out, the screens were opened for the big guns to fire. Each embrasure opening drew the relentless fire of

---

52 Owen, *In Camp and Battle with the Washington Artillery*, 424.

53 Owen, *In Camp and Battle with the Washington Artillery*, 415, 420; Philip D. Stephenson, D.D., *Civil War Memoir of Philip Daingerfield Stephenson, D.D,* ed. Nathaniel C. Hughes (Conway, AR, 1995), 358; Little and Maxwell, "A History of Lumsden's Battery."

54 Owen, *In Camp and Battle with the Washington Artillery*, 415, 420; Maury, "Defence of Spanish Fort," 132; J. A. Chalaron, "Battle Echoes from Shiloh," *Southern Historical Society Papers* 21 (1893): 220–221.

55 Minnesota Board of Commissioners on Publication of History of Minnesota in Civil and Indian Wars, *Minnesota in the Civil and Indian Wars, 1861–1865*, vol. 2 (St. Paul, 1890), 622.

Captain Cuthbert Slocomb commander, Spanish Fort's field artillery. *Dr. Glen Cangelosi*

the blue-coated riflemen; nonetheless, the artillerists continued to operate their weapons.[56]

The 5th Company never handled a larger weapon than the 8-inch iron Columbiad at Battery Blair. Mounted on a center pintle carriage, the men named it *Lady Slocomb* in honor of their captain's wife. Cast at the Tredegar Iron Works in Richmond, Virginia, in 1862, it weighed over 8,500 pounds and was 10 feet long. There were also three field guns and two coehorn mortars. Each weapon had a name: *Lady Vaught* for the wife of their only married lieutenant, a 3-inch rifle named *Cora Slocomb* after their captain's daughter, and *General Gibson*. The men called their two mortars *Louise* and *Theresa* after the peanut and apple vending girls at Mobile's Battle House Hotel, whose smiles had greeted them as they marched past to take their transport boats for Spanish Fort.[57]

At about 10:00 a.m., Cpl. Charles W. Fox, the gunner of the *Lady Slocomb*, scored a direct hit on a limber box of

56 George S. Waterman, "Afloat-Afield-Afloat," *Confederate Veteran* VIII (Feb. 1900), 53.

57 "The Lady Slocomb," *The Daily Register*, Mar. 15, 1891; George S. Waterman, "Afloat-Afield-Afloat," *Confederate Veteran* VIII (Jan 1900): 23; "Lady Slocomb," *New Orleans Times-Democrat*, Sep. 20, 1899, 7; Larry J. Daniel and Riley W. Gunter, *Confederate Cannon Foundries* (Union City, TN, 1977), 7. Some contemporary newspapers erroneously reported the Selma foundries produced the *Lady Slocomb*. Certain markings on the *Lady Slocomb* indicate the Tredegar foundry in Richmond, Virginia, built the cannon.

The *Lady Slocomb* and the 5th Company of Washington Artillery. *Rick Reeves*

the 14th Indiana Light Artillery. The 8-inch shell "came shrieking along, striking the limber chest of a caisson, shivering it instantly to atoms, igniting the shells, and spreading death and destruction around," reported one correspondent. "One unfortunate man was literally burst to a cinder, few vestiges remaining to show that the heap of blood-stained rags and clothes lying before you was, a moment before, a creature fashioned in his Creator's likeness. Oh, it was a shocking spectacle!" Others were seriously injured from the blast. One Bluecoat, Cpl. Joseph Pauling, who sat by the chest, lived though all his clothes were blown off him.[58]

Colonel William E. Burnet—a distinguished Texas-born West Pointer—answered the Confederacy's call to arms early in the crisis. His father, David Burnet, the ex-president of Texas, vehemently opposed secession, and his heart wrenched when he learned his son joined the Confederates.[59]

58 George S. Waterman, "Afloat-Afield-Afloat," *Confederate Veteran* VIII (Feb. 1900): 54; "The Mobile Expedition," *New Orleans Times-Democrat*, Apr. 8, 1865, 2; "Rebellion in the Gulf States Dead," *Chicago Tribune*, Apr. 18, 1865, 3; Gladieux, *14th Indiana*, 27.

59 Mary W. Clarke, *David G. Burnet* (Austin, TX, 1969), 236–237.

Corporal Charles W. Fox, 5th Company, Washington Artillery. *Dr. Glen Cangelosi*

Burnet served on Maury's staff as chief of artillery. His fellow officers and men liked and respected him. Maury especially held him in high regard: "Col. Burnet's range of knowledge extended far beyond the limits of the military profession, and as a scholar, a political economist, and a scientific man, he ranked foremost amongst those we ever were associated with."[60]

Early in the morning, Burnet had gone with Maury to Spanish Fort to establish a new battery. When Maury returned to Mobile, he told Burnet: "I will return for you in the steamer—remain here as long as you find necessary." Shortly after noon, he inspected the fortifications with Gibson and ordered necessary changes in the view of the encroaching Federals.[61]

A Union sharpshooter continually annoyed them with his fire, but they could not see him. Someone eventually spotted the blue-coated sniper sitting in a tree about 40 feet up and roughly five hundred yards away. Colonel Burnet borrowed some muskets from a Texas regiment nearby to take some shots at the opposing marksman. He carried a gun and knelt and took a deliberate aim, but the shot went wide of the mark. Meanwhile, the fire from the Federal sniper continued to harass them. As Burnet prepared to take another shot, a Texas soldier farther down the line fired and knocked the Bluecoat out of the tree. Two hours later, while Burnet examined the lines, a shot from near this tree struck him close to his left eye, and before he could be moved to a transport only a short distance off, he expired.[62]

Gibson wired Maury's headquarters with the sad announcement of Colonel Burnet's death. "I have never received such a shock," recalled Maury. In his after action-report, Gibson expressed the sentiments of his men: "His loss was

60 "Souvenirs of War," *The Mobile Times*, Jan. 14, 1866; N. T. M'Conaughy, "Gallant Col. William E. Burnett," *Confederate Veteran* (Aug 1909): 399; Clarke, *David G. Burnet*, 236–237.

61 "Souvenirs of War," *The Mobile Times*, Jan. 14, 1866; M'Conaughy, "Gallant Col. William E. Burnett," 399; *ORA* 49, pt. 1, 318.

62 M'Conaughy, "Gallant Col. William E. Burnett,"399; *ORA* 49, pt. 1, 318.

greatly lamented by all of us, who knew and admired him as a skillful soldier and accomplished gentleman."[63]

Burnet's death led to a scuffle between Cmdr. George W. Harrison of the CSS *Morgan* and Capt. John W. Gillespie, an ordnance officer from Maury's staff. Harrison refused a request from Maury to take Burnet's body on board the *Morgan* and demanded Gillespie, who delivered the request, to leave his ship. Maury managed to find another boat for Burnet's body to be transported to the city, where he was laid to rest on April 2.[64]

The following day, in Mobile, Gillespie confronted Harrison and forced him on his back with his "legs kicking up frantically towards heaven," then choked him with one hand and made hostile demonstrations with the other. Maury witnessed the confrontation and told Harrison "very plainly what he thought of the affair." Afterward, Farrand relieved Harrison from the command of the *Morgan*, replacing him with Capt. Joseph Fry. "Poor dog—everybody gives him a kick." Gillespie "won the undying gratitude and admiration of this community by administering a dose of corporeal chastisement to the unpopular captain," observed one soldier who witnessed the fight.[65]

Maury's wife and her friends, who thought a great deal of the young officer, assumed the duties relating to his funeral. Mrs. Twelors, in whose home Burnet had been quartered in Mobile, allowed him to be buried in her family's private lot at Mobile's Magnolia Cemetery. Maury penned a letter to David Burnet informing him of his son's death. The general noted that he relied upon his son more than anyone and found him the best-educated soldier he had ever known. "He had many excellent qualities. His courage was of the highest order. He was kind to all, had no prejudices, was modest and unobtrusive. His death was a great loss, and

63 *ORA* 49, pt. 2, 1179; Dabney H. Maury, "Col William Estey Burnet," Find A Grave, accessed June 13, 2016, https://www.findagrave.com/memorial/65156612/william-estey-burnet; *ORA* 49, pt. 1, 318.

64 "Confederate States Staff Officers—G Surnames—Access Genealogy," Access Genealogy, accessed Sep. 10, 2017, https://www.accessgenealogy.com/military/confederate-states-staff-officers-g-surnames.htm; Robert Tarleton to SBL, Apr. 3, 1865, Tarleton Family Papers, Yale University Library Archives, New Haven, CT, hereafter RT to SB, Apr. 3, 1865.

65 *ORN* 22, 60, 98; *ORN* 21, 575,577–578, 583–587; "The Fighting at Mobile," *Richmond* [VA] *Dispatch*, Aug. 16, 1864, 1; RT to SB, Apr. 3, 1865. The *Richmond Dispatch* reported that Harrison commanded the CSS *Morgan* during the battle of Mobile Bay. The vessel escaped relatively unscathed during the battle, which caused Harrison to be criticized for staying out of range of Farragut's guns and prematurely retiring from the engagement. After the battle, at 11 p.m. on the same day, he and his crew made a daring escape up the bay, while being hotly pursued by "two monitors and two double enders." He managed to guide the *Morgan* to the safety of Mobile at daybreak. Apparently, Harrison continued to command the *Morgan* during the early stages of the siege of Mobile. After this incident, Capt. Joseph Fry replaced him.

he could not be replaced. General Beauregard had been so impressed with the young soldier that he had confidently told him about important inventions he had applied to the service of artillery," acknowledged Maury. After reading the letter, the anguished Burnet took down his Bible and inscribed these words:

> William Este Burnet, born July 7, 1833, at 6 o'clock a.m. at Oakland, Harris County, Texas, was killed at Spanish Fort near Mobile on the 31st of March, 1865, a victim to an unhappy war, and I only am left, poor and desolate. Oh God! Thy will be done, and give me the grace to submit cheerfully to it. D. G. B.[66]

Benton's Division of Granger's Corps established itself close to Fort McDermott. Captain Riley B. Stearns and his men of the 7th Vermont occupied the exposed location, far beyond any continuous line of rifle pits. The Federals had not yet dug continuous approaches needed for a retreat or reinforcement. Not one to sit on his hands, Gibson ordered a sortie to dislodge them and eliminate the threat to his battery.[67]

During the day, Gibson's Brigade devoted a good deal of attention to Stearns, and from time to time, they shelled his position vigorously. Later in the afternoon, in preparation for the attack, Gibson's men started a brush fire on the right of Stearns's position; the smoke blew over and in front of him. The fire "lit up the scene to almost grandeur." Having stood the terrific shelling, Stearns now feared being burned or smoked out as the wind sent the fire in his direction. He ordered his men to fall back. The Confederates were ready; they fired a volley as soon as the first man started back, and Stearns immediately rescinded his order. Just before dusk, the fire had extended to his rear and on his left, making so dense a smoke as to seclude him entirely. The guns of the garrison were still bearing down on him without mercy. In less than 10 minutes, 15 shells exploded around the single pit where Stearns and his men were posted. Expecting an assault, he ordered his men to fix bayonets.[68]

Captain Clement S. Watson, his inspector-general, and A. E. Newton, Company E, 4th Louisiana Battalion, were in charge of the attack. Around sunset, the shelling suddenly stopped; Watson and his men moved out and swiftly attacked the Vermonters. The sudden charge left Stearns unable to resist. "I gave the order to fire, which was obeyed by the majority of my men, but the next instant, every

---

66 Clarke, *David G. Burnet*, 237.

67 Andrews, *History of the Campaign of Mobile*, 166–167; *ORA* 49, pt. 1, 316.

68 Holbrook, *7th Regiment of Vermont*, 174; Sperry, *History of the 33d Iowa Infantry*, 142; Andrews, *History of the Campaign of Mobile*, 85–86.

man had at least one musket at his head, with a summons to surrender," reported Stearns. "I found two muskets and a revolver pointed at me, with a request to come out of the pit."[69]

The sortie succeeded; Gibson reported that Watson drove the Federals back, killed a large number, and captured Captain Stearns and 21 enlisted men. With their success, the triumphant party remembered their fallen artillery chief.[70]

An officer of the 28th Wisconsin expressed a low opinion of the 7th Vermont. As he put it: "The 7th Vermont ("the White Reg't." our men call it) fell back again, like a pack of cowards as they are. This is the second or third time that they have done the same thing. They left me unsupported last Tuesday night when I was out so that it was only by doing the best I knew that I kept the rebs from flanking me & 'gobbling up' my two companies." The Wisconsinite added that the remainder of the 7th Vermont was taken from the line and put on fatigue duty, "disgraced in fact, as we consider it."

The 7th Vermont had experienced similar accusations in the past. During the defense of Baton Rouge in 1862, Gen. Benjamin Butler ordered the flag of the 7th Vermont not to be borne by them in consequence of the regiment's supposedly breaking in confusion and losing their colors, even though the enemy did not press them. Colonel Holbrook appealed for a court of inquiry, and the regiment was acquitted of the charges of abandoning its colors and disobeying orders. The court, however, determined the regiment did flee about 100 feet in a disorderly manner.[71]

After the war, a soldier of the 77th Illinois reflected: "Now I always believed there was as brave men in the 7th Vt. as in any other regiment in the field, but they certainly were not properly officered. There is but very little difference in a regiment of men, but a set of weak, inefficient officers will ruin any regiment."[72]

Despite the criticism, members of the 7th Vermont defended Stearns. Colonel Holbrook, with several officers from his own and other regiments, went to the position occupied by Stearns after the siege. Holbrook declared: "it was the

69 *ORA* 49, pt. 1, 316; *ORA* 49, pt. 2, 1178; Holbrook, *7th Regiment of Vermont*, 176.

70 *ORA* 49, pt. 1, 316; *ORA* 49, pt. 2, 1178; George S. Waterman, "Afloat-Afield-Afloat," *Confederate Veteran* VIII (Feb. 1900): 55; *Mobile Advertiser and Register*, Apr. 1, 1865. The prisoners, all belonging to Company K, 7th Vermont, arrived in Mobile on Apr. 1, 1865. The names of 20 prisoners appeared in the *Mobile Advertiser and Register* as follows: Capt. Riley B. Stearns, 1st Sgt. D. Spalding, 3rd Sgt. Charles Bailey, 4th Sgt. George R. Waterman, 5th Sgt. John Coburn, Cpl. C.W. Libbay, Cpl. W. H. Hudson, Cpl. A. McGillivery, Privates Geo. Sullivan, Levi J. Fowley, H. F. Hadlock, S. F. Small, Charles Busbey, H. E. Vernon, W. O. Cochran, Harry M. Small, Peter Meinsso, L. Goodwin, E. C. Murphy, and Hugh Lucas.

71 Stevens and Blackburn, *"Dear Carrie,"* 306, 308; "7th Vermont Was Not Properly Officered," *The National Tribune*, Sep. 2, 1886, 3; "Seventh Vermont," *Rutland Daily Herald*, 4.

72 "7th Vermont Was Not Properly Officered," *The National Tribune*, Sep. 2, 1886, 3.

opinion of all that none but a hero could have held out as he did, and it was conceded that his conspicuous bravery and that of his men deserved the highest commendation and praise."[73]

Shortly after his capture, Stearns found himself before General Gibson, whom he described as a "mild-looking man of about 35 and very pleasant speech." Gibson respectfully offered to share his supper of cold fowl and water. He told Stearns that he had never seen troops stand shelling as they had that day. He also informed him that in the morning, they had killed his artillery chief and wounded several others.[74]

Gibson heaped praise on Watson and the others of the sortie party. "These brave comrades deserve the thanks and have entitled themselves to the admiration of this army," he wired Maury's headquarters. Maury's reply fully echoed Gibson's commendation, assuring "them of the admiration of this army." A couple of days later, Gibson recommended that Watson be promoted to major for his part in the gallant sortie.[75]

Acutely aware of the importance of morale, Gibson reported that the attack "inspired our troops with a bolder spirit and the enemy with increased caution." After this charge, however, the Federals vigilantly guarded against sudden attacks, and though frequent combat at points took place and further sorties were considered, Gibson determined none could be carried out with a reasonable chance of success.[76]

Federals

Nevertheless, Gibson's bold tactics had earned the besiegers' respect. "This siege of this fort had begun five days ago, and taking it by storm was not even thinkable," remarked a private belonging to the 5th Minnesota in a letter to his sister, "for the fort is very solid, and it would take thousands of men to take it by storm."[77]

In Granger's front, artillery firing went on nearly all the time, and musketry rattled continually between the opposing skirmishers. An officer with the 26th New York Artillery recorded in his diary that they opened their battery at 8:00 a.m.,

73 Fisher Diary, Mar. 31, 1865; Holbrook, *7th Regiment of Vermont*, 181.

74 R. B. Stearns to C. C. Andrews, Apr. 13, 1866, C. C. Andrews Papers, MNHS; Andrews, *History of the Campaign of Mobile*, 87; Holbrook, *7th Regiment of Vermont*, 177, 180.

75 *ORA* 49, pt. 2, 1178, 1181, 1191.

76 *ORA* 49, pt. 1, 316.

77 Charles W. "Karl" Bachmann, *Charles W. Bachmann and Family Papers*, 1865, MNHS, St. Paul, MN, hereafter *Bachmann, Charles W. Bachmann and Family Papers*.

firing 100 rounds during the day. "Though the siege had now lasted but four days or five days, we felt already well used to it," recalled a soldier of Benton's Division. "The regular booming of the half hour guns was an accustomed sound, and the lively contest of artillery just before sun-down was looked for as a thing of course."[78]

In a private letter home to his wife, one officer from the 28th Wisconsin criticized the leadership of the XIII Corps. "I don't think our part of it is handled with the greatest ability," complained the officer. "Smith Corps is all right, I guess. Canby is here."[79]

A Confederate wharf boat, used as quarters at Huger, had somehow been cut loose and drifted down and lodged diagonally opposite McDermott and about five hundred yards distant. The Federals believed the boat gave range to the Secessionists' guns. Soldiers of Bertram's Brigade, led by 1Lt. Newton C. Ridenour, acting aide-de-camp of the 23rd Iowa, and five members of the 94th Illinois, paddled out in a small skiff to the vessel. Some of Thatcher's fleet, initially suspecting them to be Confederates, opened on them, but, by signals, they were soon made to cease. Spanish Fort then opened fire on them from all the guns pointing in that direction and with musketry. Ridenour and the men went through the shower of shots and shells to the boat, boarded, and examined it. They returned to their skiff and paddled themselves back under the cover of fire from the squadron. The Graybacks hit their skiff several times. However, they all made it back safely and were greeted by the loud cheers of thousands of their comrades, who watched them from the bluff. Even the garrison recognized and admired their bravery. That night, Gibson sent men down and burned the vessel.[80]

Just before dusk, the Confederates shelled the besiegers furiously. An officer of the 20th Wisconsin claimed the rebel mortars were the most bothersome. "One shell passed through my pit and came pretty near my head and several other men," he recorded.[81]

Gumtree Mortars

Both armies built wooden mortars from gum tree stumps to augment the conventional mortars for use in their advanced trenches. "Coehorn mortars were very useful, especially to us, because of the great scarcity of ammunition," Maury noted. The Confederate short-range gum-tree mortars were hollowed out

---

78 Sperry, *History of the 33d Iowa Infantry*, 142; Millard Diary, Mar. 31, 1865.

79 Stevens and Blackburn, *"Dear Carrie,"* 302.

80 Andrews, *History of the Campaign of Mobile*, 83–84.

81 Miller, *Captain Edward Gee Miller*, 31.

Chaplain Elijah Edwards, 7th Minnesota, Marshall's Brigade, sketched this image of a Union gumtree mortar at Spanish Fort in his journal on April 10, 1865. *DePauw University Archives*

to eight and ten-inch caliber, lined with sheet iron, and hooped with iron. "It was an exceedingly busy time, as the Confederates had improvised some mortars, made from pine logs and bound with iron bands, with which they tossed shells into the trenches almost every minute of the day," remembered one officer of the 33rd Illinois. These shells could easily be seen in their flight and were generally successfully dodged, but it kept the men very busy running back, forth, and around the corners.[82]

Union forces fired the gumtree mortars from their advanced trenches. The Federals dubbed the improvised weapons "Fighting Quakers." One soldier of the 94th Illinois described the mortars thusly: "A tough piece of gum log was selected, properly hollowed out, banded with strong iron bands and mounted on a slab." The *New Orleans Times-Democrat* declared them "small but destructive engines of war." Six wooden mortars of 4.62 caliber were made for each of Smith's two divisions at Spanish Fort, ingeniously built by Minnesotans of Wellman's Pioneers. The mortars were derived from 15-inch sections of sweetgum trees that were 12 inches in diameter, with the bore 9 inches deep. The barrels were bored with a 2-inch auger, then reamed to size (4 inches] and strapped with iron. They were conventionally bored with a powder chamber and vent and launched many 6-12 pound shells into Spanish Fort. The wooden mortars were carried into the trenches by teams of two to four men. Using a small powder charge, they could throw a shell, with a very short fuse, directly into Spanish Fort. Pleased with the

---

82 "Souvenirs of the War," *New Orleans Daily Crescent*, 4; Maury, "Defense of Spanish Fort," 135; Elliott, *Thirty-Third Regiment*, 8.

effectiveness of the Gumtree mortars, Gen. A. J. Smith reported they "rendered excellent service."[83]

"The mortars are feared more than anything else. They throw shell 120 pounds which come plump down on one," recalled Col. Thomas H. Herndon, commander of the 36th Alabama. There were niches in the walls of the earthworks that the Southern soldiers could sit in, seemingly protected on three sides. One unfortunate soldier of Holtzclaw's Brigade met a gruesome death when a Federal mortar shell, on its descent, struck him as he rested in one of the niches. A water bucket-sized mortar shell crushed his head and appeared to explode in the middle of his chest. One Alabamian recalled the horrifying details: "He was literally blown into bits, scattered to the four winds. I recollect joining in the hunt for the fragments of his body, but little of it was found." Another soldier from Holtzclaw's Brigade further described the grisly aftermath: "One arm over the breastworks one part of his body here and another there, the litter bearer gathered up his remains and rolled them up in a blanket buried near the trench."[84]

The Confederates could see the lit fuse on the shells at night and could usually dodge them. They would wait until the shell descended, then run down the line for safety before returning to their positions. "You could not rest day nor night for these mortar shells," recollected a private of the 58th Alabama. The Federals "would throw shells over the breastworks like throwing a ball over a house."[85]

Many men scattered in the open space behind the works and focused on dodging the mortar shells. Private Phillip D. Stephenson, 5th Company, Washington Artillery, became adept at anticipating where the shells would land. His fellow soldiers would look to him to guide them out of harm's way. His officer would say, "Sing out, Stephenson, and tell us which way to run!"[86]

Contrary to Colonel Lockett's assertion during the construction of Spanish Fort, bombproofs were essential protection against the intense bombardment. "It was good for us that our bombproofs were well constructed, and some surcease; otherwise human nature could not stood the strain," recalled George Waterman.[87]

83 Hubbard, "Civil War Papers," 629, LC; "Mobile Expedition," *New Orleans Times-Democrat*, 2; Allen, "Operations Against the City of Mobile," 77; *Gum-tree Mortar Barrel*, Minnesota Historical Collections Database, 4225.H576, Sep. 4, 2016, MNHS, St. Paul, MN; Reed, *Twelfth Regiment Iowa*, 229; *ORA* 49, pt. 1, 229; Bailey, *A Gazetteer of McLean County* (Chicago, IL, 1866), 50.

84 Herndon, "My Dear Wife"; Jones and Pulcrano, History of the Eighteenth Alabama, 65.

85 Jones and Pulcrano, *Eighteenth Alabama Infantry Regiment*, 64; J. S. E. Robinson, "Reminiscences of the War between the States," AUM.

86 Stephenson & Hughes, *Civil War Memoir of Philip Daingerfield Stephenson*, 363–364.

87 Waterman, "Afloat-Afield-Afloat," 1900b, 53–54.

Lithograph of bombproofs at Spanish Fort. *Alabama Department of Archives and History*

Gibson's men proved themselves as worthy adversaries during the initial stages of the siege. The U.S. skirmish lines, nevertheless, continued to advance closer each night. Gibson knew the strength of the besiegers would continue to grow, and their siege train would soon open on the fort. In a general order, he urged his brigade commanders to strengthen the main works and skirmish lines and stressed the necessity of vigilance and energy. "You must dig, dig, dig," the Louisianan ordered. "Nothing can save us but the spade."[88]

---

88 Ridge Diary, Mar. 31, 1865; *ORA* 49, pt. 2, 1180, 1181. A siege train consisted of heavy guns and mortars designed to batter and destroy fortifications with solid shot or shell, and dismount cannons.

Chapter 11

"The Rebels Do Not Seem Willing to Retreat"

Federals

Saturday, April 1, 1865: "'April's fool's day,' as this proved to a good many of our boys. The bombardment still progresses," pointed out one officer of XVI Corps. The weather was warm all day, and the cannon fire made it even hotter.[1]

Although Huger and Tracey were ordered to hold their fire due to a shortage of ammunition, the Southern gunboats and artillery batteries of Spanish Fort continued to launch their shells at the Federals, albeit more judiciously. Cannonading and sharpshooting started early in the morning and continued as usual. Despite the more deliberate expenditure of ammunition, one soldier of the 94th Illinois recorded in his diary: "The shells came over as thick almost as hail."[2]

"Our men are close up under the enemies works sapping & mining like gophers & are making remarkable progress. The enemy keeps up a terrible fire on us day & night," noted one Bluecoat. After six days of siege operations, the Federals had built extensive trenches, breastworks, and bombproofs. "Part of our men in camp live in holes dug in the ground, covered with timbers & earth, to protect them from shot & shell from the enemy's batteries," noted an officer of

---

1 Fike Diary, Apr. 1, 1865; William A. Sweet, Diary, Apr. 1, 1865, Wisconsin Veterans Museum, Madison, WI.

2 Ridge Diary, Apr. 1, 1865; Macy, "Civil War Diary of William M. Macy," 193.

the 28th Wisconsin. A soldier of the 124th Illinois jotted down in his diary: "We enjoyed a good night's rest in our bombproof."[3]

The Federals opened their cannon but were silenced by the artillery of the Southern defenders. "The cannonading and musket firing is incessant; it must not be inferred that all are fighting," Chaplain Elijah E. Edwards, 7th Minnesota, recorded. Many of the veterans had adapted to the continual artillery and musketry fire. Edwards observed: "Some are firing in a desultory manner. Some are reclining and sleeping under the shelter of bombproofs; others hide in a grave-like hollow excavated in the sides of the hills. Some are reading; some are just playing cards." Some of the soldiers even organized baseball games in camp. "Their coolness is refreshing," remarked Edwards.[4]

Although the men found time for leisure, they could not enjoy the fresh seafood they had earlier enjoyed at Dauphin Island and Mobile Point. "We have a nice camp among the pines on high ground with good water but not much to eat since we have got out of reach of the oyster fisheries nothing but pickle pork & hardtack," recognized one officer. "It is about to get me down again."[5]

To counter the Federal battery on the bluffs of Minette Bay, Liddell dispatched his garrison artillery chief, Capt. John B. Grayson, and two batteries (Culpepper's and Winston's) from Blakeley. In the morning, Grayson's artillerists opened an enfilading fire into the rear of the Indianians from the north side of Minette Bay. "It has stopped them from firing and put them to digging, and in some places run them out of the swamp," reported Gibson, who requested the fire to continue. Moreover, Grayson's fire created a dangerous environment in the camps of the XVI Corps. "Men can face almost any danger when they are engaged in it, but even old soldiers never acquire a relish for punishment when off duty. They like to be permitted to rest in safety," noted Chaplain Howard, 124th Illinois. The appearance of Major General Steele's advance, however, caused Liddell to withdraw Grayson back to Fort Blakeley.[6]

The Federals also found the Confederates had dug advance rifle pits during the night to head off their advance. The gray soldiers opened a brisk fire on the besiegers from these pits. "Those who came here under the impression that we had

---

3 JFD to wife, Apr. 1, 1865; Stevens and Blackburn, *"Dear Carrie,"* 306; Snedeker, *The Civil War Diary of Charles Henry Snedeker.*

4 Sweet Diary, Apr. 1, 1865; Edwards Journal, Mar. 30, 1865, 250.

5 JFD to wife, Apr. 1, 1865.

6 *ORA* 49, pt. 2, 1184, 1189; Howard, *124th Regiment,* 303.

During the siege, chaplain Elijah Edwards, 7th Minnesota, sketched this Union bombproof in his journal on April 2, 1865. *Depauw University Archives*

an easy job have had that idea dispelled several days since," realized an officer of the 122nd Illinois Regiment.[7]

That afternoon, Pvt. Sidney E. Weston—a 17-year-old with the 7th Vermont in his first battle—learned first-hand that the Confederates still had plenty of fight left in them. A captain of the 91st Illinois who had come up to check on the men in the rifle pits in front of Benton's Division had carelessly exposed himself, and a vigilant Confederate shot him in the hand. The officer hollered in unbearable pain and called out to comrades that he was hit. Weston thought he could help and cautiously went down the hill to the suffering man. While lying on his belly as bullets whistled over his head, Weston took the officer's sash off his body and wrapped it around his wounded hand. After helping the wounded officer, Weston returned to his position, but the Graybacks saw him and sent a volley his way. He dropped behind a log for a few minutes before crawling 15 to 20 feet on his hands and knees. According to Weston, after a few moments of waiting, he then "jumped up and ran if I ever did, dodging sideways so that they could not have a chance to aim at me and so got through safe."[8]

Gibson's efforts to create an exaggerated impression of his garrison size deceived the besiegers. One officer of Smith's Corps remarked: "They have thrown a very

7 Howard, *124th Regiment*, 303; JFD to wife, Apr. 1, 1865.

8 Weston, "Dear Parent."

heavy force into the fort & it is supposed by our Gen[era]ls that the most of the force for the defense of Mobile are in that fort. They have been reinforcing it day & night since we arrived." Gibson's bold and aggressive sorties helped perpetuate the illusion of a large force inside the fort. As one Federal officer put it, the Graybacks came down on us "like a whirlwind." In reality, Gibson lacked enough men to defend the works adequately. "We did not have enough to man the fort as it ought to have been done, not by half. We had only men enough to fill the trenches three or four feet apart," recalled a soldier of Holtzclaw's Brigade.[9]

U.S. Navy

Around 1:00 p.m., the U.S. Navy tinclad *Rodolph*, Acting Master N. M. Dyer commanding, received orders to take a barge containing apparatus for raising the *Milwaukee*. The ironclad crossed the Blakeley bar with the apparatus to the wreck of the *Milwaukee* when, at 2:40 p.m., she exploded a torpedo under her starboard bow and rapidly sank in twelve feet of water. It appeared that a hole had been made in her ten feet in diameter that exploded her boilers. The blast killed four of her crew and wounded seven, of whom five were Black sailors.[10]

The torpedoes caused the U.S. Navy to approach the works timidly. This was understandable, considering three of the five vessels lying in the channel nearest the fort had been blown up. Thatcher had lost three gunboats in just four days. "It should be said, in justice to the fleet, that they never showed fear, but rather an excess of the contrary; and that the enemy which they had to meet, to wit; concealed torpedoes and impregnable walls of piling, are those against which the best combinations and the greatest bravery are of little avail," the *New York Times* reported.[11]

Thatcher's vessels continually swept the channel to fish out torpedoes. Despite their efforts, the Confederates continued to let loose the instruments of destruction from below their obstructions to sweep down with the current. Though demoralized, the naval officers doubled their vigilance and detailed boats to search for the dreaded torpedoes. They usually caught torpedoes from a ship by dragging them with a grappling iron. Some vessels were fitted with 10-foot spars with nets attached to the bows to catch and explode the torpedoes before they struck the

9 JFD to wife, Apr. 1, 1865; Jones and Pulcrano, *Eighteenth Alabama Infantry Regiment*, 67.

10 Andrews, *History of the Campaign of Mobile*, 94.

11 JFD to wife, Apr. 1, 1865; "In Mobile Bay," *The National Tribune*, Oct. 13, 1887, 3; Truman, "The Siege of Mobile," *New York Times*, Apr. 21, 1865, 8.

The destruction of the USS *Rodolph* on April 1, 1865. *Naval History and Heritage Command*

hull. They also laid netting across the channel at the mouth of the Blakeley River to intercept the torpedoes.[12]

The *Mobile Advertiser & Register* reported: "New Orleans was conquered by the Federal navy, and (General Benjamin) Butler and the troops only occupied what the fleet had won. Here their fleet is 'out of the ring,' and ours is in. Nature and our engineers have barred the Yankee fleet out of the fight."[13]

The devastating effect of the torpedoes left a profound impression on Federal naval personnel. A few months after the war, Lt. Cmdr. Theodore B. Dubois, captain of the USS *Albatross* during the siege, declared that "the Confederate torpedoes are the greatest invention of the age, and will render forts and batteries unnecessary as harbor defenses." Dubois added he would "undertake the guardianship of any port, at a cost not greater than that of a monitor, if they will give him the man who made and laid down those torpedoes as an assistant."[14]

12 "Rebellion in the Gulf States Dead," *Chicago Tribune*, Apr. 18, 1865, 3; Waterman, "Afloat-Afield-Afloat," *Confederate Veteran* VII (Nov. 1899): 491.

13 "The War at Home," *Mobile Advertiser & Register*, Apr. 7, 1865.

14 "See Second Page of This Morning's Picayune," *Times Picayune*, Nov. 9, 1865, 4; *ORN* 22, 14, 120.

Confederates

While the disasters depressed the fleet, the Graybacks celebrated. The destruction of these mighty warships caused much jubilation among the Confederates, who fired salutes from Spanish Fort and the guns of the *Nashville*. Nowhere else in the war did torpedoes accomplish such remarkable results as Mobile Bay, which essentially paralyzed Thatcher's powerful squadron.[15]

"But for the torpedoes, Farragut's fleet would have greatly embarrassed the defense. But they could only use their guns of the greatest range because all of them who ventured close in were sunk," Maury claimed. "They usually blew out a section of the bottom eight feet by ten. The ships sunk immediately. As the water was shoal, few of the people were killed on these ships. But all the other ships were profoundly impressed and kept well away from where these torpedoes were supposed to be awaiting them." The Confederate torpedoes indeed neutralized the Union Navy and significantly diminished its ability to assist Canby's land forces. Several more vessels went down long after the Confederates left Mobile.[16]

George S. Waterman, the Confederate naval officer from New Orleans, and a comrade arrived at the fort and sought out their hometown friends in the Washington Artillery's 5th Company. They observed the tremendous damage caused by the Federal batteries: "Not a yard of ground or a house had escaped the iron and leaden scythes; the very grass was mowed." Soon, they came upon General Gibson, who intently watched the Federal lines with field glasses as he approached. Waterman's recollections reveal the characteristic courage and coolness displayed by Gibson during the siege. He asked Gibson for the location of the Washington Artillery. The general kindly invited them to have a seat as bullets whizzed by and offered to personally lead them to Battery Blair, the location of the 5th Company. "Unmindful of the bullets, he raised his glasses to survey the enemy with characteristic nonchalance for several minutes," remembered Waterman. "A bullet angrier than the others skipped past his ear, over our heads, and struck the tent at about the height of a man seated in a chair." This prompted the soldiers inside the tent to scramble out. Gibson, seemingly unconcerned, then calmly guided them to the 5th Company. "While there was grim humor in his cautious reference to the hill country, with its sharpshooters in the treetops, as well as on the hilltops, we reached the old parade ground, which had been made bare as a floor," recalled Waterman. "Here we made a stand, the General straight as an arrow, while his 'colleagues' looked 'two ways for Sunday.'" When they came within 150 yards

15 Waterman, "Afloat-Afield-Afloat,"1899a, 491.

16 Maury, "Spanish Fort," 135; Maury, "Mobile," 11.

of their journey's end, they bid the general farewell. Gibson wished them a happy arrival and returned to his observation point.[17]

Just as Waterman arrived at Battery Blair, Lt. Abe Leverich and Sgt. James F. Giffen of the Washington Artillery were both struck by the same bullet from a sharpshooter's rifle. The bullet penetrated Leverich's cheek and lodged in Giffen's shoulder.[18]

His comrades took him to the supposed safety of their bombproof, or "gopher hole," where they slept and ate. Waterman described it as a "log house covered with three layers of pine logs and six feet of earth." Even the bombproof could be a dangerous place—as roll call was being conducted, a sudden crash was heard, and a fused shell came to a halt about two feet within the door of the gopher hole. "Not a syllable was uttered, but such a display of nimbleness was never equaled before football came around, and there were more artillerists in the flesh and spirit stowed into one corner than Armour, Swift, or Morris could pack in an hour. Here we huddled—minutes? no seconds," recalled Waterman. He added: "But New Orleans boys are always equal to the emergency." Orderly Sergeant John Bartley seized the unwelcome shell and threw it out.[19]

To Gibson's dismay, Maury decided to further reduce the strength of Spanish Fort's garrison by transferring Ector's Brigade back to French's Division at Fort Blakeley to counter Steele's arrival. He immediately protested the order: "Much the largest force of the enemy is here (two corps). This place is closely invested and weaker by far than Blakeley. Large detachments from Holtzclaw's brigade are at Blakeley. The losses in my own have been heavy. There are already many more troops at Blakeley than here. Can't you let me keep Ector's Brigade a day or two longer? The withdrawal of it just now renders this position hazardous in the extreme."[20]

Gibson summoned his brigade commanders—except for Col. Julius Andrews, who commanded Ector's Brigade—to a council of war. Each officer was asked their opinion of holding their position with the reduced force. All agreed that the fort would be untenable if the Federals assaulted it. Gibson wired Maury of their collective opinion and pleaded to keep Ector's Brigade. Despite the crippling reduction of men, he made a point to say the garrison would remain steadfast in its duty. "Let me assure you of one thing," he declared, "whatever force is left

17 Waterman, "Afloat-Afield-Afloat,"1900c, 23.

18 Waterman, "Afloat-Afield-Afloat," 1900c, 23.

19 Ibid., 24. Armour, Swift, or Morris was a large national meat packing company.

20 ORA 49, pt. 2, 1185.

Sergeant James F. Giffen, 5th Company, Washington Artillery. *Dr. Glen Cangelosi*

here shall make a defense that will reflect no discredit upon our army. Every officer and man will do his whole duty."[21]

Liddell tried to console Gibson: "I regret very much the withdrawal of such a number of troops from your command, but greater credit will be due General Holtzclaw and yourself by holding out gallantly with your small force, and no one will more readily accord this credit to you, General Holtzclaw, and your garrison than myself."[22]

At Gibson's request, Liddell telegraphed Maury to request Ector's Brigade stay put. Maury responded flatly: "I decided this matter when at Blakeley. Ector's Brigade must come up to Blakel[e]y." Despite Gibson's barrage of telegrams that night, no record of Maury's reply exists. Maury, however, must have changed his mind; Ector's men remained at Spanish Fort.[23]

Sunday, April 2, 1865: The seventh day of the battle opened clear and mild. The relentless Union siege operations had begun to wear down the beleaguered garrison. Like a python squeezing its prey, the advance lines of the besiegers continued to constrict around Spanish Fort, creeping closer every day. The garrison, nevertheless, continued to resist fiercely. The besieged showed no intention of leaving without a struggle.[24]

Fort McDermott steadfastly anchored the Confederate's right flank. Captain Samuel Barnes, Company C, 22nd Louisiana, commanded the strongest position of Spanish Fort. Roughly 110 men from Barnes's own company and Owen's Arkansas Battery manned McDermott. On March 30, Massenburg's Georgia light artillery arrived from Mobile as reinforcements. The fort boasted 18 guns,

---

21 *ORA* 49, pt. 2, 1186–1187; Colonels Campbell, Jones, Patton, and General Holtzclaw were present.

22 Ibid., 1187.

23 Ibid., 1186–1187.

24 *ORA* 49, pt. 2, 1191; Macy, "Civil War Diary of William M. Macy," 194.

Lieutenant Abe Leverich, 5th Company, Washington Artillery. *Dr. Glen Cangelosi*

including six 6pdr smoothbores, two 24-pdr howitzers, six coehorn mortars, one 6.4 Brook rifle ("Dog Towser"), two 20-pdr Parrott rifles, and one 8-inch mortar.[25]

In the morning, Fort McDermott engaged in a tremendous artillery fight with two sections of Mack's 18th New York Battery. The New Yorkers opened "four 20-pounder rifles" that morning in Granger's front, about 450 yards from McDermott. The besieger's fire was exceedingly accurate. Captain Barnes's men responded with vigorous fire toward Mack's battery. Around 11:00 a.m., Slocomb's Washington Artillerists came to McDermott's support. The latter also received heavy blows from the 1st Indiana 8-inch mortars and the Massachusetts light guns on Mack's left and rear. The 5th Company of Washington Artillery nearly enfiladed Mack's position, throwing their deadly projectiles at him for almost two hours. Mack's batteries were too far from Slocomb's right to bring guns to bear on them, and he could only increase the intensity of his fire on the guns on Fort McDermott, disabling one of their howitzers and silencing all their guns by noon. But at 4:00 p.m., McDermott opened on Mack again, who returned the fire. The 5th Company again joined the fray, and the struggle continued until dark. Mack's works were hit 38 times during the day. Many of the New Yorkers narrowly escaped the hail of shot and shells. Nonetheless, Mack's command reported no casualties. Fort McDermott had suffered the most damage. Its parapet had been defaced, and an 8-inch mortar shell from the 1st Indiana had disabled the carriage of their big Brooks gun. Men on both sides spent that evening repairing the damage to their respective works.[26]

25 Andrews, *History of the Campaign of Mobile*, 71–72, 90; Charles J. Allen, "Some Account and Recollection of the Operations against the City of Mobile and Its Defences, 1864 and 1865," *Glimpse of the Nation's Struggles*, St. Paul 1887, 78.

26 Andrews, *History of the Campaign of Mobile*, 130–131.

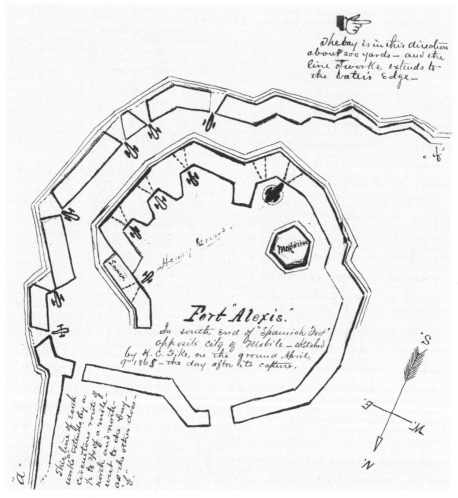

The Federals referred to Fort McDermott as Fort Alexis during the siege. Union officer Capt. Henry Fike, 117th Illinois, drew this sketch on April 9, 1865. *The State Historical Society of Missouri*

Though the Confederates continued to fire at the besiegers, they obeyed Gibson's order to economize the ever-dwindling supply of ammunition to have enough to repel an assault. At Huger, the fort held out in silence while enduring the Federal cannonading. "They annoy us but so far, thank God, have done no damage," remarked a private of the 22nd Louisiana Consolidated. "I am sitting at our big 10-inch gun where myself and the Sergt. sleep. It is about as safe a place as there is at the battery." Inside Spanish Fort, the veterans of Holtzclaw's and Ector's Brigades were more deliberate in discharging their muskets than the comparatively green troops of Thomas's Brigade. Despite the disadvantage of having an inadequate supply of ammunition, Gibson remained poised. He wired Maury: "Our losses become smaller every day, our ability to cope with him greater, and the confidence of the officers and men grows stronger and stronger." Gibson requested that one of the iron-clads come down to enfilade the U.S. Army's right flank held by the XVI Corps again. Proactive and aggressive, he informed Maury that he planned to attack Carr's Division to arrest his advance.[27]

Artillery fire from the Indiana battery on Minette Bay made landing steamers at Battery Tracey's wharf, night or day, exceedingly difficult and risky. To secure a safer means of communication with the city, men worked on a second treadway from the rear of Tracey on Bateau Bay to Conway Bayou for communication with Mobile.[28]

Federals

The Federals conducted a routine inspection, which took place at 8:00 a.m. for those not on duty. A war correspondent from the *New Orleans Times* poignantly described the dawn at Spanish Fort:

> The Sabbath was ushered in by a glorious sun shining forth, dispelling by its effulgence the shades of the dark and lonely night, and giving, by its brightness a foretaste of the bliss of heaven. The few feathered songsters which have not been startled away by the thundering din of battle warbled forth their delicious lays and sang in sweet strains their little tales of love. The bands of the various divisions and brigades burst forth almost simultaneously with ravishing and exquisite music—the atmosphere was cool and refreshing—in short, it was Sunday morning. According to one account, "the cheering strains of the brass bands" were heard all along the line. The Spanish Fort artillerists even appeared to try to blend the explosion of a shell with this agreeable music. Many soldiers on both sides started their day listening to the preaching of their respective chaplains in the operating lines and in camp. The pleasant environment, however, soon faded as the deafening racket of cannonading and musketry fire continued with more intensity.[29]

After working all day and night getting their artillery into position, the artillerists of Mack's New York Battery opened fire on Spanish Fort at 9:00 a.m.

---

27 *ORA* 49, pt. 2, 1191–1192; "The Lady Slocomb," *New Orleans Times-Democrat*, Sep. 20, 1899, 7; ML to AH, Apr. 2, 1865; Maury, "Defence of Mobile in 1865," 11; *ORA* 49, pt. 2, 1192.

28 Hewitt, *Supplement to the Official Records*, pt. 1, vol. 7, 943, 960.

29 "The Mobile Expedition," *New Orleans Times-Democrat*, Apr. 8, 1865, 2; Andrews, *History of the Campaign of Mobile*, 130.

"Got a sharp reply. We dismounted a gun for them in the afternoon," one of the battery's soldiers noted in his journal.[30]

One private of the 14th Wisconsin observed: "It is almost two years since I had to write under such circumstances as the present. We are right in the midst of a siege similar to that of Vicksburg, 'only more so,' & we have had to pass thro' a good many dangers."[31]

"It was unsafe for a man to show his head above the breastworks for a single moment. Many men were shot through pure carelessness or recklessness in exposing themselves on the line, and many were shot in holding the skirmish lines at the extreme front," recalled one U.S. officer. Another soldier of the 14th Wisconsin described it in his diary: "Death every day." Despite the dangers, Maj. Gen. Gordon Granger visited the trenches and "gave one of the boys all the tobacco he had." His presence among the men boosted morale.[32]

The wounds inflicted on the XVI Army Corps were typically from shells or their splinters, which caused horrifying gashes. In particular, gunboats shelling them from the river caused Carr's Division on the extreme right heavy casualties. Elsewhere on the Union lines, the wounds were chiefly caused by minie-balls— the men not being as exposed as Carr's men were during the early stages of the siege. The U.S. field hospitals were known to be clean and thoroughly organized; the patients carefully and efficiently treated. If capable of being transported, the seriously wounded were taken to Starke's Wharf to disembark to hospitals in New Orleans.[33]

"The rebs shot 100-pound shells at us 6.4 inches in diameter at us," pointed out an officer of the 1st Indiana Heavy Artillery. "They cut down trees 12 to 16 inches in diameter. I have seen them hit the side of a tree & go through—not changing their course apparently." A tree stump in the rear of Benton's Division had been cut down for the breastworks. Several men were standing around it, talking, when a shell came over and cut in half a musket sticking in the ground nearby, struck the stump, and passed on without hitting any person. "Those who were there said that it would seem impossible for anything to hit the stump without going through some of the men who were gathered so close around it," remembered a soldier of the 33rd Iowa.[34]

---

30 "Civil War Diary of Henry M. Dryer."

31 Newton & Ambrose, "The Siege of Mobile," 596.

32 Byers, Iowa, 406–407; Wittenberger, "Frank Wittenberger Civil War Diary"; Miller, *Captain Edward Gee Miller*, 31.

33 "The Mobile Expedition," *New Orleans Times-Democrat*, Apr. 8, 1865, 2.

34 RHC to PMC; Sperry, *History of the 33d Iowa Infantry*, 141.

Union Chaplain Elijah Edwards, 7th Minnesota, Marshall's Brigade, sketched this scene of Federals holding up a decoy over the breastworks during the siege on April 3, 1865. *DePauw University Archives*

The Federals responded to the Confederate fire in kind; they were by no means helplessly succumbing to the fire from Spanish Fort. "The 1st and 4th Indiana batteries, and the 14th Indiana heavy artillery, the nearest to the rebel works, are ceaselessly sending their missiles of death into the Spanish dwelling," observed one correspondent, adding, "Their situation must be frightful."[35]

Confederates

Monday, April 3, 1865: The eighth day of the siege presented some fine weather, but the heavy pounding of guns had kept the garrison up all night. "It is digging all night and fighting all day," Gibson telegraphed Maury.[36]

The earth trembled as the battle raged on with little intermission. "Day and night, we were in constant peril," remembered a soldier of Holtzclaw's Brigade. "If a man only lifted his hand above the breastworks a Yankee would take a crack at it."[37]

Head-logs were often knocked down on the Graycoats during the artillery duels, bruising and injuring them. Sharpshooters devoted their attention to the

35 "Rebellion in the Gulf States Dead," *Chicago Tribune*, Apr. 18, 1865, 3.

36 Andrews, *History of the Campaign of Mobile*, 136; "Civil War Diary of Henry M. Dryer"; Waterman, "Afloat-Afield-Afloat,"1900b, 54.

37 Edwards Journal, Apr. 3, 1865, 251; Jones and Pulcrano, *Eighteenth Alabama Infantry Regiment*, 67–68.

fort's portholes or embrasures and fired a steady stream of bullets through them from dusk until day. The Confederate soldiers did not fire much and were more quiet than usual. The U.S. sharpshooters kept them down, and they kept busy inside repairing their works."[38]

Sergeant Fritz Ripley, 21st Alabama, a man known for his genial disposition, displayed an unusually depressed state of mind. He told his friends that he believed he would be killed that day. His comrades tried to change his depressed mood throughout that long day. As nightfall came, he remained unharmed and yet quiet while another teased him about his intuition. Ripley took the ribbing with good nature. Standing tall and stretching back his arms, Ripley happily remarked: "Well, boys, this morning I was as sure—." He never finished the sentence; a sharpshooter's bullet fatally struck him in his expanded chest.[39]

The Confederate skirmishers remained in their advance rifle pits for 24-hour shifts. These pits were about the size and shape of a common grave, with some large logs and dirt piled up on the side facing the besiegers. The men in these holes needed to bring enough food and water to last them for the duration. One evening, Cpl. Edgar W. Jones, Company G, 18th Alabama, occupied a rifle pit with two young Alabamians who had never been under fire. In going on duty that night, Jones did not notice that he had forgotten to bring his water canteen until after daylight the following day. He inquired about the boys and found they were in the same fix. He had raw bacon, fat, and cornbread cooked with salt and water. To escape thirst, he decided not to eat. "I was kept so busy dodging shells and bullets all day that I did not get hungry or thirsty."[40]

Jones and his young companions' rifle pit was about 20 yards in front of Battery Blair, the location of the monstrous *Lady Slocomb*. A U.S. battery with several large cannons faced them about 70 yards east. When either fort fired a shot, it passed directly over them. Jones recalled the powerful concussion the fire of these big guns caused: "The men who operate the guns never remain anywhere to the front but spring back to the rear and hold their fingers thrust in their ears tightly to prevent the awful sound from making them deaf, and even then, these gunners often bleed at the ears." He added: "Every time one of these guns went off, the earth seemed to give way, and I seemed to be lifted six inches from the ground and allowed to fall back rather suddenly."[41]

38 Stephenson, "Defence of Spanish Fort," 122–123; Macy, "Civil War Diary of William M. Macy," 194.

39 William S. McNeill, "Silence of Peace," *Philadelphia Times*, 1891.

40 Jones and Pulcrano, *Eighteenth Alabama Infantry Regiment*, 68.

41 Ibid., 68.

Gibson grimly reported that eight were killed and 16 wounded during the day. One of the casualties, Pvt. James Durrett, Company E, 18th Alabama, had just written a letter to his sister. His cousin Henry, who served with him in the same company, penned a sad note to James's sister: "Dear Cousin, It was with painful regret that I inform you that Jimmy was this evening mortally wounded, being shot directly through the brain. He was wounded about 4 o'clock this evening. While standing in the ditches, he imprudently raised his head to look over at the enemy, which was firing at our line." Henry included the letter James had written and a lock of his hair.[42]

Around 3:00 p.m., the opposing batteries engaged in an artillery duel for about an hour. Jones described the bombardment as "a dozen earthquakes" turned loose. "I was bouncing like a rubber ball, or rather, the earth was dancing under me," he recalled. Federal shots were striking the logs and dirt, knocking them into the pit. The young soldiers would say things like: "I do hope and trust they will quit." "I do pray to the Lord they won't shoot anymore." "Oh, Lord, have mercy," Jones exclaimed to them, "There ain't no use in praying. It won't do any good. You had as well hush." The cannonading would resume, and the boy soldiers would get down, pray, and say, "I wish I were at home." Jones would have to pull them from under dirt and debris thrown in on them. "I never knew the names of these boys, but I think [they] were from Coffee or Covington Counties, or down that way," Jones recalled. "When the duel ceased, I was almost as deaf as a stump."[43]

The garrisons at Huger and Tracey could see and hear constant firing at Spanish Fort, but they still continued to ride out the siege in silence per their orders. "The Yankees fired about half dozen shots at us today. No damage done," observed one Louisianan at Huger. "We sleep at our guns as the shanties here are exposed to the fire of the enemy."[44]

Gibson kept up a barrage of his own during the day—telegrams requesting support. He reported: "I never saw such digging as the enemy does. He is fast converting his advanced skirmish line into his main line." Gibson's men were exhausted. To counter the ever-encroaching threats he faced, he sent dispatches to Maury and Liddell asking for "200 negroes," more entrenching tools, a supply of wooden embrasures, iron screens, hand grenades, gunboat support, and a heavy gun. At 9:00 a.m., he again wired Maury: "Is there no chance to get the gunboat? Can I get 100 negroes with 50 axes and 50 picks'?" He asked Maury if any siege

---

42 *ORA* 49, pt. 2, 1195; Henry Durrett to James's sister Jane, James A. Durrett and Henry Durrett, *The Letters of James A. Durrett,* accessed July 20, 2019, https://durrettblog.wordpress.com/.

43 Jones and Pulcrano, *Eighteenth Alabama Infantry Regiment,* 68–69.

44 ML to AH, Apr. 3, 1865.

mortars from the city's western shore defenses could be spared in yet another dispatch. Later that night, Gibson confirmed the arrival of "a 20-pounder Parrott gun and negroes," yet he remained anxious to receive mortars and the other items he requested. Maury did not have spare axes and shovels in Mobile. However, he forwarded Gibson's request for entrenching tools to Lieutenant General Taylor at his department headquarters in Meridian.[45]

Despite the threat of General Wilson's rapidly moving cavalry force from northern Alabama, Taylor had not given up hope that Forrest's horse soldiers could still help lift the siege in Baldwin County. Taylor sent a dispatch to Forrest, instructing him, depending on the movements of the Federal raiders, to prepare to "operate vigorously upon the flank and rear of the troops besieging Spanish Fort and Blakeley."[46]

Meanwhile, in Mobile Bay, the U.S. Navy continued the painstaking and dangerous process of removing torpedoes as the boats slowly inched their way up the Blakeley River. Waterman carried a letter from Gibson to Fort McDermott for Colonel Patton. From McDermott, he could plainly see the Federal ships slowly moving up the river, dragging their nets for torpedoes. During the previous August, Waterman had served aboard the CSS *Gaines* and recognized some of the vessels he fought against during the battle of Mobile Bay. He watched the monitors *Chickasaw* and *Winnebago* throw some hefty shots toward Fort McDermott. Patton showed him through his field glass the sunken *Milwaukee* and *Rodolph*.[47]

Federals

In front of Carr's Division, gumtree wooden mortars were positioned in some advance rifle pits about 100 yards from the Confederate line. One Minnesotan observed that the mortar shells shot "into the air at an angle so nearly approaching the vertical that they descend at short range, sometimes only a few yards from the mortars from which they were fired." The gumtree mortars used by the XVI Corps were described as being about 2 feet long. The Minnesota pioneers stayed busy making them.[48]

45 *ORA* 49, pt. 2, 1194, 1195, 1200, 1209.

46 *ORA* 49, pt. 2, 1195.

47 Waterman, "Afloat-Afield-Afloat," 1900b, 54.

48 Snedeker, *The Civil War Diary of Charles Henry Snedeker*; Edwards Journal, Mar. 30, 1865, 251; Ridge Diary, Apr 3, 1865.

The light draft monitor USS *Chickasaw* participated in the 1864 Battle of Mobile Bay and in the 1865 Mobile Campaign. *Naval History and Heritage Command*

Garrard's Division moved from its position at Sibley's house to join Steele's Column in the siege of Fort Blakeley.[49]

A "swamp hawk" flew between the opposing lines during the day. Both sides fired several shots at the bird, which soon dropped to the ground. Private William Rowe, 7th Minnesota, Company D, "jumped over the works and ran out in plain sight of the Confederates, picked up the bird, and returned unmolested to his place in the trench." As the reckless Yankee returned to his lines, he removed his hat in recognition of the soldierly courtesy shown him by the Confederates. Just before disappearing in the trenches, he also took the opportunity to taunt the Graycoats by shaking the bird over his head at them. Records show Rowe, who came from Ramsey County (St. Paul area), Minnesota, was only 16 years old and the youngest member of his company. Rowe's service records reveal that he mustered into service on February 11, 1865, so Spanish Fort was his first engagement. Rowe's youth and inexperience helped explain his brave but foolish behavior.[50]

Despite the daily progress made by the Federals, they were still wary of Spanish Fort's strength. In a letter to his sister and brother-in-law, Pvt. Karl Bachmann, 5th Minnesota, noted: "The rebels do not seem willing to retreat, they are well entrenched, and they also have very good positions, for they know well that when this fort will be won, Mobile will also be lost or that they cannot hold it."

49 Gerling, *One Hundred Seventeenth Illinois Infantry*,102.

50 Andrews, *History of the Campaign of Mobile*, 134-135; Brueske, *The Last Siege*, 66. H. P. Van Cleve, *Annual Report of the Adjutant General of the State of Minnesota for the Year Ending December 1, 1866, and of the Military Forces of the State from 1861 to 1866* (St. Paul, MN: Pioneer Print, 1866), 43.

Bachmann described the fort as "very solid" and believed it would "take thousands of men to take it by storm." The threat of sub-terra shells planted in the front of Spanish Fort served as a further deterrent. One evening, skirmishers of the 8th Wisconsin captured a small Confederate post of three men, including an Irishman. When asked if the Confederates had any sub-terra shells in their front, he replied, "I trod light when I came out."[51]

Though many sensed the war would soon be over, the sentiment was not a foregone conclusion. A soldier of the 12th Iowa noted in his diary a wager he made: "If the war closes by the 1st of January, 1866, I will owe Sergeant Hutchins and Corporal Jordan a dinner. If not, Hutchins will owe said dinner to us as per agreement when we were discussing the probable duration of the war."[52]

Waging the long war required effort from the leaders to lift the spirits of the men. Accordingly, the Federals issued whiskey rations. "The men really needed some stimulant to recuperate their strength. No matter what our temperance reformers preach (if they don't practice), I insist, a little whiskey, judiciously given, does the men good, aye, more, is beneficial to their health, which must be somewhat impaired by their late almost superhuman exertions," reported a correspondent from the *New Orleans Times-Democrat*.

Moreover, it finally happened after several days of talk that the quartermaster would issue tobacco. "It seemed almost too good to be true," rejoiced one soldier, "almost as welcome as payday or a mail."[53]

51 Bachmann, *Charles W. Bachmann and Family Papers*; Andrews, *History of the Campaign of Mobile*, 237.

52 Henderson Diary, Apr 3, 1865..

53 Ridge diary, Apr. 3, 1865; "The Mobile Expedition," *New Orleans Times-Democrat*, Apr. 8, 1865, 2; Sperry, *History of the 33d Iowa Infantry*, 142.

Chapter 12

"Inch by Inch"

Confederates

Tuesday, April 4, 1865: Gibson issued special orders to address the ammunition shortage. In yet another example of his characteristic ingenuity, he decided to have the ordnance department recycle ammunition shot into the fort by the besiegers. He offered 36 hours of leave to visit Mobile to any man who collected 25 pounds of solid shot and lead or six mortar shells, "The enemy gives us plenty of 10-inch shells for a mortar; we would only require fuses and a little powder," Gibson wired Maury's headquarters. He also continued his appeals to Maury for more guns and entrenching tools.[1]

While Gibson was inventive, he had no tolerance for disloyalty. As he put it, deserters would "ruin ourselves and our country by giving information to those who seek to destroy our lives and homes." After three soldiers from his brigade went to the U.S. lines, he issued orders expressly prohibiting any new soldiers from going beyond the main line of works. He ordered his soldiers to fire on and arrest anyone attempting to desert and had secret police in each company to detect them.

1 *ORA* 49, pt. 2, 1195, 1200–1201, 1205. Gibson's special orders allowed one man only from each command to be absent at a time. Gibson noted, "Any man detected in destroying serviceable cartridges, either our own or such of the enemy's that fall into our hands, will be severely punished and deprived of the privilege of the order. All lead brought to the ordnance had to bear undoubted signs of having been thrown by the enemy."

To promote vigilance and initiative, he declared a 24-hour leave for anyone who captured a prisoner and 30 days leave for catching a deserter.[2]

Back at Meridian, Taylor explored progressive ways to augment his forces under recent legislation at his headquarters. On March 13, the Confederate Congress finally approved enlisting soldiers of color "to increase the military force of the Confederate States" and "repel invasion, maintain the rightful possession of the Confederate States."[3]

General Taylor entertained a proposition from William Lyon, a prominent Marengo County, Alabama resident. Lyon informed Taylor that citizens of Marengo and adjoining counties were willing to furnish enslaved persons for military service. Receptive to the offer, Taylor assured Lyon that the lack of communication from officials at Richmond "on the subject of the late legislation with regard to the employment of negroes as soldiers" would not be an obstacle. Although he suffered a shortage of guns at the time, Taylor sought to find out how many enslaved men would be available for service on short notice.[4]

Federals

"Inch by inch, we are moving on the Gibraltar that protects Mobile. The belching of cannon and whiz of Springfields and Enfields unceasingly greet the day," reported the *Chicago Tribune*. Canby's siege indeed continued to progress. His men completed a pontoon bridge over Minette Bay that re-established direct communication between his two wings. Marshall's Brigade returned to its original position on the line. The besiegers advanced their position ever closer to the fort through vigorous toil. "Our rifle pits are some of them within 150 yards or so of the rebel fort & batteries—the men dig, dig, dig, day & night, with accouterments on & their rusty rifles by their sides in the trenches," observed an officer of the 28th Wisconsin. "The rebels dig too, and we have to be cautious not to expose ourselves too far, or whiz goes a bullet, much too close to one's head to be pleasant

2 *ORA* 49, pt. 2, 1200–1201; Andrew B. Booth, "USGenWeb Project: Louisiana Archives—War Between the States Resources," USGenWeb Archives—Census Wills Deeds Genealogy, last modified 1920, https://www.usgwarchives.net/la/military/wbts.htm?fbclid=IwAR1c9wPZ9AGJ0lOky2Gpy4aS_nVbPL7s4mf-aqRiFZU3feKs-aXZ1wukMn4. Corporal Thomas Riley, Co. B, 18th LA deserted on 3/27/65, Pvt. John W. Anderson, Co. B, 13th LA deserted on 4/2/65, and Pvt. John French, Co. B & D, 13th LA on 4/3/65. No further desertions from Gibson's Brigade occurred after 4/4/65.

3 *ORA* 49, pt. 2, 1199; "Very Late From Richmond," *New York Times*, Mar. 12, 1865, 1.

4 *ORA* 49, pt. 2, 1199.

for a timid man. Sometimes they rain around us like hail, and I wonder that the casualties are so low."[5]

By April 4, the Federals knew about the treadway bridges and the escape routes from the rear of Spanish Fort and to the rear of Tracey. "A means of escape from Spanish Fort was discovered this morning. It extended from the fort to a strip of land by the Tensaw River. They could pass along the shore under the bluffs from the fort at dark without being seen, but the trick has been discovered, and a new battery commands that pass. This, with the fleet on the south, has completely shut the rebels in," reported a *New York Herald* correspondent. "They are making a footway by which to communicate with steamers at Conway's Bayou." Another overconfident but less informed correspondent declared: "No body of troops can possibly escape from it (Spanish Fort) without being captured."[6]

The Confederates shelled the besiegers in the morning and kept up musketry firing throughout the day. However, the Federals remained relatively quiet while preparing for a massive general bombardment. At 5:00 p.m., their silence ended— they opened on Spanish Fort with 38 siege guns (including six 20-pounder rifles and 16 mortars) and 37 field guns. With orders for each gun to fire every three minutes, they relentlessly bombarded the fort for two hours. "The sudden and furious fire overwhelmed us with awe. It seemed as if heaven had opened its artillery and was avenging itself for the previous sins of man. Now are seen clouds of black smoke and dust from the parapets rolling themselves like huge mountains," noted one correspondent.[7]

One Wisconsinite belonging to the XIII Corps observed: "Fun! How we did warm the Johnnies! A caisson with a reb on top of it blown up—an awful sight." An Iowan described the bombardment as "quite grand, but not reaching the grandeur of the Vicksburg Siege."[8]

Both sides expected an assault to follow the intense bombardment. "Since our ill-fated charge on the fortifications at Vicksburg, hardly a man in the Regt can think of charging again without shuddering, & tho' we would go if we were ordered, it would not be with that spirit & belief in our success, in which every charge should be made," a Wisconsinite from Carr's Division jotted down in a

5 "Rebellion in the Gulf States Dead," *Chicago Tribune*, Apr. 18, 1865, 3; ORA 49, pt. 1, 95; Reed, *Twelfth Regiment Iowa*, 229, 231; Stevens and Blackburn, *"Dear Carrie,"* 307.

6 "Mr. J. J. Dawson's Dispatch," *New York Herald*, Apr. 19, 1865, 5; Edmund N. Hatcher, *The Last Four Weeks of the War* (Columbus, OH, 1891), 156.

7 Miller, *Captain Edward Gee Miller*, 31; Howard, *124th Regiment*, 304; "Rebellion in the Gulf States Dead," *Chicago Tribune*, Apr. 18, 1865, 3.

8 Howard, *124th Regiment*, 304; Miller, *Captain Edward Gee Miller*, 31; Henderson Diary, Apr. 5, 1865.

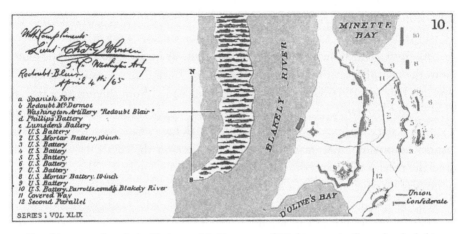

First Lieutenant Joseph A. Chalaron, 5th Company of Washington Artillery, sketched this map of Spanish Fort on April 4, 1865. *History Museum of Mobile*

letter to his parents. "If it were on an open field, I would say charge at once, for we can whip the Rebs every time at that game, & I believe too that it is a saving of life, but charging on fortifications with an almost impregnable abattis in front besides a ditch from 8 to 12 feet deep & as many wide is altogether a different matter." The bombardment lasted about two hours, but no assault occurred after the cannon fire ceased.[9]

Confederates

The earth trembled from the mighty roar of cannons, and citizens in Mobile heard the bombardment across the bay, creating a great sense of anxiety. Mary Waring, a teenager living in Mobile with her family, wrote in her journal: "This evening the firing is terrific, not a moment elapsing between the booming of heavy artillery. I trust our noble little fort will stand defiant to the assaults of the enemy."[10]

Since the beginning of the fight, the *Lady Slocomb* had terrorized the besiegers. The columbiad fired 144 charges, 1,440 pounds of powder, and over 7,500 pounds of shot and shell during the siege. The Federal artillerists, therefore, devoted particular attention to Battery Blair's big gun. A shot from the rear knocked off the right trunnion of the *Lady Slocomb*, and a shot from the front carried away its elevating screw; its carriage shattered and disabled by shots from its exposed

9 Newton and Ambrose, "The Siege of Mobile," 598; Newton, *A Wisconsin Boy in Dixie*, 148–149; "Civil War Diary of Henry M. Dryer."

10 Mary Waring-Harrison, *Miss Waring's Journal: 1863–1865*, ed. Thad Holt (Chicago, 1964), 8–12.

1Lt. Joseph A. Chalaron, 5th Company, Washington Artillery. *Dr. Glen Cangelosi*

flank. The 18th New York Battery and Battery L, 1st Indiana Artillery likely fired the shots that disabled the giant cannon. Chalaron recalled the big gun "was pointing towards the Indiana Battery when struck on the right trunnion from behind by a twenty-pound parrot shot, which must have come from Mack's Battery, that was on our right rear as the gun stood. About the same time, another shot from the direction of the Indiana Battery, passing under the gun, between the cheeks of the carriage, shattered the elevating screw." The quick-thinking artillerists of the 5th Company discreetly thrust an iron handspike under the cannon's breech, resting on the cheeks of the carriage, to keep the gun in place and horizontal, thus deceiving the besiegers as to its condition. The artillerists loaded the giant cannon with canister before seeking shelter in the bombproofs.[11]

Except for a few guns at Old Spanish Fort, the Confederates replied weakly during this terrible ordeal of fire. The Graycoats conserved the scarce supply of ammunition to repel an assault. At the first pause in the attack, the 5th Company rushed back from cover to man the guns for an expected attack. Had it come, the big gun would have fired one last charge of canister the men had loaded before leaving her.[12]

The concentrated bombardment nearly leveled Battery Blair. When the cannonading ceased, the men of 5th company quickly threw up sandbags on the damaged works until they again had enough cover around the gun to allow it to be

11 Chalaron, "Battle Echoes from Shiloh," 220–221; "The Lady Slocomb," *New Orleans Times-Democrat*, Sep. 20, 1899, 3,7.

12 "The Lady Slocomb," *New Orleans Times-Democrat*, Sep. 20, 1899, 3,7; Wittenberger, "Frank Wittenberger Civil War Diary."

dismounted that night. Under the cover of darkness, they quietly removed the big cannon and its carriage to make room for a replacement.[13]

The dismounting of the *Lady Slocomb* temporarily diminished the battery's importance. Gibson immediately reported to Maury the loss of the renowned columbiad and requested a replacement and additional mortars. "Can't you send another 64-pounder and some 10-inch mortars? I would like to have two more 64-pounders and fight the fight out in earnest."[14]

The Federal battery on the bluffs of Minette Bay fired their 30-pounder Parrotts and two Whitworth guns at Huger and Tracey during the bombardment. Nonetheless, Maj. Washington Marks and his garrison remained quietly resolute. "The Yanks shelled us for a while quite furiously; nobody hurt. We are well protected," a Louisiana artillerist wrote to his girlfriend. "So far, the Yanks have made a very poor fight as they have a host of men. I hope we will succeed in driving them back."[15]

At Spanish Fort's Red Fort (Redoubt 4), Capt. J. W. Phillips's Tennessee Battery suffered terribly from mortar shells. Maury relieved Phillips with Capt. James Garrity's Alabama Battery. The latter unit, with a strength of 67 men, like so many others in the garrison, were veterans of most of the principal battles of the Western theater.[16]

The Federals continued to shell the fort all night with mortars. "There was no shelter from these bombs—no defense from that fire. We had to stand and take it. Their force was terrible," recalled a Washington Artillery veteran. He added: "Those abominable mortars were the last item in their preparations. They practiced on us to get the range, and then we 'got it.'" The shells would bury six feet into the ground, and the explosion would tear up about 15 or 20 square feet. Sometimes, the projectiles even penetrated the bomb-proofs. The men, therefore, were constantly expecting to lose their ammunition and provisions stored in the magazine.[17]

Under a flag of truce, the Confederates obtained permission to take their wounded to Mobile by transport unmolested. The intense bombardment badly battered the earthworks and dismounted some of the guns of Spanish Fort. The

---

13 Chalaron, "Battle Echoes from Shiloh," 220–221.

14 Chalaron, "Battle Echoes from Shiloh," 220–221; *ORA* 49, pt. 2, 1199. A 64-pounder is an 8-inch cannon.

15 *ORA* 49, pt. 1, 95; ML to AH, Apr. 4, 1865.

16 Andrews, *History of the Campaign of Mobile*, 139.

17 Snedeker, *The Civil War Diary of Charles Henry Snedeker*, Stephenson, "Defence of Spanish Fort," 126.

besiegers presumed the loss in killed and wounded from the continuous onslaught must have been considerable.[18]

Gibson and his battle-hardened veterans, however, remained undaunted by the concentrated bombardment they had endured. "The enemy's batteries are very heavy," Gibson wired Liddell soon after the attack, "but they can never take this place with them. All's well." Liddell replied: "Hope you will yet drive away the Yankee devils and am delighted that you have suffered so little."[19]

Despite Gibson's optimistic facade, he knew his garrison could not hold out forever. Sickness and constant heavy details were diminishing his numbers. "For the first ten days, my artillery, aided by well-trained sharpshooters, was able to cope with that of the enemy, sometimes silencing his guns, and often broke up his working parties in handsome style; but after this time, it was evident, from his overwhelming resources in men and guns, that it would be impossible with the means at my disposal to arrest his gradual advance," he reported after the siege.[20]

Federals

Wednesday, April 5, 1865: The Federal bombardment waned; batteries fired only occasionally. Canby reported that the artillery fire had to be reduced because poor road conditions prevented an adequate supply of ammunition. Likewise, Union diary accounts indicated that no cannonading occurred from the fort. Men on both sides spent time in the morning fixing their damaged breastworks. Though artillery fire had temporarily decreased in frequency, skirmishing continued. George Brown, Company D, 7th Vermont, had his spade handle shot off by a musket ball while working.[21]

Canby's land forces were augmented by a battery of sailors led by Lt. Cmdr. James H. Gillis, the captain of the torpedoed monitor *Milwaukee*. Gillis and his sailors volunteered to join the bombardment on the land after losing their vessel. They disembarked at Starke's Wharf with three 30-pounder Parrott rifles. Gillis and his crew constructed and worked a battery in General Carr's front. Federal

18 Millard Diary, Apr. 4, 1865; "Rebellion in the Gulf States Dead," *Chicago Tribune*, Apr. 18, 1865, 3.

19 *ORA* 49, pt. 2, 1199; *Dispatch Book, Eastern Division, District of the Gulf, Mar.–Apr. 1865*, vol. 100, chapter II (War Department Collection of Confederate Records, 1865), 98.

20 *ORA* 49, pt. 1, 315.

21 *ORA* 49, pt. 2, 1204; *ORA* 49, pt. 1, 95; Gerling, *One Hundred Seventeenth Illinois Infantry*, 102; Macy, "Civil War Diary of William M. Macy," 194; Fisher Diary, Apr. 5, 1865.

reports referred to the sailor's artillery position as the naval battery. Canby later reported that the naval battery performed admirably.[22]

The besiegers did not anticipate such a stubborn defense. Indeed, many of the Federals underestimated the indomitable spirit of the Confederate defenders. Colonel Hubbard observed in a letter to his aunt: "We are considerably astonished at the character of the obstacles and the determination of the opposition with which we meet. The position against which the army is now operating is a very formidable defensive work, strongly garrisoned and held with great pertinacity. . . . Spanish Fort is regarded as the key point in the defenses of Mobile and hence is held with great obstinacy."[23]

Comrades in the 14th Wisconsin considered Pvt. Fred Mattice a brave soldier and one of the best sharpshooters in his regiment. Mattice emerged from many battles unscathed. He laughed at his comrades who hugged the dirt when the Confederates fired their mortar shells. Mattice, however, paid the price for his incaution when a piece of shell struck him in the head. He never regained consciousness and died three days later. His death cast a gloom over his company; he was well-liked by all. He left four motherless children in Wisconsin as his wife had died after he enlisted.[24]

Confederates

On the 10th day of the siege, work continued on the treadway from the rear of Tracey on Bateau Bay to Conway's Bayou. Meanwhile, Gibson's vexation became evident in his multitude of dispatches. He desperately requested more transportation, men, artillery pieces, naval support, and entrenching tools. In the morning, he wired Maury that the besiegers erected batteries on his right and left that commanded the fort and that he could not do the work necessary to defend his line against these threats with his limited number of troops. "With the small force to cover it, a force the greater part of which has been on an unbroken strain for two weeks, I must be supplied with more heavy guns, more mortars, more axes, more negroes, to make a successful and triumphant defense, and besides these some little craft, under my orders, to watch the water flanks—some fighting craft."[25]

22 *ORA* 49, pt. 1, 96, 268; *ORA* 49, pt. 2, 228, 277.

23 L. F. Hubbard to Aunt Mary, Apr. 5, 1865, "L.F Hubbard and the Fifth Minnesota Letters of a Union Volunteer," 68, Norman Nicholson Collection, Historic Mobile Preservation Society (HMPS). Hubbard became the Governor of Minnesota in 1881.

24 E. Stockwell, *Private Elisha Stockwell*, 165.

25 Hewitt, *Supplement to the Official Records*, pt. 1, vol. 7, 961; *ORA* 49, pt. 2, 1204–1205.

In a dispatch sent at 1:30 p.m., Gibson asked Maury to come over and look at his lines. "My men are wider apart than they ever were under Johnston or Hood. My works not so strong as they ordinarily were and the enemy in larger force, more active, and closer." Gibson expressed the need for light howitzers, axes, and a gunboat. He also made an unusual request: "Have you any negro troops? I would be glad to get some."[26]

Gibson sent another telegram an hour and a half later: "If I can't get howitzers, I will take mountain howitzers. I will make good soldiers of all the negroes you send me, provided I have axes and spades. I am economizing all ammunition and secure all the enemy gives. All's well. Hope to see you tomorrow." Gibson wanted at least 200 Black men, but only 100 could be sent to him then.[27]

Later, in his after-action report, Gibson noted that on the last day of the siege, "several hundred negroes arrived that evening to be employed in the defense." Considering that all the Confederate soldiers with entrenching tools were compelled to work, his specific word choice of "soldiers" and "troops" for the "several hundred negroes" carried significance. Maury's special orders on March 26, Gibson's repeated dispatches, and his after-action report suggest that these men were sent over as soldiers, not just laborers. Moreover, in a sentence from his original April 16th handwritten report—omitted from the published Official Records—Gibson reported: "Nearly all the Negro servants of the officers participated in the defense of the works—one or two of whom were wounded." Gibson capitalized the word "Negro," something he had not done in his life. It is also noteworthy that these men of color were armed when there were not enough muskets to provide for all the White soldiers. One of the men Gibson referred to, Jim McIntosh, a servant of Colonel Patton, suffered a wound on the second day of the siege.[28]

The Confederates expended from 12,000 to 36,000 rounds per day. Gibson expressed concern to his brigade commanders over the tremendous amount of ammunition expended in the previous two days. "Our supply is limited and, at this rate, will soon be exhausted," he warned them. To address the ammunition shortage, Maury called for all the besiegers' unexploded 10-inch shells fired into Spanish Fort to be gathered and sent to Battery Huger to use against them. Gibson advised his commanders to have the men collect unexploded shells and have them

26 Ibid., 1205.

27 Ibid., 1204; Hewitt, *Supplement to the Official Records*, pt. 1, vol. 7, 961.

28 *ORA* 49, pt. 1, 317; Handwritten report, RLG, Apr. 16, 1865; Dixon, "Randall Lee Gibson," 69–70; Roger Hansen, "Confederate Wounded, 1865 Mobile Campaign" (unpublished manuscript, 2020); "[Extract] Special Orders," *Mobile Advertiser & Register*, Mar. 28, 1865. Gibson reported his officer's servants participated in the defense in his original hand-written report. The published Officials Record mysteriously omitted this sentence.

piled up, ready to be loaded onto wagons, and then notify headquarters where the piles could be found every evening.[29]

In a circular to his officers, Gibson continued to urge the necessity of being prepared for an assault:

> The idea is prevalent that these works will never be assaulted. It is made the imperative duty of every officer to see that his men are so arranged that in the twinkling of an eye they may fall into their proper places; that the works are adapted to allow every gun to be concentrated and fired under the head-logs; that his picket-line is equally prepared and protected. The picket-line must be held. Regimental commanders must see that the pickets in their immediate front are encouraged and hold their lines. Brigade commanders will be expected to charge and dislodge the enemy immediately from their picket lines, should he attempt to dash on them and to occupy them. Whenever there are indications of an assault, and always when heavy shelling begins, officers must see that their men put on their accouterments and have their guns in hand. It is ordered that after shelling, or in case of an assault, every officer and man yells as loud as possible.[30]

To halt the besiegers' encroachment, Colonel Patton sent a dispatch to Captain Slocomb to open upon them along the line with guns and mortars. "Should you, however, by so doing draw upon you a greatly superior artillery fire and one which you cannot silence without too great risk of dismounting your guns, you will cease firing and put your guns and men under cover," the Virginian ordered. Patton also instructed Slocomb to deploy sharpshooters to target the Federal sharpshooters so that he could effectively work his artillery.[31]

That night, the Graybacks mockingly hollered to the besiegers to see if they wanted to borrow some artillery. The Federals shouted back that they would soon hear from their battery.[32]

Thursday, April 6, 1865: On the 11th day of the siege, Gibson telegraphed headquarters that nothing unusual occurred in the morning. He again stressed the need for a company of sappers, miners, and 200 Black men to check the besiegers' continual progress from the Federal approaches. The Bluecoats used three barges in an attempt to cut the telegraph line during the previous night before being driven off. Gibson, therefore, again requested Liddell and Maury to send him gunboat support to fire into Smith's Corps on the Federal right flank and protect

---

29 Maury, "Souvenirs of the War," 4; Handwritten orders, RLG, Apr. 6, 1865; *ORA* 49, pt. 2, 1205.

30 *ORA* 49, pt. 2, 1205.

31 *ORA* 49, pt. 2, 1206.

32 Gerling, *One Hundred Seventeenth Illinois Infantry*, 102.

the telegraph line. In the afternoon, Gibson reported "strong indications" on his left side that the fort would be assaulted at daylight.[33]

In response to Gibson's repeated dispatches, Liddell requested the support of gunboat Capt. John W. Bennett of the CSS *Nashville* and Capt. Joseph Fry of the CSS *Morgan*. He asked that the two gunboats be positioned off Spanish Fort's left flank, between Huger and Tracey, to protect their telegraph line. Liddell explained to them: "By taking your position near Battery Tracey, you will be able to enfilade the enemy's right flank and render great assistance to General Gibson and myself by depriving the enemy of the use of Bay Minette."[34]

During the day, the Graybacks completed a treadway from Battery Tracey over the marsh to Conway's Bayou, providing a new but limited line of communication for the garrison with Mobile.[35]

As the siege continued, Gibson's men hoped General Forrest's cavalry would soon come to their aid. However, they received disturbing news that Wilson's cavalry captured Selma—their critical industrial and manufacturing center—on Sunday, April 2. This was unsettling in its implications; the Mobile garrison was on its own. "I regret the fall of Selma. I presume the people of Mobile are quite despondent. It is no use. We will have to fight it out. I believe Mobile will prove a big job for the Yanks," pronounced one resilient gray-coated soldier. Gibson noticed signs of discouragement and apathy as he passed through the lines during the day. He refused to be daunted and told his officers: "This will never do." He urged his officers "to arouse, to encourage, to cheer up their subordinates and their men."[36]

Federals

Conversely, Federal morale soared upon hearing of Wilson's capture of Selma. Moreover, the men received a 10-day ration of tobacco. Even those who were not tobacco users still benefitted: "I sold mine for six postage stamps," one soldier of the 124th Illinois recorded in his diary.[37]

Certain that Mobile would soon follow Selma, Wilson made unique arrangements to communicate with Canby about their success and future course. Worried that the Graycoats still controlled the intervening country, he sent a

---

33 Thomas Diary, Apr. 6, 1865; *ORA* 49, pt. 2, 1210.

34 *ORA* 49, pt. 2, 1209–1210.

35 Andrews, *History of the Campaign of Mobile*, 143.

36 Wilson, *Under the Old Flag*, 238; ML to AH, Apr. 6, 1865; Handwritten orders, RLG, Apr. 6, 1865.

37 Snedeker, *The Civil War Diary of Charles Henry Snedeker*.

black man named Charles Marven to Canby down the Alabama River by boat. Marven was sensible, trustworthy, and well-acquainted with the river. He willingly transported a dispatch to Canby, written on tissue paper and concealed in his clothing. Wilson also took the precaution of fully explaining its contents to his messenger. "As though proud of his trust, he received it with becoming gravity and solemnly assured me he would deliver it in person to Canby within five days unless killed on the way," Wilson recalled. He added: "It is pleasant to record that he started on the 4th and, without rest, night or day, reached his destination and delivered his message safely into Canby's hands." In compliance with Wilson's request, Canby paid Marven two hundred dollars for his valuable service.[38]

With the intelligence of the fall of Selma at 1:00 p.m., the Federals celebrated the victory with a 100-gun salute from the land batteries and the fleet. "Received news of the capture of Selma by Gen. Wilson. Glorious. Siege progressing rapidly," observed an officer of the 20th Wisconsin. The Mobile newspapers dismissed the Federal celebration: "The Federal Fleet fired a jour de Joie of hundred guns over the capture of Selma, and over the defeat of Lee and Johnston by Grant and Sherman," reported one Mobile newspaper columnist. "In common with the rest of mankind, we have given the Yankees all credit for being very fast and smart people, but we have never understood that they were possessed of military clairvoyant powers and could know things by intuition before they had happened."[39]

Union forces continued to methodically dig their way closer to Spanish Fort. They took every precaution to make their trenches safe. As the Federal lines were strengthened, the number of men injured decreased despite their proximity to the fort. The safety measures did not prevent all casualties. One soldier of the 44th Missouri had his gun ready to fire, and when he looked over the top of the work to see something to shoot at, a bullet struck him in the mouth and killed him instantly. Even with an overwhelming numerical advantage, the Federals indeed had their hands full. "The Marines were ordered to help us. Strong shooting by the Rebels," Pvt. Frank Wittenberger, Company C, 14th Wisconsin, jotted down in his diary.[40]

Colonel James L. Geddes commanded the 8th Iowa on the Confederate's extreme left flank. Born in Edinburgh, Scotland, the 38-year-old Geddes was a

38 Wilson, *Under the Old Flag*, 238.

39 Miller, *Captain Edward Gee Miller*, 31; Francis F. Audsley to wife, Apr. 7, 1865, Francis Fairbank and Harriet Elizabeth Audsley Papers, The State Historical Society of Missouri-Columbia, hereafter FFA to wife, Apr. 7, 1865; Wilson, Under the Old Flag, 238; "From Mobile," *The Times Picayune*, Apr. 22, 1865, 1.

40 EBM to sister, Apr. 7, 1865; Wittenberger, "Frank Wittenberger Civil War Diary"; FFA, Apr. 7, 1865.

Colonel James L. Geddes, Third Brigade, Third Division. *State Historical Society of Iowa, Des Moines*

small, slender man weighing about 135 pounds. He had sharp features, fine brown hair, and large hazel eyes. His contemporaries described him as "active and intelligent" and "always held in high esteem by his men" and superiors.[41]

At ten years of age, Geddes immigrated to Canada. He returned to Scotland at 18, where he embarked for the East Indies and entered the British Military Academy at Calcutta. After studying there for about two years, he enlisted in the British service with the Royal Horse Artillery. He served with the British army for seven years, took part in the Punjab Campaign, and fought in the battle of Khyber Pass. He also engaged in the campaign against the Hill Tribes of the Himalayas. After leaving the British service, he returned to Canada, where Queen Victoria appointed him a cavalry colonel, and he organized a cavalry regiment. However, he soon resigned his commission and immigrated to the United States in 1857. He purchased a farm in Benton County, Iowa.[42]

General Benjamin Prentiss acknowledged Geddes's distinguished courage, coolness, and ability at Shiloh. Geddes and his regiment stood unflinchingly in the face of a relentless Confederate onslaught. On the first day of battle, he and his regiment were captured at the Hornet's Nest by men under James T. Holtzclaw, who commanded the left wing of Spanish Fort three years later. As a prisoner of

---

41 A. A. Stuart, *Iowa Colonels and Regiments: Being a History of Iowa Regiments in the War of the Rebellion* (Des Moines, IA, 1865), 194.

42 Stuart, *Iowa Colonels and Regiments*, 185.

war, Geddes penned several popular war songs, including *The Soldier's Battle-Prayer* and *The Stars and Stripes*.[43]

"The enemy has a strong position here, and seems sullen & defiant," an officer of the 28th Wisconsin remarked in a letter to his wife, "how long he can hold out is to be seen." Irritated by Gibson's dogged resistance, Canby ditched his original plan of operations and prepared to make his first blow upon Fort Blakeley. He ordered a part of his force to withdraw from Spanish Fort and concentrate with Steele at Blakeley. He ordered Carr's Division to be moved in three days. Before receiving the order to withdraw, Geddes had frequently pointed out to Carr the most vulnerable point of Spanish Fort.[44]

For some days, it was suspected that a weak place existed on the fort's left flank. The works did not extend to the water there, and the artillery on the flank was not as strong as elsewhere along the line. The Confederate's northern flank was on a high bluff that ran perpendicular to the Blakeley River. To most people, the position appeared to be strong. Moreover, the ground was thickly covered with young pines and exceedingly swampy between this bluff and the river. Undeterred by the swampy landscape, Geddes firmly believed his men could gain a lodgment at this position. Acting without orders, he initiated plans to place two companies of his regiment in the approach which had been dug down the front of the ridge. His plan called for the men to lay low while a heavy fire opened along the entire line. Under the cover of the bombardment, they would dash around the left flank of the fort through the marsh, supported by the entire regiment and brigade if needed.

After receiving the unwelcomed marching orders to Blakeley, Geddes felt the urgency to push forward his attack plan to Carr, who also seemed convinced it would work. He and Carr brought the plan to Smith. The trio then crept up within a few yards of their advanced line on the right. After a careful examination and consultation, Smith concurred that the fort's left could be turned. He forwarded Geddes's plan to Canby, who approved and issued the necessary orders.[45]

*   *   *

43 Stuart, *Iowa Colonels and Regiments*, 189; "Geddes," Department of Residence, last modified Dec. 21, 2020, https://www.housing.iastate.edu/halls/geoffroy/geddes/.

44 Stevens & Blackburn, *"Dear Carrie,"* 308; Huff, *The Annals of Iowa*, 950.

45 "The Capture of Spanish Fort," *The National Tribune*, Oct. 29, 1908, 7; Andrew Geddes, "Fighting Them Over," *The National Tribune*, Nov. 24, 1892, 4; "Our Special Report; The Preparation. The Start. The Investment of Spanish Fort," *New York Times*, Apr. 24, 1865.

Friday, April 7, 1865: Heavy rain and chilly conditions further exacerbated the miserable conditions on the 12th day of the siege. One blue-coated officer recalled it as "a damp, disagreeable day." As usual, sharpshooting and some cannonading continued.[46]

Confederates

By dawn, a replacement for the disabled *Lady Slocomb* and two coehorn mortars were in position at Battery Blair. The men brought up a spare cannon from the Old Spanish Fort (Redoubt 1) below the bluff during the night. With hushed voices and noiseless steps their work continued, undetected by the blue-coated sharpshooters 100 yards in their front, whose bullets, at the slightest sound, repeatedly came whizzing by their position at night. Chalaron recalled the remarkable feat: "Hundreds of infantry, tugging at ropes, dragged up to the redoubt a carriage and mate to our big gun. Again, with undetected movements, these were mounted on the old chassis." With the breastworks repaired and the new pieces in place, the men of Battery Blair were better prepared than ever for the expected final assault.[47]

"Enemy failed to attack. He probably discovered I was prepared and, on the alert," Gibson wired Maury. During the night, three Yankee pickets were captured. From these prisoners, Gibson confirmed that two army corps were at work against them.[48]

Though the garrison conserved their ammunition, they did not remain silent. "The Rebs are firing more today than usual," observed one soldier of the 7th Vermont. Colonel Patton directed Captain Slocomb, when ready, to open his mortars, throwing shells into the Federals picket line "leisurely." An artillery shell fired from the Confederates went through the chest of a soldier of the 40th Missouri Regiment.[49]

Gibson maintained his relentless request for support. "I must have the things I have asked for within the last three days; else disaster may happen," he pleaded. "Think of our incomplete works and of the disparity of the forces." In a subsequent dispatch, he stressed: "I can't get along without sub-terra shells, hand-grenades, more negroes, a company of sappers and miners, a cutter or launch from the navy,

46 Howard, *124th Regiment*, 305; Thomas Diary, Apr. 7, 1865; Miller, *Captain Edward Gee Miller*, 31; Ridge Diary, Apr. 7, 1865.

47 "The Lady Slocomb," *New Orleans Times-Democrat*, Sep. 20, 1899, 3, 7.

48 *ORA* 49, pt. 2, 1214. Pickets are "lookouts" in advanced positions.

49 Fisher Diary, Mar. 7, 1865; *ORA* 49, pt. 2, 1215; Wittenberger, "Frank Wittenberger Civil War Diary."

two howitzers." He pointed out that the besiegers had significantly progressed the previous day and night. As Gibson put it: "He will soon dig up to my main line at the rate he advances. Must do something to meet his night approaches." Gibson did not exaggerate; that night, Confederate Captain Garrity and a man of his battery made their way up to where the Federals dug an approach in McArthur's Division. They were so close that the digging Federals shoveled dirt on them. Garrity listened to the besiegers and heard one say, "We'll give the rebels—tomorrow." The lines in some places were almost within a stone's throw away from the Confederate works.[50]

Over in Mobile, organized citizen committees made daily preparations to visit the beleaguered garrison daily. They distributed supplies to the men in the trenches and delicacies to the wounded in the hospitals. The wounded received care each night as they arrived in the steamers from the siege.[51]

Federals

Before carrying out Geddes's plan to bombard and then assault, Canby wanted to destroy the treadway bridge to cut off the garrison's escape route. The Federals furiously shelled the spit and treadway area for several hours but failed to achieve their aim. To secure this avenue of escape, Liddell requested James Fry, captain of the CSS *Morgan*. He wanted the *Nashville* or the *Morgan* to take a position between Tracey and Huger and send picket boats to guard the treadway bridge. He also asked that every effort be made to destroy the pontoon bridge the Federal army used to cross the mouth of Minette Bay Creek and silence the battery on the bluffs of Minette Bay.[52]

"We are just hammering away at Spanish Fort and I think will get it before long," declared a soldier of Marshall's Brigade. "The mortar battery right by us is now firing on them. There are four of them throwing 120 lbs. shells. I tell you, it shakes the earth when one fires, but I guess it does more than that when the ball gets to its destination."[53]

The U.S. Army trenches provided protection and reduced casualties. "Not many are being wounded, but yet every two or three hours, some poor fellow is brought in with a frightful wound," noted a surgeon of Smith's Corps. "Our men

---

50 *ORA* 49, pt. 2, 1214–1215; Andrews, *History of the Campaign of Mobile*, 236–237.

51 Maury, "Souvenirs of the War," 4.

52 *ORA* 49, pt. 1, 96; *ORA* 49, pt. 2, 1214.

53 FFA to wife, Apr. 7, 1865. It is believed infantrymen roughly estimated "120 lbs." shell. A 10-inch mortar shell probably weighed between 91–98 lbs.

are comparatively safe, but the poor Johnnies have to suffer." Gibson reported 6 men killed and 23 wounded.[54]

Some men began to see light at the end of the tunnel. "We are beginning to look upon the capture of Mobile as a thing in the future & think when that event is consummated that we will not have long to serve & this will probably be our last campaign," an Illinoisan officer told his wife. "I hope it may be so."[55]

54 EBM to sister, Apr. 7, 1865; *ORA* 49, pt. 2, 1215. Randall Lee Gibson Papers' morning report on Apr. 7, 1865, indicates 2,575 troops and 2,047 guns present inside Spanish Fort.

55 JFD to wife, Apr. 7, 1865.

Chapter 13

"It Beat Anything I Ever Heard or Saw"

Confederates

$\mathcal{S}aturday,$ April 8, 1865: The 13th day of the siege opened cold and cloudy. With no hope of assistance from Forrest's cavalry, prospects indeed appeared gloomy. Early in the siege, Gibson received orders "not to hold the fort for a moment after the garrison was in danger of capture; not to risk, in the defense of an outpost, forces intended to occupy and defend the stronghold and the works around Mobile." Gibson and Holtzclaw agreed the time had finally come to evacuate the 2,616 soldiers present for duty. Lieutenant Colonel James Williams, 21st Alabama, however, expected to finish a battery for four 12-pounders on Holtzclaw's left to enfilade the besiegers. Williams planned to have the guns in position the following night. Gibson, therefore, decided to hold on another day to allow Williams an opportunity to try his battery.[1]

Skirmishing continued, although artillery fired less frequently during the day. At 12:25 a.m., Gibson wired Maury, stating the besiegers were drawing quite close to his lines. "His artillery is so much more powerful than ours, and his lines so well protected that we cannot use ours to arrest his progress," Gibson protested. Gibson also confirmed the arrival of hand grenades, howitzers, and the Black men that he

---

1 Morning report, RLG, Apr. 8, 1865; "Civil War Diary of Henry M. Dryer"; Andrews, *History of the Campaign of Mobile*, 159; *ORA* 49, pt. 1, 317. Gibson's papers show that the Apr. 8 morning report indicated 2,616 soldiers were present in the fort, including 2,106 total infantry (615 Gibson's Brigade, 592 Ector's Brigade, 899 Holtzclaw's Brigade) and 510 artillerists, 25 "Public" and 5 "Private" enslaved persons.

had been requesting for days. In the early afternoon, Fort McDermott opened on a Federal working party. The Union's heavy batteries, however, commanded Gibson's artillery. The Federal onslaught temporarily disabled one gun and caused a chest to explode; the concentrated fire could not be endured.[2]

Maury went to Spanish Fort to assess the situation for himself. "I took Colonel Lockett, Chief Engineer, with me into Spanish Fort," the Virginian recalled, "that we might determine what progress the enemy had made with his mining operations and how much longer it would be safe to keep the garrison in the place." He believed the Federals would not assault Spanish Fort before Wednesday and instructed Gibson to prepare his garrison to march out after dark on Tuesday night. At 4:00 p.m., Gibson ordered all the garrison artillery to open vigorously.[3]

Federals

One Illinoisan recalled that the Confederates began "shelling heavily, having commenced a little before we did, and the effect was terrific." Carr ordered Geddes's Brigade into their rifle pits in preparation for opening the Union's bombardment.[4]

Concerning General Smith, one newspaper correspondent observed: "Once a piece of shell shrieked within a few inches of his head. He coolly puffed his Havana, not deigning to make a remark about the 'close shave' which made a half dozen darkies seek, with remarkable celerity, their bombproof covers. From the general's rigid countenance, on which not a muscle moved, a person might judge that he rather liked that kind of music."[5]

Carr rode down to Geddes's quarters about 5 o'clock and asked him if he still thought that he could make a lodgment on the rebel works. Having received an answer in the affirmative, Carr then told him that a general cannonade would be opened upon the rebel lines within the hour and desired him to attack during the time of the artillery bombardment. Carr directed Geddes to press with skirmishers on his right against the rebel left, feel their strength, ascertain the nature of the ground, and take as much ground as he could hold. Geddes was sick at the time. He shook with a chill as Carr gave him instructions. Nevertheless, he executed the orders and commanded his brigade like a man in perfect health.[6]

---

2 Howard, *124th Regiment*, 305; *ORA* 49, pt. 2, 1217, 1218.

3 Maury, "Defense of Spanish Fort," 132; Andrews, *History of the Campaign of Mobile*, 159.

4 Howard, *124th Regiment*, 305.

5 "Letter from Varitas," *New Orleans Times-Democrat*, Apr. 14, 1865.

6 Huff, *The Annals of Iowa*, 950–951; *ORA* 49, pt. 1, 267.

Geddes directed Lt. Col. William Bell, 8th Iowa, to occupy his right gabion wall approach and, at the same time, let two of his companies move outside of the breastworks well to his right, advance to the slight crest, drive in the rebel sharpshooters, and entrench themselves there for the night. "How long will it take you to have the men ready to assault?" asked Geddes. Bell replied: "Just fifteen minutes." Before this movement, Geddes ordered the 108th and 124th Illinois to man the rifle pits on their front and open a continuous fire on the fort.[7]

The besiegers set 5:30 p.m. as the time for their bombardment. They had nearly 90 big guns positioned against Spanish Fort, including an astounding 53 siege guns (including ten 20-pounder rifles and 16 mortars) and 35 field pieces. Of these, ten siege rifles and five siege howitzers on the Union left center enfiladed the fort's left and center, while five siege howitzers close in on the extreme right enfiladed the center. The Bay Minette battery against Huger and Tracey consisted of two 100-pounder and four 30-pounder Parrott rifles. Lieutenant Commander James H. Gillis and his crew of the USS *Milwaukee* voluntarily manned one of the batteries with their naval guns. The fire of these guns opened at the appointed time and continued until dark, the troops being in the trenches and prepared to improve any advantage that might be gained.[8]

Batteries all along the lines fired continuously. An officer of the 26th New York Light Artillery, XIII Corps, reported firing 200 rounds at Fort McDermott. "The roar of the storm I can illustrate only by comparing it to the breaking of a thunderstorm at once," declared one soldier of the 95th Illinois.[9]

Though most of the men on both sides fought in numerous battles in the western theater—from Shiloh to Nashville—the bombardment of Spanish Fort on April 8 stood out. "It beat anything I ever heard or saw," an officer of the 1st Indiana Heavy Artillery exclaimed in a letter to his brother. Indeed, the fire of so many big guns and the brash explosion of shells produced one of those awe-inspiring scenes that rarely occurred during the war. "The scene of the rain of fire which was then falling inside of the rebel fortifications on the left of the position of the Third Brigade was simply awful and never to be forgotten," remembered one officer of the 81st Illinois. "The sharp salute of the Rodman, the tearing noise

---

7 Byers, *Iowa*, 407–408; *ORA* 49, pt. 1, 275–76.

8 *ORA* 49, pt. 1, 96.

9 Millard Diary, Apr. 8, 1865; "From the 95th Illinois," *The Woodstock* [IL] *Sentinel*, May 10, 1865, 1. The Union besiegers referred to Fort McDermott as Fort Alexis.

of the Napoleons, the dull, heavy report of the mortars, and the awful roar of the Parrotts can be better imagined than described," recalled another veteran.[10]

"Our heavy guns, having got the range, did great damage, almost completely silencing the enemy. The riflemen in the front line did their part to make life miserable for the cooped-up Johnnies," recalled one officer of the 33rd Illinois. "They had done well, but we had done better."

Friendly fire caused some tragic incidents during the bombardment. "I think it was the first Indiana battery heavy artillery that was stationed in our rear— the same one that had shot over the regiment at Vicksburg and accidentally shot into us, leaving a mark that time only can efface," remembered an officer of the XVI Corps. "They had been doing the same thing here to such an extent that we protected ourselves against them by splitting pine logs and lay them in a slanting position from the top of our outside works to the outer edge of the ditch. This made adequate protection against iron from their prematurely exploded shells and grapeshot." When the shelling commenced, most of the 33rd Illinois sought shelter in the bombproofs. Some soldiers went outside to cook supper when a case-shot from one of the guns in the Indiana battery exploded among them. Sandford Strowbridge, B Company, 33rd Illinois, suffered a mortal wound. A grapeshot shell struck him between the shoulders and lodged into his body. As they carried him away—realizing it was the final farewell to his beloved comrades—he said flatly: "Goodbye, boys." He died that night on the hospital boat. Strowbridge joined the service as a substitute, a poor man with a family. The Illinoisan had bought a house by taking the price offered him, thus virtually giving his life for that home. He was not the only such casualty. "Cuvillier of C Co. was mortally wounded in about the same manner. The cries of agony by that poor French boy were heartrending," remembered an officer of the 33rd Illinois. "To go through this terrible storm of shot and shell for eleven days and then to be killed through carelessness was the worst feature of the campaign."[11]

U.S. Navy

The fleet had finally worked its way close enough to Spanish Fort in time to join the bombardment. "The whole artillery force of our army and gunboats opened in one terrible storm of fire so concentrated on the rebel fort that it seemed almost impossible for it to endure a repetition," remembered one Iowan. The

10 RHC to PMC; Andrews, *History of the Campaign of Mobile*, 151; "Spanish Fort," *The National Tribune*, Jan. 28, 1886, 5; "The Capture of Spanish Fort," *The National Tribune*, Oct. 29, 1908, 7.

11 Elliot, *Thirty-Third Regiment*, 231.

men of Benton's Division could not see the bay from behind the wooded hills. However, the shells from Thatcher's gunboats "could be distinctly seen as with majestic slowness they described their brilliant arcs, and fell point-blank in the rebel fort almost at the instant of explosion."[12]

At first, the thick smoke soon obscured the fort from the fleet's sight, then the wind grew stronger and cleared it away, and they had a clear view. "The cannonading was incessant and after dark increased to a perfect roar," remembered Robert Lincoln, 3rd Assistant Engineer, U.S. Navy.[13]

Confederates

Residents of Mobile, nine miles to the west, distinctly heard the tremendous roaring of musketry and artillery. Mary Waring recorded in her diary that she "heard the most terrible" firing since the beginning of the attack. "We were very much alarmed, fearing that our poor, exhausted [men] could not stand such a repeated and rapid assault. The firing is still rapid and heavy while I write."[14]

"A most extraordinary fire" from the besiegers seemed to concentrate upon Battery Blair "from field guns, siege guns, ship guns, and mortars such a tempest of shot and shell that defies description," recalled a veteran of the Washington Artillery's 5th Company. "No doubt, we had done them mischief, and perhaps more mischief than the other forts, for our gunners had gained experience in a score of battles, but we were not prepared for such an especial compliment as this." The Federals launched giant 10-inch mortar shells into the fort. They were so large that Confederates could see them shortly after leaving the mortar's mouth as they ascended into the sky.[15]

Lieutenant Solomon Thompson, Company E, 18th Alabama, suffered an agonizing death during the bombardment. An Alabamian of Holtzclaw's Brigade recalled the horrifying details: "A piece of shell tore off one shoulder and opened a hole into his lungs. I looked in the wound and saw the lungs and heart. What suffering he endured for a while, but not long. He was soon dead. I remember he begged to be killed that he might be put out of his misery."[16]

---

12 "Our Special Report; The Preparation. The Start. The Investment of Spanish Fort," *New York Times*, Apr. 24, 1865; Andrew F. Sperry, *33d Iowa Infantry*, 143.

13 "In Mobile Bay," *The National Tribune*, Oct. 13, 1887, 3.

14 Waring-Harrison, *Miss Waring's Journal*, 13.

15 Stephenson, "Defence of Spanish Fort," 123; Stephenson & Hughes, *Civil War Memoir of Philip Daingerfield Stephenson*, 363.

16 Jones and Pulcrano, *Eighteenth Alabama Infantry Regiment*, 65.

Gibson could discern from the fierce fire the besieger's advance line contained men "fully equal to a strong line of battle." He knew they would soon assault. He later reported: "On the left, the ground was more favorable to the enemy, and to this fact and the want of works may be ascribed the nearness with which he was enabled to establish himself." Only a picket line guarded the marshy areas on the flank. The tremendous fire diverted the garrison's attention from the operation of the 8th Iowa, which occupied a sort of valley or wide ravine on their left. The woods, moreover, were so thick there that Geddes's Brigade massed without being seen.[17]

Federal Assault

Carr hurried to Smith's headquarters to provide an update after giving Geddes the go-ahead and ensuring the other regiments were ready in case of a repulse. After reporting, he told Smith that he must return to his command at once. However, Smith kept him from leaving—saying that "the boys were all right"— and mixed a toddy and made him take a drink. "I finally induced him to let me go, and he went with me," recalled Carr.[18]

The 8th Iowa of Geddes's Brigade attacked and took advantage of the bombardment. They set out through the supposedly impenetrable marsh— approximately 200 yards wide—on the extreme left of the fortifications. "It has been understood that they carried narrow strips of plank or rails or poles and threw them across the turf," recalled one Alabamian, "and thus got so far in that they had us on the flank, and before we knew it, they were pressing us from that direction, and to such extent that we were unable to hold them in check long." The Confederates mistakenly believed the swamp was impassible and did not construct substantial defensive works due to a lack of time.[19]

At 6:10 p.m., Lt. Col. William B. Bell, commander of the 8th Iowa, led two companies from behind the right gabion approach to view the rebel sharpshooters fully. They advanced through about a hundred yards of slashed trees, mud, and swamp that lay between them and the rebel works. Captain Henry Muhs, Company A, and Lt. Henry Vineyard, Company G, rapidly deployed their men and advanced, with Muhs leading the skirmishers. Bell accompanied the advance

---

17 Elliot, *Thirty-Third Regiment*, 231; Handwritten report, RLG, Apr. 16, 1865; *ORA* 49, pt. 1, 315; "Spanish Fort," *The National Tribune*, Nov. 24, 1892, 4; Huff, *The Annals of Iowa*, 950–951; Maury, "Souvenirs of the War"; Handwritten report, RLG, Apr. 16, 1865.

18 Carr, *First Reunion of the Survivors of the Army of Tennessee*, 26.

19 Jones and Pulcrano, *Eighteenth Alabama Infantry Regiment*, 64, 70; Andrews, *History of the Campaign of Mobile*, 151.

The gallant charge of the 8th Iowa Infantry. *Donnie Barrett*

until he felt sure the men could gain the crest in the rear of the rebel line and then returned to the rest of the regiment behind the bastion.[20]

From the defender's rifle pits and behind the stumps and logs and trees came unerring musketry into the faces of the little band struggling to climb through the fallen trees and abatis. The men of Carr's Division back in the trenches cheered, giving the impression that the whole division was about to assault. The cheering only put the Rebels more on the alert as they rapidly shot down the advancing line. Bell—fearing the result of the overpowering numbers at the front— at once sent another company to the aid of the men so rapidly falling. At that exact moment, he hurried Lieutenant Clark rearward to secure permission from Geddes to advance with the entire regiment.[21]

With anxiety, Bell recognized his three companies' increasingly vulnerable position; if left unsupported in the low swamp, they would be driven back and annihilated. Bell and the remainder of the 8th Iowa watched impatiently as their comrades fought a short distance off. Believing it too dangerous to wait any longer, and without orders, Bell shouted to his regiment to go over their breastworks and follow him to the front. Instantly, the men crossed over the gabion wall and advanced directly at the opposing ridge into the storm of bullets that had already slowed the advanced companies. Once they took the crest, the fire became too hot to endure. The blue-coated soldiers suffered through the deadly musketry fire and canister. Retreat was no longer an option. With the cry of "forward," the whole line

20 *ORA* 49, pt. 1, 277–279; Byers, *Iowa*, 407–408.

21 Byers, *Iowa*, 407–408.

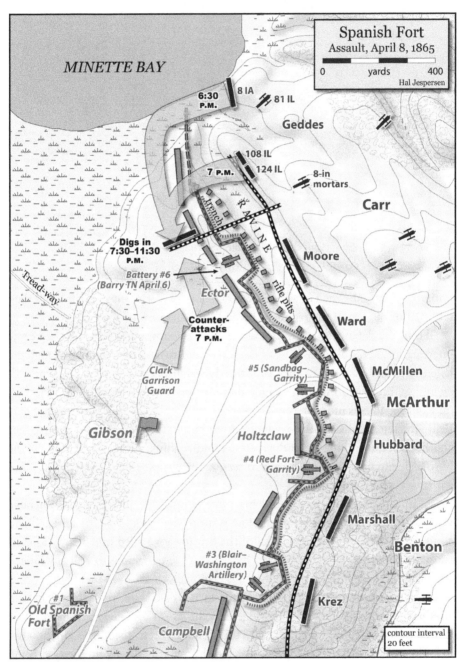

dashed for the main rebel works and, with bayonet and bullet, took the rifle pits and about 100 yards of entrenchments on the end of the works.[22]

22 Ibid.; *ORA* 49, pt. 1, 277–279.

The Confederate works in front of their mainline consisted of a series of small, unconnected rifle pits. This enabled Bell's men to attack them in detail from the rear and side as his regiment moved by the right flank in the back of the enemy's rifle pits; they either killed, wounded, or captured the men of Ector's Brigade occupying the position. The 8th Iowa took a considerable portion of the line before the rest of Ector's men realized their left was turned. The attack occurred so suddenly the line scarcely had time to form when they became bitterly engaged with Texans and North Carolina soldiers from Ector's Brigade and Capt. Robert Barry's Lookout Battery inside the fort. Although outnumbered, some Graybacks refused to surrender and fought to the death in the advance rifle pits. One Iowa veteran recalled: "Heroically and stubbornly, even stoically, the Rebels defended their rifle pits. Many, with the bayonet at their breasts, refused to surrender and were killed." Bell reported: "We here witnessed the spectacle of dying in the last-ditch, as quite a number of the rebels refused to surrender and were shot in their ditches, and on the other hand, quite a number of them who were taken prisoners ought, in justice to our men, to have been killed, as they would first fire at our men after being ordered to surrender, then throw up both hands and surrender."[23]

General Carr claimed the men in the pits were Texans. "When our men told them to surrender, they said they would never surrender to any d— Yankees," the New Yorker recalled. "They were told they were surrounded, etc., but they continued to fire and had to be killed." Once inside the works, there could be no halting, and by a right flank movement, Bell led his regiment down the inside of its rebel works, capturing roughly 300 hundred yards of the fort to Barry's Battery, where they dug in. Barry had one-third of his battery captured.[24]

Over 200 prisoners from North Carolina, Alabama, and Texas were hurried to the rear. "All of them were comfortably clad in a mixture of grey and white,

---

23 Byers, *Iowa*, 407–408; *ORA* 49, pt. 1, 277–278.

24 *ORA* 49, pt. 1, 96, 134, 267, 275–276; Carr, *First Reunion of the Survivors of the Army of Tennessee*, 26–27; Robert L. Barry, "The Lookout Battery," *Confederate Veteran* (1922): 385; Kirk Barrett, "Confederate Soldiers Captured at Spanish Fort and Imprisoned at Ship Island" (unpublished manuscript, 2018); Andrews, *History of the Campaign of Mobile*, 143. In his book, *History of the Campaign of Mobile*, C. C. Andrews claimed that Perry's Chattanooga battery relieved Lumsden's battery on Apr. 6, 1865. This is likely an error. Captain T. J. Perry led the Marion Artillery from Florida. Captain Robert L. Barry led the Chattanooga "Lookout" battery. It seems likely Andrews mistook Perry for Barry. Union after-action reports indicate about 200 Confederates were captured in the initial assault. Period references reported that the Texans held the extreme left, the Ship Island prisoner reports indicate that 159 soldiers from the 29th and 39th North Carolina were captured compared with only 53 from the Texas regiments. The bulk of the Texans captured were from the 32d Regiment. This suggests the possibility of the North Carolina troops and not the Texans that occupied the Confederate left flank that extended into the swamp.

well provided for in the way of shoes, and all remarkably intelligent," reported a newspaper correspondent.[25]

Several key members of the 8th Iowa sustained casualties during the assault, including Lt. Henry Vinyard, commanding Company G, who scaled the top of the breastworks first. The Confederates instantly shot Vinyard in the left arm, and then he suffered a fractured left thigh, an injury which proved fatal. "Pay no attention to me," Vinyard told his men as they gathered around him when he went down, "Boys—move on."[26]

Colonel Geddes came up and directed Bell to place his command outside the works of Spanish Fort and face toward them, using them for breastworks and to throw out a company as skirmishers to his right and front. Being convinced that the Confederates were taken by surprise, Geddes ordered the 81st Illinois up to support the 8th Iowa and then both the 108th and 124th Illinois, thus employing his entire brigade.[27]

Geddes did not push forward at the time because of the darkness and the fact that Granger's Corps did not know he had made a lodgment. Granger's batteries were still dropping their shells in dangerous proximity to his force, and further advance would have exposed him to the severe artillery fire coming from their lines, together with the fact that he was amid the rebel stronghold, detached from the army and cut off from immediate support in case of need. Geddes stopped at dusk, and his men commenced entrenching. As one soldier of Carr's Division put it: "We were ordered to commence entrenching to hold our ground, as no other portion of the besieging force was in concert with us." Along the rest of the Union line, shovels and picks were hurriedly gathered up and brought over to Geddes's men to help them dig a trench perpendicular to the fort. They pulled two of Barry's artillery pieces into their defensive line and held their position.[28]

By this time, Carr and Smith had come up. "We walked arm in arm down to the right and walked right into the fort, which had been abandoned by the enemy," remembered Carr. Comstock urged Smith to push his men forward. Troubled by the darkness, Smith declined. "Let me do it my way, & I will have the fort by

---

25 *ORA* 49, pt. 1, 275–76; "The Mobile Expedition," *New Orleans Times-Democrat*, Apr. 12, 1865, 2.

26 Andrew Geddes, "Fighting Them Over," *The National Tribune*, Nov. 24, 1892, 4; Andrews, *History of the Campaign of Mobile*, 153–154; *ORA* 49, pt. 1, 279. According to one officer of Geddes's Brigade, Vinyard's last words were: "Don't wait for me, boys; go ahead!"

27 *ORA* 49, pt. 1, 275–76, 277–279.

28 Howard, *124th Regiment*, 306; Handwritten letter fragment, Francis F. Audsley, 1865, SHSMC; *ORA* 49, pt. 1, 275–76.

10 a.m. tomorrow," the Pennsylvanian retorted. "Gen. C[anby] yielded to him," Comstock recorded in his journal.[29]

A private in the 14th Wisconsin complained in a letter to his parents the next day: "If they had only been driven a little further, we would have captured the whole garrison, but the Gen'l seemed to think he had done well enough for one day, so he stopped to fortify & get ready to 'give it to them' in the morning." The besiegers, however, did not recognize the importance of the point they gained and failed to press their advantage.[30]

While the 8th Iowa assaulted from the swamp, the Federal batteries and gunboats in the bay continued their fire from the Union left. The artillery cannonading initially prevented the Confederates from sending reinforcements to their left. "The charge at the right was a surprise to the rebels, and as it effectually flanked their position, threw them into confusion, and completed the demoralization our shells must have commenced," noted a soldier of the 95th Illinois.[31]

In his report on the assault, Truman criticized the lack of coordination between the XVI and XIII Corps:

Here it was the golden opportunity, by not assaulting the works all along the line, especially after Carr got inside. And yet no orders for a general assault were given. And worse than all, our brave fellows on the right, after carrying Red Fort, were driven out by nearly all the troops engaged upon the rebel side without the slightest resistance being made from 16,000 men, who were only too anxious to participate. This must reflect unhappily, at least, upon some of the General officers upon the left and in the center and will prove a hard fact to explain away. The Thirteenth Corps might have turned Alexis and captured the whole batch of prisoners.[32]

At 7:30 p.m., Canby wired Granger of Smith's lodgment and ordered him to direct the fire and operations on his part of the line to avoid coming in conflict with Carr's Division. "Smith has taken 300 yards of rifle-pits and 200 prisoners. Keep the rebels uneasy on your front by the fire of your guns and such demonstrations as will prevent the concentrating against Smith, and be prepared to take advantage of any opportunity that may offer."[33]

29 "Spanish Fort," *The National Tribune*, Jan. 28, 1886, 5; Carr, *First Reunion of the Survivors of the Army of Tennessee*, 26; Comstock, *The Diary of Cyrus B. Comstock*, 314.

30 Newton, *A Wisconsin Boy in Dixie*, 150; Maury, "Spanish Fort," 134.

31 "From the 95th Illinois," *The Woodstock* [IL] *Sentinel*, 1.

32 "Our Special Report; The Preparation. The Start. The Investment of Spanish Fort," *New York Times*, Apr. 24, 1865.

33 *ORA* 49, pt. 1, 96; *ORA* 49, pt. 2, 280.

General Osterhaus sent a follow-up telegraph: "Please order the batteries playing on the wharf at Spanish Fort to keep up during the night a continuous fire, at the rate of one shot every two minutes; besides, you will order such demonstrative operations on your whole front as may divert the enemy's attention, and prevent his massing against the troops of the Sixteenth Corps on the extreme right and driving them from their lodgment. Acknowledge receipt." It is unclear if Granger acknowledged these dispatches; however, they confirm orders were sent to the XIII Corps to continue firing in their front. This fire rendered it unsafe for the XVI Corps to advance further inside that portion of the Spanish Fort Works.[34]

Confederates

Despite the bombardment, some two dozen 14th Texas Dismounted Cavalry men answered Captain James A. Howze's call to rally around the flag in a countercharge. "He gave the word charge," remembered a soldier of Ector's Brigade, "and the boys gave the Rebel yell and charged. Here, I saw our brave young flag bearer, Billy Powers, go down. This checked us. Someone gathered up the colors, and we retreated. This was the last gun we fired." Although Howze's valiant counterattack failed to regain the captured position, it bought some time for the rest of the hard-pressed garrison to escape.[35]

Gibson had Company G, 20th Louisiana—the post provost marshal company under Lt. Alfred G. Clarke—ready for this contingency. At the head of the garrison guard, Clarke rushed to the left to dislodge Geddes. In this countercharge, he was gunned down. "On the slope of the ridge, I came across a wounded rebel officer, who said he was Captain Clarke, of Mobile, that he had charged at the head of the provost guard, and that was shot through both shoulders," recalled Union Maj. Charles J. Allen. The Federals carried Clarke off the field and provided medical attention. Despite efforts to save him, Clarke died afterward at a New Orleans hospital. His sacrifice, however, and the stubborn resistance of his comrades bought time for Gibson to execute one of the most remarkable evacuations of the war. "Louisiana has not lost during the war a truer man or a more thorough-going soldier," Gibson acknowledged in his after-action report.[36]

---

34 *ORA* 49, pt. 2, 280.

35 W. Bailey, "The Star Company of Ector's Texas Brigade," *Confederate Veteran* 22 (1914): 405; "Fourteenth Texas Cavalry," The Handbook of Texas Online, Texas State Historical Association, accessed June 9, 2016, https://tshaonline.org/handbook/online/articles/qkf14; Allen, "Operations Against the City of Mobile," 80–81; Andrews, *History of the Campaign of Mobile*, 155–156.

36 Handwritten report, RLG, Apr. 16, 1865; Allen, "Operations against the City," 81; *ORA* 49, pt. 1, 317–318. Gibson's report indicates Clarke held the rank of lieutenant, not captain.

A month after the siege, Gibson penned the following letter of condolence for Capt. John McGrath to take to Alfred Clarke's wife and family:

I feel it is my duty to claim the privilege of expressing my deep sympathy with the family of Lieut. A. G. Clarke, Provost Marshall of the Brigade who was killed while leading his command, in the most gallant manner, at Spanish Fort.

I have no words which will adequately convey my sense of his worth as a soldier. He was indeed an extraordinary man. Who was more zealous? Who could have been more attentive? Whoever exhibited under hard trials more steady fortitude, more unflinching courage? Whatever deterred him from performing promptly his whole duty and of exacting from his subordinates the most implicit obedience? In rain, in sunshine, in our prosperous days, in crushing disasters—he was ever the same brave, devoted, high-minded, prompt, soldier patriot. Would that there were more men like him in our unhappy land.

Let us not forget Clarke. Let us tell his wife & children that we all admired & loved him.

As his commanding officer, I can say he has left a rich legacy to his family—in the good services, he rendered the Country [word unclear] & in his [word unclear] character as a soldier & a man. Please take this note to them.

Yours very truly,
R. L. Gibson Brig Genl[37]

Ironically, the timeliness of the federal assault saved the life of one soldier of Ector's Brigade. The Confederates had court-martialed Pvt. James W. Harris, Company B, 29th North Carolina, for robbery and desertion. Fortunately for Harris, the same day his death sentence was published, Carr's Division captured him during the assault. Instead of being executed, the Federals sent him to Ship Island off the Mississippi Coast with the other prisoners of war.[38]

Gibson quickly ordered Holtzclaw and Colonel Andrews, commanding Ector's Brigade on the extreme left, to charge the enemy in front, flank, and drive him out. Holtzclaw reported to Gibson that there was some confusion in the troops on hand, that it was already very dark, and that the enemy was in heavy force. His staff officers brought similar intelligence. He ordered them to display a heavy line of skirmishers in front of the Federals and make every effort to connect with the part of the line in which the gap had been made. Holtzclaw informed Gibson that

37 Henry L. Clarke, "Captain Alfred Clarke," Civil War Louisiana, accessed Dec. 14, 2019, http://www.civilwarlouisiana.com/2012/06/.

38 Theresa Arnold-Scriber and Terry G. Scriber, Ship Island, *Mississippi: Rosters and History of the Civil War Prison* (Jefferson, NC, 2007), 375; Aldo S. Perry, *Civil War Courts-Martial of North Carolina Troops* (Jefferson, NC, 2012), 266.

the Federals were firmly lodged, being reinforced, and had begun to entrench. The order to charge was thus revoked, but sharp picket firing continued.[39]

At this point, Gibson withdrew the commander of his brigade, Col. Francis L. Campbell, from the right wing of the fort with a portion of his command. Part of Campbell's command attacked, driving the Unionists back, while others were posted as a rearguard at the treadway to secure the evacuation route. The besiegers were checked. Campbell's vigorous counter-attacks and the danger of being shelled by the XIII Corps compelled Carr to assume the defensive and entrench.[40]

Confederate Evacuation

At 7:30 p.m., Holtzclaw wired Liddell and Maury to inform them of the lodgment. "The left is turned after severe fighting," he reported. "We will have to withdraw tonight if we can make all arrangements you can in the way of boats, etc." Maury had just returned to Mobile from the fort when he received the urgent telegraph indicating the Federals had gained a lodgment and threatened to cut off their evacuation route. Within five minutes of receiving Holtzclaw's dispatch, Liddell anxiously telegraphed Major Marks at Battery Huger: "General Holtzclaw telegraphs the left turned at Spanish Fort. General Gibson did not [report?], and I wish to know what the news is at once and give General Gibson all the assistance you can."[41]

In compliance with Beauregard's instructions, Gibson followed his orders to abandon the position and save his garrison. Indeed, it became evident that he "could no longer judiciously protract the defense." Before the battle began, measures were taken to withdraw at the last moment. These measures were well known to Gibson, his officers, and the men who prepared the escape routes. Gibson immediately recognized the lodgment threatened to cut off his evacuation route and that a general assault would soon be ordered. He knew the time had come to withdraw his troops. "It was apparent from his superiority in heavy guns and numbers and the nearness of his approach at several points that unless extraordinary re-enforcements could be had, the moment had at length arrived

---

39 Handwritten report, RLG, Apr. 16, 1865; Andrews, *History of the Campaign of Mobile*, vi. In a January 1867 letter to Andrews, Gibson mentions a false report that the enemy was driven back on the left and attacking in force on the right, creating confusion and thus delaying reinforcements sent to check the Federals.

40 *ORA* 49, pt. 1, 317; Handwritten report, RLG, Apr. 16, 1865.

41 Handwritten telegram, James T. Holtzclaw to General Liddell, Apr. 8, 1865, Christian T. Christensen Papers, Huntington Library, San Marino, CA; Maury, "Defense of Spanish Fort," 132; *ORA* 49, pt. 2, 1217.

when I could no longer hold the position without imminent risk of losing the garrison," reported Gibson.[42]

At 8:50 p.m., Gibson wired Maury: "The enemy continues to press, but I hope for the best. He broke Ector's Brigade on the left, in the woods." Ten minutes later, he sent another dispatch informing Maury of the evacuation. "I am beginning to retire by treadway. Hope to lose nothing but artillery," he reported. "Will have a guard at the landing, so as to hold fast to the last moment."[43]

The soldiers, after spiking their guns, quietly prepared to escape after receiving whispered orders to evacuate. "The few remaining stores were issued; the sick and wounded carefully removed; the infirmary corps and several hundred negroes who arrived that evening to be employed in the defense, and, finally, in good order, the whole garrison was withdrawn," Gibson reported.[44]

The Washington Artillery's 5th Company at Battery Blair spiked their guns last. They followed Gibson's orders to man their guns to the last in case the besiegers discovered the retreat in progress. During the preparations to leave, Sgt. John Bartley concealed the company's cherished battle flag around his body.[45]

Unaware of the preplanned escape route, some gray-coated soldiers were puzzled and wondered how they could escape the Unionists surrounding them. They were directed toward the delta in their rear and moved out quickly to reach the edge of the steep bluffs overlooking the bay. The soldiers proceeded down the gorge's almost perpendicular sides, clinging to vines, saplings, anything to keep their hold until they reached the bottom, fifty feet or so below. And there, to their amazement, they found the beginning of a treadway.[46]

Colonel Thomas H. Herndon, 36th Alabama, who received severe wounds at Chickamauga and again at Atlanta, is reportedly to have been among the last to leave the Spanish Fort's trenches. He lost his sword in the marsh on their retreat from Spanish Fort. The Alabamian—utterly exhausted and not strong enough to go on his own—would not have made it without the help of his devoted men. Herndon's soldiers took turns supporting and almost carrying him. They were

42 Maury, "Souvenirs of the War," 4; Maury, "Spanish Fort," 130; *ORA* 49, pt. 1, 316, 317.

43 *ORA* 49, pt. 2, 1218, 1219.

44 *ORA* 49, pt. 1, 317.

45 Chalaron, "Battle Echoes from Shiloh," 221; Owen, *In Camp and Battle with the Washington Artillery of New Orleans*, 424.

46 Stephenson, "Defence of Spanish Fort," 126; Stephenson, *Civil War Memoir*, 364–365.

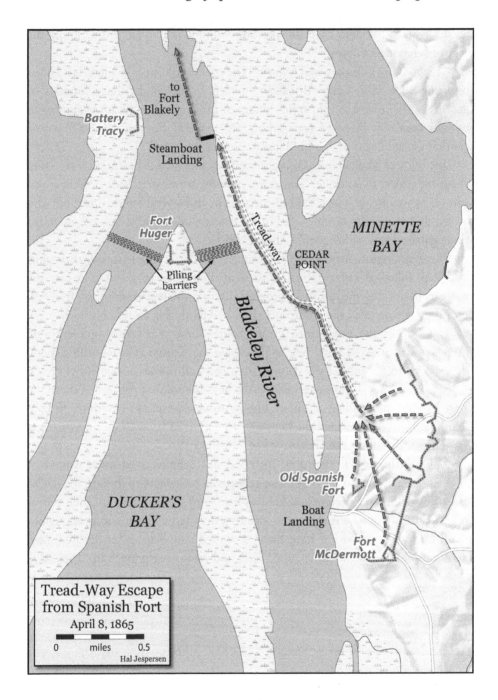

Tread-Way Escape
from Spanish Fort
April 8, 1865

0   miles   0.5

Hal Jespersen

all made to remove their shoes when they first left the fort to keep their retreat from being heard.[47]

The cover of darkness significantly aided the garrison's escape. First Lieutenant Chalaron of the Washington Artillery remembered: "With shoes removed and all articles productive of noise or glitter left behind, with muskets carried low down to hide their sheen from the keen eye of the foe's pickets, in single file, the garrison threaded down the bluff to the sea marsh, where a plank treadway led toward the boats that were stationed to pick up our escaping force." The Graybacks quietly followed the treadway, "which ran from a small peninsula from the left flank across the river, and over a broad marsh to a deep channel opposite Battery Huger." Herndon, utterly exhausted, could not get on his boots again at the end of the treadway, so he had to leave in his socks. Although within range of the Union's heavy batteries, "high grass" helped conceal them on the treadway.[48]

"The treadway first debouched upon the beach, then turning to the right, it went up the shore quite a distance. Just how far I cannot say, but I know we passed so close to the enemy's pickets stationed in the marsh that we could hear them talking, and right under the nose of their battery," remembered one Confederate. "Finally, the treadway turned and struck out into the bay. The water was shallow, and we walked just above the water's surface. Suddenly, a shot came. It was from that battery! Imagine our consternation, but it was not repeated for some time. It was evident they did not see us but were merely firing periodically across what they supposed to be the channel in order to prevent any succor reaching us."[49]

At the end of the bridge, several flat-bottomed riverboats were assembled to ferry the garrison across the river. Maury and Liddell had sent all available boats to aid in Gibson's evacuation. Once the soldiers reached the end of the treadway, they could see the outlines of the steamers their commanding officer had sent over for them in the darkness.[50]

The soldiers jumped off the treadway where it ended, into the marsh. With the Federals nearby, they were in a desperate situation, floundering off the swampy shore of the Blakeley River, waist-deep in mud. "It was a bog. I do not know

47 *Confederate Military History Extended Edition, vol. 7, Alabama* (Wilmington, NC, 1899), 616; *Account of Mrs. Herndon, wife of Thomas H. Herndon*, Confederate Regimental History Files, SG024903, Montgomery, Alabama Department of Archives and History, hereafter *Account of Mrs. Herndon*.

48 ORA 49, pt. 2, 96; "Lady Slocomb: The Silent Witness," *New Orleans Times Picayune*, 7; *Account of Mrs. Herndon*.

49 Stephenson, *Civil War Memoir*, 365–367.

50 Maury, "Spanish Fort," 131–132; Maury, "Defense of Mobile," 7; ORA 49, pt. 2, 1219; Stephenson, *Civil War Memoir*, 366.

Colonel Thomas H. Herndon, commander, 36th Alabama. *Alabama Department of Archives and History*

how far down I would have gone had it not been for a friendly log. I grabbed the end of it with both hands, pulled myself upon it, ran out to the other end, and tried the mud again. This time, I did not go so deep," remembered a veteran of the Washington Artillery.[51]

"We waded in the marshes of Mobile Bay, sometimes in mud and water up to our knees and waist," remembered one soldier of the 14th Texas Dismounted Cavalry, "and we were finally picked up by a blockade runner."[52]

"The irresponsible Dr. Sheppard was in the crowd with a jug of whiskey. He was not a very good jumper, and being burdened with his jug, he soon became hopelessly mired," remembered a soldier who escaped with the 18th Alabama, one of the first regiments to leave on the treadway. Sheppard called for help and told the soldiers that he would divide the whiskey with them when he got out. The soldiers helped pull each other out when one would jump, miss the tussock, and sink waist-deep in the mud and water. They were covered in black mud when they made it to the boats.[53]

The men found themselves sailing up the river in a relatively short time. A Union battery noticed a gunboat and took some shots that came dangerously close. Still, the boat continued to steam up the river safely to Fort Blakeley.[54]

---

51 Stephenson, *Civil War Memoir*, 366–367.

52 W. Bailey, "The Star Company of Ector's Brigade," *Confederate Veteran* XXII (June 1914): 405.

53 Jones & Pulcrano, *Eighteenth Alabama Infantry Regiment*, 70.

54 Stephenson & Hughes, *Civil War Memoir of Philip Daingerfield Stephenson*, 367.

Not all the garrison escaped by boat. The evening of April 8 was exceedingly dark, which slowed the movement of the evacuation. "The marshes about Mobile, as marshes almost everywhere else, produced a greater moral effect upon besiegers and besieged than facts justified. During ordinary stages of water, those marshes were everywhere traversable by footmen with but little difficulty," recalled Maury. To get all the troops to safety before daylight, Col. Bush Jones led about 200 men up to Blakeley using an alternate evacuation route through the marsh, rather than wait at the terminus of the treadway for the slow process of ferriage. Earlier in the siege, as an extra precaution, engineers discovered a feasible route and staked it out with help from men of the 9th Texas. "This marsh was quite practicable for infantry by that time," remembered Maury. He noted the flood had subsided, and the ground had dried. Maury noted that had the enemy known this, they could have placed troops and batteries there. This would have flanked the Confederate left and cut off their escape route.[55]

Gibson's rapid movements enabled him to march his forces away before the Federals found out they were gone or where they went. His evacuation was so stealthy that it took some time for the besiegers to realize most of the garrison had left. While they were escaping, Capt. Edward G. Miller, 20th Wisconsin, recorded in his diary: "Had a cool night in the trenches. Reb picket fired a good deal. Suspicious; things looked like preparations to leave."[56]

After the last Southerner crossed it, the Confederates burned the small flatboat bridge from the rear of Spanish Fort to the island. "It was not until about this time, the enemy discovered the works had been evacuated," stated Gibson. Father Andrew Cornette, a Spring Hill College Jesuit priest, ministered to the Spanish Fort garrison. Referring to himself in the third person, Cornette described the escape in his diary: "General Gibson determines to evacuate the fort. The evacuation is effected between eight o'clock and midnight. Father Cornette escapes with Father Turgis in a boat at 12:15 a.m.; at 12:20 a.m., the fort is taken, and at 1 o'clock, it is in flames, lighting up the retreat of the fugitives."[57]

The Federals reported apprehending another 300 Confederate soldiers in the aftermath of the assault. Some were captured in the advanced rifle pits, while others had sought shelter during the bombardment deep inside the bomb proofs

55 Andrews, *History of the Campaign of Mobile*, VI; Maury, "Souvenirs of the War," 4; *ORA* 49, pt. 1, 317; Maury, "Defense of Spanish Fort," 131.

56 Maury, "Spanish Fort," 133; Miller, *Captain Edward Gee Miller*, 31. Miller belonged to Bertram's Brigade on the southernmost flank of the fort.

57 Handwritten report, RLG, Apr. 16, 1865; Andrew Cornette, Journal, 1872, Spring Hill College Archives, Mobile, AL, 182–184. Cornette recorded his account in French.

and did not know their comrades had evacuated. They were surprised when the blue-coated soldiers dragged them out of the bombproofs with the demand to surrender. Gibson deeply lamented the capture of these men. "It is to be hoped and presumed that these accidents will be satisfactorily explained," he reported. Federal reports indicate up to 556 Confederates were captured during the siege.[58]

Federals

Around 10:00 p.m., the remainder of Carr's Division was sent to their rifle pits, where they formed a line of battle, and the order came: "Every man over the works." The men expected a blaze of fire in their faces; however, nothing happened. Moore's Brigade got on top of the works and began to move the timber and *chevaux de frise* in their front. They had a difficult time getting through the densely laid abatis.[59]

As the men made it into the fort, one officer from McMillen's Brigade recalled jumping into the vast and deep ditch. He had to climb the embankment of the fort by sticking his bayonet into the ground to pull himself up to the top. At that moment, he fully realized the soundness of Canby's judgment in using shovels instead of bayonets in a general assault. Another soldier recalled: "A moment after I jumped off the work, I noticed one of the 72nd boys a straddle of a gun calling the major's attention to that being his capture."[60]

At 11:30 p.m., Geddes notified Carr that he found no troops in Red Fort and added that he believed the Confederates were evacuating Old Spanish Fort. Carr directed him to advance a strong skirmish line and gave the same order to the brigades of Ward and Moore. A little before midnight, Carr's entire division moved up behind a strong skirmish line and, without resistance, climbed over the parapets of Spanish Fort and Red Forts. McArthur's Division swept around the front and left of Spanish Fort and marched in without opposition.[61]

After Smith's Corps realized it had complete possession of the fort, they were fired upon by the XIII Corps. "After a hard climb, we got on top and had just dropped inside of the works when a battery of the Thirteenth Corps opened on

---

58 Spink, "Capture of Spanish Fort," 7; "A Week of Victory," *Nashville* [TN] *Daily Union*, Apr. 21, 1865; *ORA* 49, pt. 1, 317–318, 207.

59 Handwritten letter fragment, Francis F. Audsley, 1865, State Historical Society Missouri Columbia, hereafter Handwritten letter fragment, Francis F. Audsley, 1865, SHSMC; "The Sixteenth Corps Did It," *The National Tribune*, Aug. 25, 1910, 3. Abatis are sharpened tree branches.

60 Elliot, *Thirty-Third Regiment*, 231; Handwritten letter fragment, Francis F. Audsley, 1865, SHSMC.

61 "The Capture of Spanish Fort," *The National Tribune*, Oct. 29, 1908, 7.

Red Fort. *Minnesota Historical Society, St. Paul's*

us," remembered a soldier of Moore's Brigade. "One shot just skimmed the top of the works and gave my comrade and me a close call and a big shower of sand. Then one of my comrades shouted at the top of his voice: "You son of a gun, who are you firing at?" The Federal gunboats and mortars kept throwing shells into the fort. It took about an hour before they understood their comrades now held the fort. Soldiers of the XVI Corps had to stand on top of the breastworks and shout to them to cease firing.[62]

A degree of competitive animosity existed between the two Union corps. "A. J. sent in his guerillas, and they had possession long before the 13th knew it," recalled one soldier of the 122nd Illinois in a letter home. "The 13th are Canby's pets, and he wanted them to have the honor." Years later, a veteran of the 124th Illinois claimed Canby did not know of the capture until an orderly "routed him out of bed."[63]

"We had a great joke on the 13th Corps; after our men had got inside the fort they mounted the breastworks & gave a cheer: the 13th Corps thought the Rebs

62 "Geddes's Brigade at Spanish Fort," *The National Tribune*, Aug. 25, 1910, 3; "The Sixteenth Corps Did It," *The National Tribune*, Aug. 25, 1910, 3.

63 William H. Peter to "Dear Ones at Home," 1865, Manuscripts Department, Abraham Lincoln Presidential Library; Arthur M. Gurnsey, "Spanish Fort and Fort Blakely Again," *The National Tribune*, Aug. 2, 1888, 3.

were going to make a charge, & they began to fire at a great rate into our own men," observed a Wisconsinite of the XVI Corps. "They felt rather sheepish when they found out who they were firing at. The Gunboats, too, threw one 11-inch shell into the fort after we had occupied it but did no damage that I am aware of."[64]

A triumphant shout rang out all along the line. With joy and tumult, they rushed in and took possession. "The thirteen days of siege at last were ended," joyfully recalled a soldier of the 33rd Iowa.[65]

After nearly two weeks of arduous labor and fighting, the Federals were irritated that most of the Confederates had slipped away. Had the bombardment and Carr's assault occurred earlier in the day, the treadway escape would likely have been unsuccessful in the daylight. The navy's failure to cut the line of water communication in the rear of Spanish Fort also made it possible for a large part of the garrison to escape "Though the visible result of the acquisition of Spanish Fort seemed at the moment a somewhat meager reward for our labor and sacrifice (the capture of but a fraction of the garrison and about fifty guns), yet we felt that we had secured an important strategic advantage and that it must prove the beginning of the end of the campaign," recalled Hubbard.[66]

The Federals were vexed by the garrison's successful escape but found joy in driving them from their stronghold. Many of the men off duty were so excited that they got out of bed and went up to see the fort by moonlight. Captain Miller, 20th Wisconsin, went to bed when the musketry firing and cannonading were incessant. He woke up when he heard the order "Fall in." Miller pulled on his boots and grabbed his sword but had no one to fight. He heard a comrade say the Rebels evacuated the fort at half-past eleven. Miller moved into the works and went into camp near the center.[67]

Inside the fort, the Federals found many commissary stores, some of which may have been supplied by the citizens of Mobile. They promptly appropriated these items without army requisition forms. "Here we stacked arms and rest a little, scrambling meantime for the possession of the guns and for the hams and cornmeal left by the garrison," noted one Illinoisan solder. Some of the Unionists even dressed up in Rebel uniforms.[68]

---

64 Newton & Ambrose, "The Siege of Mobile," 599.

65 Sperry, *33d Iowa Infantry*, 144.

66 Hill, *War Papers*, 189; Hubbard, "Civil War Papers," 630, LC.

67 Sperry, *33d Iowa Infantry*, 144; Miller, *Captain Edward Gee Miller*, 31.

68 "From the 95th Illinois," *The Woodstock* [IL] *Sentinel*, May 10, 1865, 1; Howard, *124th Regiment*, 307; Milton A. Stubbs, "Milton Stubbs Letter," U.S. Christian Commission, accessed Feb. 21, 2020, https://www.nwuscc.org/MiltonStubbsLetter.html.

Indeed, the blue-clad veterans were elated. Adjutant Wales W. Wood, 95th Illinois, recalled a few of the soldiers were so excited that they got ahead of the regimental line in its advance to the bay. Wood caught up with one of these men, Jim Barry, an Irish immigrant from Company E, 95th Illinois, who sat on a keg of tobacco under a tree. With proud feelings that animated his patriotic heart, Barry held up and saluted Adjutant Wood with an extract of his booty and offered in his peculiar Irish drawl: "Adjutant, will ye have a plug of tobaky?" The offer was so ludicrous that Barry received no reprimand, and no arrests were made of the few who outdistanced the regiment on this occasion.[69]

On the night of the evacuation, friendly fire resulted in tragedy for one Federal. Two blue-coated soldiers, being held as prisoners at Battery Tracey, managed to escape using a boat. Reaching the mainland, they moved carefully along the shore. Having followed down after the retreating garrison, other U.S. soldiers heard some rustling of the bushes and believed it to be straggling Confederates. They shouted an order to surrender. Assuming the demand came from the Southern soldiers, the two men did not respond and were fired on, with one being killed instantly. The other man cried for quarter and soon found himself among friends.[70]

69 "Capture Forts About Mobile." *Belvidere* [IL] *Republican-Northwestern*, Jan. 29, 1907, 6.

70 Andrews, *History of the Campaign of Mobile*, 236.

Chapter 14

"Until the Rebels Are Whipped"

Federals

Sunday, April 9, 1865: In the early morning, a flurry of Union dispatches revealed the competitive animosity between the XVI and XIII Corps. At 1:00 a.m., Smith wired Canby, confirming the possession of the Spanish Fort by the XVI Corps. Fifteen minutes later, Granger reported to Canby that the XIII Corps occupied Fort Alexis [Fort McDermott] and the central bastion and then sent another dispatch asking: "What news from Smith's lines?" Smith wired Granger directly: "I have possession of Spanish Fort and have relieved you from the necessity of taking any portion of it." Considering Smith's Corps had been inside the fort for hours, Granger sent a somewhat ironic response at 1:35 a.m.: "You were late! We had possession of Fort Alexis [McDermott] and Spanish Fort an hour before we heard from you. Our men are asleep inside now." Smith followed up with another report to Canby: "We have all the artillery the enemy had in the fort. The Forty-seventh Illinois, one of my regiments, took Fort Alexis while Granger was asleep."[1]

At dawn, the Federals were greeted by the sight of the Stars and Stripes floating on the heights of Spanish Fort. "The star-spangled banner was thrown to the

---

1 *ORA* 49, pt. 2, 296, 300; William R. Plum, LL.B., *The Military Telegraph During the Civil War in the United States* (Chicago, 1882), 302, 303. The Federals referred to Fort McDermott as Fort Alexis.

Fort McDermott from Old Spanish Fort. *Minnesota History Society, St. Paul's*

breeze from the three forts about 10 o'clock a.m. on the 9th," remembered one Union veteran.[2]

That morning, the besiegers at Fort Blakeley received the news of the escape of the Spanish Fort garrison. "The effect upon us all was very depressing," recalled Col. Henry C. Merriam, 73rd USCT, "for the failure to capture that garrison, after spending half a month digging them out, meant that these troops had abandoned a position no longer tenable, only to fall back to stronger fortifications covering Mobile, there to be again besieged, probably under conditions less favorable to us."[3]

Frustrated by the escape of Spanish Fort's garrison, Canby turned his full attention to Fort Blakeley. Leaving Bertram's Brigade behind to guard prisoners and property, he ordered Granger's 3rd Division and Smith's 1st and 3rd Divisions to move out "with all possible dispatch" from Spanish Fort to join the investing forces at Blakeley and "to be put in readiness for an immediate assault."[4]

The courageous conduct of the 8th Iowa led to the capture of Spanish Fort. As a special honor, Canby directed Geddes's Iowans to camp inside Spanish Fort

2 Byers, *Iowa*, 409; "The Capture of Spanish Fort," *The National Tribune*, Oct. 29, 1908, 7.

3 Henry C. Merriam, "The Capture of Mobile," *War Papers, Read Before the Commandery of the State of Maine Military Order of the Loyal Legion of the United States* 3 (1908): 244.

4 Andrews, *History of the Campaign of Mobile*, 189; *ORA* 49, pt. 2, 295, 297.

and gather trophies of the victory while the rest of Carr's Division marched to Fort Blakeley. Every officer, moreover, received a brevet rank promotion.[5]

Before marching to Fort Blakeley, several soldiers decided to tour the inside of Spanish Fort. "A strange sensation came over us as we climbed, unhindered, over the breastworks and walls, from which a few hours before we would have been swept off with a storm of fire had we attempted to scale them," remembered one Iowan. "We were glad enough no "charge" had been ordered; glad indeed that our position had been on the outside and not inside of the fort, the center of such a rain of iron and lead, it showed the marks of conflict everywhere."[6]

The interior of Spanish Fort revealed unmistakable signs of the terrible damage done by the U.S. Army's artillery. All the trees around Gibson's unenviable quarters were torn to pieces with shot and shell. Haversacks and bloodstained clothing were scattered over the ground. Deep holes and ruts covered the earth; the cabins were smashed or partly smashed, and from right to left the besieger's shells marked the parapet. "Our artillery did great damage to their works. The mortars must have caused great damage; in some places, the ground was fairly plowed up by them," a soldier of 124th Illinois recorded in his diary.[7]

After-action reports variously indicated between 540 and 556 prisoners of war, including 20 officers. "The prisoners represented principally the States of North Carolina, Texas, and Alabama. They were sufficiently well-clad and moderately well-armed and otherwise well equipped," reported the *New York Times*. Private Robert A. Spink, 14th Wisconsin, had an opportunity to talk to one of the prisoners inside the fort during most of the siege. "He said our artillery demonstration on the evening of the 4th inst[ant] and on the night before was the most awful he had ever witnessed," Spink recalled. The prisoners were marched out of the fort into the Union camp and were made to pass between rows of wooden mortars. Some cursing was heard while the bands played Yankee Doodle.[8]

Carr reported grimly: "Twenty-six of the enemy's dead were buried on the field by my men this morning." The location of the burial site of these Confederates is

5 Huff, *The Annals of Iowa*, 947–948; Byers, *Iowa*, 409; Andrew Geddes, 8th Iowa, "Spanish Fort," *The National Tribune*, Nov. 24, 1892, 4; "Spanish Fort Again," *The National Tribune*, Dec. 28, 1892, 4.

6 Sperry, *33d Iowa Infantry*, 144.

7 "Our Special Report; The Preparation. The Start. The Investment of Spanish Fort," *New York Times*, Apr. 24, 1865, 1; Stuart, *Iowa Colonels and Regiments*, 193–194; Snedeker, *The Civil War Diary of Charles Henry Snedeker*.

8 *ORA* 49, pt. 1, 229, 268; Truman, "The Siege of Mobile," *New York Times*, Apr. 21, 1865, 8; Robert A. Spink, "The Capture of Spanish Fort," *The National Tribune*, Oct. 29, 1908, 7; Edwards Journal, Apr. 10, 1865, 255.

unknown. Presumably, these men are still buried on the old battlefield, as there are no records known of the bodies being moved after the war.[9]

Smith stated that "four stands of colors" were captured from Ector's Brigade. "My Regiment might have had a greater number of flags had they been less anxious to engage the enemy," claimed Lieutenant Colonel Bell. "Where all do their duty, it is a difficult and delicate matter to make any discrimination." The battle flags were captured as follows: Sgt. Edgar A. Bras, Company K, 8th Iowa Volunteers, took one from the rebel color bearer, one by the 8th Iowa, one by the 108th Illinois, and one by the 124th Illinois. Sergeant Bras earned the Medal of Honor for capturing a flag from the standard-bearer of one of the Texas regiments, either the 10th or the 32nd Cavalry (dismounted). "A rebel battle flag, captured by the 8th Iowa, waved in front of Gen. Carr's headquarters during the day. It is red ground, blue cross, with thirteen white stars. Another flag belonging to the 39th North Carolina has Jackson, Murfreesboro, and Chattanooga inscribed on it," a correspondent from the *Times-Democrat* observed.[10]

Carr and Smith reported capturing 46 artillery pieces, but the official records indicated 47 pieces, including 20 field pieces and 27 siege/seacoast pieces. Nearly all the big guns were spiked by the Graybacks and were unserviceable. The gun carriages, implements, powder, cartridges, and fixed ammunition were in good condition. "There were some of the most improved patterns of artillery in the three forts, a greater portion of which were spiked with nails," recalled Pvt. Spink. "There were Brooke, Blakely's Napoleons, howitzers, mortars, and other patterns." Large amounts of ammunition and 270 small arms were also seized and removed

---

9 *ORA* 49, pt. 1, 268.

10 Walter Clark, *Histories of the Several Regiments and Battalions from North Carolina, in the Great War 1861–'65* (Raleigh, NC, 1901), 768; *ORA* 49, pt. 1, 229, 269, 278; "Army—Medal of Honor Recipients—U.S. Military Awards for Valor," U.S. Military Awards for Valor—Top 3, accessed June 25, 2020, https://valor.defense.gov/Recipients/Army-Medal-of-Honor-Recipients/; "Flag," American Civil War Museum: Online Collections, accessed Jan, 9, 2018, http://moconfederacy. pastperfectonline.com/webobject/8E6CAF5A-67A1-4402-B250-284917542464; Howard Michael Madaus, *The Battle Flags of the Confederate Army of Tennessee* (Milwaukee, WI, 1976), 80; "Letter from Varitas," *New Orleans Times-Democrat*, Apr. 14, 1865. The newspaper correspondent from the *Times-Democrat* misidentified the flag of the 39th North Carolina captured inside Spanish Fort. It had 12 stars, not 13 and the "Chattanooga" battle honor was actually "Chickamauga." This flag had been issued to the regiment in early 1864 (Collections report, North Carolina Museum of History). The 39th North Carolina also had a second, older flag in the fort. The ladies of Asheville presented them this regimental flag in North Carolina in May 1862. During the evacuation, Lt. R. H. Brown of Jackson County concealed the flag as he left Spanish Fort. In later years, the 39th exhibited this worn battle-flag at reunions in North Carolina.

from the battlefield. Moreover, 600 spades and shovels, 134 picks, and 203 axes fell into Federal hands.[11]

Among the appliances of war captured that were most influential in deciding the battle for Spanish Fort were the wooden mortars. One Minnesotan noted in his journal: "They were made of gum trees and were light enough to be carried." He described the mortars as looking like "harmless wooden buckets" and "iron bound buckets."[12]

The intra-service rivalry between the two Union Corps continued that morning. Lieutenant David Sanders, 81st Illinois, Carr's Division, and some other officers went over to see how the inside of the fortifications looked by daylight. One of the first things he noticed was an officer marking the guns captured by the XIII Corps. "While we were parleying with him Gen. Carr came up and at once stopped him, and sent his Chief of Ordnance over and marked every one of them captured by the Third Brigade, Third Division, Sixteenth Corps," remembered Sanders. Carr then sent Granger a scathing dispatch: "Your men are contending with mine for the possession of the captured guns and works. Let us wait until the rebels are whipped before we quarrel amongst ourselves."[13]

The rivalry between the two corps played out in the *National Tribune* for many years after the war. "It was late the next morning when I went over into the captured fort, where I charged over with my regiment, what was my surprise to see all the guns in the big fort tagged with a big card, 'Captured by Gen. Gordon Granger's Thirteenth Corps,' right where I was fired on by the same corps' battery. Reports claim that when Smith saw those cards, he ordered a detail from the 33d Wisconsin to go and take them off, saying: 'If there is any credit for this, the Sixteenth Corps should have it,'" recalled a soldier of Carr's Division 45 years later. In defense of the XIII Corps, Major General Osterhaus ordered Granger to have Bertram's Brigade take charge of all prisoners and property inside Spanish Fort.[14]

On their approximately four-mile march north to Fort Blakeley, the blue-coated soldiers received welcome news from Virginia. One of Canby's staff officers rode by the marching troops and told them that the Confederate capital had fallen seven days earlier. "Boys, Richmond has fallen," the officer on horseback announced to every regiment he passed, which resulted in loud cheers from the

11 *ORA* 49, pt. 1, 150–151, 229, 268; "The Mobile Expedition," *New Orleans Times-Democrat*, Apr. 12, 1865, 2; Spink, "The Capture of Spanish Fort," The *National Tribune*, Oct. 29, 1908, 7; Hewitt, *Supplement to the Official Records*, pt. I, vol. 7, 963.

12 Edwards Journal, Apr. 10, 1865, 254–255.

13 "Spanish Fort," *The National Tribune*, Jan. 28, 1886, 5; *ORA* 49, pt. 2, 303.

14 "The Sixteenth Corps Did It," *The National Tribune*, Aug. 25, 1910, 3; *ORA* 49, pt. 2, 297.

men. "Brig. Genls., staff and all, would off with their hats and give three Cheers for Grant and Sherman," one Iowan shared in a letter to his father. The uplifting news assured the Federals that the end was near.[15]

Confederates

As morning broke, the artillerists at Battery Tracey observed the Federal columns crossing the Minette Creek pontoon bridge. Colonel Patton—who assumed direct command of Huger and Tracey after evacuating Spanish Fort— wired Liddell the grim news that heavy columns of blue-coated soldiers were marching his way.[16]

The Spanish Fort garrison disembarked and marched ashore at Fort Blakeley in the early morning hours. After a grueling four-mile hike through the thick marsh, the 200 men under Colonel Jones arrived by daylight. They remained there long enough to make fires at the landing. Prospects were ominous, it looked as though they would have to defend against another attack. On the hill, only a few hundred feet above them, were the earthworks of Fort Blakeley, and sharp firing was heard, and balls splattered near them viciously. They wondered if they would "stay" or "go on to Mobile." Finally, they marched aboard again; the transports turned toward the city and left Fort Blakeley to its fate. Anticipating an early attack on the city, Maury ordered them to be brought over by steamboats as soon as possible for the immediate defense of the city. "Most of them had expected to be captured with the position," recalled Maury, "and when they found themselves aboard steamers bound for Mobile instead of for a Northern prison, they were happy."[17]

That morning, the Spanish Fort garrison marched down to the landing and took transports for Mobile. Their departure created a somber mood within Fort Blakeley's garrison. "Then we knew we were 'gone up' unless the enemy deferred the attack on our position until the transports (steamboats) could return for us," recalled an officer of the 1st & 3rd Missouri Cavalry (dismounted).[18]

Maury sent the troops from Spanish Fort in transports and blockade runners to Mobile in sight of the Federals. Granger notified Canby that lookouts from a tree observatory spotted a gunboat loaded with Confederate troops heading to Mobile.

15 Musser, *Soldier Boy*, 201.

16 *ORA* 49, pt. 2, 1219, 1222.

17 Stephenson & Hughes, *Civil War Memoir of Philip Daingerfield Stephenson*, 367; Hewitt, *Supplement to the Official Records*, pt. I, vol. 7, 931; Maury, "Defence of Mobile in 1865," 7; Maury, "Spanish Fort," 132.

18 Joseph Boyce & William C. Winter, *Captain Joseph Boyce and the 1st Missouri Infantry, CSA* (St. Louis, 2011), 219.

Shortly afterward, he sent another message to Canby: "Another rebel gunboat coming from Blakel[e]y loaded with troops." These reports led the Northerners to erroneously believe the men they observed leaving on the boats were the Fort Blakeley garrison.[19]

The Federals did not realize the gray-coated soldiers they observed on the boats were the garrison of Spanish Fort. Nevertheless, Canby and his generals knew the rest of the men inside Blakeley could not escape until those boats returned. This knowledge motivated them to push forth plans to assault the works directly and prevent the garrison's escape.[20]

Throughout the day, the Spanish Fort garrison came into Mobile. "Bright and early this morning I was awakened with 'Spanish Fort is evacuated' while I could hardly believe it, only it was a confirmation of my worst fears. Still, I had to believe the evidence of my own eyes, for our soldiers were passing by in squads, from an early hour, dirty, wet, and completely worn out, having been compelled to march through a marsh for a distance of four miles, in order to make their escape," Mary Waring recorded in her diary. "Poor fellows, how discouraging it must have been to abandon the fort after having so bravely defended it for two weeks."[21]

At Huger, Patton's artillerists found themselves exposed to the fire of several Federal batteries erected at Spanish Fort. The Union Navy posed another threat, as they had further cleared torpedoes on the Blakeley River, allowing the USS *Octorara* to steam up two thousand yards closer to their position. Everything remained quiet until noon when the gunboat opened fire from her new position, still nearly 3 miles from Battery Huger. The ominous puff came, followed by the shell. The men on the parapet joyously shouted that it "fell short," followed by the exclamation, "Ah, old fellow, you cannot reach us here at all events." Their optimism was short-lived, for again came another shot in a direct line with the first, which plunged into the river three hundred beyond them. Then came another shell, this time hitting the center of their battery. From that moment on, every shot told on their bomb-proofs, and by their explosions, made the boggy foundations of Huger tremble like a ship in a gale of wind.

The Confederate officers expressed the opinion that the *Octorara*'s big gun, a 100-pounder Parrott, was unlimited except by its capacity for elevation and that the gunner surpassed First Sergeant Alex Bonner of the 22nd Louisiana, who was famous in the Confederate service for his skill and efficiency with large guns.

19 Liddell & Hughes, *Liddell's Record*, 195–196; Andrews, *History of the Campaign of Mobile*, 191–192; *ORA* 49, pt. 2, 297.

20 Andrews, *History of the Campaign of Mobile*, 192.

21 Waring-Harrison, *Miss Waring's Journal*, 12–13.

Described as "an old man-of-war," Chief Boatswain's Mate, James Welsch had fired every shot. The accuracy of Welsch's shots from Huger is more remarkable, considering the fort's position was so low that the marsh reeds almost entirely obstructed it from view from the ship's spar deck. Sailors went on shore to beat down a lane through them in the line of fire with poles, as they would not burn; even then, it was with difficulty that he could discern the object of his aim.[22]

While Lee and Grant finalized the terms of surrender at the McLean House, General Steele fretted that the garrison of Fort Blakeley might also evacuate. He issued orders for an attack to begin at 5:30 p.m. The general assault overwhelmed the vastly outnumbered garrison of Fort Blakeley. By 6:00 p.m., it was all over; the U.S. flag was raised over the fort. "Thus, on the evening of the 9th of April 1865, took place the battle of Blakel[e]y, which, like that of New Orleans in 1815, was fought after the necessity for it had passed away," remembered a private from the 6th Minnesota.[23]

Liddell believed if Maury had permitted him to keep the Spanish Fort garrison, he could have repelled the assault. Without them, his inadequate force had no chance to hold the defenses. He lamented Maury's order to withdraw the Spanish Fort garrison in his memoirs. Liddell recalled: "Our lines at Blakel[e]y could not be filled by one half, except by placing the men about one yard apart, which gave no volume to the fire from the line."[24]

The possession of Spanish Fort gave the Federals command over Batteries Huger and Tracey. Immediately after the capture of the fort, the Indiana Battery sent eight shots at Huger with no reply. The two forts had remained silent for over a week. Earlier, A. J. Smith had even expressed the belief that the forts were abandoned. The Southern artillerists, however, would soon end their silence. That evening at 10:00 p.m., Maury called a council of war and decided to evacuate Mobile. With the evacuation decided, Maury issued the long-awaited orders to the eager artillerists at Huger and Tracey to open on the Federals at Spanish Fort.[25]

22 *Army and Navy Journal*, Dec. 16, 1865; Newspaper clipping, C. C. Andrews Papers, 1866, MNHS; Andrews, *History of the Campaign of Mobile*, 227–229.

23 *ORA* 49, pt. 2, 306; Andrews, *History of the Campaign of Mobile*, 193–194; Hill, *Company E–30*.

24 Liddell & Hughes, *Liddell's Record*, 195–196.

25 "Rebellion in the Gulf States Dead," *Chicago Tribune*, Apr. 18, 1865, 3; *ORA* 49, pt. 2, 182, 301; Arthur W. Bergeron, "The Twenty-Second Louisiana Consolidated Infantry in the Defense of Mobile," *The Alabama Historical Quarterly* 38, no. 3 (Fall 1976): 212; Hewitt, *Supplement to the Official Records*, 946.

Confederates

Monday, April 10, 1865: With the fall of the two eastern shore forts, Maury gave up all hope of holding Mobile. The works around the city were designed to be manned by eight thousand, but after the capture of the garrison at Blakeley, there were not enough men left to hold the place. With the loss of nearly half of his men, most of his light guns, mortars, and ammunition, Maury had little choice but to abandon Mobile. "With the means left me an obstinate or protracted defense would have been impossible, while the consequences of it being stormed by a combined force of Federal and Negro troops would have been shocking," recalled Maury. In compliance with Taylor's instructions, he ordered the evacuation of his men from the city to the vicinity of Meridian, Mississippi.[26]

"This morning, we were much startled by the ringing of the alarm bell; the object of which was to call troops together to prepare for evacuation," noted Mary Waring in her journal. "Never have I experienced such feelings as now take possession of me—perfectly miserable, as may be imagined."[27]

At noon, the evacuation of Mobile began. While dismantling their works, Maury forbade his men from making unnecessary noise or fires that might attract attention. Cannon powder was dumped into the water. Guns were spiked and filled with shells. Subsistence stores were transferred to the city government.[28]

Confederate Surgeon W. C. Cavanaugh received orders from Surgeon J. M. Williams, Director of Hospitals for the District of the Gulf, to take charge of all sick and wounded to be evacuated. Surgeon Cavanaugh immediately began moving the supplies and patients of eight different hospitals to the riverfront. Quartermaster wagons were never sent, so Cavanaugh used ambulances to transfer his supplies and patients to the steamers *Duke* and *Watson* for the next 18 hours. The *Duke* had cylinder heads removed for repair, so the Mobile post quartermaster ordered the captain of the steamer *Magnolia* to tow it to Demopolis. The steamer *Reindeer* towed the *Watson*.[29]

26 J. W. Merwin, *Roster and Monograph, 161st Reg't, N.Y.S. Volunteer Infantry* (Elmira, NY, 1902), 132; Hewitt, *Supplement to the Official Records*, pt. I, vol. 7, 931, 952; Fannie A. Beers, *Memories: A Record of Personal Experience and Adventure During Four Years of War* (Philadelphia, 1888), 241–242.

27 Waring-Harrison, *Miss Waring's Journal*, 13.

28 Report of Dabney H. Maury to Robert E. Lee, June 19, 1865, Hewitt, *Supplement to the Official Records*, pt. 1, vol. 7, 956.

29 Report of Surgeon W. C. Cavanaugh, Compiled Service Records, Record Group 94, NARA. Records of Maj. W. T. Edwards, Chief of Commissary of Subsistence, CSR, RG 94, NARA. Eight troopers of the 15th Confederate cavalry men were detailed to drive 459 head of cattle to Meridian.

At Battery Huger, the men found the news of the capture of Fort Blakeley incredibly disheartening. One soldier of the 22nd Louisiana observed: "Great many getting on logs and floating down the river were picked up by our boats. I have no doubts that as soon as the enemy makes their appearance in front of the city, it will be surrendered." The Huger garrison could hear the alarm bells ringing from Mobile. They believed the Federals had already crossed over to the western side and marched on the city. The general impression prevailed at Huger that they would be cut off and taken prisoner.[30]

After Blakeley fell, the two small outposts, Batteries Huger and Tracey, were the only obstacles left between Canby and Mobile. Union artillery continually fired on them during the siege while the fleet to the south slowly continued its approach. Low on ammunition—they only had about 200 rounds of ammunition for each cannon—they did not reply during most of the siege. Early that morning, however, Maury wired Patton: "Open all your guns upon the enemy, keep up an active fire, and hold your position until you receive orders to retire." Here, at last, was the go-ahead the isolated artillerists had sought all along. Despite their apprehension of being captured, they fired their guns to cover the evacuation of Mobile. Indeed, Patton's artillerists at the twin batteries unleashed their pent-up fury, "belching flame and smoke" on the besiegers at Spanish Fort. The continual cross-firing resembled a "grand crashing thunderstorm."[31]

Most of the Federal shots glanced harmlessly over the water. The ones that managed to hit the forts sent up clouds of dust, sand, or pieces of wood. "A shell sometimes exploded in the water and sent up a column of spray 100 feet in height," Chaplain Elijah Edwards jotted in his journal. The batteries were frequently enveloped in smoke, while their shells often ricocheted along the water, creating "a line of spray like the sparks from a rocket though not so continuous." Edwards observed what appeared to be a man standing on the parapets of Tracey throughout the galling fire. While the others on the parapets would vanish at the bursting of a shell, this heroic figure only disappeared in the smoke of the battle. "When it cleared, he was still there," Edwards recalled, "like the flag 'that so proudly we hailed at the twilight last gleaming.' How I respected that stalwart but heroic rebel till a glass kindly lent by an officer revealed the fact that he was a wooden post. Still, he furnished our gunners with an excellent mark."[32]

30 ML to AH, Apr. 10, 1865.

31 Maury, "Defence of Mobile," 9–10; Edwards Journal, Apr. 13, 1865, 256–257.

32 Edwards Journal, Apr. 13, 1865, 256–257.

Chaplain Elijah Edwards, 7th Minnesota, Marshall's Brigade, sketched the Union bombardment of Battery Huger in his journal. *DePauw University Archives*

Huger and Tracey relentlessly pounded the Federals with their heavy fire all day. With the restraint of conserving their ammunition lifted, they showed a defiant front to the Union-occupied Spanish Fort, the Bay Minette Batteries, and the double-ender *Octorara*. "So long as the obstructions at Huger held good—the ten rows of piles across Apalachee River and seven rows crossing Blakely— the Blakely River was barred to Uncle Samuel's navy," recalled Acting Master Mate George S. Waterman, CSN. "It was their last chance at the big guns, though they didn't know it, not only in the siege of Mobile but the last grand bombardment of the civil war."[33]

Ann Quigley, Head Mistress of the Barton Academy—Mobile's public school— sadly noted in her diary: "And our own brave ones—where are they? Hundreds lie sleeping in the damp tangled marshes of the Eastern Shore—hundreds are suffering in hospitals while the rest, exhausted by two weeks of unavailing efforts to defend our city, are making their way to other fields of carnage & slaughter."[34]

Federals

Union soldiers explored the deserted fort during the day. "I went over to Spanish Fort this morning to see the works. I saw a great many torpedoes planted in the ground, "one Minnesotan noted in his diary. A soldier from Iowa wandered through the interior and witnessed the giant cannon *Lady Slocomb* dismounted during the bombardment. The knocked-off trunnion lay beside the gun. He noted Gibson's unenviable headquarters, where all the trees around it were torn to pieces with shot and shell, and the timbers of several similar cabins in the immediate

33 Miller, *Captain Edward Gee Miller*, 31; Waterman 1900b, 55. There were ten rows of piles on the Blakeley River had seven rows of piles on the Apalachee River.

34 Ann Quigley, "The Diary of Ann Quigley," *Gulf Coast Historical Review* 4, no. 2 (Spring 1989): 89–98.

vicinity had been splintered by their artillery fire. Blood-stained haversacks and clothing scattered over the ground, gory streams, and little pools of blood along the trenches. "At other points, the life-blood from the bosoms of the rebel soldiery along the lines had spurted upon the walls dying them even a deeper red from the head-log to the foot of the rampart," recalled the soldier. "Oh, it was a sickening sight!"[35]

After years of bloody fighting, the men on both sides longed for the war to end. "I have seen more than I ever care to see again, and I would like to forget much that I have seen," Chaplain Edwards, 7th Minnesota, Marshall's Brigade, recorded in his journal. Edwards ministered to the wounded in the field hospitals. "Some of them from a Minn. Regiment were brought into hospitals mortally wounded. They gave no sign of pain or anxiety, and but for a faraway look in their eyes, you could not have guessed that they were conscious of their condition."[36]

That evening, an enslaved man fled Mobile in a boat and crossed over to Canby's headquarters. He informed Canby that the Confederates were evacuating, and some were moving up the river.[37]

Comstock and Osterhaus opposed trying to pass the obstructions and the two batteries on the Blakeley River. Comstock urged Canby to transport troops across Mobile Bay and land below the city instead of going up the Blakeley River and then across the delta above Mobile. "Batteries Huger & Tracey still seal the rivers to the navy & our transports & we are losing time here. Told tonight that would cross a corps if we did not have the river at once," Comstock recorded in his diary.[38]

*   *   *

Tuesday, April 11, 1865: Canby ordered the Indiana battery on Minette Bay to fire another 100-gun salute at Huger and Tracey. The salute commenced at 8:00 a.m. with great rapidity. However, Patton's men responded with continuous and vigorous concentrated fire from Huger and Tracey's heavy rifled guns. "Their shells were constantly striking my works or exploding over and around us," reported an officer of the 1st Indiana Heavy Artillery. "Everyone who witnessed this engagement of the 11th claim that on no other occasion has the fire from the enemy's artillery been so heavy and constant during the whole siege." The

---

35 Mattocks Diary, Apr. 10, 1865; Stuart, *Iowa Colonels and Regiments*, 193–194.

36 Edwards Journal, Apr. 13, 1865, 254.

37 John F. Edmond to Sister, Apr. 13, 1865, New York Historical Society, New York, NY, hereafter JFE to Sister, Apr. 13, 1865.

38 Comstock, *The Diary of Cyrus B. Comstock*, 315.

officer claimed they received nearly 400 shots during the day from the two heavily mounted earthworks on the Apalachee River.[39]

Batteries Huger and Tracey's relentless bombardment of the Union-held Spanish Fort continued throughout the day. "This forenoon, we moved about 2 miles to get out of the range of the rebel shells when our battery opened on them," a soldier of the 95th Illinois recorded in his diary.[40]

"About 10 a.m. of the 11th, we had to 'dig out' of our camp as one of the rebel batteries had got our range and with their usual 'cussedness' were dropping seven-inch shells in among us in a manner that was not very favorable to longevity or good digestion," noted a hospital steward of Hubbard's Brigade of McArthur's Division. "So out of respect for their openly expressed aversion to keeping good company, we packed up our kit' and moved up the river a mile or so out of range."[41]

Rumors created a lot of enthusiasm in the Union camps. "I found the camp in the greatest uproar and wild with excitement. It was rumored that Lee had evacuated Richmond, and this could lead to but one result—Peace—Men and officers were wild and shouted and threw up their hats and hugged each other. I could have thought them all drunk. The pine forest rang with cheers," Chaplain Edwards recalled.[42]

Confederates

In Mobile, the Confederates continued their hurried evacuation, much to the anxiety of many citizens. "All excitement still this morning, consequent upon the preparations for an evacuation. We are all perfectly miserable at the idea of being separated, for an indefinite period of time, from our dear brothers and friends," mourned Mary Waring in her diary. She took a short walk down Government Street, noting how "melancholy" everyone looked:

Very soon afterward, Holtzclaw's brigade passed by, and it made me very sad to think that so many poor fellows would never again return to Mobile. We had quite a pleasant and agreeable little surprise, however. As the brigade was passing, we noticed a young man step from the ranks and come towards the gate, and who proved to be no other person than Capt. Wells Thomson, an old friend of mine, whom I had not seen for some time. He was

39 Samuel Armstrong to Benjamin Hays, Apr. 10, 1865, C. C. Andrews Papers, MNHS.

40 Ridge Diary, Apr. 11, 1865.

41 John M. Williams, *The "Eagle Regiment": 8th Wis. Inf'ty. Vols. A Sketch of Its Marches, Battles and Campaigns. From 1861 to 1865. With a Complete Regimental and Company Roster, and a Few Portraits and Sketches of Its Officers and Commanders* (Belleville, WI, 1890), 97.

42 Edwards Journal, Apr. 13, 1865, 260.

Chaplain Elijah Edwards, 7th Minnesota, Marshall's Brigade, sketched Union soldiers running for cover during the relentless bombardment of Union-occupied Spanish Fort from Battery Huger and Tracey. *DePauw University Archives*

looking so well, and so much improved in appearance, that it was some minutes before I recognized him. I expressed my delight at seeing him, but it was only a pleasure for a moment, as he was in a hurry, and bidding us Adieu, was soon off. [43]

At 5:00 a.m., the riverboats *Magnolia* and *Reindeer* pushed off from the dock with the *Duke* and *Watson* undertow, carrying 473 patients and property of Mobile's hospitals. Another 100 dangerously wounded patients could not be moved from the Mobile hospitals. These patients were consolidated into the City Hospital on April 11 under Surgeon Charles O. Helwig, where they were surrendered on April 12 when the Unionists entered the city. A few of the wounded were transferred to Federal hospitals in New Orleans, but most remained in Mobile until they either died or were paroled. That night, on their voyage upriver to Demopolis, the *Magnolia* tied off to a tree, and the captain, engineer, and pilot deserted. Nevertheless, the Confederates were able to get the *Magnolia* to Demopolis. [44]

Major Richard C. Bond of the 1st Louisiana Artillery informed his command at Mobile's Battery Gladden that they were about to be evacuated. "It is no fault of ours," he declared in a general order. "The enemy, with his large fleet, idle at the moment, has not dared to approach within range of our battery." Bond tried to console and encourage his men. "I know that there are no cowards or faint-hearted

43 Waring-Harrison, *Miss Waring's Journal*, 14.

44 Report of Surgeon W. C. Cavanaugh, Compiled Service Records, Record Group 94, NARA.

among you," he declared. "It is easy to be gay and confident after victory; none but the really brave and true are firm and obedient under misfortune." To further encourage them, he pointed out that they would soon join two revered Southern leaders "who have never known defeat," Taylor and Forrest.[45]

Meanwhile, at Batteries Huger and Tracey, Patton's men continued firing with great vigor, trying to use up all their ammunition. "Two hundred fifty shells were hurled April 9–11 at forts and fleet by Huger and Tracey. Wasn't that 'great guns' work?" recollected George S. Waterman. The Federals at Spanish Fort responded in kind with cannon fire that killed Huger artillerists Cpl. Isidore Dinguidard and wounded Pvt. A. L. Duvigneaud during the day.[46]

Late that night, one of Maury's staff, Major Cummins, went to Battery Tracey to tell Patton they had performed their whole duty and could retire. Patton withdrew his men on a treadway bridge from the rear of Tracey. The pier reached out nearly two miles to Conway Bayou, beyond the range of the Federal guns. The first steamer Maury sent to them grounded, and at about 2:00 a.m., he dispatched another. Maury pointed out that every man was brought safely off with his small arms and ammunition. He claimed they dismantled their batteries before they abandoned them and that it was nine o'clock Wednesday morning before they left the wharf of Mobile for Demopolis.[47]

"The artillery on the Bay kept up its sullen thunder till midnight and then went silent for a while till a fearful explosion shook the air," Chaplain Edwards noted, "from the blowing up of the magazines on the islands, and we knew that there was no longer an enemy before us." Edwards's claim that the Graybacks blew up their magazines is questionable. General C. C. Andrews did not mention an explosion at Huger or Tracey in his seminal book *History of the Campaign of Mobile*.[48]

In a letter to General Andrews, written on June 17, 1866, Lt. Cmdr. William W. Low, U.S. Navy, stated that around 9:00 p.m., a cutter of the *Octorara* on picket duty just south of Huger intercepted a skiff. There were eight men aboard, deserters from Huger, who informed the officer of the boat that Huger and Tracey had been evacuated just after dark. Contrary to Maury's claim, the refugees told

45 Forrest suffered defeat at Selma while the siege of Mobile was occurring. Napier Bartlett, *Military Record of Louisiana* (Baton Rouge, 1964), 28.

46 Bergeron, "The Twenty-Second Louisiana Consolidated Infantry in the Defense of Mobile," 212; Maury, "The Defense of Mobile in 1865," 9, 10; Waterman 1900b, 55.

47 Maury, "Defence of Spanish Fort," 131; Maury, "Defence of Mobile," 10; Waterman 1900b, 55; Bergeron, "The Twenty-Second Louisiana Consolidated Infantry in the Defense of Mobile," 212. Maury incorrectly wrote Chocaloochee Bayou, but it was Conway Bayou.

48 Maury, "Defence of Mobile," 10; Edwards Journal, Apr. 13, 1865, 260; Andrews, *History of the Campaign of Mobile*, 231.

the naval officers that the armament and ordnance stores had not been destroyed. A landing was made, and the forts came into the possession of the navy. Low did not indicate a magazine explosion had occurred, although he would have certainly seen one from his vantage point aboard the *Octorara*. That evening pontoniers of the 114th Illinois learned of the evacuation and went to the forts and inscribed on the cannons: "Eleven o'clock, P.M., April 11. Captured by the One Hundred and Fourteenth Illinois" and added their names.[49]

After spiking the heavy guns at the works around the city, the small garrison left Mobile by boat and train. Maury sent two small infantry brigades with stores up to Meridian by rail on the M&O line. He sent the wagon train by the wagon road to the same city with a brigade as an escort. All the artillery troops were ordered to board the 18 steamboats at the Mobile Riverport with as many stores as they could put on in the short time allotted to them. The artillerists were given muskets to replace their cannons. "It is a heavy fall for us who have been in artillery for three years and now find ourselves as infantrymen, much to our displeasure," complained a Confederate artillerist from Fenner's Battery. "As much as I dislike it, I shall keep my musket until something better turns up."[50]

The Confederate ironclad warships *Huntsville* and *Tuscaloosa* lacked the engine power to travel upriver against the strong currents of the Mobile and Tombigbee Rivers. Instead of attempting to tow the vessels, Commodore Farrand ordered both ships scuttled by the Mobile River. The crew and materials from these two ironclads were divided among the remaining Confederate ships. Before embarking, Farrand ordered the navy yard burned. His small fleet—the ironclad *Nashville*, the ram *Baltic*, the gunboat *Morgan*, the steamers *Black Diamond* and *Southern Republic*, and the blockade runner *Virgin*—successfully escaped up the Alabama River. As the remnants of the Southern navy proceeded up the narrow and crooked Alabama and Tombigbee Rivers to Demopolis, their long and wide vessels would occasionally run into the banks. "That night was a sorry one for all of us," remembered William L. Cameron, an officer aboard the *Nashville*. Company H of the 22nd Louisiana—the last soldiers to disembark—witnessed the Federals entering the city as they departed.[51]

---

49 Andrews, *History of the Campaign of Mobile*, 231; W. W. Low to C. C. Andrews, June 17, 1866, C. C. Andrews Papers, MNHS.

50 Hewitt, *Supplement to the Official Records*, pt. 1, vol. 7, 965; Fannie A. Beers, *Memories: A Record of Personal Experience and Adventure During Four Years of War* (Philadelphia, 1888), 241–242.

51 Scharf, *History of the Confederate States Navy*, 595; Cameron, "Battles Opposite Mobile," 306; Maury, "Defence of Spanish Fort," 131; Maury, "Defence of Mobile," 10; Bergeron, "The Twenty-Second Louisiana Consolidated Infantry in the Defense of Mobile," 212.

Despite his earlier grievances with Farrand, Maury acknowledged the navy's "cordial cooperation" during the defense of Mobile. "Our own little fleet did all they could to aid the defence, but there was little opportunity for them," remembered Maury.[52]

*   *   *

Wednesday, April 12, 1865: The rear guard of Louisiana infantry, under Col. Robert Lindsay, moved out of the city at daylight. Maury, with his staff, rode out at the same time.[53]

The departure of the Confederates had a sobering effect on the residents of Mobile. "I awoke this morning with a most deserted and desolate [feeling]," lamented Mary Waring. "All our troops got off sometime during the night, and the city is entirely free of 'Graycoats' except some few scouts who will decamp upon the entrance of the enemy." After watching the last of the Confederate soldiers leave, Mobile resident Laura Pillans sadly wrote, "Perhaps I shall never look upon a gray coat again."[54]

Maury claimed "the withdrawal of troops was conducted with exact order and discipline." The observations of 2Lt. William T. Mumford, 1st Louisiana Heavy Artillery, differed from his commanding officer. In his diary, Mumford lamented, "The evacuation was badly conducted. Many more valuable stores could have been saved with proper management." They both agreed, however, that Mobile was left with great reluctance by all the men. They also agreed that the soldiers, though demoralized, behaved well.[55]

Federals

Thousands of soldiers of Granger's XIII Corps embarked from Starke's wharf that morning. An armada of transports and gunboats headed west across Mobile Bay. "The morning was foggy, but soon the sun shone out merrily upon the rippling waters and lit up a scene of military splendor such as we had never beheld," recalled a soldier of the 33rd Iowa. As the vessels neared the western shore, one gunboat advanced some distance ahead of the fleet and threw a single shell to challenge the shore, but no answer came. As one soldier of the 161st New York put it: "One 100

---

52 Hewitt, ed., *Supplement to the Official Records*, pt. I, vol. 7, 932; Maury, "Defence of Mobile," 10.

53 Hewitt, ed., *Supplement to the Official Records*, pt. I, vol. 7, 931, 936.

54 Waring-Harrison, *Miss Waring's Journal*, 15; Laura Roberts Pillans, "Diary of Mrs. Laura Roberts Pillans, 11 July 1863–2 November 1865," History Museum of Mobile, Mobile, AL.

55 "From a Confederate Diary," accessed Apr. 29, 2020, https://www.oocities.org/laheavy1/MumfordDiary.html; Hewitt, *Supplement to the Official Records*, pt. 1, vol. 7, 932.

Hotchkiss was tossed by man of 'howdy,' and the quick response was a white flag borne by two citizens, who made communications that I know not of."[56]

Granger's command disembarked on the western shore about five miles south of the city, just south of modern-day Brookley Air Field. "We expected to land under a desperate fire, found no enemy to resist us. Everything was joy and hilarity," noted General Slack. The unopposed landing occurred around 11:00 a.m. The astounded Union forces were oblivious that the Confederate troops had departed Mobile earlier that morning.[57]

Around noon, the mayor of Mobile, Robert Slough, arrived by horse and buggy, accompanied by some city councilmen, displaying a white bed sheet. He immediately surrendered the city to the army and navy representatives as soon as the latter could get ashore. Mayor Slough informed them that the Confederate garrison had left for Meridian, Mississippi, the last of them leaving that morning. It took several hours to get all the troops ashore, as the pier had rotted in places, and some of the vessels could not get near the shore. The last soldiers made it up Mobile's Bay Shell Road around dusk.[58]

As the Federal soldiers marched toward the city, they noted the variety of trees on the bay's western side: magnificent gumtrees, pitch pine, magnolias, and numerous other types abounded. As the blue-coated troops approached the city, they were in awe of the vast defensive fortifications. "The rebel works here are quite extensive & very strong," noted an officer of the 28th Wisconsin. "They evidently had not men enough to man their works, or they would have never abandoned such strong ones without giving us a fight—& a hard one."[59]

"The Yankee troops did not come in until about four o'clock in the afternoon when they were marched in to the tune of "Yankee Doodle," observed Mary Waring. "My feelings this afternoon and tonight have been anything but pleasant—I believe I was never so gloomy—but there will be a bright day for us yet."[60]

That evening around sundown, while many of Mobile's residents were sitting in their plazas and balconies, Confederate horsemen made a daring raid into the city. "Soon, a company of cavalry in the well-known gray were galloping at a

---

56 Sperry, *33rd Iowa Infantry*, 153–154; JFE to Sister, Apr. 13, 1865.

57 JFE to Sister, Apr. 13, 1865; James R. Slack & David Williamson, *Slack's War* (Jefferson, NC, 2012), 285. The XIII Corps landed near modern day Hannon Road, just south of the Brookley Air Field.

58 Waring-Harrison, *Miss Waring's Journal*, 15; JFE to Sister, Apr. 13, 1865; Stevens & Blackburn, *"Dear Carrie,"* 310–311.

59 Stevens & Blackburn, *"Dear Carrie,"* 310–311.

60 Waring-Harrison, *Miss Waring's Journal*, 15.

Federal troops marched up Bay Shell Road into the city of Mobile. *Library of Congress*

dashing speed by their doors, halting occasionally to pick up and mount behind them a sentinel in blue," remembered one citizen. The horsemen were from Capt. Frank Moore's Scouts. They succeeded in capturing two U.S. soldiers, one from the Battle House barbershop and the other from McGill's shoe shop on Dauphin Street. Carrying the prisoners behind them on horses, Captain Moore escaped through the "orange grove to the fastnesses of the swampy bottoms" north of the city. The two prisoners were sent to Maury's headquarters near Meridian. The newly created Unionist-controlled *Mobile Daily News* reported the incident as: "a few drunk and mounted men dashed through the street and gobbled up, or rather kidnapped," soldiers of Veatch's 3rd Division of the XIII Corps, calling the incident "disgraceful."[61]

---

61 R. C. Beckett, "A Sketch of the Career of Company B, Armistead's Cavalry Regiment," *Publications, The Mississippi Historical Society* 8 (Feb 1905): 48; William Rix, *Incidents of Life in a Southern City During the War: A Series of Sketches Written for the Rutland Herald* (Rutland, VT, 1880), 24; *ORA* 49, pt. 1, 175; Spence, "The Last Fight"; "Disgraceful," *Mobile Daily News*, Apr. 13, 1865; Roger Hansen, "Compiled Service Records of Captain Frank Moore" (Unpublished, 2019). Captain Frank Moore captained a steamboat before the war. His service records indicate he served as commander of Co. D, 5th Louisiana Infantry, Army of Northern Virginia before receiving a wound at Second Manassas in Virginia on Aug. 29, 1862. Since his wound limited his ability to march with infantry, he requested

One Wisconsinite pointed out in a letter to his wife: "The fall of Richmond— the surrender of Lee & his army (if he has surrendered, as reported.) all our late victories must be enough to convince the rebels & everyone else that the rebellion is nearly quelled."

Confederates at Meridian, MS

Soon after they arrived at Meridian, Mississippi, the Confederates received news of General Lee's surrender. The news caused a somber mood in the camp. "The mind of the whole community, including the army, is at present saddened, almost prostrated by the sad tidings reaching us from Yankee sources," Capt. Clement S. Watson lamented to his wife. "We hear that Gen'l Lee and his army have surrendered to Gen'l Grant. If so, our struggle for the present is at an end, and a few years of slavery will be our doom. I have abiding faith, however, in the achievement of our independence."[62]

In a letter written on April 16, Col. Samuel Lockett shared with his wife that "Genl. Maury has been very much depressed since he left Mobile and has been quite severely criticized for giving up the city. I don't think anybody could have done better with the great superiority of the enemy's forces taken into consideration."[63]

Despite the hopeless situation, Gibson tried to keep his command intact. "The attention of officers of all grades is called to the desertions taking place in some of the commands," he urged in a General Order on April 15. "This is a time when every officer should be vigilant and attentive to the wants of his men and exercise measures at once to prevent the worst of military crimes—desertion," he added. Gibson offered a 40-day furlough to any soldier who helped detect and capture a deserter.[64]

To stop further destruction and bloodshed, on April 11, 1865, John A. Campbell, assistant Confederate secretary of war, penned a letter to Taylor

---

permission from the Confederate secretary of war to raise a cavalry company at Mobile for special service. The secretary of war had him detailed to Maury from the 5th Louisiana Infantry for special duty. Maury gave Moore command of a special company of mounted scouts that reported directly to him. These scouts were reliable local men hand-picked primarily from the 15th Confederate Cavalry that were not eligible for the draft, meaning they were under 18 or over 45 years of age.

62 Stevens & Blackburn, *"Dear Carrie,"* 303; CSW to Wife, Apr. 18, 1865.

63 Samuel Lockett to Cornelia Lockett, Apr. 16, 1865, Samuel Lockett Papers #432, Southern Historical Collection, Wilson Library, University of North Carolina at Chapel Hill. Lockett also wrote that Gen. Richard Taylor seemed to agree with "the newspaper generals" and had relieved Maury from duty with his division. However, corroborating evidence currently does not exist to support his statement.

64 *ORA* 49, pt. 2, 1240.

detailing the state of the dying Confederacy. He requested Grant forward the letter to Taylor via Canby in Mobile. In the message, Campbell, who resided in Mobile before the conflict, explained the untenable situation: Petersburg and Richmond had fallen; Jefferson Davis and his cabinet had evacuated, and Lee had surrendered the Army of Northern Virginia. He also shared the generous terms Grant gave Lee. Campbell, who had met with Lincoln on April 3–4, also conveyed his generous surrender conditions. "His indispensable conditions are the restoration of the authority of the United States and the disbanding of the troops and no receding on his part from his position on the slavery question as defined in his message in December and other official documents—all other questions to be settled on terms of sincere liberality," noted Campbell. "He says that to any State that will promptly accept these terms, he will relinquish confiscation except when third persons have acquired adverse interests." Campbell ended the letter by advising Taylor "to cease hostilities."[65]

Taylor heeded Campbell's sage advice. On April 29, he met Canby at Jacob Magee's house in Kushla, Alabama, a few miles north of Mobile, and agreed to a truce. At Magee's home, Canby presented Taylor with the exact terms of surrender Sherman offered Gen. Joseph Johnston. The following day, however, Canby had the embarrassing duty to notify Taylor that he had received an "official notice that the suspension of hostilities agreed upon between Generals Johnston and Sherman has been disapproved by the President of the United States and annulled." The Presidential rejection of the terms offered to Johnston by Sherman meant Canby must resume hostilities after 48 hours. Canby then proposed surrender under the same conditions Grant offered Lee at Appomattox Court House. "Frankly, what I would not say if I did not believe that circumstances of both armies were such that you may accept them for your army without reproach from any quarter," Canby remarked to Taylor. He expressed his desire to end the fighting without further bloodshed and destruction of property. Taylor knew the jig was up and agreed to the same terms Grant had given Lee. On May 4, the final surrender ceremony between the two generals and Confederate Commodore Farrand and Union Admiral Thatcher occurred near the Mobile & Ohio Railroad in Citronelle, Alabama.[66]

On May 8, Gibson issued a farewell address to his Louisiana Brigade:

Headquarters Gibson's Brigade,
Near Meridian, Miss., May 8, 1865.

65 *ORA* 49, pt. 2, 322–323.

66 *ORA* 49, pt. 2, 455; 531–532, 559, 593, 594–595.

Fellow-Soldiers:

For more than four years, we have shared together the fortunes of war. Throughout all the scenes of this eventful revolution, you have been fully tried and now retire with the consciousness of having achieved a character for discipline, for valor, and for unselfish patriotism of which you may be justly proud. There is nothing in your career to look back upon with regret. You have always been in front of the enemy; you have never feasted in soft places at the rear, nor fought your battles at comfortable firesides. Your banners are garlanded with the emblems of every soldierly virtue. More than twenty battlefields have seen them unfurled. They were never lowered save over the bier of a comrade. Forget not the good and true men who have fallen. No sculptured marble may perpetuate the memory of their services, but you will wear their names ever green in your hearts, and they will be enshrined forever in the affections of the Southern people, in whose cause they fell. Comrades, henceforth, other duties will devolve upon you. Adversities can only strengthen the ties that bind you to your country and increase the obligations you owe to her interests and her honor. As soldiers, you have been among the bravest and most steadfast, and as citizens, be law abiding, peaceable, and industrious. You have not surrendered and will never surrender your self-respect and love of country. You separate not as friends, but brethren whom common hopes, mutual trials, and equal disasters have made kinsmen. Hereafter you shall recount to your children, with conscious pride, the story of these rugged days, and you will always greet a comrade of the old brigade with open arms. Having commanded a company and regiment in the brigade, I have known many of you from the very beginning of the struggle, have been with you through all its varied fortunes, and offer to each one of you a grateful and affectionate farewell. May God bless you.

R. L. GIBSON,
Brigadier-General, Commanding.[67]

The next evening, Gibson's Louisianans, Ector's Texans and North Carolinians, Holtzclaw's Alabamians, and Massenburg's Georgians gathered around General Maury. Gibson's Louisiana Brigade band, the only Confederate band east of the Mississippi River, played their final serenade. "Many officers of the regiments which had been serving with me waited on me in a body and gave me their last farewell," Maury remembered. The following day, the Graybacks departed for their homes. The war was finally over.[68]

---

67 *ORA* 49, pt. 1, 319.

68 Maury, *Recollections of a Virginian*, 231; Maury, "Spanish Fort," 136.

Epilogue

The siege of Spanish Fort did not end the war. It did not turn out to be a major turning point or a regionally strategic battle. In many respects, it has been overshadowed by more significant battles. Yet for the veterans who were there and risked their lives in its defense and conquest, it is remembered as intense a fight as any they had experienced.[1]

"Twelve days of exposure and labor, unequaled during the war except, perhaps, at the siege of Vicksburg, was the lot of the investing army," recalled Major Sanford W. Huff, a surgeon with the 12th Iowa. Veterans of the opposing side echoed Huff's sentiments. A soldier of the 18th Alabama, a regiment in Holtzclaw's Brigade, fought through the war in most of the Western theater's deadliest battles: Shiloh, Farmington, Chickamauga, Chattanooga, and the fighting around Atlanta, as well as at Franklin and Nashville. Looking back after the war, he wrote that Spanish Fort "was one of the hardest fights of our great war for the number engaged on the Confederate side."[2]

Indeed, soldiers on both sides were exposed to continual hardships and dangers at Spanish Fort. Despite the grueling conditions, both armies demonstrated tremendous resolve, gallantry, and perseverance. General Carr, XVI Corps, stated in his after-action report: "I cannot commend too highly the conduct of the officers and soldiers of my division during this trying, dangerous, and laborious siege. The

---

1 Newton and Ambrose, "The Siege of Mobile," 595.

2 Huff, *The Annals of Iowa*, 949; G. T. Cullins, "Siege of Spanish Fort, Near Mobile," *Confederate Veteran* XII (July 1904): 354. The siege lasted 13 days, not 12.

men were all on duty at least once in twenty-four hours. On one occasion, the officers and non-commissioned officers of a brigade held the trenches during the day while the men slept." Carr's statement could be applied to most of the men who participated in the siege.[3]

Hubbard's Brigade, for example, excavated seven thousand cubic yards of earth and expended one hundred and sixty-nine thousand rounds of musket ammunition during the siege. "The labors of the siege were very arduous," Hubbard reported. "The men worked by large details, night and day, upon fortifications and approaches, yet they bore their trials patiently and cheerfully responded to every call of whatever character."[4]

In round numbers, the severe fighting at the Spanish Fort resulted in 233 men killed and 1,000 wounded (combined estimated casualty figures of both sides). The daily Confederate casualties ranged from 15–20 men. Due to the chaotic circumstances during the evacuation, Gibson could not fully determine his exact casualties. He reported a loss of about 95 killed and 395 wounded, with an estimated 20 men killed during the assault. General Carr, however, reported that 26 Southerners were buried on the field the morning after the assault, which indicates about 99 Confederates were killed in action or mortally wounded. The research of Roger Hansen, Kirk Barrett, and myself identified 97 Confederates killed in action or mortally wounded, some dying later in April. The number of reported Confederates captured also varied. Gibson inaccurately estimated 250. Canby reported his forces took more than 600 prisoners, while Carr indicated 540 prisoners were captured by his division. Colonel Bertram, who took charge of all prisoners at Spanish Fort, reported 556. Ship Island records show that 519 prisoners captured at Spanish Fort were sent to the prison camp.[5]

The Federals reported 52 killed, 575 wounded, and 30 captured or missing. My research, however, identified 129 men killed or mortally wounded. Carr's Division, XVI Corps, endured the most casualties—246 (30 killed, 216 wounded),

3 State of Iowa, *Report of the Adjutant General and Acting Quartermaster General of Iowa* (Des Moines, 1866), 295; *ORA* 49, pt. 1, 268.

4 Minnesota Board of Commissioners on Publication of History of Minnesota in Civil and Indian Wars, *Minnesota in the Civil and Indian Wars, 1861-1865*, vol. 2 (St. Paul, 1890), 623.

5 Maury, "Defence of Mobile," 9; *ORA* 49, pt. 1, 96, 207, 269, 318, 268; Kirk Barrett, "Confederate Soldiers Captured at Spanish Fort and Imprisoned at Ship Island" (unpublished manuscript, 2018). Canby's count of 600 included soldiers that were captured in the vicinity of Blakeley and by Steele's Pensacola Column up until Apr. 8. The Ship Island records did not include about 15 wounded that were captured and sent to New Orleans hospitals. About 525 prisoners were taken at Spanish Fort on Apr. 8. The research of Roger Hansen, Kirk Barrett, and myself has identified a total of 232 men killed or mortally wounded at Spanish Fort.

with Geddes's Brigade suffering the most significant percentage of those casualties (20 killed, 87 wounded), most of which occurred during the April 8 assault.[6]

Although fatalities were less than in other similarly sized battles, the fighting at Spanish Fort was nevertheless an unforgettable experience. Colonel Ryland Todhunter, assistant adjutant general for Ector's Brigade, who fought at many significant battles in the Western Theater, proclaimed, "no engagement exceeded Spanish Fort in severity."[7]

In his post-war memoirs, Grant concluded that the campaign for Mobile got off too late to render any service for which it was designed. Grant—who had tried for more than two years to have an expedition sent to take Mobile—felt Canby moved too slowly and thus did not occupy troops that might have otherwise been used against his army in the east. He determined that by the time the city was captured, it was no longer essential and, if left alone, would have fallen within a few days without the casualties.[8]

General Comstock criticized Canby's over-cautiousness in his diary. He described the movement against Mobile as "slow and sure," pointing out several instances where Canby needlessly allowed the campaign to delay. Comstock acknowledged Canby as a "good man & safe" but lacked "experience enough with large bodies of troops to act rapidly & take risks." He believed that Mobile should have been taken sooner, considering the size of his force. Comstock, however, failed to recognize the factors that slowed Canby's progress: inclement weather, rugged terrain, strong fortifications, deadly sub-terra shells, waterborne torpedoes, and the unexpected fighting tenacity of the Confederate defenders. Moreover, Canby did not know how large a force opposed him.[9]

Colonel Hubbard also disapproved of Canby's slowness: "His efforts seemed to have been employed in collateral movements that may have had for their ultimate purpose the achievement of the general object in view, but which were altogether too slow in their development to keep pace with events transpiring elsewhere." Despite the criticism, many of Canby's soldiers believed his cautious approach saved lives.[10]

After the war, Maury penned an article for the Southern Historical Society on the defense of Mobile. In the piece, he claimed to be "infinitely relieved" when he

6 *ORA* 49, pt. 1, 102, 114–115. In the Official Records, Geddes's Brigade reports 19 men killed, but does not appear to account for the death Lt. Henry Vinyard.

7 Ryland Todhunter, "Ector's Texas Brigade," *Confederate Veteran* 7 (1899): 312.

8 Grant, *Memoirs*, 647; 585; 646–647.

9 Comstock, *The Diary of Cyrus B. Comstock*, 316.

10 Hubbard, "Civil War Papers," 620, LC.

discovers Canby attacking the eastern shore. "Had Canby landed on Dog River, west of Mobile, and invested the city, he would have found his work shorter and easier and might have captured my whole army," he noted. The Virginian claimed that the level ground at Mobile left it exposed to fire from any direction. He pointed out that nearly 40,000 non-combatants in the city would soon have paralyzed the defense by his small garrison: he would have had to evacuate earlier, and it would have been much more challenging to do so. Canby sent Gen. Frederick Steele to Pollard from Pensacola as a feint movement to screen Canby's landing at Fish River. Confederate attacks from that direction would encounter Steele first. Nonetheless, Maury believed Canby made an error. "Had Canby not made the indefensible blunder of landing his army at Fish River to attack Mobile," Maury pointed out, "the sending of Steele's Corps towards Pollard would not have been a blunder, for then I might have been forced to try and bring out my garrison on that side, and to lead it to Montgomery, and have had to drive Steele from my path or surrender to him."[11]

Most of Maury's soldiers were on the eastern shore defending Spanish Fort and Fort Blakeley during the siege. He claimed that about 3,000 artillerists garrisoned the forts and works around the city's western shore and that not more than 800 men were guarding the southern approaches to the city. "And by a bold dash, the place could have been carried any night during the operations against Spanish Fort," alleged Maury.[12]

Maury's critique failed to acknowledge the deterrent effect of the substantial earthworks surrounding Mobile. With three formidable defensive lines, the Southern engineers prioritized their works west of the city. To his credit, Canby did not believe an army should attack the enemy where he desires you to.[13]

The natural defenses surrounding Mobile also served as a potent deterrent. The Dog River meandered through the low, marshy ground close to the rear of the outside line, and it would have been tough for Union forces to have advanced across it. This obstacle would have delayed attacking land forces too long under severe fire, which they could not have answered.[14]

A period topographical map of the bay reveals that the Dog River Bar reached a significant part of the way across the bay from the mouth of that river. This shallow bar would have prevented Thatcher's fleet from approaching close enough

---

11 Maury, "Defence of Mobile in 1865," 1–2. Maury served as Chairman for the Southern Historical Society's Executive Committee.

12 Maury, "Souvenirs of the War," 4; Maury, "Defence of Mobile," 4.

13 *ORN* 21, 533–534; "Our New Orleans Correspondence."

14 Truman, "The Siege of Mobile."

to attack the western shore batteries scattered along the coast from Mobile to Dog River. Moreover, the strong man-made water obstructions outside those batteries made it nearly impossible for the shallow-draft gunboats to attack effectively.[15]

The Confederates made formidable preparations to meet the Federal forces on the water and the city's western approaches. However, they left their eastern shore land defenses comparatively vulnerable. They did not even start working on the Baldwin County forts in earnest until after the battle of Mobile Bay. Canby received credible intelligence reports, including advice from Sherman, that led him to take the eastern shore route. With the information he had at the time, the Kentuckian determined that the best route was to move first against Spanish Fort and Fort Blakeley. "Gen. Canby perceived that the rebel strength was his weakness, and did what this war abundantly taught us to do—flanked it," a *New York Times* report concluded. The eastern shore route also facilitated the movement of troops overland to Montgomery.[16]

At Spanish Fort, some thought Canby should have ordered an assault at the onset of the investment. "It was said at the time, in army circles, that it was the judgment of General [A. J.] Smith to have pushed on to the storming of the works without a halt, and that the feasibility of the movement was sustained by subsequent developments, and the probable loss would not have equaled the aggregate loss of the twelve days of siege which succeeded," Major Huff recalled. "It is probable that General Smith's judgment—knowing, as he did, so thoroughly the quality of these troops, having witnessed, as he had so frequently, their achievements under his own direction—was a clear and practical conclusion, from unmistakable data, of their capability, and that the risk of failure was of a remote and contingent character." He felt that Canby did not fully understand the capabilities of the veteran troops which formed his army since he had not personally served with them before.[17]

Canby knew an immediate assault would have been stubbornly resisted and cost many lives. The Spanish Fort garrison expected to be attacked on the first day of the investment. Some portions of the fortifications and obstructions around Spanish Fort were elaborate, made by skillful engineers, and many soldiers defending the works were veterans. They were ready and would have inflicted severe casualties on the Unionists. Had a general assault been ordered on the first day, it would have been too costly. The Federals, furthermore, did not fully understand the character of the fort. Not much would have been gained in time, as the army

15 Truman, "The Siege of Mobile."

16 *ORN* 21, 533–534; "Our New Orleans Correspondence"; Truman, "The Siege of Mobile."

17 Huff, *The Annals of Iowa*, 949.

would still have been waiting for supplies. Ordinary prudence would dictate that the besiegers should at least have one line of works behind which they could return if repulsed. To his credit, Canby decided not to take unnecessary risks.[18]

Many of Canby's men were grateful for his prudence. "Fortunately, upon a personal inspection of the works, Gen. Canby saw that the chances were altogether against the success of an assault, and so resolved to proceed by regularly investing them," remembered Colonel Holbrook. "This was a wise, judicious decision, for an attempt to storm these formidable defenses at that time would have been attended with very great slaughter."[19]

Despite his criticism, Grant acknowledged Canby's character and reasoned his lack of experience leading a large army played a role in his overcautiousness. "I presume his feelings when first called upon to command a large army against a fortified city, were somewhat like my own when marching a regiment against General Thomas Harris in Missouri in 1861. Neither of us would have felt the slightest trepidation in going into battle with someone else commanding. Had Canby been in other engagements afterward, he would, I have no doubt, have advanced without any fear arising from a sense of the responsibility," Grant noted in his memoirs.[20]

Canby expected more support from the fleet in the siege of Spanish Fort when he planned his attack. Confederate torpedoes in the lower reaches of the rivers emptying into the bay, however, were remarkably effective in stopping the U.S. Navy from playing a more substantial role in the siege. The destruction caused by the torpedoes kept Thatcher's gunboats out of the Blakeley River and thus enabled the Confederates to evacuate most of their garrison successfully. "We would have been in a box if the fleet could have approached, for it would have been in our rear," recalled one soldier of Holtzclaw's Brigade.[21]

The Confederates defended Spanish Fort to prevent the establishment of Union batteries that could bombard Huger and Tracey and to help keep the U.S. Navy out of the Blakeley River. Before the siege, Beauregard considered it a mistake to garrison any part of Baldwin County. He believed that Huger and Tracey should have been made self-sustaining forts and that the main garrison should be in Mobile. In hindsight, Maury conceded that it was, perhaps, an error to fortify or occupy the positions of Spanish Fort and Fort Blakeley. "No batteries from these bluffs

---

18 Andrews, *History of the Campaign of Mobile*, 164–165; Huff, *The Annals of Iowa*, 949.

19 Holbrook, *7th Regiment of Vermont*, 168.

20 Grant, *Memoirs*, 650.

21 Jones and Pulcrano, *Eighteenth Alabama Infantry Regiment*, 64.

could seriously harm batteries Huger and Tracey," Maury acknowledged later. The battery near Bayou Minette bridge was in as good a position as could have been selected upon that site; about 2,700 yards from battery Huger, it bombarded both forts for several days without causing severe damage.

With time, however, the Union batteries established late in the siege, north of Spanish Fort, on the shore of Minette Bay, would have made holding Huger and Tracy untenable. If the question of defending the Blakeley River were to be presented again, Maury would have made Huger and Tracey stronger, self-sustaining works as Beauregard had initially suggested. "If the Eastern Shore were to be occupied at all, a strong work on the Redoubt McDermott would accomplish the object sought," he concluded. The Southerners expended a tremendous amount of artillery ammunition during the defense of the two forts. The capture of the Selma arsenal, where their ammunition was manufactured, further exacerbated the issue. After the capture of Blakeley, not enough ammunition remained to justify an attempt to defend Mobile.[22]

There was, nonetheless, value to the Confederates in holding Spanish Fort. They could send out parties to obstruct Federal communications and cause much annoyance. This suggests the answer to the opinion of some Confederate engineers that Canby made a mistake to have noticed Spanish Fort. They claimed it would have been better to pass the fort and attempt the destruction of Huger and Tracey with batteries on Bay Minette or the shore or passing all the eastern-shore garrisons to have gone round to the confluence of the Tombigbee and Alabama Rivers, the occupation of Mobile by the Confederates being then a question of supplies. However, bypassing Spanish Fort would have been too dangerous to the Union line of communication.[23]

An obvious omission of the Confederates was the failure to construct strong and connected works on their left down across the swamp, where they were successfully assaulted. Their works there were disconnected, and the men occupying this position were captured in detail. More effort here in the months preceding the siege might have allowed them to resist the assault or even deter Carr's attack there from taking place.[24]

Gibson recognized his left flank's vulnerability from the onset of the siege. In his after-action report, he remarked that the ground there "was covered with water, and it had been utterly impossible to get earth here to make defenses or to

22 Maury, "Souvenirs of the War"; Andrews, *History of the Campaign of Mobile*, 70–71.

23 Andrews, *History of the Campaign of Mobile*, 163.

24 Ibid., 165.

make cover for our men against his batteries." This weakness, however, was not Gibson's fault; he did not have enough men to defend the works and adequately strengthen his left once the fort was invested. The Confederate engineers should have recognized and addressed the issue in the months preceding the siege.[25]

The Confederate engineers, however, were led to believe that the swamp on the northern left flank of Spanish Fort was impassable. This miscalculation proved the fort's downfall. One Alabamian of Holtzclaw's Brigade recalled the area was "left unprotected on our left and through which we had not built any works because we thought it impenetrable by mortals. But somehow the Yankees did penetrate it." Reflecting back, Maury acknowledged the mistake: "No commander should ever rely upon the reports of country people about marshes [nor even the reports of engineer officers]." More substantial works should have been built there to allow protection for more sharpshooters to be deployed before Gibson's arrival. Once the investment began, it was too late to correct the problem.[26]

An attack on Smith's Corps—while it was still disembarking and fortifying its position at Dannelly's Mill—might have been a possibility. Smith had not yet united with Granger's Corps and was thus more vulnerable. Had Maury recognized where the main thrust of the attack was coming from earlier, it was a possibility that he could have sent the bulk of his forces to the eastern shore sooner. A bold commander with good intelligence and confidence that his force could move and react rapidly might have been able to pull it off. However, there was a lack of discernible, timely, and accurate tactical information from the eastern shore cavalry. Colonel Spence did not have an adequate number of scouts available, and the nature of the terrain possibly hindered his cavalry from providing the accurate intelligence needed to make such a decision in the first place. Although Spence's horsemen made a gallant effort, communication was not streamlined, perhaps because they were from different brigades and had to cover a large territory, including the Pensacola front. Effective intelligence gathering was further complicated by Colonel Moore's successful feint to Fowl River on the western shore.

A bold attack at Dannelly's Mill, nevertheless, would have been quite difficult and risky. Advance Union scouts might have detected a large force before Smith's Corps disembarked, plus gunboats for support accompanied them. Maury would have had to strip most of his defenses to put together a credible force to bear against Smith's Corps. He would have been left vulnerable with Granger's Corps and Steele's column on the move toward them. For such an attack to have been

25 *ORA* 49, pt. 2, 1210; Handwritten report, RLG, Apr. 16, 1865.

26 Jones and Pulcrano, *Eighteenth Alabama Infantry Regiment*, 70; Maury, "Souvenirs of the War," *The New Orleans Daily Crescent*, Mar. 19, 1866, 4.

successful, it probably would have required more assets than the District of the Gulf could have mustered at the time.

After the war, Colonel Scheliha, the District of the Gulf's noted Prussian engineer, concluded that the best defense depended upon mobile forces concentrated in the interior for rail movement to threatened points. He believed important strategic areas should be strongly fortified and garrisoned, but mighty reserves must be maintained for prompt reinforcement. The fortifications of Mobile—"the last Confederate stronghold"—were strong in the approaches to the city itself. However, the Department of Alabama, Mississippi, and East Louisiana could not provide enough men to hold the position, not to mention strong mobile reserves when they were needed. General Taylor believed the cavalry under Forrest could defeat Wilson and help lift the Mobile siege if they could hold out for seven days. These predictions, however, greatly underestimated the size of Wilson's force. Hopelessly outnumbered, Forrest could only delay, not defeat Wilson. The news of Forrest's defeat at Selma dashed all hope of relief for the Mobile garrison.[27]

In hindsight, there was nothing else the Confederates could have done to hold Spanish Fort and ultimately defend Mobile. They could only hope to drag it out and make it costlier for the Federals while hoping for the help of Forrest or a miracle of some kind. Nothing else would have saved Mobile or the Confederacy at that point.

Though vastly outnumbered, the defenders of Spanish Fort were active and vigilant; they caused the Unionists to proceed with their siege operations cautiously. "I was with my company on the skirmish line 50 hours during the siege, and I never got up and swung my hat at the rebels but kept as close to the ground as I could," noted one Wisconsinite.[28]

When the besiegers finally captured the fort, they were amazed by what the Southern garrison endured. Upon touring the captured Spanish Fort, they saw evidence of the awful ordeal the gray-coated men went through during nearly two weeks of a constant storm of shots and shells. "It is not too much to say that no position was ever held by Confederate troops with greater hardihood and tenacity," recalled Maury, "nor evacuated more skillfully after the hope of further defense was gone." Indeed, the men who participated in the battle, on both sides, fought as if the war's outcome depended on them; there were instances of bravery that rivaled

---

27 Viktor Von Scheliha, *A Treatise on Coast-defence: Based on the Experience Gained by Officers of the Corps of Engineers of the Army of the Confederate States* (London, 1868), 5–6; James L. Nichols, "Confederate Engineers and the Defense of Mobile," *Alabama Review*, July 12, 1959, 194; Maury, "Defence of Mobile in 1865," 6.

28 "Amused at the Many Accounts," *The National Tribune*, Aug. 25, 1910, 3.

any major battle of the war. As historian Arthur W. Bergeron, Jr. put it: "The defense of this position for two weeks by fewer than three thousand men against eight times as many Federals certainly should stand as one of the most heroic episodes of the war."[29]

Few men saw more hard fighting during the war than Gibson; many considered his leadership at Spanish Fort the best achievement of his military career. Despite not receiving adequate reinforcements to repel Canby's well-supplied and numerically superior force, Gibson boldly inspired his garrison to fight it out. His leadership drew praise from both sides of the conflict.[30]

Shortly after the evacuation of Mobile, Capt. Clement Watson of Gibson's Brigade wrote to his wife: "Gen'l Gibson and his command gained great credit for the manner in which he held out at Spanish Fort with his small garrison against the attacks of a force ten times or greater as his own."[31]

Union Gen. C. C. Andrews acknowledged Gibson's leadership: "The garrison commander, General Gibson, was competent and active and inspired his troops with enthusiasm. He was highly complimented by his superior officers for his conduct during the siege." Andrews also noted that the garrison displayed uncommon resolution and courage in the frequency of its sorties.[32]

Gibson's commanding officers readily commended his efforts in defending Spanish Fort. "General Gibson displayed great courage and capacity during this brilliant operation. Some days before the battle ended, he received a sharp wound but did not go off duty nor let his name go in the report of wounded," observed Maury. In his memoirs, Lieutenant General Taylor praised Gibson: "Fighting all day and working all night, Gibson successfully resisted the efforts of the immense force against him until the evening of April 8th, when the enemy effected a lodgment threatening his only route of evacuation. Gibson's stubborn defense and skillful retreat make this one of the best achievements of the war."[33]

Spanish Fort's garrison represented most Confederate states; as Maury put it: "They were the very flower of our Western Army." Spanish Fort marked their final battle after four years of continuous active service. "They fitly closed the career of

29 "The Capture of Spanish Fort"; Maury, "Defence of Spanish Fort," 130; Arthur W. Bergeron, Jr., *Confederate Mobile* (Jackson, MS, 1991), 182.

30 *Life and Character of Randall Lee Gibson*, 103.

31 CSW to Wife, Apr. 18, 1865.

32 Andrews, *History of the Campaign of Mobile*, 165.

33 Maury, "Spanish Fort," 135; Taylor, *Destruction and Reconstruction*, 221.

the Confederacy by an action so brilliant that had it taken place two years sooner, it would have greatly exalted the prowess of the Confederate troops," touted Maury.[34]

The ever-humble Gibson bestowed credit and commendation on his men for being "active, vigilant & brave" against the overwhelming odds they faced, especially recognizing those who died defending the fort. "Several attempts were made by concentrated bombardment from day to day to demoralize the troops, with the intention to take advantage of any accident and likewise repeated efforts to advance his lines without digging, but in each instance, he was repulsed with a loss proportioned to the vigor of the attack," Gibson noted in his after-action report. He concluded, "if any credit shall attach to the defense of Spanish Fort, it belongs to the heroes whose sleep shall no more be disturbed by the cannon's roar."[35]

Postbellum

Confederate Commanders

Colonel Julius A. Andrews, commander of Ector's Brigade, resided in Clarke County, Mississippi, where he became a successful merchant after the surrender. By 1880, he and his family moved to Fort Worth, Texas. In 1894, he served four years as an Indian Agent for the Lemhi Tribe in the Idaho Territory before moving to Idaho Springs, Colorado, where he started a steam laundry business. In 1899, Andrews was convicted of embezzling funds from the Lemhi agency and served time in the Idaho penitentiary. In 1923, Andrews applied for a veteran's pension in Oklahoma at age 84. On December 28, 1928, he died and was buried at the Mountain View Cemetery in Kiowa County, Oklahoma.[36]

Commodore Ebenezer Farrand settled in Alabama, where he worked as an insurance representative in Montgomery. Later, he became a co-owner of the Railway Hotel in Attalla, Alabama, where he died on March 17, 1873. He was buried at the Oak Hill Cemetery in Attalla.[37]

Brigadier General Randall L. Gibson, a Democrat, served in the U.S. House of Representatives from 1874 to 1882. From 1882 until his death on December 15, 1892, he served Louisiana in the U.S. Senate. He played an instrumental role in coordinating, with wealthy New Orleans businessman Paul R. Tulane,

34 Maury, "Spanish Fort," 135.

35 Handwritten report, RLG, Apr. 16, 1865; *ORA* 49, pt. 1, 315–316, 318.

36 "Andrews, Julius A."

37 Spencer C. Tucker, *The Civil War Naval Encyclopedia*, 1st ed. (Santa Barbara, CA, 2010), 185–186.

the transition of his alma mater, the University of Louisiana, into the prestigious private Tulane University. Gibson served as Tulane's Board of Administration president from 1884 until his death. Gibson Hall at Tulane is named in his honor. He was buried at the Lexington Cemetery in Lexington, Kentucky.[38]

Brigadier General James T. Holtzclaw, commander of the left wing of Spanish Fort's defenses, remained in Alabama following the surrender. He resumed his legal practice and served on the Alabama Railroad Commission until shortly before he died in 1893. He was buried at the Oakwood Cemetery in Montgomery, Alabama.[39]

Colonel Bush Jones, commander of Holtzclaw's Brigade, returned to Perry County, Alabama, after receiving his parole at Meridian. He became a probate judge of Perry County and served in this role until his eviction from office in 1868 because of the Reconstruction Acts. Jones continued to practice law until his death (age 36) on September 27, 1872, at Uniontown, Alabama. He was buried at the Rosemont Cemetery in Uniontown.[40]

Brigadier General St. John R. Liddell, District of the Gulf, Eastern Division Commander, returned to Louisiana. He resumed his long-standing feud with a neighbor, Lt. Col. Charles Jones, who had served with the 17th Louisiana. The exact cause of the bitter Liddell-Jones family feud is unknown, although it likely began in 1847. On February 14, 1870, as he dined aboard the riverboat steamer *St. Mary* on the Black River in Louisiana, Jones and his two sons shot Liddell to death. Almost two weeks later, a mob killed Jones and one of his sons. Liddell was buried at Llanada Plantation Cemetery in Jonesville, Louisiana.[41]

Major General Dabney H. Maury, commander of the District of the Gulf, served as ambassador to Colombia from 1887 to 1889. Maury tried his hand at several ventures in the years before this appointment. He is most noted for founding the Southern Historical Society in 1868, the dominant source of literature in defense of the Confederacy. This organization produced over 52 volumes of historical writings. Maury is buried at the Confederate Cemetery in Fredericksburg, Virginia.[42]

Colonel Isaac W. Patton, Chief of Artillery of the Spanish Fort, returned to New Orleans after the war. He worked in the commission business and served

---

38 Warner, *Generals in Gray*, 104–105.

39 Ibid., 141–142.

40 Brewer, *Alabama, Her History*, 496–497; "Col Bushrod 'Bush' Jones," Find A Grave—Millions of Cemetery Records, accessed Oct. 27, 2021, https://www.findagrave.com/memorial/47502849/bushrod-jones.

41 Liddell & Hughes, *Liddell's Record*, 205–206.

42 Warner, *Generals in Gray*, 215–216.

Senator Randall L. Gibson of Louisiana. *Library of Congress*

as sheriff of the Criminal Court in 1872. He participated in the famous battle of Liberty Place in 1874. Four years later, he served as Mayor of New Orleans from 1878–1880. Patton died in New Orleans on February 9, 1890, at 62. He was buried in the Lafayette Cemetery.[43]

Lieutenant General Richard S. Taylor interceded with President Andrew Johnson on behalf of his former brother-in-law, Jefferson Davis, and proposed less punitive Reconstruction sanctions. He penned a book on his Civil War experiences entitled *Destruction and Reconstruction; Personal Experiences of the Late War*. Taylor died penniless in New York City and was buried at the Metairie Cemetery in New Orleans in 1879.[44]

Brigadier General Bryan M. Thomas, whose brigade defended the line's left wing at Spanish Fort before being relieved by Holtzclaw, served as deputy U.S. Marshal for Dalton, Georgia. He also worked as the superintendent of the Dalton public schools. On July 16, 1905, he passed away at age 69 and was buried in the Dalton West Hill Cemetery.[45]

Captain Cuthbert H. Slocomb, 5th Company, Washington Artillery, commanded all the field artillery at Spanish Fort. After the war, Slocomb resumed his successful hardware business. The well-respected businessman served as a director of the Bank of Louisiana and the New Orleans Water Works and vice president of the Mechanical & Agricultural Association of Louisiana. He also owned numerous thoroughbred horses. Slocomb died on January 31, 1873, at age 41, and is buried at the Metairie Cemetery in New Orleans, LA.[46]

43 "The Distinguished Dead," *The Times Picayune*, Feb. 10, 1890, 3.

44 Warner, *Generals in Gray*, 300.

45 Warner, *Generals in Gray*, 304–305; "General Longstreet appointed General Bryan M. Thomas," *Six Mile* [AL] *Bibb Blade*, Aug. 25, 1881, 2.

46 Edwin L. Jewell, *Crescent City Illustrated* (New Orleans, 1873), https://ia600202.us.archive. org/13/items/jewellscrescentc01jewe/jewellscresc; "Captain Cuthbert Harrison Slocomb," Find

Lieutenant Colonel Philip B. Spence, 12th Mississippi Cavalry, received an appointment as postmaster of Newport, Kentucky, by President Grover Cleveland. During his tenure as postmaster, Spence had the opportunity to name a small community in Kentucky. He chose the name Brent after his father and son. During Cleveland's second administration, the president appointed Spence as United States consul to Quebec, Canada. After a long period of illness, Spence passed away in Cincinnati in 1915 at 78. He was buried at Evergreen Cemetery, Southgate, Campbell County, Kentucky.[47]

Lieutenant Colonel James M. Williams, 21st Alabama, remained in Mobile with his wife. The couple had six children. After the war, he worked as a deputy and clerk with the Mobile County Probate Court. He died in 1903 at the age of 65.[48]

Federal Commanders

Brigadier General William P. Benton served as Collector of Internal Revenue in the City of New Orleans. On March 14, 1867, he died of yellow fever and was buried at the New Orleans Greenwood Cemetery.[49]

Brigadier General Henry Bertram returned to Wisconsin and entered local politics. He became mayor of Watertown in 1870 and served as Dodge County Sheriff in 1872. He later moved to Juneau, Wisconsin, where he worked as a merchant and hotel keeper. He died unexpectedly on September 2, 1878, and was buried in the Juneau City Cemetery.[50]

Major General E. R. S. Canby, commander of the Department of West Mississippi, stayed in the army for nearly eight more years. On April 11, 1873, however, Modoc Indian chief Captain Jack murdered him at a peace conference in northern California. Canby has the grim distinction of being the highest-ranking officer in history to be murdered by a Native American. Former Confederate enemies lamented his death. "Narrow perhaps in his view, and harsh in the discharge of duty, he was just, upright, and honorable, and it was with regret that

A Grave—Millions of Cemetery Records, accessed Nov. 27, 2021, https://www.findagrave.com/memorial/6884675/cuthbert-harrison-slocomb.

47 "Colonel Philip Brent Spence," RootsWeb.com Home Page, accessed July 19, 2015, http://www.rootsweb.ancestry.com/~kycampbe/philipspence.htm.

48 "Col. James Madison Williams," Find a Grave, accessed Feb. 15, 2022, https://www.findagrave.com/memorial/19041170/james-madison-williams.

49 Ezra J. Warner, *Generals in Blue: Lives of the Union Commanders* (Baton Rouge), 1964.

50 "Gen. Henry Bertram," *Watertown Times*, Oct. 10, 1914.

I learned of his murder by a band of Modoc savages," remarked Taylor. Canby was buried in Indianapolis, Indiana, at the Crown Hill Cemetery.[51]

Eugene A. Carr earned the rank of Brevet Major General of volunteers for his gallantry as the commander of the 3rd Division of the XVI Corps during the siege of Spanish Fort. "If convenient," President Lincoln had written on the nomination, "I would like for this promotion to be made." After the war, Carr went on numerous expeditions against the Apaches in Arizona and New Mexico. In 1892, he received a promotion to the rank of Brigadier General in the regular army before retiring in 1893. Carr passed away on Dec. 2, 1910, and was buried at the West Point Cemetery, New York.[52]

Brevet Major General Kenner Garrard resigned on November 9, 1866. He returned to his home in Cincinnati, Ohio, where he worked as a real estate broker. He died in 1879 in Cincinnati, Ohio, at the age of 51 and was interred at Spring Grove Cemetery.[53]

Colonel James L. Geddes, whose brigade gained the lodgment of Spanish Fort, served as interim president at the institution known today as Iowa State University from September 1, 1867, to June 16, 1868. Geddes' leadership skills that served him well at Spanish Fort rubbed people the wrong way during his short tenure as a university president. "Gen. James L. Geddes was a brave and accomplished soldier in the Civil War. He was an efficient superintendent, but his administration lacked unity owing to certain forces within and without the institution over which he could not gain control," recalled one observer. "His military training made him exacting in details, but he seemed not to have learned the cardinal principle of which no executive officer can afford to be ignorant; namely, in questions simply of administrative policy, to stand firm as a rock when there is a rock to stand on, but to be politic and diplomatic when there is only a bed of sand." He continued with the university in various capacities for twenty more years. Geddes also penned several popular war songs, including *The Soldiers' Battle Prayer* and *The Stars and Stripes*. He died in Ames, Iowa, on February 21, 1887. He was later buried in Evergreen Cemetery, Vinton, Iowa.[54]

---

51 Heyman, *Prudent Soldier*, 375–377, 382; Taylor, *Destruction and Reconstruction*, 226, 228–229.

52 "Promotion of Brig. Gen E.A. Carr to a Brevet Major-General," *New York Times*, May 8, 1865, 2; James T. King, *War Eagle A Life of General Eugene A. Carr* (Lincoln, NE, 1963), 70–71; Carr, *First Reunion of the Survivors of the Army of Tennessee*, 23; "Death of General Carr," *Army and Navy Journal*, Dec. 10, 1910, 407.

53 "Kenner Garrard (1827–1879)," Find A Grave, accessed Dec. 21, 2016, https://www.findagrave.com/memorial/5088/kenner-garrard.

54 "Administration of Gen. James L. Geddes," *Bulletin of Iowa Institutions* 2 (1900): 460–462; John H. Eicher and David J. Eicher, *Civil War High Commands* (Stanford, 2001), 746, 252.

Major General Gordon Granger remained in the army until his untimely death. On January 10, 1876, Granger died after a paralytic stroke at his military headquarters in Santa Fe, New Mexico. He was buried in the Lexington Cemetery, Lexington, Kentucky, where his Spanish Fort opponent, Randall L. Gibson, also rests.[55]

Lucius Hubbard earned the brevetted rank of Brigadier General. He became the ninth governor of Minnesota in 1881 and served until 1887. He later served as a delegate to the 1898 Republican National Convention and fought in the Spanish-American War as commander of the 3rd Division. On February 5, 1913, Hubbard was buried in the Oakwood Cemetery in Red Wing, Minnesota. Hubbard County, Minnesota, is named in his memory.[56]

Brigadier General William Marshall became the fifth governor of Minnesota, serving from 1865 to 1870. He later served as the railroad and warehouse commissioner from 1874 to 1882. On January 8, 1896, Marshall passed away and was buried in the Oakland Cemetery in St. Paul, Minnesota. The city of Marshall, Minnesota, was named after him.[57]

Brigadier General John McArthur was involved in several occupations after the war, including Commissioner of Chicago Public Works during the Chicago fire, Postmaster General of Chicago, and the Chicago and Vert Island Stone Company general manager. McArthur died and was buried at the Rosehill Cemetery and Mausoleum, Chicago, Illinois, on May 15, 1906.[58]

Major General A. J. Smith of the XVI Corps remained in the army until 1869. President Ulysses Grant then appointed him postmaster of St. Louis, Missouri, where he lived until his death in 1897 at the age of 82. He was buried in the Bellefontaine Cemetery in St. Louis.[59]

Admiral Henry K. Thatcher remained in the navy and commanded the North Pacific Squadron until he retired at 62 in 1868. He passed away in 1880 at his home

---

55 Conner, *Gordon Granger*, 216.

56 "Lucius F. Hubbard Biography: Governors of Minnesota: Mnhs.org," MNHS, accessed Nov. 5, 2020, https://collections.mnhs.org/governors/inde.php/10004136.

57 "William R. Marshall Biography : Governors of Minnesota : Mnhs.org," MNHS, accessed Nov. 5, 2020, https://collections.mnhs.org/governors/index.php/10004001.

58 Alfred T. Andreas, *History of Chicago*, vol. 3 (Chicago, 1886), 86–87.

59 "A. J. Smith," *The Annals of Iowa*, vol. 3 (1897), 76–77, Iowa Research Online | University of Iowa Research, accessed Feb. 14, 2016, http://ir.uiowa.edu/cgi/viewcontent.cgi?article=2219&context=annals-of-iowa; L. R. Hamersly, *Officers of the Army and Navy (Regular and Volunteer) Who Served in the Civil War* (Philadelphia, 1894), 324.

in Winchester, Massachusetts. Thatcher was buried at the Forest Hills Cemetery in Jamaica Hills, Massachusetts.[60]

General James C. Veatch, commander of the 1st Division, XIII Corps, returned to Indiana, where he practiced law. In 1870, he worked as the collector of internal revenue taxes until August 1883. Veatch died December 22, 1895, in Rockport, Indiana, where he was buried at the Sunset Hill Cemetery.[61]

60 Porter, *Naval History of the Civil War*, 780.

61 "James Clifford Veatch (1819–1895)," Find A Grave, accessed July 2, 2020, https://www.findagrave.com/memorial/5897067/james-clifford-veatch.

Confederate Order of Battle:
Siege of Spanish Fort, March 27–April 8, 1865

(Including those actively engaged at Spanish Fort and Batteries Huger and Tracey)

DEPARTMENT OF EAST LOUISIANA, MISSISSIPPI, & ALABAMA

Lt. Gen. Richard S. Taylor, Commander, Headquarters—Meridian, Mississippi

DISTRICT OF THE GULF: Maj. Gen. Dabney H. Maury, Headquarters—Mobile, Alabama; Col. William E. Burnet, Chief of Artillery[1]

EASTERN DIVISION, DISTRICT OF THE GULF:[2] Brig. Gen. St. John R. Liddell, Headquarters—Blakeley, Alabama (Commander of the Blakeley Garrison)[3]

Armistead's Cavalry Brigade:[4]
12th Mississippi Cavalry: Lt. Col. Phillip B. Spence[5]
Detachments, 15th CS Cavalry: 2Lt. Artemus O. Sibley

---

1 *ORA* 49, pt. 1, 318. Graduate of Kentucky Military Institute and in 1857 commissioned lieutenant from Texas in 1st Infantry Regiment. Appointed 1Lt in Confederate Army in Mar. 1861 age 28 and served on Gen. A. S Johnston's staff in Sep. and was appointed post commander of Grenada, Mississippi from Nov. 1861–Apr 1862. In May and June, commanded Orleans Guard Battery as a captain, and by the battle of Corinth, achieved the rank of major and chief of artillery for Maury's Division. In Aug. 1863, Burnet received a promotion to colonel and chief of artillery for the Department of the Gulf and commander of the Bay Batteries. Killed in action on Mar. 31, 1865, at Spanish Fort while reviewing the defenses at Fort McDermott. Colonel John A. Brown replaced him.

2 *ORA* 49, pt. 1, 252. The Eastern Division consisted of all troops on the Eastern Shore including the Spanish Fort garrison under Gibson. The Western Division comprised the defenses directly around the city of Mobile, commanded by General Thomas in late 1864 up to the arrival of the Army of Tennessee units in Feb. 1865. After this time, Maury directed the complex operations of the Western District through the various brigade/division commanders in the area.

3 Service records show that he was captured at Blakeley on Apr. 9, 1865.

4 *ORA* 49, pt. 1, 1047; *ORA* 49, pt. 2, 1206. The brigade operated as company size elements of couriers and scouts across the entire front of the Pensacola, Fort Morgan, and Fish River Federal columns. Remnants of the brigade entered into the Blakeley lines on Apr. 1 with the exception of a couple of companies that operated in the enemy's rear. Spence commanded the remnant inside the Blakeley works consisting primarily of the 12th Mississippi Cavalry and a few companies of the 8th Alabama (Ball's). The troops under Spence were withdrawn from the rifle pits of Cockrell's Division on Apr. 6, and returned by transport to Mobile by orders issued by Maury on Apr. 5. Prisoner rolls indicate only a few mounted men from the 8th AL cavalry remained in the Blakeley works, apparently performing courier service for the garrison headquarters.

5 *ORA* 49, pt. 1, 1047; *ORA* 49, pt. 2, 1148. The War Department combined the 12th MS Cavalry Regiment with Lewis's Alabama Battalion and re-designated it as the 16th Confederate Cavalry Regiment in 1864. On Mar. 24, 1865, the ten companies of Mississippi cavalry were again re-designated the 12th MS Cavalry as the Alabama companies were transferred.

SPANISH FORT GARRISON: Brig. Gen. Randall L. Gibson

Col. Isaac W. Patton, Chief of Artillery[6]

Maj. John H. Henshaw, Chief Quartermaster

Maj. W. V. Couch, Commissary Officer

Capt. Clement S. Watson, Assistant Inspector General

Capt. George Norton, Assistant Adjutant General

Capt. W. P. Richardson, Ordnance Officer

Capt. Leverett H. Hutchinson, Co. C, 2nd Regt Engineer Troops

1Lt. Albert G. Clarke, Post Commandant, and Provost Marshal[7]

1Lt. S. L. Ware, Aide-de-Camp[8]

1Lt. Cartwright Eustis, Aide-de-Camp[9]

1Lt John T. Elmore, Engineer Corps in charge of SF works and treadway construction[10]

J. L. Adams, Telegrapher, detailed from 22nd Louisiana.

Mr. Mark D. Crane, Telegrapher

ARTILLERY: Col. Isaac W. Patton

Redoubt 1 (Old Spanish Fort Water Battery)

22nd Louisiana Consolidated (Heavy Artillery) Co. A, D, F: Capt. James C. Theard

Redoubt 2, Fort McDermott (Fort Alexis): Capt. Samuel Barnes[11]

22nd Louisiana Consolidated (Heavy Artillery) Co. C

6 *ORA* 49, pt. 2, 226, 1206. Captain, Co. F, 21 LA, 1861 and promoted regimental colonel in 1862; surrendered at Vicksburg; appointed colonel of 22nd LA Consolidated (7 regiments) Jan. 1864; commanding Eastern District of the Gulf before the arrival of Liddell. In Jan. 1864, he commanded the Apalachee Batteries. At Spanish Fort, Liddell assigned him chief of artillery for the garrison with his headquarters in the old Spanish Fort River Battery.

7 Mortally wounded through both shoulders while leading a counterattack on Apr. 8 with the provost guard consisting of Company G, 20th LA, against the 8th IA. He died on Apr. 22 after being transported to the U.S. Hospital in NO. His remains were transferred to Greenwood Cemetery, NO. Though no commission records exist, Clarke is listed as captain in the Federal hospital records.

8 Served on Gibson's staff for two years. Ware suffered a severe wound during the Atlanta campaign.

9 Eustis had been on Gibson's staff for about a year. He belonged to Co. F, 20th LA

10 Elmore was a graduate of the Charleston Military Academy and worked as a civil engineer for 6 years prior to the war. He enlisted in the 3rd Alabama Infantry in 1861 and was on detached engineer duty during most of his service. In 1862, he received a commission as a 2Lt. In 1863, he was assigned to the torpedo department under Gen. Gabriel Raines in Charleston, SC. In October 1864, he was transferred to Mobile Engineer Department. In March 1865, he was assigned as engineering officer in charge of the earthworks of Spanish Fort on General Gibson's staff and tasked to build the treadway from Spanish Fort to Apalachee Batteries. 2Lt George B. McClellan of the Engineer Corps had a detachment of Mobile engineer troops and reported to First Lieutenant Elmore specifically to build the treadway. Later on during the siege, Lt. Col. John H. Gindrat of the engineer department assisted Elmore in completing the treadway and telegraph line between Blakeley and the Apalachee Batteries.

11 Joined Louisiana Volunteers Oct. 1, 1861, as junior lieutenant Co. B, 23. Surrendered at Vicksburg. Reorganized in 1863 as Co. K, 22 LA and sent to Mobile. Promoted captain of Co. C, 22 LA Heavy Artillery in 1864 and assigned to various Bay batteries. Commanded Fort McDermott during the siege until severely wounded and evacuated to Mobile on Apr. 7, 1865.

Owen's 3rd Arkansas Light Battery: 1Lt.William C. Howell[12]
Massenburg's Georgia Battery, Capt. Thomas L. Massenburg, deployed March 30.

Field Artillery Battalion: Capt. Cuthbert H. Slocomb
Redoubt 3, Battery Blair
5th Company, Washington Louisiana Artillery: 1Lt. Joseph A. Chalaron

Redoubts 4 and 5
Phillip's Tennessee Battery: Capt. J. W. Phillips
Garrity's Alabama Battery: Capt. James Garrity (relieved Phillip's night of April 5)

Redoubt 6
Lumsden's Alabama Battery:[13] 1Lt. Andrew C. Hargrove[14]
Barry's Tennessee Battery:[15] Capt. Robert L. Barry
Third Missouri Battery Section: 1Lt. D. T. Hartshorn[16]

APALACHEE RIVER BATTERIES: Lt. Col. John A. Brown [17]
Battery Tracey: Capt. Ambrose A. Plattsmier
22nd Louisiana Consolidated (Heavy Artillery) Companies G, H, I
Battery Huger: Maj. Washington Marks[18]
22nd Louisiana Consolidated (Heavy Artillery) Companies B, K
1st Mississippi Artillery Company C (Turner's Battery): Capt. Lauderdale A. Collier

RIGHT WING, SPANISH FORT GARRISON:
Gibson's Brigade: Col. Francis L. Campbell

12 The National Park Service indicates that after Nashville, Owen's Battery AK Light Battery broke up and transferred to McCown-Hubbard's-Thrall's Battery.

13 Compiled service records show they were transferred to Mobile on Apr. 6 and relieved by Barry's Tennessee Battery (Lookout Artillery).

14 Service records show Hargrove was shot in the head on Apr. 4, 1865. He survived for 30 years, but committed suicide later, reportedly because of the severe pain.

15 Transferred from Mobile to the Spanish Fort garrison on Apr. 5, and relieved Lumsden's Battery.

16 Compiled Service Records, RG 109, NA. On Mar. 26, 1865, one detachment of the 3rd MO Battery transferred to Spanish Fort with a 20-pounder Parrott. On Apr. 1, a second gun detachment was moved to Spanish Fort. Lieutenant Hartshorn, who reported to Captain Slocomb, commanded the two-gun section.

17 *ORA* 49, pt. 2, 1179. Appointed from Maryland, graduated from West Point in 1846, and was assigned to the 4th Artillery. Commissioned Confederate captain of artillery and ordnance in July 1861. In 1862 transferred to Fort Caswell in North Carolina. He held the temporary rank of colonel and post commander. Promoted to lieutenant colonel in Mar. 1863 and assigned as chief of ordnance in the Trans-Mississippi Department at Shreveport. La. On Feb. 1864 Brown was ordered to Mobile, and by Aug. he commanded the city redoubts A to G. On Mar. 18, 1865, he assumed command of the Apalachee Batteries under Colonel Patton. Promoted colonel on Apr. 3, 1865, and sent to Mobile to replace Colonel Burnet on Maury's Staff. Paroled on May 10, 1865, at Meridian, MS.

18 Appointed captain, Co. G, 22 LA in 1861, promoted major 1862; surrendered at Vicksburg in 1863; command and construction of Apalachee Batteries in 1864. During Mobile campaign commanded Battery Huger.

Capt. Lewel Gustave, Acting Assistant Adjutant General
Surgeon J. S. Holt
1st, 16th, 20th Louisiana: Lt. Col. Robert H. Lindsay
4th Battalion & 25th Louisiana: Col. Francis C. Zacharie
19th Louisiana: Maj. Camp Flournoy[19]
4th, 13th, 30th, and 14th Battalion Sharpshooters, Louisiana: Unknown[20]

LEFT WING, SPANISH FORT GARRISON:
Thomas's Brigade: Brig. Gen. Bryan M. Thomas (3/23-30/65)[21]
Chief-of-Staff: Capt. James A. Wiggs
Ordnance Officer: Lt. Charles L. Huger[22]
62nd Alabama (1st Reserves): Col. Daniel E. Huger
63rd Alabama (2nd Reserves): Lt. Col. Junius A. Law
Brig. Gen. James T. Holtzclaw (3/31- end of siege)[23]
Capt. J. H. Pickens, Acting Assistant Adjutant General
Lt. John T. Holtzclaw, Aide-de-Camp
Surgeon J. F. Fryar

Holtzclaw's Brigade: Col. Bush Jones [24]
21st Alabama (-2 companies): Lt. Col. James Williams
18th Alabama: Capt. Augustus C. Greene
32nd & 58th Alabama: Col. Bush Jones
36th Alabama: Col. Thomas H. Herndon

19 Flournoy was only 22 years old at Spanish Fort.

20 *ORA* 49, pt. 1, 1045–1046. Gibson's Brigade listed a total effective force of 558 men on Mar. 10, 1865. An unknown captain commanded this consolidated regiment.

21 *ORA* 49, pt. 2, 1179. Thomas' Brigade on Mar. 23 consisted of the 21st, 62nd, and 63rd AL Infantry. Directed to Blakeley under the command of Cockrell. Transferred to Spanish Fort soon after arriving at Blakeley. Heavily engaged on Mar. 26–27. On Mar. 30, the brigade moved back to Blakeley. Holtzclaw's and Ector's Brigades from Blakeley were transferred to Spanish Fort to relieve Thomas' Brigade. The 21st AL, after participating in an execution of a deserter, went back to Spanish Fort on Apr. 1 and was assigned to Holtzclaw's Brigade.

22 Originally from 1st LA Regular Infantry, Huger served as General Gibson's acting assistant adjutant general in 1864.

23 *ORA* 49, pt. 2, 1179. Holtzclaw assumed command of the left wing of Spanish Fort on Mar. 31, 1865.

24 *ORA* 49, pt. 2, 1179. The 21st AL joined Thomas' Brigade. This brigade fought the opening battles at Spanish Fort Mar 27–29, 1865. On Mar. 30, the brigade transferred to Blakeley, presumably to take the reserves out of the fierce fighting. After Thomas' Brigade arrived at Blakeley, it participated in the execution of two privates from the 21st AL. The regiment then transferred back to Spanish Fort as part of Holtzclaw's Brigade. Two companies of the 21st AL remained at Blakeley as the Post Provost Guard.

38th Alabama: Capt. Charles E. Bussey[25]

Ector's Brigade, Cockrell's Division: Col. Julius A. Andrews[26]
Surgeon Ramon T. De Aragon[27]
2Lt. John A. Beall, Acting Ordnance officer
29th North Carolina: Capt. John W. Gudger
39th North Carolina: Maj. Pascal C. Hughes
9th Texas Infantry: Lt. Col. Miles A. Dillard
10th Texas Cavalry–dismounted: Capt. Jacob Ziegler
14th Texas Cavalry–dismounted: Lt. Col. Abram Harris
32nd Texas Cavalry–dismounted: Capt. Nathan Anderson

Special thanks to Roger Hansen who researched and compiled the Confederate Order of Battle.[28]

25 *ORA* 49, pt. 2, 1046; *ORA* 49, pt. 2, 1241. Bussey appears in the Official Records as commanding the 38th AL on Mar. 10, 1865. It is possible, however, that Col. Augustus Lankford resumed command of the 38th AL at Spanish Fort. Lankford's service record indicates his release from a POW camp on Feb. 25, 1865, in time to rejoin his command at Spanish Fort. Although his name did not appear in any official record dispatches during the siege, his name appeared in a dispatch on Apr. 15, 1865 from Maury to Spence. His service record also indicates that he commanded the 38th Alabama after parole.

26 Andrews, of the 32nd TX Dismounted Cavalry, commanded Ector's Brigade at Spanish Fort. Colonel David Coleman of the 39th NC and Andrews both led Ector's Brigade at different times. It is unclear, however, if Coleman commanded at Spanish Fort.

27 Cuban born and educated, emigrated to U.S. in 1850s to Tennessee. Enlisted in 13th TN. Quickly assigned as a hospital steward he participated at Shiloh. Promoted assistant surgeon of the 9th TX in June of 1862 and to regimental surgeon in Apr. of 1863. At Spanish Fort he served as brigade surgeon and evacuated with the garrison.

28 *ORA* 49, pt. 1, 1046–1048. Roger Hansen, *Confederate Command & Staff Mobile Campaign* (Roger Hansen, 2019). U.S. War Department, Compiled Service Records of Soldiers from the Confederate States, RG 94, NARA; The Confederate command structure varied during the siege. Maury shifted regiments and batteries to meet the Federal threat.

Appendix 2

Federal Order of Battle:
Siege of Spanish Fort, March 27–April 8, 1865

ARMY OF WEST MISSISSIPPI: Maj. Gen. Edward R. S. Canby[1]

General Staff

Chief-of-Staff: Maj Gen. Peter J. Osterhaus
Provost Marshal: Brig. Gen. George L. Andrews
Aide-de-Camp: Brevet Brig. Gen. Cyrus B. Comstock
Chief Engineer: Brevet Col. Miles D. McAlester
Assistant Adjutant-General: Lt. Col. Christian T. Christensen
Assistant Inspector General: Lt. Col. John M. Wilson
Quartermaster: Lieut. Col. Charles G. Sawtelle
Commissary of Subsistence: Lt. Col. Chester Bingham Hinsdill

Headquarters Units

Engineer Brigade: Brig. Gen. Joseph A. Bailey
1st Company of Pontoniers: Capt. John J. Smith
96th US Colored Troops: Col. John C. Cobb
97th US Colored Troops: Lt Col. George A. Harmount, Col. George D. Robinson

Siege Trains: Brig. Gen. James Totten
1st Indiana Heavy Artillery (7 companies): Col. Benjamin F. Hays
18th Battery, New York Light Artillery: Capt. Albert G. Mack

FIRST CAVALRY DIVISION: Brig. Gen. Joseph F. Knipe
First Brigade
12th Indiana: Maj. William H. Calkins
2nd New Jersey: Lt. Col. P. Jones Yorke
4th Wisconsin: Col. Webster P. Moore

Second Brigade
10th Indiana: Maj. George R. Swallow
13th Indiana: Lt. Col. William T. Pepper
4th Tennessee: Lt. Col. Jacob M. Thornburgh

---

1 *ORA* 49, pt. 1, 105–108.

XIII CORPS: Maj. Gen. Gordon Granger

FIRST DIVISION: Brig. Gen. James C. Veatch

First Brigade: Brig. Gen. James R. Slack

99th Illinois (five companies): Lt. Col. Asa C. Matthews

47th Indiana: Lt. Col. John A. McLaughlin

21st Iowa: Lt. Col. Salue G. Van Anda

29th Wisconsin: Lt. Col. Bradford Hancock

Second Brigade: Brig. Gen. Elias S. Dennis

8th Illinois: Col. Josiah A. Sheetz

11th Illinois: Col. James H. Coates

46th Illinois: Col. Benjamin Dornblaser

Third Brigade: Col. William B. Kinsey

29th Illinois: Lt. Col. John A Callicott

30th Missouri (4 companies): Lt. Col. William T. Wilkinson

161st New York: Maj. Willis E. Craig

23rd Wisconsin: Maj. Joseph E. Greene

Artillery: Capt. George W. Fox

4th Battery, Massachusetts Light Artillery: Lt. George W. Taylor

7th Battery, Massachusetts Light Artillery: Capt. Newman W. Storer

SECOND DIVISION[2]

First Brigade: Col. Henry Bertram

94th Illinois: Col. John McNulta

19th Iowa: Lt. Col. John Bruce

23rd Iowa: Col. Samuel L. Glasgow

20th Wisconsin: Lieut. Col. Henry A. Starr

Battery F, 1st Missouri Light Artillery: Capt. Joseph Foust

THIRD DIVISION: Brig. Gen. William P. Benton

First Brigade: Col. David P. Grier

28th Illinois: Lt. Col. Richard Ritter

77th Illinois: Lt. Col. John B. Reid 77th Illinois

96th Ohio (5 companies): Lt. Col. Albert H. Brown

35th Wisconsin: Col. Henry Orff

Second Brigade: Col. Henry M. Day

91st Illinois: Lt. Col. George A. Day

50th Indiana (5 companies): Lt. Col. Samuel T. Wells

29th Iowa: Col. Thomas H. Benton, Jr.

---

2 The second and third brigades of Gen. C. C. Andrews Division marched with Maj. Gen. Frederick Steele's column out of Pensacola before eventually besieging Fort Blakeley Apr. 1–9, 1865.

7th Vermont: Col. William C. Holbrook

Third Brigade: Col. Conrad Krez
33rd Iowa: Col. Cyrus H. Mackey
77th Ohio: Lt. Col. William E. Stevens
27th Wisconsin: Capt. Charles H. Cunningham
28th Wisconsin: Lt. Col. Edmund B. Gray

Artillery
21st Battery, New York Light Artillery: Capt. James Barnes
26th Battery, New York Light Artillery: Lieut. Adam Beattie

XVI CORPS: Maj. Gen. Andrew Jackson Smith

FIRST DIVISION: Brig. Gen. John McArthur
First Brigade: Col. William L. McMillen
33rd Illinois: Col. Charles E. Lippincott
26th Indiana: Col. John G. Clark
93rd Indiana: Col. De Witt C. Thomas
10th Minnesota: Lt. Col. Samuel P. Jennison
72nd Ohio: Lt. Col. Charles G. Eaton
95th Ohio Col. Jefferson Brumback

Second Brigade: Col. Lucius F. Hubbard
47th Illinois: Maj. Edward Bonham
5th Minnesota: Lt. Col. William B. Gere
9th Minnesota: Col. Josiah F. Marsh
11th Missouri: Maj. Modesta J. Green
8th Wisconsin: Lt. Col. William B. Britton

Third Brigade: Col. William R. Marshall
12th Iowa: Maj. Samuel G. Knee
35th Iowa: Lt. Col. William B. Keeler
7th Minnesota: Lt. Col. George Bradley
33rd Missouri: Lt. Col. William H. Heath

Artillery
3rd Battery, Indiana Light Artillery: Capt. Thomas J. Ginn
2nd Battery, Iowa Light Artillery: Capt. Joseph R. Reed

SECOND DIVISION: Brig. Gen. Kenner Garrard
First Brigade: Col. John I. Rinaker
119th Illinois: Col. Thomas J. Kinsey
122nd Illinois: Lt. Col. James F. Drish (wounded April 9), Maj. James F. Chapman
89th Indiana: Lt. Col. Hervey Craven
21st Missouri: Capt. Charles W. Tracy

Second Brigade: Brig. Gen. James I. Gilbert
117th Illinois: Col. Risdon M. Moore
27th Iowa: Maj. George W. Howard
32nd Iowa: Lt. Col. Gustavus A. Eberhart
10th Kansas (4 companies): Lt. Col. Charles S. Hills
6th Minnesota: Lieut. Col. Hiram P. Grant

Third Brigade: Col. Charles L. Harris
58th Illinois (four companies): Capt. John Murphy
52nd Indiana: Lt. Col. Zalmon S. Main
34th New Jersey: Col. William Hudson Lawrence
178th New York: Lt. Col. John B. Gandolfo
11th Wisconsin: Maj. Jesse S. Miller

THIRD DIVISION: Brig. Gen. Eugene A. Carr
First Brigade: Col. Jonathan B. Moore
72nd Illinois: Lt. Col. Joseph Stockton
95th Illinois: Col. Leander Blanden
44th Missouri: Capt. Frank G. Hopkins
33rd Wisconsin: Lt. Col. Horatio H. Virgin

Second Brigade: Col. Lyman M. Ward
40th Missouri: Col. Samuel A. Holmes
49th Missouri: Col. David P. Dyer
14th Wisconsin: Maj. Eddy F. Ferris

Third Brigade: Col. James L. Geddes
81st Illinois: Lt. Col. Andrew W. Rogers
108th Illinois: Col. Charles Turner
124th Illinois: Brevet Col. John H. Howe
8th Iowa: Lt. Col. William B. Bell

Artillery Brigade: Capt. John W. Lowell
Cogswell's Battery, Illinois Light Artillery: Lt. William R. Elting
Battery G, 2nd Illinois Light Artillery: Lt. Perry Wilch
1st Battery, Indiana Light Artillery: Capt. Lawrence Jacoby
14th Battery, Indiana Light Artillery: Capt. Francis W. Morse
17th Battery, Ohio Light Artillery: Capt. Charles S. Rice

Appendix 3

Spanish Fort: Known Confederate Soldiers Killed in Action or Mortally Wounded

Name	Rank	Regiment	Co.	Date	Notes
Adair, F. M.	PVT	32nd TX DC	D	4/8/65	Gunshot wound to the left leg. Died at the U.S. Hospital in NO on 4/22/65. GWC
Alexander, C. W.	PVT	25th LA	B	4/26/65	Mortally wounded 3/28/65, died 4/26/65 in Mobile Hospital.
Anderson, William B.	PVT	Garrity's AL Artillery			MAC
Andrus, Lewis T.	PVT	16th LA	K	4/6/65	
Ayers, William H.	PVT	10th TX DC	B	4/3/65	MAC
Baker, Jonathan A.	CPL	19th LA	I	4/8/65	
Beckton, James B.	CPL	10th TX DC	G	3/30/65	
Becton, Joseph H.	SGT	10th TX DC	G		
Blakey, A. A.	PVT	10th TX DC	I		
Bledsoe, Francis M.	PVT	18th AL	K	4/8/65	
Buffalo, William H.	PVT	Phillips AL Light Artillery		4/2/65	Killed by a sharpshooter while firing his piece. MAC
Burnet, William E.	COL	Chief of Artillery, District of the Gulf		3/31/65	Chief of Artillery, highest ranking CSA officer killed in the siege of Mobile. MAC.
Campbell, William M.	PVT	9th TX	H	3/30/65	Mortally wounded 4/8/65. MAC.
Conn, William H.	PVT	19th LA	G	4/25/65	
Corban, William C.	PVT	39th NC	B	4/4/65	
Casey, A.	PVT	39th NC	E	4/8/65	MAC

Childers, Harris	PVT	18th AL	A	4/6/65	Mortally wounded. Died on a steamboat to Montgomery, AL.
Clarke, Alfred	CPT	20th LA	G		GWC
Cottrill, John	PVT	20th LA	E	4/23/65	
Engel, Henry	PVT	1st LA	F	4/2/65	
Daily, Luther A.	PVT	38th AL	A	3/28/65	Gunshot wound to the head. MAC
Dinguidard, Isido	CPL	22nd LA	B	4/3/65	Battery Huger
Donnelly, John	PVT	20th LA	G	4/11/65	Mortally wounded 3/29/65. MAC
Durret, James A.	PVT	18th AL	E	4/7/65	Shot in the forehead. MAC
Engle, Henry	PVT	1st LA	F	4/3/65	Killed while detailed to Col. Garners' staff in Mobile; staff visit to Spanish Fort
Erwin, Frank	PVT	62nd AL	I	3/28/65	
Etheridge, George	PVT	Massenburg's Light Artillery		3/28/65	Mortally wounded 4/1/65. MAC
Ford, Joseph	PVT	19th LA	C		Mortally wounded 3/29/65. MAC
Flynn, Michael	PVT	4th LA Battalion	D	4/2/65	Gunshot to abdomen.
Frason, S. L.	PVT	22nd LA	F	3/28/65	Mortally wounded. MAC
Gilliland, Hiram J.	PVT	32nd & 58th AL	G	4/11/65	Mortally wounded. MAC
Gould, Emile Strader	PVT	21st AL	K	4/1/65	MAC
Graves, George W.	PVT	25th LA	K	4/1/65	
Greer, J. L.	PVT	19th LA	C	3/28/65	Mortally wounded 3/27/65.
Hamilton, John G.	PVT	21st AL	B	3/29/65	Mortally wounded 4/1/65. MAC
Haney, Charles	PVT	39th NC	I	4/13/65	Mortally wounded.
Hartnett, William R.	PVT	21st AL	C	4/8/65	MAC. Was also listed in E company.
Hodges, Christian	PVT	20th LA	F	4/4/65	MAC
Holland, Gilbert G.	CPT	32nd AL	H	4/10/65	Mortally wounded. MAC
Kennedy, J.	PVT	30th LA	D		MAC
Kenny, John	PVT	16th LA	F	4/16/65	MAC

James, Henry J.	CPT	19th LA	I	3/27/65	Died aboard the steamer Dorrance while being transported to Mobile.
Johnston, E. L.	1LT	63rd AL	H	3/28/65	MAC
Johnson, A. J.	PVT	18th AL	I	4/10/65	Mortally wounded 4/7/65.
Johnson, William	PVT	19th LA	E	3/10/65	Date is suspect.
Jones, Richard A	PVT	14th LA	A	3/28/65	
Lacuse, M.	PVT	19th L	E	3/28/65	
Landrum, John	PVT	1st LA	D	4/12/65	
Lee, John	PVT	39th NC	I	5/3/65	Mortally wounded 4/8/65. GWC
Lightsey, David M.	PVT	19th LA	D	3/28/65	
Ligon, William H.	SGT	19th LA	I	4/3/65	MAC
Lindsey, Steven A.	PVT	19th LA	C	4/4/65	
Lord, Daniel	PVT	25th LA		3/28/65	Head.
Lyles, Richard	1LT	10th TX DC	H	3/31/65	
Malone, D. L.	PVT	19th LA	E	3/30/65	
McGraw, John B.	PVT	14th LA Battalion of Sharpshooters	A	3/28/65	Aka–Ned
McEntruff, James F.	PVT	10th TX DC	E	4/6/65	Mortally wounded 4/1/65, left shoulder, hip, and back. MAC
McFarland, D. (Ned)	PVT	62nd AL	I	3/30/65	Mortally wounded 3/26/65. MAC
McIlHenny, Edward S.	CPL	Washington Light Artillery	5th	3/29/65	
Miller, Benjamin R.	PVT	Washington Light Artillery	5th	3/30/65	
Miller, Isaac	PVT	58th AL	B	4/1/65	MAC
Mitchell, Ben L	PVT	Massenburg's GA Battery		4/1/65	31 years of age.
Montgomery, William C.	PVT	19th LA	K	4/8/65	
Moore, John A.	PVT	16th LA	E	4/6/65	Mortally wounded 4/5/65. MAC
Mosely, William D.	1LT	62nd AL	A	3/27/65	MAC
Moses, Oliver	PVT	63rd AL	G		
Mount, Samuel C.	CPT	39th NC	C	4/8/65	Mortally wounded.
Nidee, Pierce	2LT	13th LA	K	3/28/65	MAC

Pack, John R.	PVT	39th NC	D	4/27/65	GWC
Patton, Frank M.	SGT	25th LA	F	4/7/65	
Pond, W. M.	SGT	16th Confederate Cavalry	A	3/26/65	
Powers, William A.	PVT	14th TX DC	C	4/8/65	
Pullen, T. N.	PVT	4th LA	E	3/27/65	Mortally wounded. Left arm.
Reach, Sr., Jeremiah M.	PVT	62nd AL	A	3/27/65	
Reach, Jr., Jeremiah M.	PVT	62nd AL	A	3/27/65	
Read, James M.	PVT	62nd AL	A	4/2/65	Mortally wounded 3/31/65. Serious head fracture, right arm and foot, captured. Died in field hospital of 3rd Division, XVI Corps.
Ripley, Fritz Henry	SGT	21st AL	E	4/3/65	MAC
Rusha, Henry	PVT	14th LA	B		
Sampson, James W.	PVT	Garrity's AL Light Artillery		4/8/65	
Schults, Thomas J.	PVT	Lumsden's Battery		4/10/65	Mortally wounded. MAC
Shepard, J. O.	SGT	62nd AL	B	4/2/65	Mortally wounded 3/29/65.
Shirley, J. H.	PVT	62nd AL	E	3/26/65	MAC
Sims, Charles W.	2LT	62nd AL	H	4/5/65	Mortally wounded 3/29/65. MAC
Sauzenburger, John	PVT	20th LA	D	3/27/65	Shot in the abdomen.
Strickland, Ed	PVT	25th LA	K	3/28/65	
Thompson, Solomon M.	LT	18th AL	E	4/8/65	Killed by shell. MAC
Tisdale, Nat.	PVT	30th LA	A	3/28/65	Mortally wounded in head 3/28/65.
Wansden, Simeon	PVT	63rd AL	G		
Watlins, Frank B. P.	1st SGT	62nd AL	A	3/27/65	Gunshot wound to lung. Died while walking home 7/65.
Ware, H. M.	PVT	21st AL	H	4/9/65	Mortally wounded 3/28/65. MAC
Weil, Conrad	PVT	16th LA	H	5/31/65	Mortally wounded 3/28/65. OHC
Wells, Joseph	PVT	22nd LA	D	4/1/65	

Wiggins, Tim	PVT	62nd AL	H	3/31/65	Mortally wounded 3/30/65. MAC
Wilson, G. W.	PVT	62nd AL	H	4/2/65	MAC
Wilson, Moses	PVT	62nd AL	C	3/30/65	Mortally wounded 4/4/65. MAC
Wise, George F.	PVT	19th LA	D	4/7/65	Mortally wounded 4/4/65.
Wood, Isom (Levi)	PVT	29th NC	F	4/17/65	Mortally wounded 4/8/65. Gunshot wound shoulder. Died in U.S. Hospital NO. GWC

Dismounted Cavalry (DC); Mobile National Cemetery (MNC), Mobile Magnolia Cemetery (MAC), NO Greenwood (GWC), Mobile's Old Hebrew Cemetery (OHC), New Orleans (NO).

Appendix 4

Spanish Fort: Known Federal Soldiers Killed in Action or Mortally Wounded

Name	Rank	Regiment	Co.	Date	Notes
Adams, Samuel	PVT	124th IL	F	4/3/65	Shot in head and killed on picket just before sundown. MNC
Alger, Delos	PVT	8th IA	A	4/8/65	MNC
Allard, Charles W.	PVT	7th Vt	C	4/8/65	Mortally wounded on or before 3/29. CNC
Allen, Arnold	PVT	21st IA	C	3/26/65	
Anton, Nelson	PVT	50th IN	E	4/5/65	MNC
Bartholomew, Yost	PVT	108th IL	C	4/7/65	MNC
Bangle, Charles	PVT	8th WI	A	5/7/65	Mortally wounded. MNC
Battis, John	PVT	161st NY	K		MNC
Black, George C.	PVT	124th IL	K	3/28/65	Shot through the bowels on 3/27/65.
Boyer, Frank	SGT	8th IA	G	4/8/65	MNC
Brennan, Bernard	CPL	5th MN	I	4/2/65	MNC
Bringwold, William H.	PVT	49th MO	F	4/6/65	Shot in the head.
Brown, Robert	PVT	91st IL	B	4/8/65	Mortally wounded 4/2/65. MNC
Carr, Robert	PVT	33rd WI	F	4/19/65	Mortally wounded 3/28/65. Died in NO.
Cameron, Joseph	PVT	12th IA	I	5/8/65	Mortally wounded 4/6/65. CNC
Cannell, William	PVT	35th WI	A	4/8/65	MNC
Courtney, Patrick	PVT	35th IA	E		MNC
Culliver, Francois	PVT	33rd IL	C		Mortally wounded 4/8/65 "friendly fire" from 1st IN Artillery. Died at NO.
Curry, Alonzo	PVT	28th IL	C	4/7/65	MNC

Dace, Charles	PVT	11th MO	A	3/30/65	MNC
Daly, John	PVT	21st NY Light Artillery		3/29/65	MNC
Dillon, George	PVT	47th IN	F	3/27/65	Shot through the hips. MNC
Donahoe, Peter	PVT	81st IL	H	3/27/65	MNC
Dwire, David	1SGT	8th IA	A	4/8/65	MNC
Easley, Thomas	PVT	117th IL	B	4/7/65	Mortally wounded 4/6/65. Gunshot wound stomach, gunshot shoulder, left arm amputated.
Edward, Radley	PVT	27th WI	I	4/4/65	MNC
Edwards, James W.	PVT	28th IL	B	4/28/65	Mortally wounded 3/26/65. Sent to Jefferson Barracks, NO where he died.
Elam, L. A.	PVT	33rd WI	A	6/5/65	Died of wounds in NO.
Erwin, James M.	CPL	108th IL	H	3/28/65	MNC
Erwin, William	CPT	11th MO	D	4/7/65	MNC
Fadden, Charles	PVT	7th MN	I	3/27/65	MNC
Fawbush, Doctor W.	PVT	50th IN	E	3/27/65	MNC
Fielman, Wilheim	PVT	8th IA	F		MNC
Fisk, Rasalva	CPL	124th IL	B	4/21/65	Mortally wounded 3/31/65. Died Jackson Barracks Hospital.
Flood, Philip	CPL	28th WI	H	3/31/65	MNC
Ganstow, Knud K.	PVT	91st IL	E	3/29/65	MNC
George, Major	CPL	19th IL	B	3/27/65	MNC
George, Richards	PVT	8th WI	D	3/29/65	MNC
Godwin, Samuel	PVT	29th IL	G	4/1/65	MNC
Grimm, Fritz	PVT	8th IA	B	4/9/65	Mortally wounded. MNC
Hancock, William	PVT	20th WI	B	3/28/65	MNC
Haty, Joseph	PVT	50th IN	E	3/27/65	Killed by a shell.
Hauter, Samuel	PVT	40th WI	I	4/2/65	MNC
Hazzard, William	PVT	124th IL	D	6/5/65	Mortally wounded 3/29/65. Gunshot wound to the abdomen. Died in NO.

Hervett, John	PVT	124th IL	A	3/30/65	Killed by shell from gunboat.
Hill, Henry	PVT	14th WI	F	4/8/65	MNC
Hogg, Samuel D.	PVT	28th WI	B	3/30/65	Died of wounds received 3/30/65. MNC
Hogue, William	PVT	1st IN Artillery		4/1/65	
Holiday, William N.	CPL	19th IA	I	4/11/65	Mortally wounded 3/27/65. MNC
Holy, Joseph	PVT	50th IN	D		MNC
Holtz, Joseph	PVT	50th IN	E	3/28/65	MNC
Howell, James C.	CPL	28th IL	E	3/28/65	Head, died on the field. MNC
Hudson, Frank P.	CPL	91st IL	K	3/27/65	Shot through the brain. MNC
Hughes, William H	PVT	33rd WI	C	4/30/65	Mortally wounded 3/30/65. Died Jefferson Barracks Hospital, NO.
Hunter, Sam	PVT	40th MO	I		MNC
Hutchinson, Henry S.	PVT	29th IA	H	3/31/65	MNC
Johnson, James	CPL	27th WI	B	4/2/65	MNC
Kridelbaugh, Frank	PVT	23rd IA	F	3/27/65	Mortally wounded 3/26/65, left shoulder and thigh.
Lafond, Peter	PVT	20th WI	F	4/24/65	Mortally wounded by own shell 4/4/65.
Langford, Silas	PVT	19th IA	H	3/29/65	Killed by concussion of shell.
Leach, Douglas	PVT	124th IL	F	7/7/65	Mortally wounded. MNC
Lee, William	PVT	14th WI	K	4/1/65	Shot through the head. MNC
Leighton, John	SGT	33rd WI	D	4/15/65	Mortally wounded 3/30/65. Died in NO.
Lester, George W.	PVT	124th IL	A	4/3/65	Killed in camp. Minie ball to his head. MNC
Long, James	PVT	8th IA	G	4/8/65	MNC
Majors, George	CPL	19th IA	A	3/27/65	MNC
Manning, Mathew	PVT	124th IL	C	4/6/65	Killed in the rifle pits. MNC
Mathews, George	PVT	35th WI	K	3/30/65	MNC

Mattice, Frederick B.	PVT	14th WI	I	4/8/65	MNC. Mortally wounded by shell 4/5/65.
McCanley, J.	PVT	58th IL	D	4/3/65	
McGinnis, John	PVT	33rd WI	K	3/30/65	
McGuire, John	SGT	40th MO	C	4/1/65	Instantly killed by a splinter while sitting in his tent.
McGuire, Michael	PVT	11th MO	C	4/2/65	MNC
Metz, John	PVT	33rd IA	G	4/22/65	Mortally wounded 4/1/65. Shot right shoulder, right arm amputated. Sent to Jefferson Barracks Hospital in NO.
Miner, Henry	PVT	49th MO	E	4/13/65	Shot in the arm 4/4/65, mortally wounded.
Montgomery, James E.	PVT	19th IA	E	3/28/65	
New, Sandy	PVT	28th IL	A	4/1/65	
Newton, William	CPL	33rd WI	I	3/31/65	MNC
Norton, Joel	CPL	29th WI	C	3/27/65	Killed by a shell when advancing on the fort. MNC
Oaks, George	PVT	40th MO	B	3/31/65	MNC
O'Brien, Timothy	PVT	28th WI	H	4/2/65	MNC
Oglesby, Joseph R.	PVT	29th IL	G	3/30/65	
O'Reilly, J.	PVT	11th MO	C	4/4/65	Mortally wounded 4/3/65
Owen, Robert	PVT	14th WI	G	4/8/65	Shot in right shoulder, severed artery. MNC
Pember, Merritt C.	PVT	33rd WI	A	4/11/65	Died of wounds.
Perkins, Henry C.	SGT	7th VT	C	4/1/65	Mortally wounded by shell 3/25/65. Both legs amputated. Sent to Jefferson Barracks, NO.
Peterson, Andrew	PVT	5th MN	C	4/4/65	Mortally wounded. MNC
Picket, Lewis	PVT	7th VT	G	4/11/65	Mortally wounded 3/26/65. Sent to Jefferson Barracks, NO.
Polk, Hudson	SGT	91st IL	K	3/27/65	Shot through the brain.
Radley, Edward S.	PVT	27th WI	I		MNC

Reaser, George	PVT	47th IN	F	3/27/65	Killed instantly by rifle ball through the head. MNC
Reed, Henry	PVT	33rd WI	F	4/8/65	Killed in action. MNC
Reese, Martin	PVT	91st IL	C	3/27/65	Fractured skull 3/26/65. Died in Division hospital. MNC
Richards, George W.	PVT	8th WI	D	4/8/65	MNC
Robinson, John G.	CPL	1st MO Cavalry	I	4/9/65	Mortally wounded. MNC
Schroeder, John H.	1SGT	19th IA	A	3/28/65	Killed by shell. MNC.
Shabino, Joseph	PVT	28th WI	I	3/30/65	Shot through the head. MNC
Short, Joseph	PVT	19th IA	H	4/7/65	Mortally wounded 3/26/65 by shell, back. Sent to Jefferson Barracks Hospital, NO, LA.
Smith, Daniel	PVT	14th IN Artillery		6/16/65	Mortally wounded 3/27/65.
Smith, William A.	CPL	95th IL	I	3/28/65	MNC
Stephenson, T. J.	CPL	95th OH	B		MNC
Sterrett, David	PVT	8th IA	K	3/28/65	MNC
Stetson, Carlton G.	CPT	33rd WI	I	4/2/65	MNC
Stone, Emory F.	CPT	20th WI		4/7/65	Mortally wounded 3/27/65.
Stoers, Charles (Aka Storrs, Stoors, Stowers)	PVT	7th VT	K	4/10/65	Mortally wounded 3/31. MNC
Strowbridge, Sanford	PVT	33rd IL	B	4/8/65	Mortally wounded 4/8/65 "friendly fire" from 1st IN Artillery. Died in route to NO.
Thomas, Cicero	PVT	19th IA	F	4/9/65	Shot in bowels. Mortally wounded 4/8/65. MNC.
Thompson, Edward	PVT	33rd IL	I	4/4/65	MNC
Thumb, William	CPL	91st IL	E	3/29/65	MNC
Tift, John	PVT	33rd WI	K	3/31/65	MNC
Turner, George	PVT	8th IA	G	4/8/65	MNC
Vanmarter, Eli	PVT	34th NJ	B	4/2/65	MNC

Vineyard, Henry	LT	8th IA	G	4/26/65	Mortally wounded 4/8/65. CNC
Wallace, William	PVT	95th IL	A	3/28/65	MNC
Wallace, Alexander	PVT	26th IN	E	4/1/65	MNC
Wallis, George J.	PVT	7th VT	G	4/16/65	Mortally wounded 4/8/65. Bullet hit him in the breast and came out his back. CNC
Weech, John	PVT	11th MO	C	4/5/65	MNC
Weeks, Spencer J.	CPL	28th WI	I	4/4/65	Killed by premature explosion of a Union shell. MNC
Wilhelm, Fielman	PVT	8th IA	F	4/8/65	MNC
Williams, James	PVT	40th MO	K	3/26/65	Head blown off. MNC
Williams, John	PVT	20th WI	A	3/28/65	MNC
Williams, Joseph C.	CPL	23rd IA	H	4/13/65	Mortally wounded 3/30/65. Sent to Jefferson Barracks Military Hospital in NO. (Gangrene)
Williams, Seymour	PVT	23rd IA	H	4/2/65	Mortally wounded 3/30/65. Chest. MNC
Wilson, John	PVT	21st NY Light Artillery		3/27/65	MNC
Wilson, Thomas	PVT	94th IL	A	4/1/65	MNC
Wing, Cyrus	PVT	72nd OH	I	4/8/65	MNC
Wooten, William R.	CPL	81st IL	A	4/4/65	MNC
Yost, Bartholomew	PVT	108th IL	C	4/7/65	MNC
Ziebarth, August	PVT	27th WI	E	3/28/65	MNC

Chalmette National Cemetery (CNC), Mobile National Cemetery (MNC), New Orleans (NO)

Appendix 5

Confederate Vessels Operating in Upper Mobile Bay from March 15–April 12, 1865[1]

Commodore Ebenezer Farrand: Commanding Naval forces
in the waters of the state of Alabama

Name	Guns	Description	Cmdg. Officer
Baltic		Once an ironclad, later served as a transport. Length: 186 feet. Draft: 6 feet 5 inches.	Unknown
Black Diamond		Small, high-pressure riverboat. Length: 156 feet.	Unknown
Heroine	1	Blockade runner. Armament: "one small brass gun."	Unknown
Huntsville	4	Ironclad. Scuttled at Spanish River. Length: 150 feet. Beam: 7–8 feet. Draft: 7–8 feet. Armament: two rifled 7-inch Brooke guns, two rifled 6.4-inch Brooke guns.	Lt. Julian Myers
Mary	1	Blockade runner. Armament: "one small brass gun."	Unknown
Morgan	6	Side wheel steamship. Length: 202 feet. Draft: 7 feet, 2 inch. Armament at surrender included: one 6.4-inch double-banded Brooke gun, two 32-pounder rifled and banded guns, two long 32-pounder smooth bores, one VII-inch double-banded Brooke gun.	Cmdr. George W. Harrison (removed 4/1/65); Lt. Joseph Fry
Nashville	4	Side wheel steamship Ironclad. Length: 271 feet. Draft: 10 feet, 9 inches. Armament: three 7-inch Brooke rifles, one 24-inch Howitzer.	Lt. J. W. Bennett
Red Gauntlet		Blockade runner	Unknown
Southern Republic		Side wheel river steamboat	Lt. Julian Myers

---

1 "Surrender of Rebel Navy Officers," *New Orleans Times-Democrat*, May 15, 1865, 6; *ORN*, 22, 59–60, 180, 187, 225–229, 231, 263; Sidney H. Schell and Allen R. Saults, The CSS *Huntsville* and CSS *Tuscaloosa Project, Report of 1985 Activities* (Mobile, AL, 1985).

Tuscaloosa[2]	4	Ironclad. Scuttled at Spanish River. Length: 150 feet. Draft: Between 7–8 feet. Armament: two rifled 7-inch Brooke guns, two rifled 6.4-inch Brooke guns.	Lt. C. P. McGary
Virgin[3]		Blockade runner	Unknown

2 The *Huntsville* and *Tuscaloosa* were scuttled in the Spanish River during the evacuation. *ORN* 22, 95.

3 The *Heroine, Mary, Red Gauntlet,* and *Southern Republic* were purchased and under the control of Maj. Gen. Dabney H. Maury and the Confederate Army. *ORN* 22, 180, 263.

Appendix 6

U.S. Navy Vessels Operating in Mobile Bay from March 15–April 15, 1865

Western Blockading Squadron: Admiral Henry K. Thatcher, Commanding

Name	Guns	Class	Cmdg. Officer
Albatross	6	screw	Acting Vol. Lt. T. B. Du Bois
Althea	1	screw	Acting Ensign F. A. G. Bacon
Anderson, W. G.	8	bark	Acting Master H. Tibbits
Buckthorn	2	screw	Acting Vol. Lt. W. Godfrey
Chickasaw	4	ironclad	Lt. Cmdr. G. H. Perkins
Cincinnati	13	ironclad	Lt. Cmdr. Geo. Brown
Corypheus	2	schooner	Acting Master and Pilot W. Stewart
Cowslip	3	paddle wheel	Acting Master Wm. T. Bacon
Elk	6	stern wheel	Acting Vol. Lt. N. Kirby
Genesee	8	paddle wheel	Lt. Cmdr. John Irwin
Glasgow	2	paddle wheel	Acting Master E. Kemble
Itasca	4	screw	Lt. Cmdr. N. Green
Ida	1	screw	Acting Ensign F. Ellms
Kickapoo	4	ironclad	Lt. Cmdr. M. P. Jones
Kittatinny	6	schooner	Acting Ensign N. J. Blasdell
Metacomet	10	paddle wheel	Cdr. P. Crosby
Milwaukee	4	ironclad	Lt. Cmdr. J. H. Gillis
Meteor	6	stern wheel	Acting Master M. Jordan
New London	5	screw	Acting Vol. Lt. Wash Godfrey
Nyanza	6	stern wheel	Acting Vol. Lt. C. A. Boutelle
Octorara	10	paddle wheel	Lt. Cmdr. W. W. Low
Osage	2	ironclad	Lt. Cmdr. W. M. Gamble
Pink	3	screw	Acting Master Samuel Belden
Richmond	22	screw	Capt. T. P. Greene
Rodolph	6	stern wheel	Acting Master N. M. Dyer
Rose	2	screw	Acting Ensign W. D. Maddocks
Sciota	4	screw	Acting Lt. J. W. Magune
Sebago	10	paddle wheel	Lieut. Cmdr. D. B. Harmony

Stockdale	6	stern wheel	Acting Vol. Lt. Thos. Edwards
Sam Houston	1	schooner	Acting Vol. Lt. and Pilot M. Freeman
Tallahatchie	6	stern wheel	Acting Master T. J. Linnekin
Trefoil	3	screw	Acting Master C. C. Wells
Tritonia	1	paddle wheel	Acting Vol. Lt. Geo. Wiggin
Winnebago	4	ironclad	Lt. Cmdr. W. A. Kirkland
Wood, M. A.	3	schooner	Acting Master John Ross

During the Mobile Campaign, 36 armed vessels operated in Mobile Bay (11 screws, 1 bark, 8 paddle wheels, 4 schooners, 6 stern wheels, and 6 ironclads).[1]

1 *ORN* 22, 106–107, 121–122, 128–129.

Appendix 7

U.S. Navy Vessels Sunk by Confederate Torpedoes in Mobile Bay

Vessel	Place	Date	Killed	Wounded
Tecumseh, monitor[1]	Mobile Bay	8/5/1864	92–94	
Narcissus, gunboat[2]	Mobile Bay	12/7/1864	0	
Milwaukee, monitor[3]	Blakeley River	3/28/1865	0	
Osage, monitor[4]	Blakeley River	3/29/1865	5	11
Rodolph, tinclad[5]	Blakeley River	4/1/1865	4	11
Althea, tug[6]	Blakeley River	4/12/1865	2	4
Ida, tug[7]	Mobile Bay	4/13/1865	3	2
Sciota, gunboat[8]	Mobile Bay	4/14/1865	5	5
Cincinnati's launch[9]	Blakeley River	4/14/1865	3	
St. Mary's, transport[10]	Alabama River			

1 *ORN* 21, 417, 442, 521–522, 599; Ben LaBree, ed., *The Confederate Soldier in the Civil War*, 1861–1865 (Louisville, 1897), 439; Henry L. Abbot, "The School of Sub-Marine Mining at Willet's Point," *Journal of the Military Service Institution of the United States* 1 (1880): 205; Jack Friend, *West Wind, Flood Tide: The Battle of Mobile Bay* (Annapolis, 2014), 182. Reports on the total killed aboard the Tecumseh varied from 92–94.

2 *ORN* 21, 752–753.

3 *ORN* 22, 71.

4 Ibid., 72–75, 132–133.

5 Ibid., 74, 132–133.

6 Ibid., 93, 132–133.

7 Ibid., 132–133.

8 Ibid., 130, 132–133, 237.

9 Ibid., 130–131.

10 *From Mobile*; "The R. B. Hamilton Strikes a Torpedo—She is Blown Up—Loss of Life," *New York Times*, May 7, 1865, 1; Scharf, *Confederate Navy*, 767–768; Bree, *Confederate Soldier*, 439. The sinking of the *St. Mary's* by torpedo is also highly questionable, although there is a reference to the sinking of the *St. Mary* in the *New York Times* on May 7, 1865. There is, however, no mention of the *St. Mary* being sunk in the Official Records.

R. B. Hamilton, army transport[11]	Mobile Bay	5/12/1865	6	9
		Total[12]	122–124	42

11 *ORN*, Series 2, Vol. 1, 195; *ORN* 22, 61, 67, 70–75, 96, 106–107, 121, 129–133, 171–172, 188–189, 237. The *Tecumseh* and *Narcissus* sank prior to the 1865 campaign. *Althea, Ida, Sciota*, tug of the *Cincinnati, St. Mary*, and *R. B. Hamilton* sank after the fall of Mobile.

12 Bree, *Confederate Soldier*, 439; Scharf, *Confederate Navy*, 767–768; *ORN*, Series 2, Vol. 1, 110, 195. *ORN* 22, 61,67,70–75, 96, 106–107, 121, 129–133, 171–172, 188–189, 237; Abbot, "Sub-Marine Mining," 205. Gaines, *Shipwrecks*, 6; Some sources list the USS *Itasca* and the USS *Rose* as having struck a torpedo in Apr. of 1865.

Appendix 8

Known U.S. Naval Personnel Killed in Action or Mortally Wounded[1]

3/29–4/14/1865

Name	Rank	Vessel	Date	Notes
Nicholas Heydenger	ordinary seaman	*Osage*	3-29-65	
Lewis De Wall	master at arms	*Osage*	" "	
William Paigher	seaman	*Osage*	" "	
John Everhart	ordinary seaman	*Osage*	" "	
Charles Taylor	ordinary seaman	*Osage*	" "	
Theodore Texada	landsman	*Rodolph*	3-31-65	
Jule Baltour	first-class boy	*Rodolph*	" "	
Michael Driscoll	landsman	*Rodolph*	" "	
Johnson Smith	landsman	*Rodolph*	" "	
G. D. Andrews	first-class boy	*Althea*	4-12-65	
J. Glen	landsman	*Althea*		
Phillip Williams	landsman	*Ida*	4-13-65	Drowned
Thomas Burns	first-class fireman	*Ida*	" "	
Sanford Curran	acting third engineer	*Ida*	" "	
Leon De Wolf	acting master's mate	*Launch of Cincinnati*	4-14-65	
C. H. Howard	captain forecastle	*Launch of Cincinnati*	" "	
John Drion	ordinary Seaman	*Launch of Cincinnati*	" "	
John W. Bayard	boatswain's mate	*Sciota*	4-14-65	
J. S. Robinson	captain forecastle	*Sciota*	" "	
Jeremiah Horrigan	coxswain	*Sciota*	" "	
Jacob Brown	boatswain's mate	*Sciota*	" "	
George Creighton	landsman	*Sciota*	" "	Attached to Elk
Maurice O'Brien	surgeon's steward	*Sciota*	Unknown	Died between 4/14–19/65

1 *ORN* 22, 131–133.

Appendix 9

Ordnance and Principal Ordnance Stores Captured at Spanish Fort[1]

Field Artillery	Quantity
6-pounder field guns, bronze, smooth-bore	9
6-pounder field guns, iron, smooth-bore	2
6-pounder field guns, bronze, rifled	2
6-pounder field gun, iron, rifled	1
12-pounder light guns, bronze, smooth-bore	4
12-pounder mountain howitzers, bronze, smooth-bore	2
Total number of pieces	20

Siege, Garrison, and Sea Coast Artillery	
20-pounder rifled guns, Parrott pattern	2
30-pounder rifled gun, Parrott pattern	1
24-pounder boat howitzers, bronze, smooth-bore	2
24-pounder siege howitzer, iron, smooth-bore	1
24-pounder coehorn mortars, iron, smooth-bore	14
8-inch siege mortar, iron, old pattern	1
6.4-inch Brooke, rifled, iron	4
8-inch columbiad, iron, CS Army	1
8-inch columbiad, iron, CS Army, disabled (*Lady Slocomb*)	1
Total number of pieces	27

Stand of small-arms	270

Artillery Projectiles	
8-inch columbiad	160
30-pounder, rifled	120
20-pounder, rifled	300
6.4-inch	507

1 *ORA* 49, pt. 1, 150–151.

24-pounder, smooth-bore	200

Fixed Ammunition, Cartridges, Powder

6-pounder ammunition	1,850
12-pounder gun and howitzer ammunition	1,000
24-pounder howitzer ammunition	100
rifled musket elongated ball cartridges, caliber .577	63,000
rifled musket elongated ball cartridges, caliber .54	92,000
rifled musket ball cartridges, caliber .69	15,000
rampart grenades	170
24-pounder fire-balls	48
powder	700 lbs.
Brooke rifle cartridges	463
8-inch columbiad cartridges	350
24-pounder siege howitzer cartridges	190
24-pounder boat howitzer cartridges	240

Appendix 10

Confederates Captured at Spanish Fort and Imprisoned at Ship Island[1]

Alabama

18th Regiment	30
21st Regiment	6
32nd–58th Regiment	14
36th Regiment	62
38th Regiment	38
6th Cavalry Regiment	3
8th Cavalry Regiment	2
Total	155

Georgia

Massenburg's Artillery Battery	1
Total	1

Louisiana

4th Battalion, 25th Regiment	29
1st, 16th, 20th Regiment	19
4th, 13th, 30th Regiment, 14th Battalion Sharpshooter	70
19th Regiment	25
Total	143

North Carolina

29th Regiment	80
39th Regiment	77
Total	157

---

1 Kirk Barrett researched and compiled this list.

Tennessee

Barry's Artillery Battery	19
Total	19

Texas

9th Regiment	6
10th Cavalry (Dismounted) Regiment	4
14th Cavalry (Dismounted) Regiment	13
32nd Cavalry (Dismounted) Regiment	30
Total	53
Grand Total	519

Appendix 11

The Lady Slocomb

One of the more interesting stories that occurred in the postwar years involves the fate of the cannon, *Lady Slocomb*. Named in honor of Washington Artillery Capt. Cuthbert Slocomb's wife, the Tredegar Iron Works, in Richmond, Virginia, manufactured the cast iron cannon in 1862. The 5th Company of the Washington Artillery skillfully manned the 8-inch iron columbiad at Battery Blair.[1]

The Blue and Gray Veterans Union, a group of Union and Confederate veterans living in the Mobile Bay area, was organized on July 4, 1890, on the battlefield of Spanish Fort. On March 7, 1891, Artemus O. Sibley, owner of the land where the siege of Spanish Fort took place, sold the title to the cannon to the Blue and Gray Union for one dollar. The following week the veterans transported *Lady Slocomb*, at a cost of $285.25, to downtown Mobile where it became a peace monument commemorating the "Valor of American Soldiers and the Sweet Dawn of Peace." The veterans discovered and removed a charge of canister still inside it before moving the big gun over to Mobile.[2]

Dr. Seymour Bullock and Thomas P. Brewer were instrumental in bringing the cannon to Mobile. Bullock, a 49-year-old former Bluecoat, served as president of the Blue and Gray Union. He served with the 24th New York Cavalry Regiment as quartermaster sergeant. After the war, he relocated to Mobile to practice medicine. Brewer, an ex-Confederate, held the positions of vice president of the Blue and Gray Union and lieutenant commander of the Admiral Semmes Camp of the United Confederate Veterans. He served as a captain with Hood's Texas Brigade

---

1 Jeff Kinard, *Artillery: An Illustrated History of Its Impact* (Santa Barbara, CA, 2007), 213; "Lady Slocomb: The Silent Witness," *New Orleans Times Picayune*, 3; "Last Shot," *Los Angeles* [CA] *Herald*, 8; "The Lady Slocomb," *Mobile Daily Register*; Larry J. Daniel and Riley W. Gunter, *Confederate Cannon Foundries* (Union City, TN, 1977), 7. Although contemporary newspaper reports stated that the Selma foundries built the cannon, an official at the Confederate Memorial Hall claimed that certain markings on the *Lady Slocomb* indicate the Tredegar Foundry in Virginia built the cannon. Tredegar cannons were generally marked with the year of their manufacture on the left trunnion and, on the right "J. R. A & Co." The foundry stamped the manufacturing number into the piece's muzzle face.

2 Donnie Barrett, "Lady Slocomb," *Spanish Fort Historical Society News Letter* 2, no. 2 (Aug. 1996).

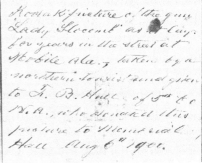

The Lady Slocomb at Mobile, Alabama's Government Street, circa 1891–1899. *Tulane University Special Collections*

in Virginia, surrendered his company at Appomattox Court House, and even ran for mayor of Mobile.[3]

Although neither Bullock nor Brewer fought at Spanish Fort, they helped organize the Blue and Gray Union in Mobile, where they both resided. The two became close friends through their association with the Union and even traveled together to Washington, D.C., where they received confirmation that the Treasury Department had no claim to the title of the *Lady Slocomb*.[4]

However, a falling-out in their friendship occurred, causing them to become mortal enemies. Bullock's wife claimed the two had an argument at a Blue and Gray Union meeting, the details of which have been lost to history. Their feud led to a tragedy at Navy Cove, 4 miles from Fort Morgan, where both men had summer cottages.[5]

Brewer attempted to avoid a confrontation after a family member warned that Bullock intended to shoot him. As he fished from the shore of Navy Cove on Thursday, October 15, 1891, Bullock approached in his boat and fired his shotgun at Brewer, missing, due to the rocking of the boat. Before Bullock could shoot again, Brewer returned fire with his shotgun and killed Bullock. Following the shooting Brewer surrendered himself to the sheriff. There were no witnesses, however, and a subsequent investigation found both double-barrel shotguns used

3 "A Shotgun Duel," *Mobile Daily Register*, Oct. 16, 1891, 1; "Capt. Thomas Brewer," *Confederate Veteran Magazine* (Dec. 1914); "Deaths Here and Elsewhere," *Pittsburgh Dispatch*, Oct. 23, 1891, 5.

4 "A Shotgun Duel," 1; Department of Treasury Archives, "Letters Sent by the Miscellaneous Division ('EK' Series), 1887–1906," vol. 12, pp. 148, 170, 248, RG 56, NARA.

5 "A Shotgun Duel"; Dr. Seymour Bullock Slain," *Atlanta Constitution*, Oct. 16, 1891, 1.

had discharged only one round. Brewer never served time for the shooting as it was determined to be a case of self-defense.[6]

The shotgun duel between Bullock and Brewer may have ultimately led to Mobile losing the cannon to New Orleans. It is believed that the tragedy at Navy Cove led the Blue and Gray Union to dissolve and allowed veterans of the Washington Artillery the opportunity to make a strong bid for the *Lady Slocomb*.[7]

Henry Badger, a prominent Confederate veteran and citizen of Mobile, paid for the transportation of the *Lady Slocomb* from Spanish Fort to Mobile in 1891. When the Blue and Gray Union ceased to exist, ownership of the big gun transferred to Badger, since he had paid for it to be transported. After he passed away on May 28, 1896, newspaper reports indicated his estate proposed selling the *Lady Slocomb* to the highest bidder.[8]

Veterans of the 5th Company of the Washington Artillery, led by 1Lt. Joseph A. Chalaron, had wanted the cannon in New Orleans ever since it came to Mobile. They had even petitioned the secretary of the U.S. Treasury for the right to purchase it. On June 4, 1891, Randall L. Gibson, who was then serving in the U.S. Senate, contacted the Secretary of the Treasury on the veterans' behalf. He tried to have the cannon turned over to the survivors of Slocomb's Battery as a memorial to honor their brave captain. When Badger's estate offered the cannon to the highest bidder in 1896, they took advantage of the opportunity to acquire it.[9]

After much deliberation, a group Washington Artillery veterans bought the cannon and brought it back to their hometown of New Orleans. In March, 1899, Chalaron and other veterans of the 5th Company of the Washington Artillery arrived in Mobile to complete the purchase of the cannon. Veterans of the Washington Artillery and the 14th Texas Cavalry then shared the expense of having the big gun moved to New Orleans, where veterans dedicated it to the memory of Capt. Cuthbert Slocomb and "the men who gave their lives for its defense." The unveiling ceremony occurred on September 19, 1899.[10]

Today, the *Lady Slocomb* can be seen outside the Confederate Museum on Camp Street in New Orleans. Many citizens of Mobile resented the removal of the cannon. The topic remains a bitter subject with some residents of the city to this day.

---

6 "A Shotgun Duel."

7 "Gleanings of General Interest from the Gulf City," *New Orleans Times Picayune*, Mar. 2, 1899.

8 *Washington* [DC] *Evening Times*, Sep. 16, 1896, 4.

9 Department of Treasury Archives, "Letters Sent by the Miscellaneous Division ('EK' Series), 1887–1906," vol. 12, pp. 148, 170, 248, RG 56, NARA.

10 "Gleanings of General Interest from the Gulf City," *New Orleans Times Picayune*, Mar. 2, 1899; "The Lady Slocomb," *Mobile Daily Register*, 3.

Appendix 12

Origins of Spanish Fort

After the war, Major General Maury recalled that the Spanish built and occupied the earthen fort known as Spanish Fort during the colonial period. However, no record of its construction during the 1780–1813 period has surfaced in Spanish archives.[1]

"The name remains rather mysterious," states Dr. Gregory Waselkov of the University of South Alabama's Center for Archaeological Studies. In 1998, Waselkov directed a field school excavation across the parapet and postern tunnel of the Confederate earthwork of that name. Unfortunately, a house built in the 1960s destroyed part of the fort site, but the northeastern third of the fort still stands. Beneath the earthwork, Waselkov found a layer of soil cultivated during the British colonial era, an indication of farming associated with the nearby Augustin Rochon plantation before 1780; however, there were no artifacts of Spanish colonial date, just Civil War munitions from the 1865 siege.

Only later did Waselkov locate a map that clarified the relationship between the fort, which Spaniards presumably built, and the Civil War structure of that name. A manuscript map drafted by Confederate army engineers during the summer of 1864 shows proposed trenches and other fortifications surrounding an existing "Spanish Fort," which appears in plain view just as the surviving portion looks today. Considering that evidence for a pre-existing earthwork before the Civil War, Waselkov reexamined photographs of the archaeological excavation profiles, which reveal a stratigraphic break between a lower colonial-era parapet and an upper zone added under the direction of Confederate Lt. Col. Scheliha. Evidently, the Southerners strengthened the colonial fort by raising the parapet height.

As to the origin of that earlier fort, "the Confederate engineers believed the earthwork dated to the Spanish colonial period," noted Waselkov. He pointed out that a map by Maxfield Ludlow of the Gulf Coast, commissioned in 1817 by Gen.

---

1 Maury, "Defence of Spanish Fort," 133.

Old Spanish Fort. The so-called Spanish Fort was originally constructed during the Revolutionary War era. During the Civil War, the Confederates improved it and renamed it Redoubt 1. *Alabama Department of Archives and History*

Andrew Jackson, shows a "British fort" in roughly the same location. "But, as for who actually built the original Spanish Fort, that remains an open question."[2]

2 Interview with Dr. Gregory Waselkov, University of South Alabama, Mobile, Alabama, Jan. 7, 2019.

Appendix 13

Spanish Fort Battlefield Postbellum

Other than timber harvesting and some minor development, the earthworks of Spanish Fort remained undisturbed for many years after the war. In 1867, 2Lt. Artemus O. Sibley of the 15th Confederate Cavalry, the man who led the attack on Veatch's Division supply train on March 24, 1865, inherited the property where the siege of Spanish Fort took place from his father, Cyrus.

The Fuller Brothers Co. later developed the land into a residential subdivision called Spanish Fort Estates from the 1950s through the early 2000s. Although many of Spanish Fort earthworks have been destroyed, several key positions remain. Historical markers are located throughout the neighborhood denoting key locations of various regiments and fortifications from the siege.

The remnants of the original Spanish Fort (Redoubt 1) and some portions of Red Fort (Redoubt 3) are located on private property and are still visible today. Fort McDermott (Redoubt 2), the strongest and highest position at Spanish Fort, remains remarkably well preserved. In 2011, Mrs. George [Anne] Fuller Jr. donated Fort McDermott to the Raphael Semmes Camp 11 of the Sons of Confederate Veterans. The Semmes Camp cleared 150 years' growth of vegetation and dedicated the site as Fort McDermott Confederate Memorial Park on April 11, 2015. The Semmes Camp entirely funded the reclamation thereof without public funding. Though a private park, it is open to the public and comprises a three-acre site containing the lower parapet, moat, upper parapet, parade ground, and artillery emplacements of the original fortifications.[1]

The Mobile Bay area also features a "Civil War Trail" available as a guide for enthusiasts interested in visiting the locations mentioned in this book. The website featuring this self-guided tour can be found at: http://www.battleofmobilebay. com/about-the-trail/default.aspx.

---

1 Description of Fort McDermott courtesy of A. J. Dupree, Mobile, Alabama.

Author at Fort McDermott. *Pam Swan*

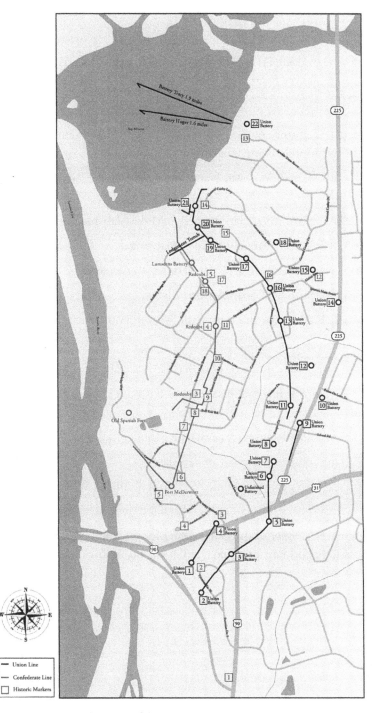

Modern map of the Spanish Fort Estates subdivision. *Kirk Barrett*

Appendix 14

Summary of Events of the Siege of Spanish Fort

March 17, 1865: The advance of the Union forces under Major General Canby moves forward from Mobile Point, Alabama.

March 18–22, 1865: Expedition from Dauphin Island to Fowl River, Alabama, and skirmishes.

March 23–24, 1865: Skirmishes near Dannelly's Mills, Alabama.

March 24, 1865: Affair near Dannelly's Mills, Alabama.

March 25, 1865: Skirmishes near the Deer Park Road, Alabama

March 26, 1865: Skirmish near Spanish Fort, Alabama.

March 27–April 8, 1865: Siege and capture of Spanish Fort, Alabama.

April 1, 1865: Skirmish near Blakeley, Alabama.

April 2–9, 1865: Siege and capture of Fort Blakeley, Alabama.

April 9–11, 1865: Bombardment and capture of Batteries Huger and Tracey, Alabama.

April 10–12, 1865: Confederate forces evacuate Mobile, Alabama.

April 12, 1865: Union forces occupy Mobile, Alabama.

April 13, 1865: Skirmish near the Mobile & Ohio Rail Line at Whistler, Alabama.

April 29, 1865: Armistice agreement at McGhee farm at Kushla, Alabama.

May 4, 1865: Final Surrender of the Confederate forces of the Department of Alabama, Mississippi, and East Louisiana, at Citronelle, Alabama.

Bibliography

Primary Sources

Manuscript Collections

Abraham Lincoln Presidential Library, Manuscript Department, Springfield, IL
> Ridge, Robert. *Diary, 1865*
> Peter, William H. *"Dear Ones at Home, 1865"*

Alabama Department of Archives and History, *Montgomery, AL*
> *Confederate Regimental History Files*
> Lyons, Mark. "The War Letters of Mark Lyons"

Auburn University Libraries, Auburn, AL
> Millard, Alexander. *Diary, 1865*

Auburn University Montgomery Library, Archives and Special Collections, Montgomery, AL
> Robinson, J. S. E. "Experience-observations of J. S. E. Robinson, Private, Co. G, 58th Ala. Volunteers: Reminiscence of the War between the States."

Blakeley State Park, Spanish Fort, AL
> Dispatch Book, Eastern Division, District of the Gulf, 1865

Charles H. Hooper Collection, John Pelham Historical Association, Hampton, VA
> Nye, Edward O. Diary, 1865

DePauw University and Indiana University Archives, Greencastle, IN
> Edwards, Elijah E. Diary, 1865

Dolph Briscoe Center Archives, University of Texas, Austin, TX
> Thomas, John. Diary, 1864–1865

Gilderman Institute of American History, New York, NY
> Gibson, Randall L. "Randall Lee Gibson to Tobias Gibson," Dec. 2, 1861
> Gibson, Randall L. "Randall Lee Gibson to Tobias Gibson," Dec. 9, 1861

History Museum of Mobile. Mobile, AL
> Herndon, Thomas H. Papers

Huntington Library, Art Collections. San Marino, CA
> Christensen, Christian T. Papers, 1862–1906, James T. Holtzclaw telegram

Illinois State Historical Society, Springfield, IL

Drish, James F. Papers, 1865

Indiana State Library, James R. Slack Collection. Rare Books and Manuscripts, Indianapolis, IN
Slack, James R. Papers, *Mar. 28, 1865*

Library of Congress, Washington, D.C.
Hubbard, Lucius. Papers, 1908

Louisiana and Lower Mississippi Valley Collections, Louisiana State Univ., Baton Rouge, LA
Gibson, Randall L. Papers, 1865

Louisiana Research Collection, Tulane University, New Orleans, LA
Watson, Clement Stanford. Papers, Apr. 18, 1865
Taylor, Richard. Papers, Manuscript Collection 40, 1865

L. Tom Perry Special Collections, Brigham Young University, Provo, UT
Davis, William E. "William E. Davis Diaries 1865"

Minnesota Historical Society, St. Paul, MN
Andrews, C. C. "C. C. Andrews Papers," 1865–1866.
Bachmann, Karl. "Charles W. Bachmann and Family Papers," 1865
Edwards, Elijah E. "Elijah E. Edwards Civil War Journal," Mar. 10–Oct. 6, 1865
Mattocks, Ebenezer B. "Diary of E. Mattocks, 1864–1865"
Merwin, J. W. "Roster and Monograph, 161st Reg't, N.Y.S. Volunteer Infantry,"
Microfiche, 1902
Nelson, John. Papers, 1865

Missouri Historical Society, St. Louis, MO
Bartlett, Aurelius T. "Reminiscences of Aurelius T. Bartlett," 1890
Typescript

National Archive and Record Service, Washington, D.C.
Camp Jefferson Davis 1848 Rosters, Record Group 94
Confederate Papers Relating to Citizens or Business Firms, complied 1874–1899,
documenting the period 1861–1865

Nebraska State Historical Society, Lincoln NE
Chilvers, William B. "William Burnham Chilvers, 1835–1914"

New York Historical Society, New York City, New York
Coan, Titus M. "Titus Munson Coan Papers," 1865
Francis, John F. "Edmund Family Collection: Correspondence," 1865

New York Military Museum, Division of Military and Naval Affairs, Saratoga Springs, NY
Kinsey, William B. "Journal of the March of the Third Brigade," 1865

Norman Nicolson Collection, Historic Mobile Preservation Society, Mobile, AL
"L. F. Hubbard and the Fifth Minnesota, Letters of a Union Volunteer, 1862–1865," Typescript

Pennsylvania State University, Special Collections, University Park, PA
Fisher, William H. H. "William H. H. Fisher Civil War Diary, 1865"

Southern Historical Collection, University of North Carolina, Chapel Hill, NC
Buchanan, Franklin. Franklin Buchanan Letterbook, Sep. 12, 1862–Nov. 20, 1863

Spring Hill College Archives. Mobile, AL

Cornette, Andrew. "Father Cornette's Notes from the Annals of Spring Hill College," 1872

State Historical Society of Missouri-Columbia, Columbia, MO

Audsley, Francis. Papers, 1865

Fike, Henry C. "Henry C. Fike Diaries, 1865"

University of Iowa Libraries, Iowa City, IA

Henderson, William L. "William L. Henderson Diary, 1861–1866"

University of North Carolina, Southern Historical Collection, Wilson Library, Chapel Hill, NC

Lockett, Samuel H. "Samuel Lockett Papers, 1864–1865"

West Virginia and Regional History Center, West Virginia University Libraries, Morgantown, West VA.

Perrigo, George W. *Diary*, 1865

Wisconsin Veterans Museum, Madison, WI

Sweet, William A. Diary, 1865–1866. Typescript

Yale University Library, Manuscripts and Archives, New Haven, CT

Tarleton Family Papers, 1861s1865. Typescript

Online Collections

"Civil War Journal of James B. Lockney WIS. 28th Regiment, Co. G." James R. Shirey. Accessed Oct. 25, 2014. http://jshirey.brinkster.net/CivilWar/.

"Confederate Law Authorizing the Enlistment of Black soldiers, Mar. 13, 1865, As Promulgated in a Military order." Freedmen and Southern Society Project. Accessed June 14, 2020. https://www.freedmen.umd.edu/csenlist.htm.

Barker, Lauren S. "28th Wisconsin Regiment: The Captain's Goose and What Became of It." Twenty-Eighth Wisconsin Volunteer Infantry. Last modified 1888. https://www.28thwisconsin.com/campfire/goose.html.

"Citizen File." *Fold3*. Accessed Dec. 30, 2020. https://www.fold3.com/.

"Civil War Diary of Henry M. Dryer." GenWeb of Monroe County, NY. Accessed Sep. 27, 2021. https://mcnygenealogy.com/book/diary.htm.

Clarke, Henry L. "Captain Alfred Clarke." Civil War Louisiana. Accessed Dec. 14, 2019. http://www.civilwarlouisiana.com/2012/06/.

Cleve, H. P. "Annual Report of the Adjutant General of the State of Minnesota." Minnesota. Adjutant General's Office. Last modified Dec. 15, 1866. http://www.archive.org/stream/annualreport01minn#page/334/mode/2up.

"Flag." American Civil War Museum: Online Collections. Accessed Jan. 9, 2018. http://moconfederacy.pastperfectonline.com/webobject/8E6CAF5A-67A1-4402-B250-284917542464.

"From a Confederate Diary." Accessed Apr. 29, 2020. https://www.oocities.org/laheavy1/MumfordDiary.html.

"Geddes." Department of Residence. Last modified Dec. 21, 2020. https://www.housing.iastate.edu/halls/geoffroy/geddes/.

"Illinois Civil War Muster and Descriptive Rolls Database." Illinois State Archives. Accessed Nov. 28, 2016. http://www.ilsos.gov/isaveterans/civilMusterSearch.do?key=49031.

Johansson, Jane M. "Gibson's Louisiana Brigade During the 1864 Tennessee Campaign." *Tennessee Historical Quarterly* 64, no. 3 (Fall 2005): 186–195. Accessed Sep. 23, 2014. http://www.jstor.org/stable/42627901.

"Illinois Civil War Muster and Descriptive Rolls Database." Illinois State Archives. Accessed Nov. 28, 2016. http://www.ilsos.gov/isaveterans/civilMusterSearch.do?key=49031.

Little, George, and James Maxwell. "A History of Lumsden's Battery, C. S. A." Gutenberg. Accessed July 2, 2020. https://www.gutenberg.org/files/26455/26455-h/26455-h.htm.

"M214 Chambers (William Pitt) Diary." University of Southern Mississippi Libraries. Accessed Aug. 1, 2016. http://lib.usm.edu/legacy/archives/m214.htm.

"Robert Angelo Spink." Oshkosh Public Museum. Accessed Aug. 1, 2016. http://oshkosh.pastperfect-online.com/20004cgi/mweb.exe?request=field;fldseq=359109.

Stubbs, Milton A. "Milton Stubbs Letter." U.S. Christian Commission. Accessed Feb. 21, 2020. https://www.nwuscc.org/MiltonStubbsLetter.html.

"The Texas Collection—Far From Home: The Journey of a Union Soldier in the South." Blogs @ Baylor University. Last modified July 15, 2019. https://blogs.baylor.edu/texascollection/.

Throne, Mildred. "Nashville and Mobile." *The Palimpsest 50 / University of Iowa Research*. Last modified 1969. https://ir.uiowa.edu/palimpsest/vol50/iss2/10.

Tichenor, Willis V. "Reminiscences of the capture of Mobile." Twenty-Eight Wisconsin Volunteer Infantry. Accessed Apr. 11, 2020. http://www.28thwisconsin.com/letters/tichenor_1893.html.

Weston, Sidney E. "Dear Parent." Vermont Civil War, Lest We Forget. Accessed Apr. 4, 2020. https://vermontcivilwar.org/get.php?input=32074.

Whipple, Henry P. "The Diary of a Private Soldier." *Wisconsin Historical Society*. Accessed Dec. 8, 2021. https://content.wisconsinhistory.org/digital/collection/quiner/id/24928.

Wittenberger, Frank. "Frank Wittenberger Civil War Diary." Richfield Historical Society, Richfield, WI. Accessed Apr. 8, 2020. https://richfieldhistoricalsociety.org/story_frank_wittenberger.html.

Wolf, Otto E. "Otto E. Wolf Civil War Letters." Fort Pickering, Tennessee - Madison County Historical Society. Accessed Mar. 19, 2018. http://madcohistory.org/wp-content/uploads/2017/11/OW_1865_final.pdf.

Books

Andrews, Christopher C. *History of the Campaign of Mobile: Including the Cooperative Operations of Gen. Wilson's Cavalry in Alabama*. New York: D. Van Nostrand, 1867.

Avery, A. C. *Five Points in the Record of North Carolina in the Great War of 1861–5*. Goldsboro, NC: Nash Brothers, 1904.

Bailey, J. C. W., ed. *A Gazetteer of McLean County [...]*. Chicago, IL: Bailey & Hair, 1866.

Beers, Fannie A. *Memories: A Record of Personal Experience and Adventure During Four Years of War*. Philadelphia: J. B. Lippincott Company, 1888.

Bentley, William H. *History of the 77th Illinois Volunteer Infantry: Sept. 2, 1862–July 10, 1865*. Peoria, IL: Edward Hine, Printer, 1883.

Benton, James G. *A Course of Instruction in Ordnance & Gunnery Prepared for the Use of the Cadets of the United States Military Academy*. N.Y.: D. Van Nostrand, 1867.

Boyce, Joseph, and William C. Winter. *Captain Joseph Boyce and the 1st Missouri Infantry, C.S.A.* St. Louis: Missouri Historical Society Press, 2011.

Bryner, Byron C. *Bugle Echoes: The Story of Illinois 47th*. Springfield, IL: Phillips Bros, Printers and Binders, 1905.

Byers, Samuel H. *Iowa in War Times*. Des Moines: W.D. Condit & Co., 1888.

Carr, Eugene A. *First Reunion of the Survivors of the Army of Tennessee, And Its Four Corps*. Logansport, IN: Wilson, Humphreys & Co., 1892.

Chamberlin, John N. *Captaining the Corps d'Afrique: The Civil War Diaries and Letters of John Newton Chamberlin*. Jefferson, NC: McFarland, 2016.

Clark, Walter. *Histories of the Several Regiments and Battalions from North Carolina, in the Great War 1861—'65*. Raleigh, NC: E. M. Uzzell, Printer and Binder, 1901.

Cleveland, Moses A. *The Civil War Diary of Moses A. Cleveland: 7th Battery Mass. Light Artillery; the Red River Campaign and the Campaign Against Port of Mobile, Alabama, 1864–1865*. Edited by Olga Fairfax. Nacogdoches, TX: Erickson Books, 2011.

Comstock, Cyrus B. *The Diary of Cyrus B. Comstock*. Edited by Marlin E. Sumner. Dayton, OH: Morningside House, Inc., 1987.

Crooke, George. *The Twenty-first Regiment of Iowa Volunteer Infantry: A Narrative of Its Experience in Active Service, Including a Military Record of Each Officer, Non-commissioned Officer, and Private Soldier of the Organization*. Milwaukee, WI: King, Fowle & Co., Book Printers, 1891.

Dispatch Book, Eastern Division, District of the Gulf, March–April 1865, Vol. 100, Chapter II. War Department Collection of Confederate Records, 1865.

Donald C. Elder, III, ed. *A Damned Iowa Greyhound: The Civil War Letters of William Henry Harrison Clayton*. Iowa City: University of Iowa Press, 1998.

Duncan, James I. *History of the Nineteenth Regiment, Iowa Volunteer Infantry*. Davenport, IA: Publishing House of Luse & Griggs, 1865.

Eggleston, Edmund T. *To Succeed Or Perish: The Diaries of Sergeant Edmund Trent Eggleston, Company G, 1st Mississippi Light Artillery Regiment*. Edited by Lawrence L. Hewitt, Thomas E. Schott, and Marc Kunis. Knoxville, TN: The University of Tennessee Press, 2015.

Elliott, Isaac H. *History of the Thirty-Third Regiment Illinois Veteran Volunteer Infantry*. Gibson, IL: Thirty-Third Illinois Regimental Association, 1902.

Farragut, Loyall. *The Life of David Glasgow Farragut: First Admiral of the United States Navy, Embodying His Journal and Letters*. New York: D. Appleton and Company, 1879.

Foote, Shelby. *The Civil War: A Narrative, Volume 3, Red River to Appomattox*. New York: Random House, 1974.

Fremantle, Sir A. *The Fremantle Diary: Being the Journal of Lieutenant Colonel James Arthur Lyon Fremantle, Coldstream Guards, on His Three Months in the Southern States*. London: Andre Deutsch, 1956.

Gerling, Edwin G. *The One Hundred Seventeenth Illinois Infantry Volunteers: (The McKendree Regiment) 1862–1865*. Highland, IL 1992.

Gladieux, Rolland J. *The 14th Indiana Light Artillery*. Kenmore, New York: Work Experience Press, 1978.

Grant, Ulysses S. *The Personal Memoirs of U. S. Grant [Two volumes in one]*. Mount MacGregor, New York: Konecky & Konecky, 1885.

Hatcher, Edmund N. *The Last Four Weeks of the War*. Columbus, OH: Edmund N. Hatcher, 1891.

Hill, Alfred J. *History of Company E, of the Sixth Minnesota regiment of volunteer infantry*. St. Paul, MN, 1899.

Hill, Charles S. *War Papers and Personal Reminiscences: 1861–1865. Read Before the Commandery of the State of Missouri, Military Order of the Loyal Legion of the United States*. St. Louis: Becktold & Co., 1892.

Holbrook, William C. *A Narrative of the Services of the Officers and Enlisted Men of the 7th Regiment of Vermont Volunteers (Veterans), From 1862 to 1866*. New York: American Bank Company, 1882.

Holtzclaw, Benjamin C. *The Genealogy of the Holtzclaw Family, 1540–1935*. Richmond: Old Dominion Press, Inc., 1936.

Howard, Richard L. *History of the 124th Regiment Illinois Infantry Volunteers: Otherwise Known as the "Hundred and Two Dozen," from August, 1862, to August, 1865*. Springfield, IL: H. W. Rokker, 1880.

Jones, Edgar W., and C. David A. Pulcrano. *Eighteenth Alabama Infantry Regiment*. Birmingham: C. D. A. Pulcrano, 1994.

Liddell, St. John R. *Liddell's Records*. Edited by Nathaniel C. Hughes. Baton Rouge: Louisiana State University Press, 1985.

Maury, Dabney H. *Recollections of a Virginian in the Mexican, Indian, and Civil Wars*. New York: Charles Scribner's Sons, 1894.

M'Conaughy, N. T. "Gallant Col. William E. Burnett." *Confederate Veteran* (August 1909): 399

Miller, Edward G. *Captain Edward Gee Miller of 20th Wisconsin: His War 1862-1865*. Edited by W. J. Lemke. Fayetteville, AK: No. 37, Washington County Historical Society, 1960.

Minnesota Board of Commissioners on Publication of History of Minnesota in Civil and Indian Wars. *Minnesota in the Civil and Indian Wars, 1861–1865*, Vol. 2. St. Paul: Pioneer Press Company, 1890.

Miscellaneous Document of the House of Representatives for the First Session of the Fifty-Second Congress, 1891–1892. Washington D.C.: Government Printing Office, 1892.

Musser, Charles O. *Soldier Boy: The Civil War Letters of Charles O. Musser, 29th Iowa*. Iowa City: University of Iowa Press, 1995.

Napier, III, John H. "Martial Montgomery: Ante Bellum Military Activity." *Alabama Historical Quarterly* (Fall 1967): 107–131.

Newton, James K. *A Wisconsin Boy in Dixie: Civil War Letters of James K. Newton*. Edited by Stephen E. Ambrose. Madison: University of Wisconsin Press, 1961.

Owen, Thomas M. *History of Alabama and Dictionary of Alabama Biography*, Vol. III. Chicago: The S. J. Clarke Publishing Company, 1921.

Owen, William M. *In Camp and Battle with the Washington Artillery of New Orleans: A Narrative of Events During the Late Civil War from Bull Run to Appomattox and Spanish Fort*. Boston: Ticknor and Company, 1885.

Palfrey, John C. "The Capture of Mobile, 1865." In *The Mississippi Valley, Tennessee, Georgia, Alabama, 1861–1864*. 8th ed. Boston: The Military Historical Society of Massachusetts, 1910.

Plum, LL. B., William R. *The Military Telegraph During the Civil War in the United States*. Chicago: Jansen, McClurg, & Company, Publishers, 1882.

Porter, David D. *The Naval History of the Civil War*. New York: The Sherman Publishing Company, 1886.

Porter, David D. *Incidents and Anecdotes of the Civil War*. New York: D. Appleton and Company, 1886.

Reed, David W. *Campaigns and Battles of the Twelfth Regiment Iowa Veteran Volunteer Infantry*. Evanston, IL, 1903.

Report of the Adjutant General and Acting Quartermaster General of Iowa. Des Moines, IA: F. W. Palmer, State Printer, 1867.

Rix, William. *Incidents of Life in a Southern City During the War: A Series of Sketches Written for the Rutland Herald*. Rutland, VT: Rutland Herald, 1880.Robinson, Arthur J. *Memorandum and Anecdotes of the Civil War, 1862 to 1865*. 1912.

Scott, John. *Story of the Thirty Second Iowa Infantry Volunteers*. Nevada, IA: John Scott, 1896.

Shirley Thorsen, Ruth S., and Naomi Struthers. *The Struthers Family*. Ottosen, IA: Struthers Family, 1973.

Slack, James R., and David Williamson. *Slack's War*. Williamson Books, 2012.

Smith, Austin W. "Service Sketch with the 4th Louisiana Battalion." *Confederate Veteran*, n.d.

Smith, Walter G. *Life and Letters of Thomas Kilby Smith, Brevet Major-General, United States Volunteers, 1820–1887*. New York: G. P. Putnam's Sons, 1898.

Snedeker, Charles Henry, Karen Hitchcock Nilsen, Mildred Britton, and Juline Hitchcock Jenkins. *The Civil War Diary of Charles Henry Snedeker*. Auburn, AL: Auburn University Archives, 1966.

Sperry, Andrew F. *History of the 33d Iowa Infantry Volunteer Regiment: 1863–6*. Des Moines, IA: Mills & Company, 1866.

State of Iowa. *Report of the Adjutant General and Acting Quartermaster General of Iowa*. Des Moines: F. W. Palmer State Printer, 1866.

Stephenson, Philip D. *Civil War Memoir of Philip Daingerfield Stephenson, D. D.* Edited by Nathaniel C. Hughes. Conway, AR: UCA Press, 1995.

Stevens, Thomas N., & George M. Blackburn. *"Dear Carrie...": The Civil War Letters of Thomas N. Stevens*. Mount Pleasant, MI: Clarke Historical Library, 1984.

Stockwell, E. *Private Elisha Stockwell, Jr., sees the Civil War*. Edited by B. R. Abernathy. University of Oklahoma Press, 1958.

Taylor, Richard. *Destruction and Reconstruction: Personal Experiences of the Late War*. New York: D. Appleton, 1879.

Tunnard, W. H. *A Southern Record. The History of the Third Regiment Louisiana Infantry*. Baton Rouge, LA, 1866.

United States War Department. *Compiled Service Records of Soldiers from the Confederate States*, Record Group 94. Washington, D.C.: National Archives, 1907.

United States War Department. *The War of the Rebellion: A Compilation of the Official Records of the Union and Confederate Armies*. Washington, D.C.: Government Printing Office, 1897.

United States War Department. *Official Records of the Union and Confederate Navies in the War of the Rebellion*, Washington, D.C.: Government Printing Office, 1894–1922.

United States. Congress. *Memorial Addresses on the Life and Character of Randall Lee Gibson, (a Senator from Louisiana,): Delivered in the Senate and House of Representatives, March 1, 1893, and April 21, 1894*. Washington D.C.: Government Printing Office, 1894.

United States. War Department. Office of Commissary General of Prisoners. United States. National Archives and Records Service. *Selected Records of the War Department Relating to Confederate Prisoners of War, 1861–65*. Washington: National Archives, National Archives and Records Service, General Services Administration, 1965. Roll 136, Vol. 406–408

Van Cleve, H. P. *Annual Report of the State of Minnesota for the Year Ending December 1, 1866 and of the Military Forces of the State from 1861–1866*. Saint Paul, MN: Pioneer Printing Company, 1866.

Von Sheliha, Viktor. *A Treatise on Coast-Defence: Based on the Experience Gained by Officers of the Corps of Engineers of the Army of the Confederate States.* London: E. & F. N. Spon, 1868.

Waring-Harrison, Mary. *Miss Waring's Journal: 1863–1865.* Edited by Thad Holt. Chicago: Wyvern Press of S. F. E., 1964.

Waselkov, Gregory. University of South Alabama, Mobile, Alabama. Interview, 7 January 2019.

Williams, James M. *From That Terrible Field: Civil War Letters of James M. Williams, 21st Alabama Infantry Volunteers.* Tuscaloosa: University of Alabama Press, 1981.

Williams, John M. *The "Eagle Regiment": 8th Wis. Inf'ty. Vols. A Sketch of Its Marches, Battles and Campaigns. From 1861 to 1865. With a Complete Regimental and Company Roster, and a Few Portraits and Sketches of Its Officers and Commanders.* Belleville, WI: Recorder Print, 1890.

Wilson, James H. *Under the Old Flag; Recollections of Military Operations in the War for the Union, the Spanish War, the Boxer Rebellion, Etc.* Vol. II. New York: D. Appleton and Company, 1912.

Wood, Wales W. *A History of the Ninety-Fifth Regiment.* Chicago: Tribune Company's Book and Job Printing Office, 1865.

Articles

Allen, Charles J. "Some Account and Recollection of the Operations against the City of Mobile and Its Defences, 1864 and 1865." *Glimpse of the Nation's Struggles* (1887): 54–88.

Bailey, W. "The Star Company of Ector's Brigade." *Confederate Veteran* XXII (June 1914).

Beckett, R. C. "A Sketch of the Career of Company B, Armistead's Cavalry Regiment." *Publications, The Mississippi Historical Society* 8 (February 1905): 33–50.

Cameron, William L. "The Battles Opposite Mobile." *Confederate Veteran* 23 (1915), 305–308.

Carter, T. G. "That Charge at Spanish Fort." *Confederate Veteran* XIII (1906).

Chalaron, Joseph A. "Battle Echoes from Shiloh." *Southern Historical Society Papers* 21 (1893): 215–224.

Cullins, G. T. "Siege of Spanish Fort, Near Mobile." *Confederate Veteran* XII (July 1904).

Davis, Eli. "That Hard Siege of Spanish Fort." *Confederate Veteran* XII (1904).

Dispatch Book, Eastern Division, District of the Gulf, March–April 1865, Vol. 100, Chapter II. War Department Collection of Confederate Records. (1865).

Lee, Stephen D. "Battle of Jonesboro." *Southern Historical Society Papers* 5 (Winter 1878): 130–131.

Macy, William M. "Civil War Diary of William M. Macy." *Indiana Magazine of History* 30, no. 2 (June 1934): 181–197.

Maury, Dabney H. "Defence of Mobile in 1865." *Southern Historical Society Papers* 3, no. 1 (January 1877): 1–11.

_____ "Defence of Spanish Fort." *Southern Historical Society Papers* 39 (April 1914): 130–136.

_____ "How the Confederacy Changed Naval Warfare." *Southern Historical Papers* 22 (1894): 75–81.

M'Conaughy, N. T. "Gallant Col. William E. Burnett." *Confederate Veteran* (August 1909): 399.

Merriam, Henry C. "The Capture of Mobile." *War Papers, Read Before the Commandery of the State of Maine Military Order of the Loyal Legion of the United States* 3 (1908): 23–250.

Napier, III, John H. "Martial Montgomery: Antebellum Military Activity." *Alabama Historical Quarterly* (Fall 1967): 107–131.

Newton, James K., and Stephen E. Ambrose. "The Siege of Mobile." *The Alabama Historical Quarterly* 20 (Winter 1958): 595–600.

Nichols, James L. "Confederate Engineers and the Defense of Mobile." *Alabama Review* (July 12, 1959).

Palfrey, John C. "The Capture of Mobile, 1865." In *The Mississippi Valley, Tennessee, Georgia, Alabama, 1861–1864*, 8th ed. Boston: The Military Historical Society of Massachusetts, 1910.

Smith, Austin W. "Service Sketch with the 4th Louisiana Battalion." *Confederate Veteran*, n.d.

Stephenson, Phillip D. "Defence of Spanish Fort." *Southern Historical Society* 39, no. 1 (April 1914): 121–129.

Tarleton, Robert, and William Still. "The Civil War Letters of Robert Tarleton." *The Alabama Historical Quarterly* 32, no. 1 (Spring 1970): 78–80.

Waterman, George S. "Afloat-Afield-Afloat." *Confederate Veteran* VII (November 1899): 490–492.

_____ "Afloat-Afield-Afloat." *Confederate Veteran* VIII (February 1900): 53–55.

_____ "Afloat-Afield-Afloat." *Confederate Veteran* VIII (January 1900): 21–24.

Wight, Ambrose S. "The Flag first hoisted at Mobile." *The Century Illustrated Monthly Magazine* (November 1890).

Newspapers

Advertiser and Register [Mobile, AL]

Allentown [PA] *Leader*

Army and Navy Journal [Washington D.C.]

Atlanta Constitution

Bibb Blade [Six Mile, Alabama]

Boston Daily Advertiser

Burlington [IA] *Weekly Hawk-Eye*

Canyon City [TX] *News*

Chicago Tribune

Cincinnati Enquirer

Cleveland Daily Leader

Courier Journal [Louisville, KY]

Daily Crescent [New Orleans, LA]

Daily Kansas Tribune [Lawrence, KS]

Daily Milwaukee News

Daily Progress [Raleigh, NC]

Daily Register [Mobile, AL]

Daily Standard [Raleigh, NC]

Harper's Weekly

Highland Weekly News [Hillsboro, OH]

Home Journal [Winchester, TN]

Liberator [Boston]

Los Angeles Herald

Mobile [AL] *Daily News*

Mobile [AL] *Evening Telegraph*

Press Register [Mobile, AL]

Mobile [AL] *Times*

Morning Herald [Demopolis, AL]

Nashville Daily Union

National Tribune [Washington, D.C.]

New York Herald

New York Times

Knoxville News Sentinel

Osage [KS] *City Free Press*

Pantograph [Bloomington, IL]

Perrysburg [OH] *Journal*

Philadelphia Inquirer

Phillipsburg Herald

Pittsburgh Daily Commercial

Republican Northwestern [Belvidere, IL]

Richmond [VA] *Dispatch*

Richmond [IN] *Weekly Palladium*

Rutland [VT] *Daily Herald*

Times Democrat [New Orleans, LA]

Times Picayune [New Orleans, LA]

Saint Paul's Globe

San Francisco Call

Selma [AL] *Morning Reporter*

St. Joseph County Independent [Mishawaka, IN]

St. Louis Dispatch

Sun [New York, NY]

Sunny South [Atlanta, GA]

Watertown [WI] *Times*

Weekly Republican—Traveler [Arkansas City, KS]

Woodstock [IL] *Sentinel*

Republican-Northwestern [Belvidere, IL]

Secondary Sources

Books

Allardice, Bruce S. *Confederate Colonels: A Biographical Register*. Columbia: University of Missouri Press, 2008.

Andreas, Alfred T. *History of Chicago*, Vol. 3, 3rd ed. Chicago: A. T. Andreas, 1886.

Anonymous. *The American Annual Cyclopedia and Register of Important Events of the Year 1865*. Vol. 5. New York: D. Appleton & Company, 1870.

Arnold-Scriber, Theresa, and Terry G. Scriber. *Ship Island, Mississippi: Rosters and History of the Civil War Prison*. Jefferson: McFarland, 2007.

Bartlett, Napier. *Military Record of Louisiana*. Baton Rouge: Louisiana State University Press, 1964.

Bergeron, Arthur W. *Confederate Mobile*. Jackson: University of Mississippi Press, 1991.

Bounds, Ben H., and Charles L. Bounds. *Ben H. Bounds, 1840–1911, Methodist Minister and Prominent Mason: Biography and Highlights from His Early Life and Civil War Memoirs*. Columbus, OH: J. O. Moore, 1962.

Brewer, Willis. *Alabama, Her History, Resources, War Record, and Public Men: From 1540 to 1872*. Montgomery, AL: Barrett and Brown, 1872.

Burns, Zed H. *Ship Island and the Confederacy*. Hattiesburg: University and College Press of Mississippi, 1971.

Clarke, Mary W. *David G. Burnet*. Austin, TX: Jenkins Publishing Company, 1969.

Conner, Robert. *General Gordon Granger: The Savior of Chickamauga and the Man Behind "Juneteenth."* Havertown: Casemate, 2013.

Daniel, Larry J. *Cannoneers in Gray: The Field Artillery of the Army of Tennessee*. Tuscaloosa: University of Alabama Press, 2005.

Daniel, Larry J., and Riley W. Gunter. *Confederate Cannon Foundries*. Union City, TN: Pioneer Press, 1977.

Evans, Clement A. *Confederate Military History: A Library of Confederate States History*. Atlanta, GA: Confederate Pub. Co, 1899.

_____ *Confederate Military History: A Library of Confederate States History*, Vol. VII. Atlanta: Confederate Publishing Company, 1899.

_____ *Confederate Military History: A Library of Confederate States History*, Vol. X. Atlanta: Confederate Military History, 1899.

Huff, M.D., Sanford. *The Annals of Iowa*, 13th ed. Iowa City: Iowa State Historical Society, 1866.

Hughes, Nathaniel Cheairs. *The Pride of the Confederate Artillery: The Washington Artillery in the Army of Tennessee*. Baton Rouge: Louisiana State University Press, 1997.

Iseminger, William R. *From McLean to Mobile: A History of the 94th Illinois Infantry Regiment Volunteers, 1862–1865 (The McLean Regiment)*. William R. Iseminger, 2022.

Johnson, Charles W. "Narrative of the Sixth Minnesota." In *Minnesota in the Civil and Indian Wars, 1861–1865*, 300–346. Salem, Mass: Higginson Book Company, 1866.

King, James T. *War Eagle A Life of General Eugene A. Carr*. Lincoln: University of Nebraska Press, 1963.

Levine, Bruce. *The Fall of the House of Dixie: The Civil War and the Social Revolution That Transformed the South*. New York: Random House, 2013.

Madaus, Howard Michael. *The Battle Flags of the Confederate Army of Tennessee*. Milwaukee, WI: Milwaukee Public Museum, 1976.

McBride, Mary G. *Randall Lee Gibson of Louisiana: Confederate General and New South Reformer*. Baton Rouge: Louisiana State University Press, 2007.

McPherson, James M. *Battle Cry of Freedom: The Civil War Era*. New York: Oxford University Press, 1988.

McPherson, James M. *For Cause and Comrades: Why Men Fought in the Civil War.* New York: Oxford University Press, 1997.

O'Brien, Sean. *Mobile, 1865: Last Stand of the Confederacy.* Santa Monica: Praeger, 2001.

Parrish, T. Michael. *Richard S. Taylor, Soldier Prince of Dixie.* Chapel Hill: University of North Carolina Press, 1992.

Perry, Aldo S. *Civil War Courts-Martial of North Carolina Troops.* Jefferson, NC: McFarland, 2012.

Perry, Milton F. *Infernal Machines: The Story of Confederate Submarine and Mine Warfare.* Baton Rouge: Louisiana State University Press, 1985.

Plum, William R. *The Military Telegraph During the Civil War in the United States: With an Exposition of Ancient and Modern Means of Communication, and of the Federal and Confederate Cipher Systems; Also, a Running Account of the War Between the States,* Vol. 2. Chicago: Jansen, McClurg & Company, 1882.

Schell, Sidney H., and Allen R. Saults. *The CSS Huntsville and CSS Tuscaloosa Project,* Mobile River, Alabama, Report of 1985 Activities.

Smith, Sidney A., and C. C. Smith. *Mobile: 1861–1865.* Mobile, AL: Wyvern Press of S.F.E, 1964.

Stuart, A. A. *Iowa Colonels and Regiments: Being a History of Iowa Regiments in the War of the Rebellion.* Des Moines, IA: Mills & Company, 1865.

United States. *The Medal of Honor of the United States Army.* Washington, D.C.: U.S. G.P.O., 1948.

Warner, Ezra J. *Generals in Gray: Lives of the Confederate Commanders.* Baton Rouge: LSU Press, 1959.

_____ *Generals in Blue: Lives of the Union Commanders.* Baton Rouge: LSU Press, 1964.

Articles

"Administration of Gen. James L. Geddes." *Bulletin of Iowa Institutions,* 2 (1900): 460–462.

Barrett, Donnie, "Lady Slocomb," *Spanish Fort Historical Society News Letter, no. 2* (Aug 1996).

Barrett, Kirk. "Confederate Soldiers Captured at Spanish Fort and Imprisoned at Ship Island." Unpublished manuscript, 2018.

Bergeron, Arthur W. "The Twenty-Second Louisiana Consolidated Infantry in the Defense of Mobile." *The Alabama Historical Quarterly* 38, no. 3 (Fall 1976): 204–213.

Bergeron, Jr., Arthur W. "They Bore Themselves with Distinguished Gallantry: The Twenty-Second Louisiana Infantry." *The Journal of the Louisiana Historical Association* 13, no. 3 (Summer 1972): 253–282.

Hansen, Roger. *Confederate Command & Staff Mobile Campaign.* Ellijay, GA: Roger Hansen, 2019.

_____ "Captain Frank Moore." Unpublished manuscript, 2019.

_____ "Confederate Wounded, 1865 Mobile Campaign." Unpublished manuscript, 2020.

Johansson, Jane M. "Gibson's Louisiana Brigade During the 1864 Tennessee Campaign." *Tennessee Historical Quarterly* 64, no. 3 (Fall 2005): 186–195. Accessed September 23, 2014. http://www.jstor.org/stable/42627901.

Newton, James K., and Stephen E. Ambrose. "The Siege of Mobile." *The Alabama Historical Quarterly* 20 (Winter 1958): 595–600.

Throne, Mildred. "Nashville and Mobile." *The Palimpsest* 50 (1969): 127–134.

Trenerry, Walter N. "When the Boys Came Home." *Minnesota History* 38, no. 6 (June 1963): 287–297.

Walmsley, James E. "The Last Meeting of the Confederate Cabinet." *The Mississippi Valley Historical Review* 6, no. 3 (1919): 336–349. doi:10.2307/1886329.

Online sites

"21st Alabama Infantry Regiment." Alabama Department of Archives and History. Accessed Apr. 28, 2020. https://archives.alabama.gov/referenc/alamilor/21stinf.html.

"63rd Alabama Infantry Regiment." Alabama Department of Archives and History. Accessed Apr. 29, 2020. https://archives.alabama.gov/referenc/alamilor/63rdinf.html.

"A. J. Smith." The Annals of Iowa 3 (1897), 76–77. Iowa Research Online, University of Iowa Research. Accessed Feb. 14, 2016. http://ir.uiowa.edu/cgi/viewcontent.cgi?article=2219&context=annals-of-iowa.

"Andrew Fuller Sperry." Find A Grave. Accessed Aug. 1, 2016. http://www.findagrave.com/cgi-bin/fg.cgi? page=gr&GRid=31211891.

"Andrews, Julius A." Texas State Historical Association. Accessed Jan. 8, 2018. https://tshaonline.org/handbook/online/articles/fan61.

"Army—Medal of Honor Recipients—U.S. Military Awards for Valor." U.S. Military Awards for Valor—Top 3. Accessed June 25, 2020. https://valor.defense.gov/Recipients/Army-Medal-of-Honor-Recipients/.

"Battle Unit Details—The Civil War." U.S. National Park Service. Accessed Mar. 22, 2016. http://www.nps.gov/civilwar/search-battle-units-detail.htm?battleUnitCode=CAL0001BA.

"Biographies of Butler County Alabama." Genealogy Trails History Group—Start Your Free Family Research Here. Accessed Sep. 9, 2017. http://genealogytrails.com/ala/butler/bios_1.html#wattsthomas.

"Captain Cuthbert Harrison Slocomb." Find A Grave—Millions of Cemetery Records. Accessed Nov. 27, 2021. https://www.findagrave.com/memorial/6884675/cuthbert-harrison-slocomb.

"Cargo of Blockade Runner Denbigh Reveals Much About Civil War-era Mobile AL.com." AL.com. Accessed Jan. 29, 2017. http://blog.al.com/entertainment-press-register/2011/11/cargo_of_blockade_runner_denbi.html.

"Catron, Thomas Benton Biographical Information." Accessed Dec. 20, 2017. http://bioguide.congress.gov/scripts/biodisplay.pl?index=C000253.

"Civil War Diary of Henry M. Dryer." GenWeb of Monroe County, NY. Accessed Sep. 27, 2021. https://mcnygenealogy.com/book/diary.htm.

Clarke, Henry L. "Captain Alfred Clarke." Civil War Louisiana. Accessed Dec. 14, 2019. http://www.civilwarlouisiana.com/2012/06/.

"Col Isaac W. Patton (CSA), Mayor of New Orleans." Geni_family_tree. Last modified June 29, 2019. https://www.geni.com/people/Col-Isaac-W-Patton-CSA-Mayor-of-New-Orleans/6000000004088656026.

"Colonel Philip Brent Spence." RootsWeb.com Home Page. Accessed July 19, 2015. http://www.rootsweb.ancestry.com/~kycampbe/philipspence.htm.

"Confederate States Staff Officers—G Surnames—Access Genealogy." Access Genealogy. Accessed Sep. 10, 2017. https://www.accessgenealogy.com/military/confederate-states-staff-officers-g-surnames.htm.

"Conscription." Essential Civil War Curriculum. Accessed July 1, 2020. https://www.essentialcivilwarcurriculum.com/conscription.html.

Crist, Robert H. "1861-1865: Robert H. Crist to his Father." Spared & Shared 10. Last modified July 28, 2015. https://sparedshared10.wordpress.com/2015/07/27/1865-robert-h-christ-to-father/.

"Dauphin Island Park and Beach Fort Gaines." Dauphin Island Park and Beach. Accessed Oct. 8, 2016. http://dauphinisland.org/fort-gaines/.

Durrett, James A., and Henry Durrett. *The Letters of James A. Durrett.* Accessed July 20, 2019. https://durrettblog.wordpress.com/.

"Ebenezer Farrand." CSN Foundation. Accessed Sep. 21, 2016. https://sites.google.com/site/290foundation/290-standing-orders/ebenezer-farrand-csn.

"Ector, Mathew Duncan." Texas State Historical Association. Accessed May 1, 2020. https://tshaonline.org/handbook/online/articles/fec02.

"Ector's Brigade." Texas State Historical Association. Accessed May 1, 2020. https://tshaonline.org/handbook/online/articles/qke01.

"Edward Dorr Tracy (1833–1863)—Find A Grave Memorial." Find A Grave—Millions of Cemetery Records. Accessed Feb. 14, 2016. http://www.findagrave.com/cgi-in/fg.cgi?page=gr&GRid=9093.

"Edward R. S. Canby." National Park Service. Accessed Mar. 10, 2016. http://www.nps.gov/resources/person.htm?id=57.

"A Former New Mexico Governor Served As Monrovia's Second Mayor." Monrovia, CA Patch. Accessed Feb. 17, 2016. http://patch.com/california/monrovia/a-former-new-mexico-governor-served-as-monrovias-second-mayor.

"Fourteenth Texas Cavalry." The Handbook of Texas Online. Accessed June 9, 2016. https://tshaonline.org/handbook/online/articles/qkf14.

"Geddes." Department of Residence. Last modified Dec. 21, 2020. https://www.housing.iastate.edu/halls/geoffroy/geddes/.

"General Joseph Bailey—Hero of the Red River." Accessed Feb. 14, 2016. http://www.generaljosephbailey.com/josephbailey/.

Slocum, Charles E. *History of the Slocums, Slocumbs and Slocombs of America: Genealogical and Biographical, Embracing Twelve Generations of the First-named Family from A.D. 1637 to 1908, with Their Marriages and Descendants in the Female Lines as Far as Ascertained.* Defiance, OH: Charles E. Slocum, 1908. https://archive.org/details/historyofslocums00sloc/page/n7/mode/2up?q=Cuthbert.

"History of Spring Hill College." Spring Hill College. Accessed Dec. 1, 2015. http://www.shc.edu/page/history-spring-hill-college.

"Lucius F. Hubbard Biography: Governors of Minnesota: Mnhs.org," Research Minnesota Historical Society, accessed Nov. 5, 2020, https://collections.mnhs.org/governors/index.php/10004136.

"James Clifford Veatch (1819–1895)." Find A Grave. Accessed July 2, 2020. https://www.findagrave.com/memorial/5897067/james-clifford-veatch.

Jean R. Freedman. "Albert Cashier's Secret." Opinionator. Last modified Jan. 28, 2014. https://opinionator.blogs.nytimes.com/2014/01/28/albert-cashiers-secret/.

Jewell, Edwin L. *Crescent City Illustrated.* New Orleans: Edwin L. Jewell, 1873. https://ia600202.us.archive.org/13/items/jewellscrescentc01jewe/jewellscrescentc01jewe.pdf.

"John P. Halligan." Find A Grave—Millions of Cemetery Records. Accessed Dec. 21, 2016. http://findagrave.com/cgi-bin/fg,cgi?page=gr&GRid=26753869.

"Kenner Garrard (1827–1879)." Find A Grave. Accessed Dec. 21, 2016. https://www.findagrave.com/memorial/5088/kenner-garrard.

Lacey, John F. "Major-General Frederick Steele." Iowa Research Online University of Iowa Research. Accessed Oct. 15, 2016. http://ir.uiowa.edu/annals-of-iowa/vol3/iss5/8.

"Major Samuel H. Lockett." Official Site: The Battle of Champion Hill (May 16, 1863). Accessed Sep. 2, 2017. http://battleofchampionhill.org/lockett1.htm.

"William R. Marshall Biography: Governors of Minnesota : Mnhs.org." Research Minnesota Historical Society. Accessed Nov. 5, 2020. https://collections.mnhs.org/governors/index. php/10004001.

Maury, Dabney H. "Col William Estey Burnet." Find A Grave. Accessed June 13, 2016. https:// www.findagrave.com/memorial/65156612/william-estey-burnet.

"NH 48925 Lieutenant Thomas B. Huger, CSN." Naval History and Heritage Command. Accessed Feb. 14, 2016. http://www.history.navy.mil/our-collections/photography/numerical-list-of-images/nhhc-series/nh-series/NH-48000/NH-48925.html.

"Representative William Bell." https://legis.iowa.gov/legislators/legislator?ga=26&personID=3767. Accessed Aug. 8, 2016.

"Robert Angelo Spink." Oshkosh Public Museum. Accessed Aug. 1, 2016. http://oshkosh.pastperfect-online.com/20004cgi/mweb.exe?request=field;fldseq=359109.

Robertson, Thomas C. "4th Louisiana at Shiloh Part 1." Civil War Louisiana. Last modified Apr. 6, 1862. https://www.civilwarlouisiana.com/.

"Rousseau's Raid." Encyclopedia of Alabama. Accessed April 29, 2020. https://www. encyclopediaofalabama.org/article/h-3596.

"Samuel Lockett." Alabama Department of Archives and History. Accessed Sep. 2, 2017. http:// www.archives.state.al.us/marschall/S_Lockett.html.

"Sixteenth Confederate Cavalry Aka The Twelfth Mississippi Cavalry." Sixteenth Confederate Cavalry Aka The Twelfth Mississippi Cavalry. Accessed Aug. 12, 2015. http://www.16thconfederatecavalry. com/index.html.

"Tenth Texas Cavalry" Texas State Historical Association. Accessed Dec. 14, 2014. http://www. tshaonline.org/handbook/online/articles/qkt13.

"Thomas McMillian Blair." Find A Grave. Accessed May 12, 2020. https://www.findagrave.com/ memorial/40613117/thomas-mcmillian-blair.

"Thomas Seay." 18th Century History—The Age of Reason and Change. Accessed Oct. 15, 2016. http://history1700s.com/index.php/articles/14-guest-authors/109-three-governors-from-greensboro-alabama.html?showall=&start=3.

"Warfare History Network » General George S. Patton, Sr.: Civil War Veteran." Accessed May 16, 2017. http://warfarehistorynetwork.com/daily/civil-war/general-george-s-patton-sr-civil-war-veteran/.

Weston, Sidney E. "Dear Parent." Vermont Civil War, Lest We Forget. Accessed Apr. 4, 2020. https:// vermontcivilwar.org/get.php?input=32074.

"William Rainey Marshall." National Governors Association. Accessed Oct. 15, 2016. http://www. nga.org/cms/home/governors/past-governors-bios/page_minnesota/col2-content/main-content-list/title_marshall_william.html.

Dissertation and Theses:

Dixon, Donald E. "Randall Lee Gibson." Master's thesis, Louisiana State University, 1971.

Index

About the Author

Paul Brueske, a lifelong resident of the Gulf Coast, has been studying the Civil War history of northwest Florida and south Alabama for the past 20 years. He is the president and founder of the Mobile Area Civil War Round Table and the head track and field coach at the University of South Alabama. Brueske is a regular speaker on Gulf Coast-related Civil War topics and a member of the Friends of Historic Blakeley State Park, the Historic Mobile Preservation Society, and Friends of the History Museum of Mobile. He is the author of *The Last Siege: The Mobile Campaign, Alabama 1865* (2018).